THC

European

12-LANGUAGE
PHRASEBOOK

Thomas
Cook

Publishing

Published by Thomas Cook Publishing
Thomas Cook Holdings Ltd
PO Box 227
The Thomas Cook Business Park
Units 19-21, Coningsby Road
Peterborough PE3 8XX
United Kingdom

Telephone: 01733 416477
email: books@thomascook.com

First published as *The Thomas Cook European Travel Phrasebook* in 1995
Reprinted with revisions 1996, 2000
This edition 2001

ISBN 1 841570 16 8

Whilst every care has been taken in compiling this publication, using the most up-to-date information available at the time of going to press, all details are liable to change and cannot be guaranteed. The publishers and Thomas Cook Holdings Ltd cannot accept any liability whatsoever arising from errors or omissions, however caused.

Editor: Giovanna Battiston
Revisions: Studio 183, Peterborough

Cover design: Pumpkin House
Cover picture: Neil Setchfield

Translations by UPS Translations, London, and Transtec, Stamford, Lincs
Typeset by Thomas Cook Publishing using Advent 3B2
Printed in Spain by GraphyCems, Navarra

Contents

Editor's Introduction

This phrasebook contains a selection of vocabulary essential to English-speaking tourists travelling across Europe through countries where English is not widely spoken.

Languages of countries where English *is* widely spoken or understood (such as the northern European destinations of the Netherlands, Norway, Sweden, Denmark and Finland) are not included; however, any attempts to speak a few words in the native tongue of these countries would no doubt be greatly appreciated. French, Italian and German, which are spoken in more than one European country, are included and between them they cover a large area of central Europe. The Eastern European languages that have been selected for this phrasebook are those spoken in countries with the greatest tourist appeal.

Comment utiliser ce recueil d'expressions

Les expressions contenues dans chaque section de langue sont numérotées pour que les personnes ne parlant pas l'anglais puissent les retrouver facilement dans d'autres langues. Par exemple, une personne parlant le français et recherchant une traduction en polonais de l'expression 57 de la section Français (Où est la boutique hors-taxe?), la trouvera au numéro 57 de la section Polonais (Gdzie jest sklep wolno-cłowy?).

Benutzung dieses Sprachführers

Die Redewendungen sind in den einzelnen Sprachen jeweils numeriert, sodaß man auch ohne Kenntnis der englischen Sprache leicht die entsprechende Übersetzung finden kann.

Zum Beispiel: Jemand mit deutscher Muttersprache schlägt im deutschen Teil die Redewendung Nummer 57 nach (Wo ist der zollfreie Laden?), und weiß dann, daß die Redewendung mit der Nummer 57 im polnischen Teil die genaue Übersetzung wiedergibt (Gdzie jest sklep wolno-cłowy?).

Empleo del libro de frases

La sección correspondiente a cada idioma comprende frases numeradas que remiten al usuario a otros idiomas y facilitan el manejo del libro por parte de quienes no sepan inglés. Por ejemplo, los hispanohablantes que quieran saber el equivalente polaco de la frase numero 57 (¿Dónde está el duty free?) no tienen más que ver la frase del mismo número en la sección de ese idioma (Gdzie jest sklep wolno-cłowy?), que denota lo mismo exactamente.

Como Usar este Livro de Frases

As frases em cada secção de idioma numeradas de modo a que leitores de língua não-inglesa possam encontrar facilmente referências cruzadas. Por exemplo, um leitor de língua Portuguesa pode procurar a frase 57 na secção portuguesa (Onde é a loja duty-free?) e sabe que a frase 57 na secção polaca (Gdzie jest wolno-clowy?) é uma tradução exacta da mesma.

Come utilizzare questo frasario

Le frasi contenute nella sezione di ciascuna lingua sono numerate in modo che chi non parla inglese possa consultarle facilmente. Ad esempio una persona di lingua italiana può cercare la frase 57 nella sezione italiana (Dov'è il duty free?) e sapere che la frase 57 nella sezione polacca (Gdzie jest sklep wolno-cłowy?) ne è l'esatta traduzione.

MAP OF EUROPE

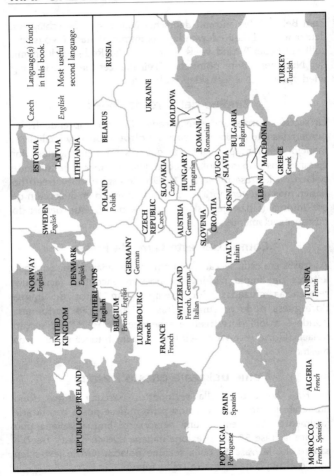

Czech   Language(s) found in this book.

English   Most useful second language.

RUSSIA

TURKEY
Turkish

UKRAINE

BELARUS

MOLDOVA

ESTONIA
LATVIA
LITHUANIA

ROMANIA
Romanian

BULGARIA
Bulgarian

MACEDONIA

SLOVAKIA
Czech

HUNGARY
Hungarian

YUGO-
SLAVIA

GREECE
Greek

ALBANIA

SWEDEN
English

POLAND
Polish

CZECH
REPUBLIC
Czech

AUSTRIA
German

SLOVENIA

CROATIA

BOSNIA

NORWAY
English

DENMARK
English

GERMANY
German

ITALY
Italian

TUNISIA
French

NETHERLANDS
English

BELGIUM
French, *English*

SWITZERLAND
French, German, Italian

LUXEMBOURG
French

UNITED
KINGDOM

FRANCE
French

REPUBLIC OF IRELAND

ALGERIA
French

PORTUGAL
Portuguese

SPAIN
Spanish

MOROCCO
French, Spanish

6

Introduction

Bulgarian is a Slavic language and like Russian, to which it is distantly related, it uses Cyrillic script, which is a development of the Greek alphabet. Russian itself is widely understood in Bulgaria; English and German may also be spoken to a degree in larger cities.

As with Greek, body language can be confusing if you are unaware that Bulgarians traditionally nod their heads up and down to signify no and shake them from side to side to mean yes. As Western influences increase, younger and Westernised Bulgarians have begun to adopt the opposite conventions, which increases confusion.

Addresses for travel and tourist information

Australia: *Consulate-General,* 14 Carlotta Road, Double Bay, Sydney, NSW 2028; tel: (2) 9327 08067.
Canada: *Embassy,* 325 Stewart St, Ottawa, Ontario, K1K 6K5; tel: (613) 789 3215.
South Africa: *Embassy,* Techno Plaza E., 305 Brooks St, Melo Park, Pretoria; tel: (12) 342 3720.
UK: *Balkan Holidays (National Tourist Office),* Sofia House, 19 Conduit St, London, W1R 9TD; tel: (020) 7543 5555.

ESSENTIALS

ESSENTIALS

Alphabet

А *ah*	Б *bah*
В *vah*	Г *gah*
Д *dah*	Е *eh*
Ж *zhe*	З *ze*
И *ee*	Й *iy*
К *kah*	Л *lah*
М *meh*	Н *neh*
О *o*	П *pe*
Р *re*	С *ce*
Т *te*	У *ou*
Ф *fa*	Х *ha*
Ц *tsa*	Ч *ch*
Ш *sh*	Щ *shch*
Ъ *eu*	ь *y*
Ю *yu*	Я *ya*

Basic Words and Phrases

1 **Yes**   **No**
   Да   Не
   Da   *Ne*

2 **Please**   **Thank you**
   Моля   Благодаря Ви
   Molya   *Blagodarya vi*

3 **That's O.K.**   **Perhaps**
   Няма проблеми Може би
   Nyama problemi Mozhe bi

4 **To**   **From**
   До   От
   Do   *Ot*

5 **Here**   **There**
   Тук   Там
   Took   *Tam*

6 **None**   **Also**
   Нищо   Също
   Nishto   *Sushto*

7 **How**   **When**
   Как   Кога
   Kak   *Koga*

8 **What**   **Why**
   какво   Защо
   Kakvo   *Zashto*

9 **I don't understand.**
   Не разбирам.
   Ne razbiram.

10 **I don't speak Bulgarian.**
   Не говоря български.
   Ne govorya bulgarski.

11 **Do you speak English?**
   Говорите ли английски?
   Govorite li angliyski?

12 **Can you please write it down?**
Може ли да го напишете,
моля?
Mozhe li da go napishete, molya?

13 **Can you please speak more slowly?**
Може ли да говорите по-
бавно, моля?
Mozhe li da govorite po-bavno, molya?

14 **How much does it/this cost?**
Колко струва това?
Kolko stroova tova?

Days

15 **Monday**
Понеделник
Ponedelnik

Tuesday
Вторник
Ftornik

16 **Wednesday**
Сряда
Sryada

Thursday
Четвъртък
Chetvurtuk

17 **Friday**
Петък
Petuk

Saturday
Събота
Subota

18 **Sunday**
Неделя
Nedelya

Morning
Сутрин
Sootrin

19 **Afternoon**
Следобед
Sletobet

Evening
Вечер
Vecher

20 **Night**
Нощ
Nosht

Week
Седмица
Sedmitsa

21 **Yesterday/Today/Tomorrow**
Вчера/днес/Утре
Fchera/Dnes/Ootre

Numbers

22 **Zero**
Нула
Noola

One
Едно
Edno

23 **Two**
Две
Dve

Three
Три
Tri

24 **Four**
Четири
Chetiri

Five
Пет
Pet

25 **Six**
Шест
Shest

Seven
Седем
Sedem

26 **Eight**
Осем
Osem

Nine
Девет
Devet

27 **Ten**
Десет
Deset

Eleven
Единадесет
Edinadeset

28 **Twelve**
Дванадесет
Dvanadeset

Thirteen
Тринадесет
Trinadeset

29 **Fourteen**
Четиринадесет
Chetirinadeset

Fifteen
Петнадесет
Petnadeset

30 **Sixteen**
Шестнадесет
Shestnadeset

Seventeen
Седемнадесет
Sedemnadeset

31 **Eighteen**
Осемнадесет
Osemnadeset

Nineteen
Деветнадесет
Devetnadeset

32 **Twenty**
Двадесет
Dvadeset

Twenty-one
Двадесет и едно
Dvadeset i edno

33 **Twenty-two**
Двадесет и две
Dvadeset i dve

Thirty
Тридесет
Trideset

34 **Forty**
Четиридесет
Chetirideset

Fifty
Петдесет
Petdeset

35 **Sixty**
Шестдесет
Shestdeset

Seventy
Седемдесет
Sedemdeset

36 **Eighty**
Осемдесет
Osemdeset

Ninety
Деветдесет
Devetdeset

37 **One hundred**
Сто
Sto

Five hundred
Пет стотин
Petstotin

38 **One thousand**
Хиляда
Hilyada

One million
Един милион
Edin milion

Time

39 **9.00**
Точно девет часа
Tochno devet chasa

40 **9.05**
Девет часа и пет минути
Devet chasa i pet minooti

41 **9.10**
Девет часа и десет минути
Devet chasa i deset minooti

42 **9.15**
Девет часа и петнадесет
минути

Devet chasa i petnadeset minooti

43 **9.20**
Девет часа и двадесет
минути
Devet chasa i dvadeset minooti

44 **9.25**
Девет часа и двадесет и
пет минути
Devet chasa dvadeset i pet minooti

45 **9.30**
Девет часа и тридесет
минути
Devet chasa i trideset minooti

46 **9.35**
Девет часа и тридесет и
пет минути
Devet chasa i trideset i pet minooti

47 **9.40**
Девет часа и четиридесет
минути
Devet chasa i chetirideset minooti

48 **9.45**
Девет часа и четиридесет и
пет минути
*Devet chasa i chetirideset i pet
minooti*

49 **9.50**
Девет часа и петдесет
минути
Devet chasa i petdeset minooti

50 **9.55**
Девет часа и петдесет и пет
минути
Devet chasa i petdeset i pet minooti

B U L G A R I A N

51 ↑ 64

51 12.00/Midday/Midnight
Точно дванадесет часа/
обед/полунощ
*Tochno dvanadeset chasa/Obet/
Poloonosht.*

52 What time is it?
Колко е часът?
Kolko e chasa?

53 It is . . .
Часът е . . .
Chasa e . . .

ARRIVING AND DEPARTING

Airport

54 Excuse me, where is the
check-in desk for . . . airline?
Извинявайте, къде е
гишето за авиолиния . . ?
*Izvinyavayte, kude e gisheto za
avioliniya . . ?*

55 What is the boarding gate/
time for my flight?
Къде е изходът за (В колко
часа е) моят полет?
*Kude e izhodut za (F kolko chasa e)
moyat polet?*

56 How long is the delay likely
to be?
Колко може да продължи
закъснението?
*Kolko mozhe da produlzhi
zakusnenieto?*

57 Where is the duty-free shop?
Къде е безмитният
магазин?
Kude e bezmitniyat magazin?

58 Which way is the baggage
reclaim?
Къде се получава багажът?
Kude se poloochava bagazhut?

59 Where can I get the bus to
the city centre?
Къде мога да взема
автобус до центъра на
града?
*Kude moga da vzema aftoboos do
tsentura na grada?*

Train Station

60 Where is the ticket office/
information desk?
Къде е касата/
информацията?
Kude e kasata/informatsiyata?

61 Which platform does the
train to . . . depart from?
От кой перон тръгва
влакът за . . ?
Ot koy peron trugva vlaka za . . ?

62 Where is platform . . ?
Къде е . . . перон?
Kude e . . . peron?

63 When is the next train to . . ?
Кога е следващият
влак за . . ?
Koga e sledvashtiya vlak za . . ?

64 Is there a later train to . . ?
Има ли по-късен влак
за . . ?
Ima li po-kusen vlak za . . ?

**B
U
L
G
A
R
I
A
N**

**65
↕
84**

Port

65 **How do I get to the port?**
Как да стигна до
пристанището?
Kak da stigna do pristanishteto?

66 **When is the next sailing to . . ?**
Кога е следващият рейс
за . . ?
Koga e sledvashtiya reys za . . ?

67 **Can I catch an earlier ferry
with this ticket?**
Мога ли да се кача на по-
ранен ферибот с този
билет?
*Moga li da se kacha na po-ranen
feribot s tozi bilet?*

Notices and Signs

68 **Вагон-ресторант**
Vagon-restorant
Buffet (Dining) Car

69 **Автобус**
Aftoboos
Bus

70 **Питейна/непитейна вода**
Piteyna/Nepiteyna voda
Drinking/Non-drinking water

71 **Вход**
Vhot
Entrance

72 **Изход**
Ishot
Exit

73 **Информация**
Informatsiya

Information

74 **Гардероб за багаж**
Garderop za bagash
Left Luggage (Baggage Claim)

75 **Сейфове за багаж**
Seyfove za bagash
Luggage Lockers

76 **Поща**
Poshta
Post Office

77 **Перон**
Peron
Platform

78 **Железопътна гара**
Zhelezoputna gara
Railway (Railroad) Station

79 **Аерогара/Летище**
Aerogara/Letishte
Airport

80 **Пристанище**
Pristanishte
Port

81 **Ресторант**
Restorant
Restaurant

82 **Пушачи/непушачи**
Pooshachi/Nepooshachi
Smoking/Non-smoking

83 **Телефон**
Telefon
Telephone

84 **Билетна каса**
Biletna kasa
Ticket Office

12

⁸⁵ **Гише за регистриране за полета/Чек-ин**
Gishe za registrirane za poleta/Check-in
Check-in Desk

⁸⁶ **Разписание**
Raspisanie
Timetable (Schedule)

⁸⁷ **Тоалетна**
Toaletna
Toilets (Restrooms)

⁸⁸ **Мъже**
Muzhe
Gentlemen

⁸⁹ **Жени**
Zheni
Ladies'

⁹⁰ **Трамвай**
Tramvay
Tram (Streetcar)

⁹¹ **Метро**
Metro
Underground (Subway)

⁹² **Чакалня**
Chakalnya
Waiting Room

Buying a ticket

⁹³ I would like a first-class/second-class single (one-way)/return (round-trip) ticket to . . .
Искам билет първа/втора класа/ведна посока за отиване и връщане ндо . . .
Iskam bilet purva/ftora clasa/fedna posoka za otivane i vrushtane ndo . . .

⁹⁴ Is my rail pass valid on this train/ferry/bus?
Картата ми за пътуване с влак важи ли за този влак/ферибот/автобус?
Kartata mi za putoovane s vlak vazhi li za tozi vlak/feribot/aftoboos?

⁹⁵ I would like an aisle/window seat.
Искам място от вътрешната страна/до прозореца.
Iskam myasto ot vutreshnata strana/do prozoretsa.

⁹⁶ No smoking/smoking, please.
Не пушете/пушете, моля.
Ne pooshete/pooshete, molya.

⁹⁷ We would like to sit together.
Искаме да седим заедно.
Iskame da sedim zaedno.

⁹⁸ I would like to make a seat reservation.
Искам да запазя място.
Iskam zapazeno myasto.

⁹⁹ I would like to reserve a couchette/sleeper for one person/two people/my family.
Искам място в кушет/спален вагон за един/двама/за семейството ми.
Iskam myasto f kooshet/spalen vagon za edin/dvama/za semeystvoto mi.

ARRIVING AND DEPARTING

100 I would like to reserve a cabin.
Искам да резервирам кабина/каюта.
Iskam da rezerviram kabina/ kayoota.

Timetables (Schedules)

101 Пристига
Pristiga
Arrive

102 Спира На
Spira na
Calls (Stops) at

103 Хранене
Hranene
Catering Service

104 Прехвърляне
Prehvurlyane na
Change at

105 Връзка
Vruska
Connection

106 Дневно
Dnevno
Daily

107 На всеки четиридесет минути
Na vseki chetirideset minooti
Every 40 Minutes

108 Първа класа
Purva clasa
First-class

109 Всеки час
Vseki chas
Hourly

110 Препоръчват се запазени места
Preporuchvat se zapazeni mesta
Seat reservations are recommended

111 Втора класа
Ftora clasa
Second-class

112 Допълнително заплащане
Dopulnitelno zaplashtane
Supplement Payable

113 През
Pres
Via

Luggage

114 How much will it cost to send (ship) my luggage in advance?
Колко струва да изпратя багажа си предварително?
Kolko stroova da ispratya bagazha si predvaritelno?

115 Where is the left luggage (baggage claim) office?
Къде е гардеробът за багаж?
Kude e garderoba za bagash?

116 What time do you open/close?
Кога отваряте/затваряте?
Koga otvaryate/zatvaryate?

117 Where are the luggage trolleys (carts)?
Къде са количките за багаж?
Kude sa kolichkite za bagash?

AT THE TOURIST OFFICE

118 Where are the lockers?
Къде са сейфовете за
багаж?
Kude sa seyfovete za bagash?

119 I have lost my locker key.
Загубих ключа за сейфа.
Zagoobih klyoocha za seyfa.

On Board

120 Is this seat free?
Свободно ли е това място?
Svobodno li e tova myasto?

121 Excuse me, you are sitting in
my reserved seat.
Извинете, седите на моето
запазено място.
*Izinete, sedite na moeto zapazeno
myasto.*

122 Which station is this?
Коя е тази гара?
Koya e tazi gara?

123 What time is this train/bus/
ferry/flight due to arrive/
depart?
Кога трябва да пристигне/
замине този влак/автобус/
ферибот/полет?
*Koga tryabva da pristigne/zamine
tozi vlak/aftoboos/feribot/polet?*

124 Will you wake me just before
we arrive?
Можете ли да ме събудите
малко преди да
пристигнем?
*Mozhete li da me suboodite malko
predi da pristignem?*

Customs and Passports

125 Passports, please!
Паспортите, моля!
Pasportite, molya!

126 I have nothing/wine/spirits
(alcohol)/tobacco to declare.
Нямам нищо/вино/
концентрати/цигари да
декларирам.
*Nyamam nishto/vino/
kontsentrati/tsigari da deklariram.*

127 I shall be staying for . . .
days/weeks/months.
Ще пребивавам . . .дни/
седмици/месеци.
*Shte prebivavam . . . dni/sedmitsi/
mesetsi.*

AT THE TOURIST OFFICE

128 Do you have a map of the
town/area?
Имате ли карта на града/
областта?
Imate li karta na grada/oblasta?

129 Can I reserve accommodation
here?
Мога ли да резервирам
стая тук?
Moga li da rezerviram staya took?

130 Do you have a list of
accommodation?
Имате ли списък на
местата за нощуване?
*Imate li spisuk na mestata za
noshtoovane?*

ACCOMMODATION

ACCOMMODATION

Hotels

131 I have a reservation in the name of . . .
Имам резервация на името на . . .
Imam rezervatsiya na imeto na . . .

132 I wrote to/faxed/telephoned you last month/last week in . . .
Аз ви писах/телефонирах/изпратих факс миналия месец/миналата седмица в . . .
Az vi pissah/telefonirah/izpratih faks minaliya mesets/minalata sedmitsa f . . .

133 Do you have any rooms free?
Имате ли свободни стаи?
Imate li svobodni stayi?

134 I would like to reserve a single/double room with/without bath/shower.
Искам да резервирам единична/двойна стая с/без баня/душ.
Iskam da rezerviram edinichna/dvoyna staya s/bes banya/doosh.

135 I would like bed and breakfast/(room and) half board/(room and) full board.
Искам стая със закуска/половин пансион/пълен пасион.

Iskam staya sus zakooska/polovin pansion/pulen pansion.

136 How much is it per night?
Колко е за една нощ?
Kolko e za edna nosht?

137 Is breakfast included?
Включва ли се закуска?
Vklyoochva li se zakooska?

138 May I see the room?
Може ли да видя стаята?
Mozhe li da vidya stayata?

139 Do you have any cheaper rooms?
Имате ли по-евтини стаи?
Imate li po-eftini stai?

140 I would like to take the room.
Искам да наема стаята.
Iskam da naema stayata.

141 I would like to stay for . . . nights.
Искам да пребивавам . . . дни.
Iskam da prebivavam . . . dni.

142 The shower/light/tap doesn't work.
Душът/осветлението/кранът не работи.
Dooshut/osvetlenieto/kranut ne raboti.

143 At what time/where is breakfast served?
Кога/къде сервирате закуска?
Koga/kude servirate zakooska?

16

144 What time do I have to check-out?
Кога трябва да се отпиша?
Koga tryabva da se otpisha?

145 Can I have the key to room no . . ?
Може ли да ми дадете ключа за стая номер . . ?
Mozhe li da mi dadete klyucha za staya nomer . . ?

146 My room number is . . .
Номерът на стаята ми е . . .
Nomera na stayata mi e . . .

147 Do you accept travellers' cheques/Eurocheques/credit cards?
Приемате ли туристически чекове/еврочекове/кредитни карти?
Priemate li tooristicheski chekove/evrochekove/kreditni karti?

148 May I have the bill, please?
Може ли сметката, моля?
Mozhe li smetkata, molya?

149 Excuse me, I think there is a mistake in this bill.
Извинявайте, мисля, че в сметката ми има грешка.
Izvinyavaite, mislya, che f smetkata mi ima greshka.

Youth Hostels

150 How much is a dormitory bed per night?
Колко е легло в обща стая?
Kolko e leglo f opshta staya?

151 I am/am not an HI member.
Аз съм/не съм ГУНА член.
As cum/ne sum ГУНА chlen.

152 May I use my own sleeping bag?
Мога ли да ползвам спалния си чувал?
Moga li da polzvam spalniya si chooval?

153 What time do you lock the doors at night?
Кога заключвате през нощта?
Koga zaklyoochvate pres noshta?

Camping

154 May I camp here for the night/two nights?
Мога ли да прекарам нощта/две нощи?
Moga li da prekaram noshta/dve noshti?

155 Where can I pitch my tent?
Къде да сложа палатката си?
Kude da slozha palatkata si?

156 How much does it cost for one night/one week?
Колко струва за една нощ/една седмица?
Kolko srtoova za edna nosht/edna sedmitsa?

157 Where can we park our caravan?
Къде може да паркираме караваната си?
Kude mozhe da parkirame karavanata si?

158 Where are the washing facilities?
Къде е умивалнята?
Kude e oomivalnyata?

159 Is there a restaurant/ supermarket/swimming pool on site/nearby?
Има ли ресторант/ супермаркет/басейн тук/ наоколо?
Ima li restorant/supermarket/ baseyn took/naokolo?

160 Do you have a safety deposit box?
Имате ли сейф?
Imate li seyf?

EATING AND DRINKING

Cafés and Bars

161 I would like a cup of/two cups of/another coffee/tea.
Искам чаша/две чаши/ още едно кафе/чай.
Iskam chaha/dve chashi/oshte edno kafe/chay.

162 With/without milk/sugar.
С/без мляко/захар.
S/bes mlyako/zahar.

163 I would like a bottle/glass/ two glasses of mineral water/ red wine/white wine, please.
Искам бутилка/чаша/две чаши минерална вода/ червено вино/бяло вино, моля.
Iskam bootilka/chasha/dve chashi mineralna voda/cherveno vino/ byalo vino, molya.

164 I would like a beer/two beers, please.
Искам една бира/две бири, моля.
Iskam edna bira/dve biri, molya.

165 May I have some ice?
Ли малко лед?
Li malko led?

166 Do you have any matches/ cigarettes/cigars?
Имате ли кибрит/цигари/ пури?
Imate li kibrit/tsigari/poori?

Restaurants

167 Can you recommend a good/ inexpensive restaurant in this area?
Препоръчайте ми добър/ евтин ресторант наоколо?
Preporuchayte mi dobur/eftin restorant naokolo?

168 I would like a table for . . . people.
Искам маса за . . . човека.
Iskam masa za . . . choveka.

169 Do you have a non-smoking area?
Имате ли място за непушачи?
Imate li myasto za nepooshachi?

170 Waiter/Waitress!
Келнер!
Kelner!

171 Do you have a set menu/children's menu/wine list?
Имате ли меню за деня/детско меню/листа за вината?
Imate li menyoo za denya/detsko menyoo/lista za vinata?

172 Do you have any vegetarian dishes, please?
Имате ли нещо вегетарианско, моля?
Imate li neshto vegetariyansko, molya?

173 Are there any local specialities?
Има ли някакви местни специалитети?
Ima li nyakakvi mestni spetsialiteti?

174 Are vegetables included?
Това включва ли гарнитура/зеленчуци?
Tova fklyuchva li garnitoora/zelenchootsi?

175 Could I have it well-cooked/medium/rare please?
Искам го добре сготвено/средно/ал англе, моля

Iskam go dobre sgotveno/sredno/al angle, molya.

176 What does this dish consist of?
Какво има в яденето?
Kakvo ima f yadeneto?

177 I would like the set menu, please.
Искам менюто за деня, моля.
Iskam menyooto za denya, molya.

178 We have not been served yet.
Още не са ни сервирали.
Oshte ne sa ni servirali.

179 Excuse me, this is not what I ordered.
Извинявайте, аз не поръчах това.
Izvinyavayte, az ne poruchah tova.

180 May I have some/some more bread/water/coffee/tea?
Може ли да ми дадете/още хляб/вода/кафе/чай?
Mozhe li da mi dadete/oshte hlyap/voda/kafe/chay?

181 May I have the bill, please?
Може ли сметката, моля?
Mozhe li smetkata, molya?

182 Does this bill include service?
Обслужването включва ли се в сметката?
Opsloozhvaneto fklyoochva li se f smetkata?

183 **Do you accept travellers' cheques (travelers' checks)/Eurocheques/MasterCard/US dollars?**
Приемате ли туристически чекове/еврочекове/мастер кард/долари?
Priemate li tooristicheski chekove/Evrochekove/MasterCard/dolari?

184 **Can I have a receipt, please?**
Може ли да ми дадете разписка/фактура, моля?
Mozhe li da mi dadete razpiska/faktoora, molya?

185 **Where is the toilet (restroom), please?**
Извинете, къде е тоалетната?
Izvinete, kude e toaletnata?

On the Menu

186 **First courses**
Предястия
Predyastiya

187 **Soups**
Супи
Soopi

188 **Main courses**
Главни/втори ястия
Glavni/ftori yastiya

189 **Fish dishes**
Рибни ястия
Ribni yastiya

190 **Meat dishes**
Месни ястия
Mesni yastiya

191 **Vegetarian dishes**
Вегетариански ястия
Vegetarianski yastiya

192 **Cheese**
Сирене
Sirene

193 **Desserts**
Десерти
Deserti

194 **Specialities**
Специалитети
Spetsialiteti

GETTING AROUND

Public Transport

195 **Where is the bus stop/coach station/nearest metro (subway) station?**
Къде е автобусната спирка/автогарата/най-близката гара на метрото?
Kude e aftoboosnata spirka/aftogarata/nay-bliskata gara na metroto?

196 **When is the next/last bus to . . ?**
Кога е следващият/последният автобус за . . ?
Koga e sledvashtiya/posledniya aftoboos za . . ?

197 **How much is the fare to the city centre (downtown)/railway (railroad) station/airport?**

Колко е билетът до
центъра/гарата/летището?
*Kolko e bileta do tsentura/garata/
letishteto?*

198 Will you tell me when to get
off?
Бихте ли ми казали кога
да сляза?
Bihte li mi kazali koga da slyaza?

199 Does this bus go to . . ?
Този автобус отива ли
до . . ?
Tozi aftoboos otiva li do . . ?

200 Which number bus goes to . . ?
Кой номер автобус отива
до?
Koy nomer aftoboos otiva do . . ?

201 May I have a single (one
way)/return (round trip)/day
ticket/book of tickets?
Искам билет в един
посока/билет за отиване и
връщане/дневна карта/
кочан билети.
*Iskam bilet f edna posoka/bilet za
otivane i vrushtane/dnevna karta/
kochan bileti?*

Taxis

202 I would like to go to . . . How
much will it cost?
Искам да отида до . . . Колко
ще струва?
*Iskam da otida do . . . Kolko shte
stroova?*

203 Please stop here.
Спрете тук, моля.
Sprete took, molya.

204 I would like to order a taxi
today/tomorrow at 2pm to
go from . . . to . . .
Искам да поръчам такси
за днес/утре в 14 часа
от . . . до . . .
*Iskam da porucham taksi za dnes/
ootre f 14 chasa ot . . . do . . .*

Asking the Way

205 Excuse me, do you speak
English?
Извинете, говорите ли
английски?
Izvinete, govorite li angliyski?

206 Excuse me, is this the right
way to . . ?
Извинявайте, това ли е
пътят за . . ?
Izvinyavayte, tova li e putyat za . . .

207 . . . the cathedral/the tourist
information office/the castle/
the old town
. . . катедралата/
туристическата
информация/замъкът/
старият град?
*. . . katedralata/tooristicheskata
informatsiya/zamukut/stariyat
grat?*

208 Can you tell me the way to the railway (railroad) station/bus station/taxi rank (stand)/city centre (downtown)/beach?

Можете ли да ми кажете къде е гарата/автогарата/колонката за таксита/центъра/плажа?

Mozhete li da mi kazhete kude e garata/aftogarata/kolonkata za taksita/tsentura/plazha?

209 First/second/left/right/straight ahead.

Първата/втората/наляво/надясно/направо.

Purvata/ftorata/nalyavo/nadyasno/napravo.

210 Where is the nearest police station/post office/doctor/hospital/pharmacy?

Къде е най-близкият полицейски участък/най-близката поща/най-близкият doктор/най-близката болница/най-близката аптеца?

Kude e nay-bliskiya politseyski oochastuk/nay-bliskata poshta/nay-bliskiya doktor/nay-bliskata bolnitsa/nay-bliskata apteka?

211 Is it far?

Далече ли е?

Dalache li e?

212 Do I need to take a taxi/catch a bus?

Трябва ли да взема такси/автобус?

Tryabva li da vzema taksi/aftobus?

213 Can you point to it on my map?

Покажете ми го на картата, моля?

Pokazhete mi go na kartata, molya?

214 Thank you for your help.

Благодаря Ви за помощта.

Blagodarya vi za pomoshta.

SIGHTSEEING

215 Where is the Tourist Information Office?

Къде е туристическата информация?

Kude e tooristicheskata informatsiya?

216 Where is the cathedral/church/museum?

Къде е катедралата/църквата/музея?

Kude e katedralata/tsurkvata/moozeya?

217 How much is the entrance (admission) charge?

Колко е входът?

Kolko e fhoda?

218 Is there a discount for children/students/senior citizens?

Има ли намаление за деца/студенти/пенсионери?

Ima li namalenie za detsa/stoodenti/pensioneri?

219 What time does the next guided tour start?
Кога е следващата обиколка с екскурзовод?
Koga e sledvashtata obikolka s ekskoorzovod?

220 One/two adults/children, please.
Един/двама възрастни/деца, моля.
Edin/dvama vuztrastni/detsa, molya.

221 May I take photographs here?
Мога ли да правя снимки тук?
Moga li da pravya snimki took?

ENTERTAINMENT

222 Can you recommend a good bar/nightclub?
Препоръчайте ми добър бар/нощен клуб?
Preporuchayte mi dobur bar/noshten cloop?

223 Do you know what is on at the cinema (playing at the movies)/theatre at the moment?
Знаете ли какво дават в киното/театъра в момента?
Znaete li kakvo davat f kinoto/teatura f momenta?

224 I would like to book (purchase) . . . tickets for the matinée/evening performance on Monday.
Искам да запазя (купя) . . . билети за сутрешното/вечерното представление в понеделник.
Iskam da zapazya koopya . . . bileti za sootreshnoto/vechernoto predstavlenie f ponedelnik.

225 What time does the film/performance start?
Кога започва филмът/представлението?
Koga zapochva filma/predstavlenieto?

MEETING PEOPLE

226 Hello/Goodbye.
Здравейте/Довиждане.
Zdraveyte/Dovizhdane.

227 Good morning/good afternoon/good evening/goodnight.
Добро утро/добър ден/добър вечер/лека нощ.
Dobro ootro/dobur den/dobur vecher/leka nosht.

228 Pleased to meet you.
Радвам се да се запозная с вас.
Radvam se da se zapoznaya s vas.

229 How are you?
Как сте?
Kak ste?

230 Fine, thank you. And you?
Благодаря, добре. А Вие?
Blagodarya, dobre. A Vie?

231 My name is . . .
Аз се казвам . . .
Az se kazvam . . .

232 This is my friend/boyfriend/
girlfriend/husband/wife/
brother/sister.
Това е приятелят ми/
приятелката ми/съпругът
ми/съпругата ми/брат ми/
сестра ми.
*Tova e priyatelya mi/priyatelkata
mi/suprooga mi/suproogata mi/
brat mi/sestra mi.*

233 Where are you travelling to?
За къде пътувате?
Za kude putoovate?

234 I am/we are going to . . .
Аз/ние отивам/е до . . .
As/nie otivam/e do . . .

235 How long are you travelling
for?
За колко дълго пътувате.?
Za kolko dulgo putoovate?

236 Where do you come from?
От къде сте?
Ot kude ste?

237 I am/we are from . . .
Аз/ ние съм/сме от . . .
As/nie sum/sme ot . . .

238 We're on holiday.
Ние сме на почивка.
Nie sme na pochifka.

239 This is our first visit here.
За първи път сме тук.
Za purvi put sme took.

240 Would you like/May I have a
cigarette?
Искате ли/може ли
цигара?
Iskate li/Mozhe li tsigara?

241 I am sorry, but I do not
understand.
Извинете, не разбирам.
Izvinete, ne razbiram.

242 Please speak slowly.
Моля, говорете бавно.
Molya, govorete bavno.

243 Do you mind if I smoke?
Мога ли да пуша?
Moga li da poosha?

244 Do you have a light?
Имате ли огънче?
Imate li ogunche?

245 I am waiting for my husband/
wife/boyfriend/girlfriend.
Чакам мъжа/жена/
приятеля/приятелката си.
*Chakam muzhu/zhena/
priyatelya/priyatelkata si.*

TRAVELLING WITH CHILDREN

246 Do you have a high chair/
baby-sitting service/cot?
Имате ли детски стол/
детски гледачки/детско
легло?
*Imate li detski stol/detski
gledachki/detsko leglo?*

247 Where is the nursery/
playroom?
Къде е занималнята/
детската стая?
*Kude e zanimalnyata/detskata
staya?*

248 Where can I warm the baby's
bottle?
Къде мога да стопля
бебешката бутилка?
*Kude moga da stoplya bebeshkata
bootilka?*

COMMUNICATIONS

Post

249 How much will it cost to send
a letter/postcard/this
package to Britain/Ireland/
America/Canada/Australia/
New Zealand?
Колко струва да изпратя
писмо/картичка/този
колет до Англия/
Ирландия/Америка/
Канада/Австралия/Нова
Зеландия?
*Kolko stroova da ispratya pismo/
kartichka/tozi kolet do Angliya/
Irlandiya/Amerika/Kanada/
Afstraliya/Nova Zelandiya?*

250 I would like one stamp/two
stamps.
Искам една марка/две
марки.
Iskam edna marka/dve marki.

251 I'd like . . . stamps for
postcards to send abroad,
please.
Искам . . . марки за
изпращане на картички в
чужбина, моля.
*Iskam . . . marki za izprashtane na
kartichki f choozhbina, molya.*

Phones

252 I would like to make a
telephone call/reverse the
charges to (make a collect call
to) . . .
Искам да се обадя/за
тяхна сметка до . . .
*Iskam da se obadya/za tyahna
smetka do . . .*

253 Which coins do I need for the
telephone?
Какви монети ми трябват
за телефон?
*Kakvi moneti mi tryabvat za
telefon?*

254 The line is engaged (busy).
Линията е заета.
Liniyata e zaeta.

255 The number is . . .
Номерът е . . .
Nomera e . . .

256 Hello, this is . . .
Ало, обажда се . . .
Allo, obazhda se . . .

257 May I speak to . . ?
Мога ли да говоря с . . ?
Moga li da govorya s . . ?

**B
U
L
G
A
R
I
A
N**

**258
↕
273**

258 He/She is not in at the moment. Can you call back?
Той/тя не е тук в момента.
Може ли да се обадите пак?
Toy/tya ne e took f momenta.
Mozhe li da se obadite pak?

MONEY

259 I would like to change these travellers' cheques (travelers' checks)/this currency/this Eurocheque.
Искам да обменя тези туристически чекове/тази валута/този Еврочек.
Iskam da obmenya tezi tooristicheski chekove/tazi valuta/tozi Evrochek.

260 How much commission do you charge? (What is the service charge?)
Колко е комисионната?
Kolko e komisionnata?

261 Can I obtain money with my MasterCard?
Мога ли да използвам мастер кард?
Moga li da ispolzvam MasterCard?

SHOPPING

Names of Shops and Departments

262 Книжарница/Книжарски стоки
Knizharnitsa/Knizharski stoki
Bookshop/Stationery

263 Бижутерия/Подаръци
Bizhooteriya/Podarutsi
Jeweller's/Gifts

264 Обувки
Oboofki
Shoes

265 Железария
Zhelezariya
Hardware

266 Антики
Antiki
Antiques

267 Фризьорски/бръснарски салон
Frizyorski/Brusnarski salon
Hairdresser's (men's)/(women's

268 Будка/щанд за цигари
Bootka/Shtant za tsigari
Tobacconist

269 Хлебарница
Hlebarnitsa
Baker's

270 Супермаркет
Soopermarket
Supermarket

271 Фотомагазин
Fotomagazin
Photo shop

272 Играчки
Igrachki
Toys

273 Туристическа агенция
Tooristicheska agentsiya
Travel Agent

274 Парфюмерия/Тоалетни принадлежности
Parfyumeriya/Toaletni prinadlezhnosti
Toiletries

275 Грамофонни плочи
Gramofonni plochi
Records

In the Shop

276 What time do the shops open/close?
Кога отварят/затварят магазините?
Koga otvaryat/zatvaryat magazinite?

277 Where is the nearest market?
Къде е най-близкият пазар?
Kude e nay-bliskiyat pazar?

278 Can you show me the one in the window/this one?
Може ли да ми покажете онова от витрината/това.
Mozhe li da mi pokazhete onova ot vitrinata/tova?

279 Can I try this on?
Може ли да пробвам това?
Mozhe li da probvam tova?

280 What size is this?
Какъв размер е това?
Kakuf razmer e tova?

281 This is too large/too small/too expensive.
Това е твърде голямо/малко/скъпо.

Tova e tvurde golyamo/malko/skupo.

282 Do you have any others?
Имате ли и други?
Imate li i droogi?

283 My size is . . .
Моят размер е . . .
Moyat razmer e . . .

284 Where is the changing room/childrens'/cosmetic/ladieswear/menswear/food department?
Къде е пробната/детският щанд/козметиката/дамското облекло/мъжкото облекло/щандът за храна?
Kude e probnata/detskiya shtand/kozmetikata/damskoto obleklo/muzhkoto obleklo/shtanda za hrana?

285 I would like . . .
Искам . . .
Iskam . . .

286 I would like a quarter of a kilo/half a kilo/a kilo of bread/butter/cheese/ham/tomatoes.
Искам четвърт/половин/един килограм хляб/масло/сирене/шунка/домати.
Iskam chetvurt/polovin/edin kilogram hlyap/maslo/sirene/shoonka/domati.

B
U
L
G
A
R
I
A
N

274
↕
286

27

287 **How much is this?**
Колко струва Това?
Kolko stroova Tova?

288 **I'll take this one, thank you.**
Ще взема това, благодаря.
Shte vzema tova, blagodarya.

289 **Do you have a carrier (shopping) bag?**
Имате ли торба?
Imate li torba?

290 **Do you have anything cheaper/larger/smaller/of better quality?**
Имате ли нещо по-евтино/по-голямо/по-малко/по-качествено?
Imate li neshto po-eftino/po-golyamo/po-malko/po-kachestveno?

291 **I would like a film for this camera.**
Искам филм за този фотоапарат.
Iskam film za tozi fotoaparat.

292 **I would like some batteries, the same size as this old one.**
Искам батерии, същият размер като тази старата.
Isakm baterii, sushtiya razmer kato tazi starata.

293 **Would you mind wrapping this for me, please?**
Може ли да ми опаковате това, моля?

Mozhe li da mi opakovate tova, molya?

294 **Sorry, but you seem to have given me the wrong change.**
Извинете, но ми връщате неточно ресто.
Izvinete, no mi vrushtate netochno resto.

MOTORING

Car Hire (Rental)

295 **I have ordered (rented) a car in the name of . . .**
Поръчах наех кола на името на . . .
Poruchah naeh kola na imeto na . . .

296 **How much does it cost to hire (rent) a car for one day/two days/one week?**
Колко струва да наема кола за един ден/два дни/седмица?
Kolko stroova da naema kola za edin den/dva dni/sedmitsa?

297 **Is the tank already full of petrol (gas)?**
Пълен ли е резервоарът с бензин?
Pulen li e rezervoara s benzin?

298 **Is insurance and tax included? How much is the deposit?**
Включени ли са застраховката и данък? Колко е депозитът?

F klyoocheni li sa zastrahofkata i danuk? Kolko e depozita?

299 By what time must I return the car?

Кога трябва да върна колата?

Koga tryabva da vurna kolata?

300 I would like a small/family car with a radio/cassette player.

Искам малка/голяма кола с радио/касетофон.

Iskam malka/golyama kola s radio/kasetofon.

Asking the Way

301 Excuse me, can you help me please?

Извинявайте, може ли да ми помогнете, моля?

Izvinyavayte, mozhe li da mi pomognete, molya?

302 How do I reach the motorway/main road?

Как да стигна до автомагистралата/ главния път?

Kak da stigna do aftomagistralata/glavniya put?

303 I think I have taken the wrong turning.

Мисля, че завих неправилно.

Mislya, che zavih nepravilno.

304 I am looking for this address.

Търся този адрес.

Tursya tozi adres.

305 I am looking for the . . . hotel.

Търся хотел . . .

Tursya hotel . . .

306 How far is it to . . . from here?

Колко е от тук до . . .

Kolko e ot took do . . .

307 Carry straight on for . . . kilometres.

Продължете направо около . . . километра.

Produlzhete napravo okolo . . . kilometra.

308 Take the next turning on the right/left.

Завийте на следващата пресечка на дясно/ляво.

Zaviyte na sledvashtata presechka na dyasno/lyavo.

309 Turn right/left at the next crossroads/traffic lights.

Завийте надясно/наляво на следващото кръстовище/следващия светофар.

Zaviyte nadyasno/nalyavo na sledvashtoto krustovishte/ sledvashtiya svetofar.

310 You are going in the wrong direction.

Вие се движите в грешната посока.

Vie se dvizhite f greshnata posoka.

MOTORING

Parking

311 **How long can I park here?**
За колко време мога да
паркирам тук?
Za kolko vreme moga da parkiram took?

312 **Is there a car park near here?**
Има ли паркинг наблизо?
Ima li parking nablizo?

313 **At what time does this car park close?**
Кога затварят този
паркинг?
Koga zatvaryat tozi parking?

Signs and Notices

314 Еднопосочна улица
Ednoposochna oolitsa
One way

315 Влизането забранено
Vlizaneto zabraneno
No entry

316 Паркирането забранено
Parkiraneto zabraneno
No parking

317 Отклонение.
Otklonenie
Detour (diversion)

318 Спри/Стоп
Spri/Stop
Stop

319 Дай път
Dai put
Give way (yield)

320 Хлъзгав път
Hluzgaf put
Slippery road.

321 Изпреварването
забранено
Isprevarvaneto zabraneno
No overtaking

At the Filling Station

322 **Unleaded (lead-free)/
Standard/Premium**
Бензин без олово/
обикновен/супер
*Benzin bes olovo/obiknoven/
sooper.*

323 **Fill the tank please.**
Напълнете резервоара,
моля
Napulnete rezervoara, molya

324 **Do you have a road map of this area?**
Имате ли пътна карта на
този район?
Imate li putna karta na tozi rayon?

325 **How much is the car-wash?**
Колко струва измиването
на кола?
Kolko stroova izmivaneto na kola?

Breakdowns

326 **I've had a breakdown at . . .**
Колата ми се повреди в . . .
Kolata mi se povredi f . . .

327 **I am on the road from . . . to . . .**

Аз съм на пътя от . . .
за . . .
*Az sum na putya ot . . .
za . . .*

328 I can't move the car. Can you send a tow-truck?
Не мога да подкарам колата. Може ли да изпратите камион за теглене?
Ne moga da potkaram kolata. Mozhe li da ispratite kamiyon za teglene?

329 I have a flat tyre.
Спуках гума.
Spookah gooma.

330 The windscreen (windshield) has smashed/cracked.
Предното стъкло е счупено/спукано.
Prednoto stuklo e schupeno/spookano.

331 There is something wrong with the engine/brakes/lights/steering/gearbox/clutch/exhaust.
Двигателят/спирачките/светлините/кормилото/скоростната кутия/амбреажът/ауспухът ми не е/са в ред.
Dvigatelyat/spirachkite/svetlinite/kormiloto/skorostnata kootiya/ambreazhut/aspoohut mi ne e/ sa f ret.

332 It's overheating.
Прегрява.
Pregryava.

333 It won't start.
Не иска да пали.
Ne iska da pali.

334 Where can I get it repaired?
Къде могат да я поправят?
Kude mogat da ya popravyat?

335 Can you take me there?
Може ли да ме заведете там?
Mozhe li da me zavedete tam?

336 Will it take long to fix?
Много ли време трябва, за да се поправи?
Mnogo li vreme tryabva, za da se popravi?

337 How much will it cost?
Колко ще струва?
Kolko shte stroova?

Accidents

338 Can you help me? There has been an accident.
Може ли да ми помогнете? Стана катастрофа.
Mozhe li da mi pomognete? Stana katastrofa.

339 Please call the police/an ambulance.
Моля, повикайте полиция/линейка.
Molya, povikayte politsiya/lineyka.

340 Is anyone hurt?
Има ли ранени?
Ima li raneni?

Traffic Offences

341 I'm sorry, I didn't see the sign.
Съжалявам. Не видях знака.
Suzhalyavam, ne vidiyah znaka.

342 Must I pay a fine? How much?
Трябва ли да платя глоба? Колко?
Tryabva li da platya globa? Kolko?

343 Show me your documents.
Покажете ми документите си.
Pokazhete mi dokoomentite si.

HEALTH

Pharmacy

344 Do you have anything for a stomachache/headache/sore throat/toothache?
Имате ли нещо за стомах/глава/гърло/зъби?
Imate li neshto za stomah/glava/gurlo/zubi?

345 I need something for diarrhoea (diarrhea)/constipation/a cold/a cough/insect bites/sunburn/travel (motion) sickness.

Трябва ми нещо за разстройство/запек/настинка/кашлица / ухапване от насекоми/слънчево изгаряне/гадене при пътуване.
Tryabva mi neshto za rastroystvo/zapek/nastinka/kashlitsa/oohapvane ot nasekomi/slunchevo izgaryane/gadene pri putoovane.

346 How much/how many do I take?
Колко се взема?
Kolko se vzema?

347 How often do I take it/them?
Колко често се взема?
Kolko chesto se vzema?

348 How much does it cost?
Колко струва?
Kolko stroova?

349 Can you recommend a good doctor/dentist?
Можете ли да ми препоръчате добър доктор/зъболекар?
Mozhete li da mi preporuchate dobur doktor/zubolekar?

350 Is it suitable for children?
Подходящо ли е за деца?
Pothodyashto li e za detsa?

Doctor

351 I have a pain here/in my arm/leg/chest/stomach.
Боли ме тук/ръката/крака/гърдите/стомахът.

*Boli me took/rukata/kraka/
gurdite/stomaha.*

352 **Please call a doctor, this is an emergency.**
Извикайте лекар, това е
спешен случай.
*Izvikayte lekar, tova e speshen
sloochay.*

353 **I would like to make an appointment to see a doctor.**
Искам час за преглед.
Iskam chas za pregled.

354 **I am diabetic/pregnant.**
Аз съм диабетик/
бременна.
As sum diabetik/bremenna.

355 **I need a prescription for . . .**
Искам рецепта за . . .
Iskam retsepta za . . .

356 **Can you give me something to ease the pain?**
Можете ли да ми дадете
болкоуспокояващо?
*Mozhete li da mi dadete
bolkooospokoyavashto?*

357 **I am/he is/she is allergic to penicillin.**
Имам/има алергия към
пеницилин
Imam/ima alergiya kum penitsilin.

358 **Does this hurt?**
Боли ли?
Boli li?

359 **You must/he must/she must go to hospital.**

Вие/той/тя трябва да
отиде/те в болница.
*Vie/toy/tya tryabva da otide/te f
bolnitsa.*

360 **Take these once/twice/three times a day.**
Вземайте от тези веднъж/
два/три пъти на ден.
*Vzemayte ot tezi vednuzh/dva/tri/
puti na den.*

361 **I am/he is/she is taking this medication.**
Аз вземам/той/тя взема
това лекарство.
*Az vzemam/toy/tya vzema tova
lekarstvo.*

362 **I have medical insurance.**
Имам медицинска/
здравна застраховка.
*Imam meditsinska/zdravna
zastrahovka.*

Dentist

363 **I have toothache.**
Боли ме зъб.
Boli me zup.

364 **My filling has come out.**
Падна ми пломба.
Padna mi plomba.

365 **I do/do not want to have an injection first.**
Искам/не искам първо
инжекция.
Iskam/ne iskam purvo inzhektsya.

EMERGENCIES

366 **Help!**
Помощ!
Pomosht!

367 **Call an ambulance/a doctor/
the police!**
Извикайте линейка/
доктор/полицията!
*Izvikayte lineyka/doktor/
politsiyata!*

368 **I have had my travellers'
cheques (travelers' checks)/
credit cards/purse/handbag/
rucksack (knapsack)/
luggage/wallet stolen.**
Откраднаха ми
туристическите чекове/
кредит картите/
портмонето/чантата/
раницата/багажа
портфейла.
*Orkradnaha mi tooristicheskite
chekove/kredit kartite/
portmoneto/chantata/ranitsata/
bagazha portfeyla.*

369 **Can you help me, I have lost
my daughter/son?**
Може ли да ми помогнете,
загубих дъщеря/сина си?
*Mozhe li da mi pomognete,
zagoobih dushterya si/sina si?*

370 **Please, go away/leave me
alone.**
Оставете ме на мира.
Ostavete me na mira.

371 **Fire!**
Пожар!
Pozhar!

372 **I want to contact the British/
American/Canadian/Irish/
Australian/New Zealand/
South African consulate.**
Искам да се свържа с
британското/
американското/
канадското/ирландското/
австралийското/
новозеландското/
южноафриканското
консулство.
*Iskam da se svurzha s britanskoto/
amerikanskoto/kanatskoto/
irlandskoto/afstraliyskoto/
novozelandskoto/
yuzhnoafrikanskoto konsulstvo.*

Introduction

Czech is the official language of the Czech Republic. The language spoken in neighbouring Slovakia is Slovak, but the two are so closely related that speakers of one can easily understand the other. Both belong to the Slavic family of languages that includes Russian and Polish. In larger cities, particularly in the Czech Republic, English is spoken, and German is often a second language for many Czechs. Russian is also widely understood, but not popular.

C
Z
E
C
H

Addresses for travel and tourist information

The following addresses are the tourist authorities for both the Czech Republic and for Slovakia.

South Africa: *Embassy,* 936 Pretorius St, Arcadia 0083, PO Box 3326, Pretoria 0001; tel: 27 12 3423477 / 4303601

UK: *Cedok Travel Limited,* Suite 22–23, 5th Floor, Morley House, 314–322 Regent Street, London, W1B 3BG; tel: (020) 7580 3778.

ESSENTIALS

Alphabet

A	B
ah	*bey*
C	D
tsey	*dey*
E	F
ey	*ef*
G	H
gey	*hah*
CH	I
khah	*ee*
J	K
yeh	*kah*
L	M
el	*em*
N	O
en	*oh*
P	Q
pey	*koo*
R	S
yer	*es*
T	U
tey	*oo*
V	W
veh	*dvoyiteh veh*
X	Y
iks	*oopsi-lon*
Z	
tset	

Basic Words and Phrases

1. **Yes** / **No**
   Ano / Ne
   Unnoh / *neh*

2. **Please** / **Thank you**
   Prosím / Děkuji
   Prosseem / *Dyekoo-yi*

3. **That's o.k.** / **Perhaps**
   Prima / Možná
   Preemmah / *Mozhnah*

4. **To** / **From**
   Do / Od
   Doh / *odd*

5. **Here** / **There**
   Zde / Tam
   Zdhe / *Tahm*

6. **None** / **Also**
   Žádný / Také
   Zhadnee / *Tukeh*

7. **How** / **When**
   Jak / Kdy
   Yuck / *Gdy*

8. **What** / **Why**
   Co / Proč
   Tsoh / *Prroch*

9. **I don't understand.**
   Nerozumím.
   Nerohzuhmeem.

10. **I don't speak Czech.**
    Nemluvím česky.
    Nemluhveem chesky.

11. **Do you speak English?**
    Mluvíte anglicky?
    Mluhveete ahnglitsky?

CZECH

01 ↑ 11

36

12 **Can you please write it down?**
Můžete to, prosím, napsat?
Moozheteh toh, prohseem, nahpsaht?

13 **Can you please speak more slowly?**
Můžete, prosím, mluvit pomaleji?
Moozheteh, prohseem, mluhvit pohmahlayi?

14 **How much does it/this cost?**
Kolik to/tohle stojí?
Kollick toh/toh-hleh stoyee?

Days

15 **Monday**
pondělí
Pondyellee

Tuesday
úterý
Ooteree

16 **Wednesday**
středa
Stzheddah

Thursday
čtvrtek
Shtvertek

17 **Friday**
pátek
Pahtek

Saturday
sobota
Sobbottah

18 **Sunday**
neděle
Neddyelleh

Morning
ráno
Rahnoh

19 **Afternoon**
odpoledne
Odpoledneh

Evening
večer
Vesherr

20 **Night**
noc
Nots

Week
týden
Teeden

21 **Yesterday/Today/Tomorrow**
včera/dnešek/zítra
Fcherah/dnehshceck/zeetrah

Numbers

22 **Zero**
nula
Noola

One
jedna
Yednah

23 **Two**
dvě
Dvyeh

Three
tři
Tzhee

24 **Four**
čtyři
Shteezhee

Five
pět
Pyet

25 **Six**
šest
Shest

Seven
sedm
Seddoom

26 **Eight**
osm
Ossoom

Nine
devět
Devyet

27 **Ten**
deset
Desset

Eleven
jedenáct
Yeddenahtst

28 **Twelve**
dvanáct
Dvunnahtst

Thirteen
třináct
Tzheenahtst

29 **Fourteen**
čtrnáct
Shtrnahtst

Fifteen
patnáct
Puttnahtst

30 **Sixteen**
šestnáct
Shestnahtst

Seventeen
sedmnáct
Seddoomnahtst

31 **Eighteen**
osmnáct
Ossoomnahtst

Nineteen
devatenáct
Devvuttehnahtst

C
Z
E
C
H

12
↕
31

ESSENTIALS

32 Twenty
dvacet
Dvutset

Twenty-one
dvacet jeden
Dvutset yedden

33 Twenty-two
dvacet dva
Dvutset dvah

Thirty
třicet
Tzhitset

34 Forty
čtyřicet
Shteezhitset

Fifty
padesát
Puddessaht

35 Sixty
šedesát
Sheddessaht

Seventy
sedmdesát
Seddoomdessaht

36 Eighty
osmdesát
Ossoodessaht

Ninety
devadesát
Devvuddessaht

37 One hundred
sto
Stoh

Five hundred
pět set
Pyet set

38 One thousand
tisíc
Tyisseets

One million
milión
Meeleeon

Time

39 9.00
devět hodin
Devvyet hoddyinn

40 9.05
devět pět
Devvyet pyet

41 9.10
devět deset
Devvyet desset

42 9.15
čtvrt na desset
Shtvert naa desset

43 9.20
devět dvacet
Devvyet dvutset

44 9.25
devět dvacet pět
Devvyet dvutset pyet

45 9.30
půl desáté
Pool dessahte

46 9.35
devět třicet pět
Devvyet tzhitset pyet

47 9.40
devět čtyřicet
Devvyet shteezhitset

48 9.45
tříčtvrtě na deset
Tzheeshtvertye naa desset

49 9.50
za deset minut deset
Zaa desset minnoot desset

50 9.55
za pět minut deset
Zaa pyet minnoot desset

51 12.00/Midday/Midnight
dvanáct/poledne/půlnoc
Dvunnahtst/poledne/poolnots

52 What time is it?
Kolik je hodin
Kollick yeh hoddin

53 It is . . .
Je . . .
Yeh . . .

ARRIVING AND DEPARTING

Airport

54 **Excuse me, where is the check-in desk for . . . airline?**
Promiňte, kde se odbavuje letecká společnost . . .?
Prohminyete, gde sse ohdbahvuhyeh letetskar spohletchnost . . ?

55 **What is the boarding gate/ time for my flight?**
Kterou branou/V kolik hodin se nastupuje na můj let?
Kteroe brahnoe/Fkollick hodyin sse nahstuhpuhyeh nah mooy let?

56 **How long is the delay likely to be?**
Jak velké asi bude to zpoždění?
Yuck velkeh ahssee buhdeh toh zpozhdyenyee?

57 **Where is the duty-free shop?**
Kde je bezcelní obchod?
Gdeh yeh beztselnyee ophod?

58 **Which way is the baggage reclaim?**
Kde je výdej zavazadel?
Gdeh yeh veedey zahvahzahdel?

59 **Where can I get the bus to the city centre?**
Odkud jede autobus do centra města?

Otkuhd yede aootobuhs dotsentrah mnyesta?

Train Station

60 **Where is the ticket office/ information desk?**
Kde je výdejna jízdenek/Kde jsou informace?
Gdeh yeh veedeynah yeezdenek/ gdeh sow informatse?

61 **Which platform does the train to . . . depart from?**
Z kterého nástupiště odjíždí vlak do . . ?
Z ktehraihoh nahstoopishtyeh odyeezhdee vluck doh . . ?

62 **Where is platform . . ?**
Kde je . . . nástupiště?
Gdeh yeh . . . nahstoopishtyeh?

63 **When is the next train to . . ?**
Kdy jede další vlak do . . ?
Gdy yeddeh daalshee vluck do . . ?

64 **Is there a later train to . . ?**
Jede později vlak do . . ?
Yeddeh pozdyeyee vluck doh . . ?

Port

65 **How do I get to the port?**
Jak se dostanu do přístavu . . ?
Yuck seh dostahnoo doh pzheestavoo . . ?

66 **When is the next sailing to . . ?**
Kdy jede příští loď?
Gdy yedeh pzheeshtee lodye?

39

CZECH

54 ↑ 66

⁶⁷ **Can I catch an earlier ferry with this ticket?**
Mohu jet na tenhle lístek dřívější lodí?
Mohuh yet nah tenhleh leestek drzheevyeyshee lodyee?

Notices and Signs

⁶⁸ **Bufetový vůz**
Boofetovee vooz
Buffet (Dining) Car

⁶⁹ **Autobus**
Aootohbooss
Bus

⁷⁰ **Pitná voda/nepitná voda**
Peetnah voddah
Drinking/Non-drinking water

⁷¹ **Vchod**
Vkhod
Entrance

⁷² **Východ**
Veekhod
Exit

⁷³ **Informace**
Informatseh
Information

⁷⁴ **Úschovna zavazadel**
Ooskhovnah zuvvahzuddel
Left Luggage (Baggage Claim)

⁷⁵ **Skříňky na zavazadla**
Skzheenkee nah zuvvahzuddlah
Luggage Lockers

⁷⁶ **Pošta**
Poshtah
Post Office

⁷⁷ **Nástupiště**
Nahstoopishtyeh
Platform

⁷⁸ **Železniční nádraží**
Zheleznechnee nahdrahzhee
Railway (Railroad) Station

⁷⁹ **Letiště**
Letyishtye
Airport

⁸⁰ **Přístav**
Przheestahf
Port

⁸¹ **Restaurace**
Restauratse
Restaurant

⁸² **Kuřáci/nekuřáci**
Koozhahtsi/nehkoozhatsi
Smoking/Non-smoking

⁸³ **Telefon**
Tellefohn
Telephone

⁸⁴ **Pokladna**
Pokludnah
Ticket Office

⁸⁵ **Odbavovací přepážka**
Ohdbahvohvahtsee przhepashka
Check-in Desk

⁸⁶ **Jízdní řád**
Yeezdnyee zhaht
Timetable (Schedule)

⁸⁷ **Záchod**
Zahkhot
Toilets (Restrooms)

88 **Páni**
Pahni
Gentlemen

89 **Dámy**
Dahmy
Ladies'

90 **Tramvaj**
Trumvahay
Tram (Streetcar)

91 **Podzemní dráha**
Podzemnee draahah
Underground (Subway)

92 **Čekárna**
Chekaarnah
Waiting Room

Buying a Ticket

93 **I would like a first-class/
second-class single (one-
way)/return (round-trip)
ticket to . . .**
Prosím jízdenku první/druhé
třídy/zpáteční do . . .
*Prosseem yeezdenkooh pervnee
tzheedy/droohe tzheedy/
zpaatechnee doh . . .*

94 **Is my rail pass valid on this
train/ferry/bus?**
Platí moje sí ťová železniční
jízdenka na tento vlak/na tuto
loď/na tento autobus?
*Plahtyee moye seetyovar
zheleznyichnee yeezdenkah nah
tentoh vluck/nah tuhtoh lodye/
nah tentoh aootohbuhs?*

95 **I would like an aisle/**

window seat.
Přeji si místo u chodbičky/u okna.
*Pzheye ssi meestoh oo
khodbichky/oo ocknah.*

96 **No smoking/smoking,
please.**
Nekuřáci/kuřáci, prosím.
*Nehckuzhaatsi/kuzhaatsi,
prosseem.*

97 **We would like to sit
together.**
Chceme sedět spolu.
Khtsemeh ssedyet spohloo.

98 **I would like to make a seat
reservation.**
Rád(a) bych si rezervoval(a)
místenku.
*Rahd(ah) bikh sih
rezerrvoval(ah) meestenkuh.*

99 **I would like to reserve a
couchette/sleeper for one
person/two people/for my
family.**
Rád bych rezervoval lehátko/
lůžko pro jednu osobu/dvě
osoby/pro rodinu.
*Rahd bykh rezervohvahl
lehhahtkoh/loozhkoh proh
yednoo osohboo/dvyeh osohby/
proh rodyeenoo.*

100 **I would like to reserve a
cabin.**
Rád(a) bych si rezervoval(a)
kabinu.
*Rahd(ah) bikh sih
rezerrvoval(ah) kahbinuh.*

C
Z
E
C
H

88
↑
100

ARRIVING AND DEPARTING

Timetables (Schedules)

¹⁰¹ **Přijede**
Pzhiyeddeh
Arrive

¹⁰² **Zastavuje . . .**
Zustahvooye . . .
Calls (Stops) at . . .

¹⁰³ **Dodávky jídla**
Dohdaafkee yeedlah
Catering Service

¹⁰⁴ **Přestupte . . .**
Pzhestoopteh . . .
Change at . . .

¹⁰⁵ **Spojení**
Spoyenee
Connection

¹⁰⁶ **Denně**
Denye
Daily

¹⁰⁷ **Každých čtyřicet minut**
Kazhdeekh shteezhitset minnoot
Every 40 minutes

¹⁰⁸ **První třída**
Pervnee tzheedah
First-class

¹⁰⁹ **Každou hodinu**
Kahzhdoow hoddyinoo
Hourly

¹¹⁰ **Doporučují se místenky**
Dohporuchoyee seh meestenky
Seat reservations are
recommended

¹¹¹ **Druhá třída**
Droohah tzheedah

Second-class

¹¹² **Platí se příplatek**
Plahtee seh pzheeplahtek
Supplement Payable

¹¹³ **Přes**
Pzhez
Via

Luggage

¹¹⁴ **How much will it cost to
send (ship) my luggage in
advance?**
Kolik stojí poslat zavazadlo
dopředu?
*Kohlick stohyee poslaht
zuvvahzuddlah dohpzhedoo?*

¹¹⁵ **Where is the left luggage
(baggage claim) office?**
Kde je úschovna?
Gde yeh ooskhohvnah?

¹¹⁶ **What time do you open/
close?**
Kdy otvíráte/zavíráte?
Gdy ohtveerahteh/zuvveerahteh?

¹¹⁷ **Where are the luggage
trolleys (carts)?**
Kde jsou vozíky na
zavazadla?
*Gde ysow vohzeeky nah
zuvvazuddlah?*

¹¹⁸ **Where are the lockers?**
Kde jsou skříňky na
zavazadla?
*Gdeh soe skrzheenyeki
nahzahvahzahddah?*

119 I have lost my locker key.
Ztratil jsem klíč od skříňky.
Ztrahtil sehm kleech odh skzheenky.

On Board

120 Is this seat taken?
Je toto místo volné?
Yeh tohotoh meestoh vohlneeh?

121 Excuse me, you are sitting in my reserved seat.
Promiňte, to je moje rezervované místo.
Prohminyteh, toh yeh mohye rezervohvahneeh meestoh.

122 Which station is this?
Která je to stanice?
Ktehraah yeh toh stanitseh?

123 What time is this train/bus/ferry/flight due to arrive/depart?
V kolik hodin tenhle vlak/tenhle autobus/tahle loď/tohle letadlo přijíždí/odjíždí?
Fkollick hodyin tenhleh vluck/tenhleh aootohbuhs/tahhleh lodye/tohhleh lehtadloh przhiyeezhdyee/odyeezhdyee?

124 Will you wake me just before we arrive?
Probudíte mě než zastavíme?
Prohbudyteh mnye nezh zahstahveemeh?

Customs and Passports

125 Prosím pasy!
Prosseem passy!
Passports, please!

126 I have nothing/wine/spirits (alcohol)/tobacco to declare.
Nemám nic/Mám víno/alkohol/tabák k proclení.
Nemaahm nits/Maahm veenoh/alckohol/tabaack kh protslenee.

127 I shall be staying for . . . days/weeks/months.
Budu zde . . . dní/týdnů/měsíců.
Boodoo zdeh . . . dnee/teednoo/mnyeseetsoo.

AT THE TOURIST OFFICE

128 Do you have a map of the town/area?
Máte mapu města/okolí?
Mahteh mahpoo mnyestah/ohkohlee?

129 Can I reserve accommodation here?
Mohu si zde rezervovat ubytování?
Mohhooseezdeh rezervohvaht oobytovaanyee?

130 Do you have a list of accommodation?
Máte seznam možností ubytování?
Mahteh seznam mozhnostyee ubitohvahnyee?

ACCOMMODATION

ACCOMMODATION

Hotels

131 I have a reservation in the name of . . .
Mám rezervaci na jméno . . .
Mahm rezervatsi nah mehnnoh . . .

132 I wrote to/faxed/telephoned you last month/last week in . . .
Psal(a)/faxoval(a)/telefonoval(a) jsem vám minulý měsíc/minulý týden v . . .
Psal(ah)/fahksoval(ah)/ telefohnoval(ah) sem vahm minuhlee mnyesseets/minuhlee teeden v . . .

133 Do you have any rooms free?
Máte nějaké volné pokoje?
Mahte nyeyakeh volneh pockoyeh?

134 I would like to reserve a single/double room with/ without bath/shower.
Rád bych rezervoval jednolůžkový/dvojlůžkový pokoj s koupelnou/bez koupelny/se sprchou.
Rahd bykh rezervohvahl pockoy ss kowpelnow/bess kowpelny/ seh sperkhow.

135 I would like bed and breakfast/(room and) half board/(room and) full board.
Rád bych pokoj se snídaní/

polopenzí/plnou penzí.
Rahd bykh pockoy seh sneedanee/pohlohpenzee/plnow penzi.

136 How much is it per night?
Kolik to stojí za jednu noc?
Kollick toh stoyee zah yednoo nots?

137 Is breakfast included?
Je to se snídaní?
Ye toh seh sneedahnee?

138 May I see the room?
Smím se na pokoj podívat?
Smeem seh nah pokoy podeevaht?

139 Do you have any cheaper rooms?
Máte lacinější pokoje?
Mahte latsinyeyshee pockoyeh?

140 I would like to take the room.
Vezmu si tento pokoj.
Vezmoo si tento pockoy.

141 I would like to stay for . . . nights.
Rád bych zůstal . . . nocí.
Rahd bykh zoostahl . . . notsee.

142 The shower/light/tap doesn't work.
Sprcha/světlo/kohoutek nefunguje.
Sprhah/svyetloh/kohoetek nefunguyeh.

143 At what time/where is breakfast served?

44

Kdy a kde se podává snídaně?
Gdy a gde se pohdahvah sneedahnye?

144 What time do I have to check-out?
Kdy musím uvolnit pokoj?
Gdy moozem oovolniht pockoy?

145 Can I have the key to room no . . ?
Můžu dostat klíč od pokoje číslo . . ?
Moozhuh dohstaht kleech ot pockohyeh cheesloh . . ?

146 My room number is . . .
Číslo mého pokoje je . . .
Cheesloh mehoh pockoyeh yeh . . .

147 Do you accept travellers' cheques/Eurocheques/ credit cards?
Přijímáte cestovní šeky/ Eurošeky/kreditní karty?
Prziyeemahteh tsestovnee sheki/ eoorosheki/kreditnyee karti?

148 May I have the bill please?
Účet, prosím?
Oochet, prosseem?

149 Excuse me, I think there is a mistake in this bill.
Promiňte, myslím, že v tomto účtu je chyba.
Prominyete, misleem zhe ftomtoh oochtuh yeh hibah.

Youth Hostels

150 How much is a dormitory bed per night?

Kolik stojí lůžko v noclehárně?
Kollick stoyee loozhkoh v notslehahrnye?

151 I am/am not an HI member.
Jsem/nejsem členem HI.
Sem/neysem chlehnehm ee, oopsi-lon, hah, ah.

152 May I use my own sleeping bag?
Můžu používat vlastní spacák?
Moozhoo powsheevath vlastnee spatsahck?

153 What time do you lock the doors at night?
Kdy v noci zamykáte?
Gdy v notsi zahmykahteh?

Camping

154 May I camp here for the night/two nights?
Můžu zde stanovat jednu noc/dvě noci?
Moozhoo zdeh stahnovaht jehdnoo nots/dvye notsi?

155 Where can I pitch my tent?
Kde můžu postavit stan?
Gde moozhoo postahvit stahn?

156 How much does it cost for one night/one week?
Kolik stojí jedna noc/jeden týden?
Kollick stoyee yednah nots/yeden tyhdehn?

C Z E C H

157 Where can we park our caravan?
Kam můžeme zaparkovat náš obytný přívěs?
Kam moozhemeh zaparrkohvat nahsh obitnee przheevyes?

158 Where are the washing facilities?
Kde jsou umývárny?
Gde sow oomyhvahrny?

159 Is there a restaurant/ supermarket/swimming pool on site/nearby?
Je tady/blízko restaurce/ supermarket/plovárna?
Yeh tahdyh/bleezkoh restauratseh/supermarkeht/ plohvahrnah?

160 Do you have a safety deposit box?
Máte trezor?
Mahteh trehzohr?

EATING AND DRINKING

Cafés and Bars

161 I would like a cup of/two cups of/another coffee/tea.
Prosím šálek/dva šálky kávy/ ještě kávu/čaje.
Prosseem shahleck/dvah shahlkyh/yeshtye kahvoo/chaye.

162 With/without milk/sugar.
S mlékem/cukrem. Bez mléka/ cukru.
Ss mlaikehm/tsookrehm. Behz mlaikah/tsookroo.

163 I would like a bottle/glass/ two glasses of mineral water/red wine/white wine, please.
Prosím láhev/sklenku/dvě sklenky minerální vody/ červeného vína/bílého vína.
Prosseem lahhehv/sklehnku/ dvye sklehnkyh minehrahlnee voddy/chervehnehoh veenah/ beelehhoh veenah.

164 I would like a beer/two beers, please.
Prosím pivo/dvě piva.
Prosseem pivoh/dvye pivah.

165 May I have some ice?
Led, prosím.
Lehd, prosseem.

166 Do you have any matches/ cigarettes/cigars?
Máte zápalky/cigarety/ doutníky?
Mahte zahpalkyh/tsigartyh/ dowtneekyh?

Restaurants

167 Can you recommend a good/inexpensive restaurant in this area?
Můžete doporučit dobrou/ lacinou restauraci v okolí?
Moozheteh dohporuhchit dobrow latsinow restauratsi vh ohkohlee?

168 I would like a table for . . . people.
Přeji si stůl pro . . . osoby.

*Pzheyee sih stool proh . . .
ohsohby.*

169 Do you have a non-smoking area?
Máte nekuřáckou část?
Mahteh nehkuhrzhahtskoe chahst?

170 Waiter/Waitress!
Číšníku/číšnice!
Cheeshneekoo/cheeshnitse!

171 Do you have a set menu/children's menu/wine list?
Máte sestavené menu/ dětské menu/ceník nápojů?
Mahteh sehstahveneh menuh/ dyetskeh menuh/tseneek nahpojoo?

172 Do you have any vegetarian dishes, please?
Máte, prosím, vegetariánská jídla?
Mahteh, prosseem, veghetahriahnskeh yeedlah?

173 Are there any local specialities?
Máte nějaké místní speciality?
Mahte nyeyakeh meestnye spetsialiti?

174 Are vegetables included?
Je v tom také zelenina?
Yeh ftom tahkeh zelenyinah?

175 Could I have it well-cooked/medium/rare please?
Mohl(a) bych to dostat dobře/středně/jen lehce propečené, prosím?

Mohl(ah) bikh toh dostat dobrzhe/strzhednye/yen lehtse propetcheneh, prosseem?

176 I would like the set menu, please.
Sestavené menu, prosím.
(Sestahveneh menuh, prosseem.)

177 I would like the set menu, please.
Sestavené menu, prosím.
Sestahveneh menuh, prosseem.

178 We have not been served yet.
Ještě jsme nebyli obslouženi.
Yeshtye smeh nehbyhli obslowzhenih.

179 Excuse me, this is not what I ordered.
Promiňte, ale tohle jsem si neobjednal(a).
Prohminyete, ahleh toh-hle sem si ne-ohbyednal(ah).

180 May I have some/some more bread/water/coffee/tea?
Přeji si/více chleba/vody/kávy/čaje.
Pzheyi sih/veetse khbleba/voddy/chaye.

181 May I have the bill, please?
Účet, prosím?
Oochet, prosseem?

182 Does this bill include service?
Zahrnuje účet obsluhu?
Zahrnooye oochet obsloohoo?

CZECH

169 ↕ 182

183 Do you accept travellers'
cheques (travelers' checks)/
Eurocheques/MasterCard/
US dollars?
Berete cestovní šeky/
Eurošeky/MasterCard/
americké dolary?
*Bereteh tsestovnee shehkyh/
Euroshekyh/Masterkard/
ahmehritskeh dohlaryh?*

184 Can I have a receipt, please?
Můžete mi vystavit účtenku,
prosím?
*Moozhetemi vistahvit
oochtenkuh, prosseem?*

185 Where is the toilet
(restroom), please?
Prosím, kde jsou toalety?
Prosseem, gde sow toaletyh?

On the Menu

186 First courses
Předkrmy
Przhetkrmi

187 Soups
Polévky
Polehvki

188 Main courses
Hlavní jídla
Hlavnyee yeedlah

189 Fish dishes
Rybí pokrmy
Ribee pohkrmi

190 Meat dishes
Masitá jídla
Mahssitah yeedlah

191 Vegetarian dishes
Vegetariánská/Bezmasá jídla
*Vehgehtahrianskah/Bezmahssah
yeedlah*

192 Cheese
Sýry
Seerri

193 Desserts
Moučníky/Zákusky
Moechnyeeki/Zahkooski

194 Specialities
Speciality
Spetsialiti

GETTING AROUND

Public Transport

195 Where is the bus stop/
coach station/nearest metro
(subway) station?
Kde je autobusová zastávka/
autokarová stanice/nejbližší
metro zastávka?
*Gde yeh aoothoboosovah
zahstahvkah/auuthokahrovah
stanitseh/neyblizhshee metroh
zahstahvkah?*

196 When is the next/last bus
to . . ?
Kdy jede další/poslední
autobus do . . ?
*Gdy yedeh dalshee/poslednee
aoothobos doh . . ?*

197 How much is the fare to the
city centre (downtown)/
railway (railroad) station/
airport?

GETTING AROUND

Kolik stojí jízdenka do středu
města/na železniční nádraží/
na letiště?
*Kollick stoyee yeezdehnkah doh
stzhedoo mystah/nah
zheleznichnee nahdrazhee/nah
lehtishtye?*

**198 Will you tell me when to
get off?**
Reknete mi kde vystoupit?
*Zheknyeteh mee gdeh
vyhstowpith?*

199 Does this bus go to . . ?
Jede tento autobus do . . ?
*Yedeh tentoh aoothoboos
doh . . ?*

**200 Which number bus goes
to . . ?**
Které číslo autobusu jede do . . ?
*Ktehreh cheesloh aoothoboosoo
yedeh doh . . ?*

**201 May I have a single (one-
way)/return (round-trip)/
day ticket/book of tickets?**
Prosím jízdenku/zpáteční/
denní lístek/svazek lístků.
*Prosseem yeezdehnkoo/
zpahtechnee/dehnee leesteck/
svahzeck leestkoo.*

Taxis

**202 I would like to go to . . .
How much will it cost?**
Jedu do . . . Kolik to stojí?
*Yedoo doh . . . Kollick toh
stoyee?*

203 Please stop here.
Zastavte zde, prosím.
Zahstahvteh zdeh, prosseem.

**204 I would like to order a taxi
today/tomorrow/at 2pm to
go from . . . to . . .**
Rád bych objednal taxi na
dnešek/zítra/ve čtrnáct hodin
od . . . do . . .
*Rahd bykh ohbyednahl taxi nah
dnehsheck/zeetrah/ve shternahtst
hoddinh od . . .doh . . .*

Asking the Way

**205 Excuse me, do you speak
English?**
Promiňte, mluvíte anglicky?
*Prohmihnyete, mlooveeteh
ahnlitskyh?*

**206 Excuse me, is this the
right way to . . ?**
Promiňte, jdu tudy
správně . . .
*Prohminyete, jduh toodi
sprahvnye . . .*

**207 . . . the cathedral/the
tourist information office/
the castle/the old town**
. . . ke katedrále/k turistické
informační kanceláři/ke
hradu/ke starému městu
*ke kahtedrahleh/ktooristitskeh
informmachnyee kahntselahrzhi/
ke hradoo/ke stahrehmuh
mnyestuh.*

C
Z
E
C
H

198
↑
207

49

C
Z
E
C
H

208 Can you tell me the way to the railway station/bus station/taxi rank (stand)/ city centre (downtown)/ beach?
Jak se dostanu na nádraží/ autobusové nádraží/ stanoviště autotaxi/střed města/pláž?
Yuck seh dostahnoo nah nahdrazhee/aootohboosoveh nahdrahzhee/stahnovishtye aoototaxi/stzhed mnyestah/ plazh?

209 First/second/left/right/ straight ahead.
První/druhá/nalevo/napravo/ rovně.
Pervnee/droohah/nahlevoh/ naprahvoh/rovnye.

208
↓
219

210 Where is the nearest police station/post office/doctor/ hospital/pharmacy?
Kde je nejbližší policejní stanice/pošta/doktora/ nemocnice/lékárna?
Gde yeh neyblizhsee politseynee stanitseh/poshtah/doctorah/ nehmohtsnyitseh/leckarnah?

211 Is it far?
Je to daleko?
Yeh toh dahlekoh?

212 Do I need to take a taxi/ catch a bus?
Musím jet taxíkem/autobusem?
Mooseem yeht taxeekehm/ aoothoboosehm?

213 Can you point to it on my map?
Ukažte to na mapě.
Ookazhte toh nah mahpye.

214 Thank you for your help.
Děkuji za Vaši pomoc.
Dyekooyi zah vashi pohmots.

SIGHTSEEING

215 Where is the Tourist Information office?
Kde jsou turistick informace?
Gde sow tooristitskeh informatseh?

216 Where is the cathedral/ church/museum?
Kde je katedrála/kostel/ muzeum?
Gde ye kahtehdrahlah/kohstehl/ moozeoom?

217 How much is the entrance (admission) charge?
Kolik je vstupné?
Kollick yeh vstoopneh?

218 Is there a reduction for children/students/senior citizens?
Je sleva pro děti/studenty/ důchodce?
Yeh slehvah proh dyetee/ stoodehnty/dookhodtseh?

219 What time does the next guided tour start?
Kdy jde další skupina s průvodcem?
Gdy ydeh dahlshee skoopinah ss proovohdtsehm?

²²⁰ **One/two adults/children, please.**
Jeden/dva dospělí/děti, prosím.
Yedehn/dvah dohspyelee/dyetee, prosseem.

²²¹ **May I take photographs here?**
Smím tady fotografovat?
Smeem tahdi fotografohvaht?

ENTERTAINMENT

²²² **Can you recommend a good bar/nightclub?**
Doporučíte dobrý bar/noční podnik?
Dohpohrucheeteh dohbree bahr/ nochnee pohdnick?

²²³ **Do you know what is on at the cinema (playing at the movies)/theatre at the moment?**
Co dávají v kině/v divadle?
Tsoh dahvahyee vh kihnye/vh divahdleh?

²²⁴ **I would like to book (purchase) . . . tickets for the matinée/evening performance on Monday.**
Rád bych zamluvil . . .
vstupenek na pondělní odpolední/večerní představení.
Rahd bykh zahmloovil . . . vstoopehnehck nah pohndyelnee ohdpohlehdnee pzhedstahvehnee.

²²⁵ **What time does the film/ performance start?**
Kdy začíná film/představení?

Gdy zacheenah film/ pzhedstahvehnee?

MEETING PEOPLE

²²⁶ **Hello/Goodbye**
Nazdar/Na shledanou
Nahzdahr/Nah-skhleddunnow

²²⁷ **Good morning/good afternoon/good evening/ goodnight.**
Dobré jitro/dobrý den/dobrý večer/dobrou noc.
Dohbreh yitroh/dohbree den/ dohbree vecherr/dohbroe nots.

²²⁸ **Pleased to meet you.**
Těší mě.
Tyehshee mnye.

²²⁹ **How are you?**
Jak se daří?
Yuck seh dazhee?

²³⁰ **Fine, thank you. And you?**
Dobře, děkuji. A vy?
Dobrzhe, dyekuhyi. A vi?

²³¹ **My name is . . .**
Jmenuji se . . .
Menooyi seh . . .

²³² **This is my friend/ boyfriend/girlfriend/ husband/wife/brother/ sister.**
To je můj přítel/chlapec/ dívka/manžel/manželka/ bratr/sestra.
Toh jeh mooy pzheetehl/ khlahpets/dyeefkah/mahnzhel/ mahnzhelkah/brahtr/sehstrah.

**C
Z
E
C
H**

**220
↕
232**

TRAVELLING WITH CHILDREN

²³³ **Where are you travelling to?**
Kam jedete?
Kahm yehdehteh?

²³⁴ **I am/we are going to . . .**
Jedu/jedeme do . . .
Yehdoo/yehdehmeh doh . . .

²³⁵ **How long are you travelling for?**
Jak dlouho cestujete?
Yuck dlowhoh tsehstooyeteh?

²³⁶ **Where do you come from?**
Odkud jste?
Odkood steh?

²³⁷ **I am/we are from . . .**
Jsem/jsme z . . .
Sem/sme z . . .

²³⁸ **We're on holiday.**
Jsme tu na dovolené.
Smeh tuh nahdohvohleneh.

²³⁹ **This is our first visit here.**
Jsme tady na návštěvě poprvé.
Smeh tahdi nah nahfshtyevye pohpreveh.

²⁴⁰ **Would you like/May I have a cigarette?**
Přejete si/Můžu si vzít cigaretu?
Pzheyeteh sih/Moozhuu sih vzeet tsigahrehtoo?

²⁴¹ **I am sorry, but I do not understand.**
Promiňte, nerozumím Vám.
Prohminyteh, nehrozoomeem vahm.

²⁴² **Please speak slowly.**
Mluvte, prosím, pomalu.
Mloofteh, prosseem, pohmahloo.

²⁴³ **Do you mind if I smoke?**
Smím si zapálit?
Smeem sih zahpahlit?

²⁴⁴ **Do you have a light?**
Můžu si připálit?
Moozhoo sih pzhipahlit?

²⁴⁵ **I am waiting for my husband/wife/boyfriend/girlfriend.**
Čekám na svého manžela/svou ženu/svého přítele/svou přítelkyni.
Chekahm na svehhoh mahnzhela/svoe zhenuh/svehhoh przheeteleh/svoe przheetelkynyi

TRAVELLING WITH CHILDREN

²⁴⁶ **Do you have a high chair/baby-sitting service/cot?**
Máte dětskou židli/opatrovatelskou službu/postýlku?
Mahteh dyetskow zhidli/ohpahtrohvahtelskow sloozhboo/posteelkoo?

²⁴⁷ **Where is the nursery/playroom?**
Kde jsou jesle/dětský pokoj?
Gde sow yesleh/dyetskee pockoy?

²⁴⁸ Where can I warm the
baby's bottle?
Kde můžu ohřát lahvičku?
*Gde moozhoo ohzhaht
lahvichkoo?*

COMMUNICATIONS

Post

²⁴⁹ How much will it cost to
send a letter/postcard/this
package to Britain/Ireland/
America/Canada/Australia/
New Zealand?
Kolik stojí dopis/pohlednice/
tento balík do Británie/Irska/
Ameriky/Kanady/Australie/
na Nový Zéland?
*Kollick stoyee dohpis/
pohlehdnitseh/tehntoh bahleeck
doh Britahnie/Irskah/
Ahmehrickyh/Kahnahdy/
Aoostrahliah/nah nohvee
zehlahnd?*

²⁵⁰ I would like one stamp/two
stamps.
Prosím známku/dvě známky.
*Prosseem znahmkoo/dvye
znahmky.*

²⁵¹ I'd like . . . stamps for
postcards to send abroad,
please.
Potřebuji . . . poštovní známky
na pohlednice do ciziny,
prosím.
*Potrzhebuhyi . . . pohshtovnyee
znahmki nahpohhlednyitse do
tsizini, prosseem.*

Phones

²⁵² I would like to make a
telephone call/reverse the
charges to (make a collect
call to) . . .
Rád bych zatelefonoval/na
účet volaného do . . .
*Rahd bykh zahtelephonohvahl/
nah oochet vohlahnehoo doh . . .*

²⁵³ Which coins do I need for
the telephone?
Jaké mince potřebuji pro
telefon?
*Yuckeh mintseh pohtzhebooyee
proh telephohn?*

²⁵⁴ The line is engaged (busy).
Linka je obsazena.
Linkah yeh obsazhenah.

²⁵⁵ The number is . . .
Číslo je . . .
Cheesloh yeh . . .

²⁵⁶ Hello, this is . . .
Haló, tady je . . .
Hulloh, tahdiye . . .

²⁵⁷ May I speak to . . ?
Mohu mluvit s . . ?
Mohu mluhvit s . . ?

²⁵⁸ He/She is not in at the
moment. Can you call back?
Momentálně tady není.
Můžete zavolat později?
*Mohmentahlnye tahdi
nenyee. Moozheteh zahvolat
pohzdyeyi?*

C
Z
E
C
H

248
↑
258

MONEY/SHOPPING

MONEY

259 I would like to change these travellers' cheques (travelers' checks)/this currency/this Eurocheque.
Rád bych vyměnil tyto cestovní šeky/tuto měnu/tento Eurošek.
Rahd bykh vymnyenil tytoh tsehstovnee shecky/tootoh mnyenoo/tehntoh Ehurohsheck.

260 How much commission do you charge? (What is the service charge?)
Kolik účtujete provize?
Kollick oochtooyeteh prohvizeh?

261 Can I obtain money with my MasterCard?
Můžu vybrat peníze s MasterCard?
Moozhoo vybraht pehneezeh ss MasterCard?

259
↕
274

SHOPPING

Names of Shops and Departments

262 Knihkupectví/Papírnictví
Knyihkoopetstvee/Pahpeernyictvee
Bookshop/Stationery

263 Klenotnictví/Dárky
Klehnotnyitstvee/Dahrrki
Jeweller's/Gifts

264 Obuv
Ohbuhf
Shoes

265 Železářství
Zhelezahrzhstvee
Hardware

266 Starožitnosti
Starrozhitnohstyi
Antiques

267 Holič/Kadeřník
Holich/Kahdehrzhnyeek
Hairdresser's (men's)/(women's)

268 Tabák
Tahbahk
Tobacconist

269 Pekárna
Pehkahrrnah
Baker's

270 Samoobsluha
Sahmoh-opsloohah
Supermarket

271 Fotografické potřeby
Fotografitskeh pohtrzhebi
Photoshop

272 Hračky
Hrachki
Toys

273 Cestovní kancelář
Tsestovnyee kahntselahrzh
Travel Agent

274 Drogerie/Parfumerie
Drohgueriyeh/Parrfuhmehriye
Toiletries

275 Desky
Dahski
Records

In the Shop

276 What time do the shops open/close?
Kdy jsou obchody otevřené/zavřené?
Gdy sow obkhody ohtevzheneh/zavzheneh?

277 Where is the nearest market?
Kde je nejbližší trh?
Gdeye neyblizhshee treh?

278 Can you show me the one in the window/this one?
Můžete mi ukázat to ve výloze/tady to?
Moozhetemi uhkahzat toh veveelozeh/tahdi toh?

279 Can I try this on?
Můžu to vyzkoušet?
Moozhoo toh vyzkowshet?

280 What size is this?
Jaká je to velikost?
Yuckah yeh toh vehlikohst?

281 This is too large/too small/too expensive.
Je to příliš velké/příliš malé/příliš drahé.
Yeto przheelish velkeh/przheelish mahleh/przheelish drah-heh.

282 Do you have any others?
Máte nějaké jiné?

Mahte nyeyakeh yineh?

283 My size is . . .
Moje velikost je . . .
Moyeh velikohst ye . . .

284 Where is the changing room/childrens'/cosmetic/ladieswear/menswear/food department?
Kde jsou tady převlékárny/dětské oddělení/kosmetika/dámské/pánské oddělení/potraviny?
Gde sow tahdy pzhevlehkahrny/dyetskeh otdyelehnee/kohsmehtickah/dahmskeh/pahnskeh otdyelehne/potrahviny?

285 I would like . . .
Rád(a) bych . . .
Rahd(ah) bikh . . .

286 I would like a quarter of a kilo/half a kilo/a kilo of bread/butter/cheese/ham/tomatoes.
Prosím čtvrt kila/půl kila/kilo chleba/másla/sýra/šunky/rajčat.
Prosseem chtvert kilah/pool kilah/kiloh khlebbah/mahslah/seerah/shoonky/rahychat.

287 How much is this?
Kolik to stojí?
Kollick toh stoyee?

288 I'll take this one, thank you.
Vezmu si tuhle, děkuji.
Vezmoossi toohle, dyekuyi.

SHOPPING/MOTORING

289 Do you have a carrier (shopping) bag?
Máte sáček?
Mahteh sahcheck?

290 Do you have anything cheaper/larger/smaller/of better quality?
Máte něco lacinější/větší/menší/kvalitnější?
Mahteh nyetsoh latsinyejshee/vyetshee/menshee/kvahlitnyeyshee?

291 I would like a film for this camera.
Rád bych film pro tento aparát.
Rahd bykh film proh tentoh aparaht.

292 I would like some batteries, the same size as this old one.
Rád bych baterie, stejné velikosti jako tato stará.
Rahd bykh bahterhieh, stehyneh vehlikohsti yuckoh ttahtoh stharah.

293 Would you mind wrapping this for me, please?
Zabalte mi to, prosím.
Zahbahlteh mee toh, prosseem.

294 Sorry, but you seem to have given me the wrong change.
Promiňte, vrátil jste mi peníze špatně.
Prohminyteh, vrahtil steh mee pehneezeh shpatnye.

MOTORING

Car Hire (Rental)

295 I have ordered (rented) a car in the name of . . .
Zamluvil jsem auto pod jménem . . .
Zahmloovil sehm aootoh pohd mehnehm . . .

296 How much does it cost to hire (rent) a car for one day/two days/one week?
Kolik stojí vypůjčení auta na den/dva dny/na týden?
Kollick stoyee vypoojchenee aootah nah den/dvah dnyh/nah teeden?

297 Is the tank already full of petrol (gas)?
Je nádrž plná benzínu?
Yeh nahdrsh plnah behnzeenoo?

298 Is insurance and tax included? How much is the deposit?
Zahrnuje to pojištění a daně?
Kolik je záloha?
Zahrnooye toh poyeeshtyenee ah dahneh? Kollick ye zahlohah?

299 By what time must I return the car?
Do kdy musím vrátit auto?
Doh gdyh moosseem vrahtit aootoh?

300 I would like a small/family car with a radio/cassette player.

Přeji si malé/rodinné auto s radiem/kazetou.
Pzheyee sih mahleh/roddineh aootoh ss rahdiehm/kazetow.

Asking the Way

301 Excuse me, can you help me please?
Promiňte, můžete mi, pomoci, prosím?
Prohminyeteh, moozhetemi pohmohtsi, prohsseem?

302 How do I reach the motorway/main road?
Jak se dostanu na dálnici/na hlavní silnici?
Yakseh dohstahnuh nadahlnyitsi/nahlavnyee silnyitsi?

303 I think I have taken the wrong turning.
Myslím, že jsem špatně odbočil.
Misleem zhessem shpatnyeh odbohchil.

304 I am looking for this address.
Hledám tuto adresu.
Hlehdahm tuhtoh adrehsuh.

305 I am looking for the . . . hotel.
Hledám hotel . . .
Hlehdahm hotel . . . .

306 How far is it to . . . from here?
Jak daleko je odsud do . . ?

Yak dahlekoh yeh odsuhd doh . . ?

307 Carry straight on for . . . kilometres.
Jeďte pořád rovně asi . . . kilometrů.
Yedye-teh porzhahd rovnyeh ahsee . . . kilohmehtroo.

308 Take the next turning on the right/left.
Na příští odbočce zahněte doprava/doleva.
Na przheeshtye odboch-tse zahnyehteh doprahvah/ dohlehvah.

309 Turn right/left at the next crossroads/traffic lights.
Odbočíte doprava/doleva na nejbližší křižovatce/u nejbližšího semaforu.
Odbohcheeteh dohprahvah/ dohlehvah nah neyblish-shee krzhizhovaht-tse/uh neyblish-sheehoh sehmahforuh.

310 You are going in the wrong direction.
Jedete špatným směrem.
Yedyete shpahtneem smnyerem.

Parking

311 How long can I park here?
Jak dlouho tady můžu parkovat?
Yak dloehoh tahdi moozhu parrkohvaht?

MOTORING

312 Is there a car park near here?
Je tady někde blízko parkoviště?
Yeh tahdi nyegdeh bleeskoh parrkohveeshtye?

313 At what time does this car park close?
V kolik hodin se tohle parkoviště zavírá?
Fkollick hohdyin se toh-hle parrkohveeshtye zaveerah?

Signs and Notices

314 Jednosměrný provoz.
Yednohsmnyernee prohvohs.
One way.

315 Zákaz vjezdu.
Zahkaz vyezduh.
No entry.

316 Parkování zakázáno.
Parrkohvahnyee zahkahzahnoh.
No parking.

317 Objížďka
Obyeezhdyekah
Detour (diversion)

318 Stůj/Stop.
Stooy/Stop.
Stop.

319 Dej přednost v jízdě.
Dey przhednost vyeezdyeh.
Give way (yield).

320 Kluzká vozovka/
Nebezpečí smyku.
*Kluhzkah vohzovkah/
Nebespechee smikuh.*

Slippery road.

321 Zákaz
předjíždění.
Zahkaz przhedyeezhdyenyee.
No overtaking.

At the Filling Station

322 Unleaded (lead-free)/
Standard/Premium
Bezolovnatý/Normál/Super
*Besolovnahtee/Norrmahl/
Suhperr*

323 Fill the tank please.
Plnou nádrž, prosím.
Pulnoe nahdrzh, prohseem.

324 Do you have a road map of this area?
Máte silniční mapu této oblasti?
Mahteh silnyichnee mahpuh tehtoh oblahstyi?

325 How much is the car-wash?
Kolik stojí umytí auta?
Kolik stoyee uhmytyee owtah?

Breakdowns

326 I've had a breakdown at . . .
Porouchalo se mi auto u . . .
Poroekhahloh seh mi outoh uh . . .

327 I am on the road from . . .
to . . .
Jsem na silnici z . . . do . . .
*Sehm na silneetsi z . . .
doh . . .*

328 I can't move the car. Can you send a tow-truck?
Nemohu s autem odjet.
Můžete poslat havarijní odtahovou službu?
Nehmohhu soutehm odyeht.
Moozhete pohslat hahvahriynyee ohdtahhovoe sluhzhbuh?

329 I have a flat tyre.
Píchl(a) jsem pneumatiku.
Peekhl(a) sehm pneuhmahtikuh.

330 The windscreen (windshield) has smashed/cracked.
Mám rozbité/prasklé přední sklo.
Mahm rozbihteh/prahskleh przhednyee skloh.

331 There is something wrong with the engine/brakes/lights/steering/gearbox/clutch/exhaust.
Něco není v pořádku s motorem/s brzdami/se světly/s převodovkou/se spojkou/s výfukem.
Nyetso nehnyee v pohrzhahdkuh smohtohrem/s br-zdahmee/sesvyetly/sprzehvohdohvkoe/se spoykoe/sveefookem

332 It's overheating.
Přehřívá se to.
Przhehrzheevahsseh toh.

333 It won't start.
Nechce to nastartovat.
Nekhtse toh nahstahrtohvat.

334 Where can I get it repaired?
Kde si to můžu nechat opravit?
Gdehsi toh moozhu nekhaht ohprahvit?

335 Can you take me there?
Můžete mě tam zavézt?
Moozhete mnye tahm zahvehst?

336 Will it take long to fix?
Bude oprava trvat dlouho?
Buhde ohprahva turvaht dloehoh?

337 How much will it cost?
Kolik to bude stát?
Kollick toh boodeh staht?

Accidents

338 Can you help me? There has been an accident.
Můžete mi pomoct? Stala se nehoda.
Moozheteh me pomotst? Stahlah seh nahodah.

339 Please call the police/an ambulance.
Zavolejte, prosím, policii/záchranku.
Zahvohlehyteh, prohseem, pohlitssiyi/zahhrankooh.

340 Is anyone hurt?
Je někdo zraněný?
Jeh nyekdoh zranyehnee?

Traffic Offences

341 **I'm sorry, I didn't see the sign.**
Moc mě to mrzí, neviděl jsem tu značku.
Mohts mnye toh mrrzeeh, nevidyel sem to znachkooh.

342 **Must I pay a fine? How much?**
Musím zaplatit pokutu? Kolik?
Muhseem zahplahtyit pohkuhtuh? Kolik?

343 **Show me your documents.**
Ukažte mi své doklady.
Ookazhte me sveh dohklahdi.

HEALTH

Pharmacy

344 **Do you have anything for a stomachache/headache/ sore throat/toothache?**
Máte něco proti bolení břicha/hlavy/v krku/zubu?
Mahteh nyetso prohti bohlehnee bzhikha/vh krckoo/zooboo?

345 **I need something for diarrhoea (diarrhea)/ constipation/a cold/a cough/insect bites/ sunburn/travel (motion) sickness.**
Potřebuji něco proti průjmu/zácpě/rýmě/kašli/poštípání hmyzem/spálení sluncem/ cestovní nevolnosti.
Pohtzhehbooyi nyetsoh prohti prooymoo/zahtzpye/reemnye/ kashli/poshteenahnee hmyzehm/ spahlehnee slontsehm/ tsehstovnee nehvohlnohsti.

346 **How much/how many do I take?**
Kolik toho mám vzít?
Kollick tooho mahm vzeet?

347 **How often do I take it/ them?**
Jak často to mám brát?
Yuck chashstoh toh mah braht?

348 **How much does it cost?**
Kolik to stojí?
Kollick toh stoyee?

349 **Can you recommend a good doctor/dentist?**
Můžete doporučit dobrého lékaře/zubaře?
Moozheteh dopohroochit dohbrehoh lehkazhe/zoobazhe?

350 **Is it suitable for children?**
Je to vhodné pro děti?
Yeh toh vhohdneh pro dyeti?

Doctor

351 **I have a pain here/in my arm/leg/chest/stomach.**
Bolí mě tady/v paži/v noze/ hrudi/žaludku.
Bohlee mnye tahdy/vh pazhi/ vh nohzeh/hroodi/zhahloodkoo.

352 **Please call a doctor, this is an emergency.**
Prosím zavolejte doktora, je to náhlá příhoda.

*Prosseem zahvohleyteh
dohktohrah, yeh toh nahlah
pzheehodah.*

353 I would like to make an
appointment to see a
doctor.
Rád bych se objednal u
doktora.
*Rahd bykh seh ohbyednahl oo
dohktohrah.*

354 I am diabetic/pregnant.
Mám cukrovku/jsem v jiném
stavu.
*Mahm tsookrovkoo/sem vh
yeenehm stahvoo.*

355 I need a prescription for
. . .
Potřebuji předpis na . . .
*Pohtzhehbooyi pzhehdpiss
nah . . .*

356 Can you give me
something to ease the
pain?
Můžete mi dát něco na
ulehčení bolesti?
*Moozhehteh mee daht nyetso
nah oolehchenee bohlehstee?*

357 I am/he is/she is allergic
to penicillin.
Mám alergii/Má alergii/Má
alergii na penicilin.
*Mahm ahlehrguiyi/Mah
ahlehrguiyi/Mah ahlehrguiyi
nah pehnitsileen.*

358 Does this hurt?
Bolí to?
Bohlee toh?

359 You must/he must/she
must go to hospital.
Musíte/On musí/Ona musí
do nemocnice.
*Muhsseeteh/On muhsee/Onah
muhsee dohnehmohtsnyitseh.*

360 Take these once/twice /
three times a day.
Užívejte je jednou/dvakrát/
třikrát denně.
*Oozheeveyteh yeh yednoe/
dvahkraht/trzikraht denye.*

361 I am/he is/she is taking
this medication.
Užívám/On užívá/Ona užívá
tyhle léky.
*Oozheevahm/On oozheevar/
Onah oozheevar teehleh lahky.*

362 I have medical insurance.
Mám lékařské pojištění.
*Mahm lehkahrzhskeh
poyishtyenyee.*

Dentist

363 I have toothache.
Bolí mě zub.
Bohlee mnye zoob.

364 My filling has come out.
Vypadla mně plomba.
Vypahdlah mnye plohmbah.

365 I do/do not want to have an injection first.
Přeji si/nepřeji si nejdříve injekci.
Pzheyee ssi/nehpzheyee ssi neydzheeveh inyeksti.

EMERGENCIES

366 Help!
Pomoc!
Pohmots!

367 Call an ambulance/a doctor/the police.
Zavolejte sanitku/doktora/policii!
Zahvohleyteh sahnitkoo/docktorah/pohlitsiyee!

368 I have had my travellers' cheques (travelers' checks)/credit cards/purse/handbag/rucksack (knapsack)/luggage/wallet stolen.
Byly mi ukradeny cestovní šeky/kreditní karty/peněženka/kabelka/ruksak/zavazadlo/náprsní taška.
Byly mee ookrahdehny tsehstohvnee shecky/krehditnih kahrty/pennyehzhenkah/kubbelkah/rooksack/zuvvahzuddloh/nahprsnee tashkah.

369 Can you help me, I have lost my daughter/son?
Pomozte mi, ztratil jsem dceru/syna.
Pohmohsteh mee, ztrahtil sem tseroo/seenah.

370 Please go away/leave me alone.
Běžte pryč/nechte mě být.
Byezhteh prych/nekhteh mnye byt.

371 Fire!
Hoří!
Hohrzhee!

372 I want to contact the British/American/Canadian/Irish/Australian/New Zealand/South African consulate.
Rád(a) bych se spojil(a) s britským/americkým/kanadským/irským/australským/novozélandským/jihoafrickým konzulátem.
Rahd(ah) byh seh spohyilah s britskeem/ahmehritskeem/kahnahtskeem/irskeem/aoostralskeem/nohvoh zehlahntskeem/yihoh-ahfritskeem konsuhlahtem.

Introduction

French is spoken as a first language not only in France but also in Monaco, in south and west Belgium and Brussels, in western Switzerland and as a second language in Luxembourg. English may also be spoken, but it will pay dividends to at least attempt some French.

F
R
E
N
C
H

Addresses for travel and tourist information

Australia: *French National Tourist Office,* BNP Building, 12th Floor, 12 Castlereigh Street, Sydney, NSW 2000; tel: (2) 92 315244.
Canada: *French National Tourist Office,* 1981 McJill College, 490 Montreal, Quebec, H3A 2W9; tel: (514) 876 9881, or tel: (514) 876 4264.
New Zealand: *French Embassy,* 34–42 Manners St, PO Box 11, Wellington; tel: (4) 384 50 42/43.
South Africa: *French Tourist Office,* Box 41022, Craighall, Johannesburg 2024; tel: (11) 880 8062.
UK: *Maison de la France,* 178 Piccadilly, London, W1V 0AL; tel: (0906) 8244123. *Belgian Tourism Office,* 31 Peper St, London, E14 9RW. *Swiss National Tourist Office,* Swiss Centre, 10 Wardour St, London, W1D 6QF; tel: (020) 7734 1921.
USA: *French Tourist Office,* 444 Madison Ave (16th Flr), New York, NY 10022; tel: (212) 838 7800. *Belgian National Tourist Office,* 780 Third Avenue (Suite 1501), New York, NY 10017; tel: (212) 758 8130. *Swiss National Tourist Office,* Swiss Center, 608 Fifth Avenue, New York, NY 10020; tel: (212) 757 5944.

ESSENTIALS

Alphabet

A *ah*	B *beh*
C *seh*	D *de*
E *eur*	F *eff*
G *ge*	H *ash*
I *ee*	J *ji*
K *ka*	L *elle*
M *emme*	N *enne*
O *o*	P *pe*
Q *ku*	R *erre*
S *esse*	T *te*
U *u*	V *ve*
W *dooble ve*	X *iks*
Y *ee grec*	Z *zede*

(left margin: F R E N C H · 01 ↕ 12)

Basic Words and Phrases

1 Yes
Oui
Wee

No
Non
nawng

2 Please
S'il vous plaît
Seel voo pleh

Thank you
Merci
Mehrsee

3 That's O.K.
Ça va
Sahr vahr

Perhaps
Peut-être
Purtehtr

4 To
à
ah

From
De
der

5 Here
Ici
Eesee

There
Là
lah

6 None
Aucun
Okang

Also
Aussi
Ossee

7 How
Comment
Kommahng

When
Quand
kahng

8 What
Quel
kehl

Why
Pourquoi
poorkwah

9 I don't understand.
Je ne comprends pas.
Zher ner kawngprahng pah.

10 I don't speak French.
Je ne parle pas français.
Zher ner pahrl pah frahngsay.

11 Do you speak English?
Vous parlez anglais?
Voopahrlay ahnglay?

12 Can you please write it down?
Pouvez-vous l'écrire s'il vous plaît?
Poovehvoo laycreer seelvooplay?

13 Can you please speak more slowly?
Pouvez-vous parler plus lentement s'il vous plaît?
Poovehvoo pahrlay plew lahntermahng seelvooplay?

14 How much does it/this cost?
Quel est le prix?
Kehl eh ler pree?

Days

15 Monday **Tuesday**
Lundi Mardi
Langdee *Mahrdee*

16 Wednesday **Thursday**
Mercredi Jeudi
Mehrkrerdee *Zhurdee*

17 Friday **Saturday**
Vendredi Samedi
Vahndrerdee *Sahmdee*

18 Sunday **Morning**
Dimanche Le matin
Deemahngsh *Ler mahtang*

19 Afternoon **Evening**
L'après-midi Le soir
Lahpreh meedee *Ler swahr*

20 Night **Week**
La nuit La semaine
Lah nwee *Lah sermehn*

21 Yesterday/Today/Tomorrow
Hier/Aujourd'hui/Demain
Yehr/Ojoordewee/Dermang

Numbers

22 Zero **One**
Zéro Un

Zayroa *Ang*

23 Two **Three**
Deux Trois
Dur *Trwah*

24 Four **Five**
Quatre Cinq
Kahtr *Sangk*

25 Six **Seven**
six Sept
Seess *Seht*

26 Eight **Nine**
Huit Neuf
Weet *Nurf*

27 Ten **Eleven**
Dix Onze
Deess *Awngz*

28 Twelve **Thirteen**
Douze Treize
Dooz *Trehz*

29 Fourteen **Fifteen**
Quatorze Quinze
Kahtorz *Kangz*

30 Sixteen **Seventeen**
Seize Dix-sept
Sehz *Deess seht*

31 Eighteen **Nineteen**
Dix-huit Dix-neuf
Deez weet *Deez nurf*

32 Twenty **Twenty-one**
Vingt Vingt et un
Vang *Vang tay ang*

33 Twenty-two **Thirty**
Vingt-deux Trente
Vangt dur *Trahngt*

F
R
E
N
C
H

13
↕
33

F R E N C H

34 ↕ 54

³⁴ **Forty** **Fifty**
Quarante Cinquante
Kahrahngt *Sangkahnt*

³⁵ **Sixty** **Seventy**
Soixante Soixante-dix
Swahssahngt *Swassahngt deess*

³⁶ **Eighty** **Ninety**
Quatre-vingts Quatre-vingt-dix
Kahtrer vang *Kahtrer vang deess*

³⁷ **One hundred Five hundred**
Cent Cinq cents
Sahng *Sang sahng*

³⁸ **One thousand One million**
Mille Un million
Meel *Ang meelyawng*

Time

³⁹ **9.00**
Neuf heures
Nurv urr

⁴⁰ **9.05**
Neuf heures cinq
Nurv urr sangk

⁴¹ **9.10**
Neuf heures dix
Nurv urr deess

⁴² **9.15**
Neuf heures et quart
Nurv urr eh kahr

⁴³ **9.20**
Neuf heures vingt
Nurv urr vang

⁴⁴ **9.25**
Neuf heures vingt-cinq
Nurv urr vang sangk

⁴⁵ **9.30**
Neuf heures et demie
Nurv urr eh dermee

⁴⁶ **9.35**
Dix heures moins vingt-cinq
Dee zurr mwang vang sangk

⁴⁷ **9.40**
Dix heures moins vingt
Dee zurr mwang vang

⁴⁸ **9.45**
Dix heures moins le quart
Dee zurr mwang le kahr

⁴⁹ **9.50**
Dix heures moins dix
Dee zurr mwang deess

⁵⁰ **9.55**
Dix heures moins cinq
Dee zurr mwang sangk

⁵¹ **12.00/Midday/Midnight**
Douze heures/Midi/Minuit
Doowz urr/meedee/meenurhee

⁵² **What time is it?**
Quelle heure est-il?
Kel urr ehteel?

⁵³ **It is . . .**
Il est. . .
Eel eh . . .

ARRIVING AND DEPARTING

Airport

⁵⁴ **Excuse me, where is the check-in desk for . . . airline?**
Excusez-moi, où est le comptoir d'enregistrement de . . ?
Ekskewsehmwah, oo eh ler

*kongtwahr
dahngrehzheestrehmahng der . . ?*

**55 What is the boarding gate/
time for my flight?**
Quelle est la porte
d'embarquement/l'heure
d'embarquement de mon vol?
*Kehl eh lah pohrt
dahngbahrkehmahng/lurr
dahngbahrkehmahng der mawng
vohl?*

**56 How long is the delay likely
to be?**
Le retard est de combien?
Ler rurtahr eh der kawngbyang?

57 Where is the duty-free shop?
Où est la boutique hors-taxe?
Oo eh lah bootik ohrtahks?

**58 Which way is the baggage
reclaim?**
Où se trouve l'aire de réception
des bagages?
*Oo ser troov lair der
rehssehpsseeawng deh bahgahzh?*

**59 Where can I get the bus to
the city centre?**
Où puis-je prendre le bus pour
le centre-ville?
*Oo pweezh prahngdr ler bews poor
ler sahngtr veel?*

Train Station

**60 Where is the ticket office/
information desk?**
Où se trouve le guichet/le
bureau de renseignements?
Oo ser troov ler geesheh/ler

bewroa der rahngsehniehmahng?

**61 Which platform does the
train to . . . depart from?**
De quel quai part le train
pour . . ?
Der kehl kay pahr ler trang poor . . ?

62 Where is platform . . ?
Où se trouve le quai . . ?
Oo ser troov ler kay . . ?

63 When is the next train to . . ?
Quand est le prochain train
pour . . ?
Kahng eh ler proshang trang poor . . ?

64 Is there a later train to . . ?
Y-a-t-il un train plus tard pour
. . ?
*Ee ahteel ang trang plew tahr
poor . . ?*

Port

65 How do I get to the port?
Pour aller au port, s'il vous
plaît?
Poor ahleh oh por, seelvooplay?

**66 When is the next sailing
to . . ?**
Quand est le prochain départ
pour . . ?
*Kahng eh ler proshang dehpahr
poor . . ?*

**67 Can I catch an earlier ferry
with this ticket?**
Puis-je prendre un ferry plus tôt
avec ce billet?
*Pweezh prahngdrer ang ferry plew
tow ahvehk ser beeyeh?*

F
R
E
N
C
H

55
↑
67

ARRIVING AND DEPARTING

Notices and Signs

68 **Voiture-restaurant**
Vwature restorahn
Buffet (Dining) Car

69 **Autobus**
Otoebewss
Bus

70 **Eau potable/Eau non potable**
Oa poatahbl/Oa nawng poatahbl
Drinking/Non-drinking water

71 **Entrée**
Ahngtray
Entrance

72 **Sortie**
Soartee
Exit

73 **Renseignements**
Rahngsehnyermahng
Information

74 **Consigne**
Kawngsseeñ
Left Luggage (Baggage Claim)

75 **Consigne automatique**
Kawngsseeñ oatomahtick
Luggage Lockers

76 **Poste**
Peost
Post Office

77 **Quai**
Kay
Platform

78 **Gare**
Gahr
Railway (Railroad) Station

79 **Aéroport**
Ahehrohpohr
Airport

80 **Port**
Pohr
Port

81 **Restaurant**
Rehstoarahng
Restaurant

82 **Fumeurs/non fumeurs**
Fewmurh/nawng fewmurh
Smoking/Non-Smoking

83 **Téléphone**
Taylayphone
Telephone

84 **Guichet**
Gueechay
Ticket Office

85 **Enregistrement des bagages**
Ahngrehzheestrehmahng day bahgahzh
Check-in Desk

86 **Horaires**
Oarayrh
Timetables (Schedules)

87 **Toilettes**
Twahlayt
Toilets (Restrooms)

88 **Hommes**
Ommh
Gentlemen

89 **Femmes**
Fam
Ladies'

⁹⁰ **Tramway**
Trahmway
Tram (Streetcar)

⁹¹ **Métro**
Maytroa
Underground (Subway)

⁹² **Salle d'attente**
Sahldahtahngth
Waiting-Room

Buying a Ticket

⁹³ **I would like a first-class/
second-class single (one-
way)/return (round-trip)
ticket to . . .**
Je voudrais un billet de première
classe/deuxième classe aller/
aller-retour pour . . .
*Zher voodray ang beeyeh der
premryehr/durzyehm klahss
ahlay/ahlay rertoor poor . . .*

⁹⁴ **Is my rail pass valid on this
train/ferry/bus?**
Est-ce que ma carte ferroviaire
est valable pour ce train/ce
ferry/ce bus?
*Ehss ker mah kahrt fehrohveeair
eh vahlahblh dahng ser trang/ser
ferry/ser bewss?*

⁹⁵ **I would like an aisle/window
seat.**
Je voudrais être près de l'allée/la
fenêtre.
*Zher voodray aytr pray der
lahlaeh/lah fernaytr.*

⁹⁶ **No smoking/smoking, please.**
Non fumeur/fumeur.

Nawng fewmur/fewmur.

⁹⁷ **We would like to sit
together.**
Nous aimerions être assis
ensemble.
*Noo aymerreeawng ehtr ahssee
ahngsahngbl.*

⁹⁸ **I would like to make a seat
reservation.**
Je voudrais réserver une place.
*Zher voodray rehzehrveh ewn
plahss.*

⁹⁹ **I would like to reserve a
couchette/sleeper for one
person/two people/for my
family.**
Je voudrais réserver une
couchette/place de voiture-lit
pour une personne/deux
personnes/pour ma famille.
*Zher voodray rehzehrveh ewn
kooshayt/plahss der vwature-lee
poor ewn pehrson/dur perhson/
poor mah fahmeeye.*

¹⁰⁰ **I would like to reserve a
cabin.**
Je voudrais réserver une cabine.
*Zher voodray rehzehrveh ewn
kahbeen.*

Timetables (Schedules)

¹⁰¹ **Arrive**
Ahrivh
Arrive

¹⁰² **S'arrête à. . .**
Sahrayth ah. . .
Calls (Stops) at. . .

F
R
E
N
C
H

90
↕
102

69

103 Restauration
Restoarahseeawng
Catering Service

104 Changez à
Chahngzay ah . . .
Change at . . .

105 Correspondance
Koarespawngdahngss
Connection

106 Tous les jours
Too ley joorh
Daily

107 Toutes les quarante minutes
Tooth lay kahrahngt menewt
Every 40 Minutes

108 Première classe
Prermeeayrh class
First-Class

109 Toutes les heures
Toot lay zur
Hourly

110 Il est recommandé de
réserver sa place
*Eel eh rekomahngday der
rayzayrvay sa plahs*
Seat reservations are
recommended

111 Deuxième classe
Dersieme class
Second-class

112 Supplément à payer
Sewplaymahng ah payay
Supplement Payable

113 Par
Pah
Via

Luggage

114 How much will it cost to send
(ship) my luggage in
advance?
Quel est le prix pour envoyer
mes bagages en avance?
*Kehl eh ler pree poor ahngwahllay
meh bahgahz ahng ahvahngss?*

115 Where is the left luggage
(baggage claim) office?
Où se trouve la consigne?
Oo ser troov lah kawngseen?

116 What time do you open/
close?
A quelle heure ouvrez-vous/
fermez-vous?
*Ah kehl ur oovrayvoo/
fairmehvoo?*

117 Where are the luggage
trolleys (carts)?
Où se trouve les chariots à
bagages?
*Oo ser troov leh shahryo ah
bahgahzh?*

118 Where are the lockers?
Où se trouve la consigne
automatique?
*Oo ser troov lah kawngseen
awtoematique?*

119 I have lost my locker key.
J'ai perdu la clé de mon casier.
*Zhay payrdew lah kleh der
mawng kahzeeay.*

On Board

120 Is this seat taken?
Est-ce que cette place est libre?
Ehsker sayt plahss eh leebr?

121 Excuse me, you are sitting in my reserved seat.
Excusez-moi, vous occupez la place que j'ai réservée.
Ehskewzaymwah voo okewpeh lah plahss ker zay rehzehrveh.

122 Which station is this?
Quelle est cette gare?
Kehl eh sayt gahr?

123 What time is this train/bus/ ferry/flight due to arrive/ depart?
A quelle heure arrive/part le train/le bus/le ferry?
Ah kehlur ahrivh/pahr ler trang/ ler bewss/ler ferry?

124 Will you wake me just before we arrive?
Pouvez-vous me réveiller avant l'arrivée?
Poovay voo mer rehvehlleh ahvahng lahreeveh?

Customs and Passports

125 Les passeports, s'il vous plaît!
Leh pahsspor, seelvooplay!
Passports, please!

126 I have nothing/wine/spirits (alcohol)/tobacco to declare.
Je n'ai rien à déclarer/J'ai du vin/de l'alcool/du tabac à déclarer.

Zher neh reeang ah dehklahreh/ zhay dew vang/der lahlkol/dew tahbah ah dehklahreh.

127 I shall be staying for . . . days/weeks/months.
Je vais rester . . . jours/ semaines/mois.
Zhe veh resteh . . . zoor/sermehn/ mwah.

AT THE TOURIST OFFICE

128 Do you have a map of the town/area?
Avez-vous une carte de la ville/ région?
Ahveh-voo ewn cart der lah veel/ rehjyawng?

129 Can I reserve accommodation here?
Puis-je réserver un logement ici?
Peweezh rehzehrveh ang lozhmahng eesee?

130 Do you have a list of accommodation?
Vous avez une liste d'hôtels?
Voozahveh ewn leesst dohtehl?

ACCOMMODATION

Hotels

131 I have a reservation in the name of . . .
J'ai fait une réservation au nom de . . .
Zheh feh ewn rehsehrvahssyawng o nawng der . . .

132 I wrote to/faxed/telephoned you last month/last week in . . .
Je vous ai écrit/faxé/téléphoné le mois dernier/la semaine dernière.
Zher voozeh ehkree/faxeh/ tehlehfoneh ler mwah dehrnyeh/ lah sermayn dehrnyair.

133 Do you have any rooms free?
Vous avez des chambres disponibles?
Voozahveh deh shahngbr deesspohneebl?

134 I would like to reserve a single/double room with/without bath/shower.
Je voudrais réserver une chambre pour une personne/ pour deux personnes avec/sans salle de bain/douche.
Zhe voodray rehsehrveh ewn shahngbr poor ewn pehrson/poor dur pehrson avek/sawns sal der banne/doosh.

135 I would like bed and breakfast/(room and) half board/(room and) full board.
Je voudrais le petit-déjeuner/la demi-pension/la pension complète.
Zher voodray ler pewtee-dehjewneh/ lah dermee-pahngsyawng/lah pahngsyawng kawngplait.

136 How much is it per night?
Quel est le prix pour une nuit?
Khel eh ler pree poor ewn nuwy?

137 Is breakfast included?

Est-ce que le petit-déjeuner est compris?
Ehsker ler pertee dehjerneh eh kawngpree?

138 May I see the room?
Puis-je voir la chambre?
Pweezh vwahr lah shahngbr?

139 Do you have any cheaper rooms?
Avez-vous des chambres moins chères?
Ahvehvoo deh shahngbr mooang shayr?

140 I would like to take the room.
Je prends la chambre.
Zhe prahng lah shangbr.

141 I would like to stay for . . . nights.
Je voudrais rester . . . nuits.
Zhe voodray resteh . . . newyh.

142 The shower/light/tap doesn't work.
La douche/la lumière/le robinet ne marche pas.
Lah doosh/lah luhmiair/ler rohbeenay ner marsh pah.

143 At what time/where is breakfast served?
A quelle heure/où servez-vous le petit-déjeuner?
Ah khel ur/ooh serveh-voo ler perteedehjerneh?

144 What time do I have to check-out?
A quelle heure dois-je laisser la chambre?
Ah khel ur dwahz lehseh lah shahngbr?

145 Can I have the key to room no . . . ?

Je voudrais la clé de la chambre . . .

Zher voodray lah klay der lah shahngbr . . .

146 My room number is . . .

Le numéro de ma chambre est . . .

ler newmehro der mah shahngbr eh . . .

147 Do you accept travellers' cheques/Eurocheques/credit cards?

Vous acceptez les chèques de voyage/les Eurochèques/les cartes de crédit?

Voos aksepteh leh sheck der vwoyazh/laze eurosheck/leh kart der krehdee?

148 May I have the bill please?

Pouvez-vous me donner la note, s'il vous plaît?

Poovehvoo mer doneh lah nott seelvooplay?

149 Excuse me, I think there is a mistake in this bill.

Excusez-moi, mais je crois qu'il ya a une erreur dans la note.

Ehskewzaymwah, zhe kwaw ke eel ee ah oon errer don la not.

Youth Hostels

150 How much is a dormitory bed per night?

Quel est le prix d'un lit en dortoir par nuit?

Kehl eh ler pree dang lee ahng

dortwarr pahr newy?

151 I am/am not an HI member.

Je suis/Je ne suis pas membre d'une Auberge de Jeunesse.

Zhe sewy/zhe ner sewy pah mahngbr dewn obehrz der jurnehss.

152 May I use my own sleeping bag?

Est-ce que je peux me servir de mon propre sac de couchage?

Ehsker zhe pur mer sairvyr der mawng proprer sahk der kooshahz?

153 What time do you lock the doors at night?

A quelle heure fermez-vous la porte le soir?

Ah kehlur fehrmehvoo lah port ler swahr?

Camping

154 May I camp here for the night/two nights?

Puis-je camper ici pour la nuit/deux nuits?

Pweehze kahngpeh ysee poor lah newy/dur newy?

155 Where can I pitch my tent?

Où puis-je dresser ma tente?

Oo pweehze dresseh mah tahngt?

156 How much does it cost for one night/week?

Quel est le prix par nuit/par semaine?

Kehl eh ler pree pahr newy/pahr sermayn?

F R E N C H

157
↕
167

157 Where can we park our caravan?
Où pouvons-nous garer notre caravane?
Oo poovong noo gahreh nohtr kahrahvahn?

158 Where are the washing facilities?
Où se trouve le bloc sanitaire?
Oo ser troov ler block sanitaire?

159 Is there a restaurant/supermarket/swimming pool on site/nearby?
Y-a-t-il un restaurant/supermarché/piscine sur place/près d'ici?
Yahteel ang restorahng/supermahrsheh/peassinn sewr plahss/pray deessee?

160 Do you have a safety deposit box?
Avez-vous un coffre-fort?
Ahvehvoo ang koffr-for?

Cafés and Bars

161 I would like a cup of/two cups of/another coffee/tea.
Je voudrais une tasse de/deux tasses de/encore une tasse de café/thé.
Zher voodray ewn tahss der/der tahss der/oncaw ewn tahss der kafeh/teh.

162 With/without milk/sugar.
Avec/sans lait/sucre.
Ahvek/sahng lay/sewkr.

163 I would like a bottle/glass/two glasses of mineral water/red wine/white wine, please.
Je voudrais une bouteille/un verre/deux verres d'eau minérale/de vin rouge/de vin blanc, s'il vous plaît.
Zhe voodray ewn bootayy/ang vair/der vair doa mynehral/der vang roozh/der vang blahng, sylvooplay.

164 I would like a beer/two beers, please.
Je voudrais une bière/deux bières, s'il vous plaît.
Zhe voodray ewn byair/der byair, sylvooplay.

165 May I have some ice?
Puis-je avoir de la glace?
Pweezh ahvoar der lah glass?

166 Do you have any matches/cigarettes/cigars?
Avez-vous des allumettes/des cigarettes/ des cigares?
Ahveh-voo dehzahlewmaitt/deh cigaraytt/deh ssigar?

Restaurants

167 Can you recommend a good/inexpensive restaurant in this area?
Pouvez-vous recommander un bon restaurant/un restaurant bon marché dans les environs?
Pooveh-voo rekomahngdeh ewn bawng restorahng/ewn restorahng bawng mahrcheh dahng lehzahngvyrawng?

168 I would like a table for . . . people.

Je voudrais une table pour . . . personnes.

Zher voodray ewn tabl poor . . . pehrson.

169 Do you have a non-smoking area?

Vous avez une zone non-fumeurs?

Voozahvah ewn zohn nong fewmur?

170 Waiter/Waitress!

Monsieur/Mademoiselle, s'il vous plaît!

Mawnsewr, madmwahzel, sylvooplay!

171 Do you have a set menu/children's menu/wine list?

Avez-vous un table d'hôte/un menu pour enfants/la carte des vins?

Ahvehvoo ewn tabler d'ot/ewn menew poor ahngfahng/lah list deh vang?

172 Do you have any vegetarian dishes, please?

Avez-vous des plats végétariens, s'il vous plaît?

ahvehvoo der plah vehgehtahryang, sylvooplay?

173 Are there any local specialities?

Y-a-til des spécialités locales?

Eeahteel deh spayseeahleeteh locahl?

174 Are vegetables included?

Est-ce que les légumes sont compris?

Essker leh lehgewm sawng kohngpree?

175 Could I have it well-cooked/medium/rare please?

Je le voudrais bien cuit/ à point/ saignant.

Zher ler voodray beeang kwee/ah pwang/saynyang.

176 What does this dish consist of?

En quoi consiste ce plat?

Ahng koah kawngsist ser plah?

177 I would like the set menu, please.

Je voudrais la carte, s'il vous plaît.

Zher voodray lah cart, sylvooplay.

178 We have not been served yet.

Nous n'avons pas été encore servis.

Noo nahvawng pazehteh ahngkor sehrvee.

179 Excuse me, this is not what I ordered.

Excusez-moi, ce n'est pas ce que j'ai commandé.

Ekskewzaymwah, ser nay pah ser ker zheh komandeh.

180 May I have some/some more bread/water/coffee/tea?

Puis-je avoir du pain/encore du pain/de l'eau/du café/du thé?

Pweezh ahvoar dew pang/ahngkor dew pang/der lo/dew kafeh/dew teh?

EATING AND DRINKING

181 **May I have the bill, please?**
L'addition, s'il vous plaît!
Laddyssyawng, sylvooplay!

182 **Does this bill include service?**
Est-ce que le service est
compris?
Ehsk ler sehrveess eh kawngpree?

183 **Do you accept travellers'
cheques (travelers' checks)/
Eurocheques/MasterCard/US
dollars?**
Prenez-vous les chèques de
voyage/les eurochèques/la
Mastercard/les dollars
américains?
*Prernehvoo leh cheque der
vwahahzh/leh eurocheque/lah
Mastercard/leh dolar
ahmehrykang?*

184 **Can I have a receipt, please?**
Je pourrais avoir un reçu sil
vous plaît?
*Zher pooray avwahr ahng rerssew
seelvooplay?*

185 **Where is the toilet
(restroom), please?**
Où sont les toilettes, s'il vous
plaît?
Oo sawng leh twahlaitt, sylvooplay?

On the Menu

186 **First courses**
Entrées
Ahngtray.

187 **Soups**
Soupes
Soup

188 **Main courses**
Plats principaux
Plah prangseepo.

189 **Fish dishes**
Poissons
Pooahsong

190 **Meat dishes**
Viandes
Veeanhd

191 **Vegetarian dishes**
Plats végétariens
Plah vehzhehtahryang

192 **Cheese**
Fromages
Frohmahzh

193 **Desserts**
Desserts
Dehser

194 **Specialities**
Spécialités
Spehsseeahleeteh

GETTING AROUND

Public Transport

195 **Where is the bus stop/coach
station/nearest metro
(subway) station?**
Où se trouve l'arrêt d'autobus le
plus proche/la gare routière/la
station de métro la plus proche?
*Oo ser troov lahreh dotobewss la
plew prosh/lah gahr rootyair/lah
stassion der mehtro lah plew
prosh?*

196 When is the next/last bus to . . ?

A quelle heure est le prochain/ dernier autobus pour . . ?

Ahkehlur eh ler prochang/ dehrneeyeh otobewss poor . . ?

197 How much is the fare to the city centre (downtown)/ railway (railroad) station/ airport?

Quel est le prix du billet pour le centre-ville/la gare/l'aéroport?

Kehl eh ler pree dew beeyeh poor ler sahngtr-veel/lah gahr/ lahehropor?

198 Will you tell me when to get off?

Pouvez-vous me le dire quand je devrai descendre?

Poovehvoo mer der kahng zher deuvreh dehssahngdr?

199 Does this bus go to . . ?

Est-ce que cet autobus va à . . ?

Ehsk sayt otobewss vah ah . . ?

200 Which number bus goes to . . ?

Quel est le numéro de l'autobus qui va à . . ?

Khel eh ler newmehro de lotobewss kee vah ah . . ?

201 May I have a single (one-way)/return (round-trip)/day ticket/book of tickets?

Puis-je avoir un aller/un aller-retour/un ticket pour la journée/un carnet de tickets?

Pweezh ahvwahr ewn ahleh/ewn ahleh-retoor/ewn tickeh poor lah joorneh/ewn kahrneh der tickeh?

Taxis

202 I would like to go to . . . How much will it cost?

Je voudrais aller à . . . Quel est le prix?

Zhe voodray ahleh ah . . . kehl eh ler pree?

203 Please stop here.

Arrêtez ici, s'il vous plaît.

Ahrehteh yssy, sylvooplay.

204 I would like to order a taxi today/tomorrow/at 2pm to go from . . . to . . .

Je voudrais réserver un taxi aujourd'hui/demain/à deux heures pour aller de . . . à . . .

Zher voodray rehzehrveh ewn taxi ojoordewee/dermang/ah derzur poor ahleh der . . . ah . . .

Asking the Way

205 Excuse me, do you speak English?

Excusez-moi, parlez-vous anglais?

Ekskewsehmwah, pahrlehvoo ahnglay?

206 Excuse me, is this the right way to . . ?

Excusez-moi, c'est la bonne direction pour . . ?

Ekskewzaymwah, seh lah bon deerekseeawng poor . . ?

F
R
E
N
C
H

207
↕
217

207 . . . the cathedral/the tourist information office/the castle/the old town.

. . . la cathédrale/l'office de tourisme/le château/la vieille ville.

. . lah kahtehdrahl/lohfeece de tooreezm/ler chateau/lah veeay veel

208 Can you tell me the way to the railway (railroad) station/bus station/taxi rank (stand)/city centre (downtown)/beach?

Pour aller à la gare/gare routière/station de taxis/au centre ville/à la plage, s'il vous plaît?

Poor ahleh ah lah gahr/gahr rootyair/stahssion der taxi/oh sahngtr veel/ah lah plahzh, sylvooplay?

209 First/second left/right/straight ahead.

Première/deuxième à gauche/à droite/tout droit.

Prermeyair/derzeaim ah goash/ah drwaht/too drwah.

210 Where is the nearest police station/post office/doctor/hospital/pharmacy?

Où se trouve le poste de police/le bureau de poste/le médicin/l'hôpital /la pharmacie le/la plus près?

Oo ser troov ler post der poliss/ler bewro der post/ler medeesang/lopeetahl/lah fahrmasi ler/lah plew pray?

211 Is it far?

C'est loin?

seh looang?

212 Do I need to take a taxi/catch a bus?

Faut-il prendre un taxi/un autobus?

Foteel prahngdr ewn taxi/ewn otobewss?

213 Can you point to it on my map?

Pouvez-vous me le montrer sur la carte?

Poovehvoo mer ler mawngtreh sewr lah kart?

214 Thank you for your help.

Merci pour votre aide.

Mehrsee poor votrayd.

SIGHTSEEING

215 Where is the Tourist Information office?

Où se trouve l'office de tourisme?

Oo ser troov loffyss de toorism?

216 Where is the cathedral/church/museum?

Où se trouve la Cathédrale/l'Église/le Musée?

Oo ser troov lah katehdral/lehglyz/ler mewzeh?

217 How much is the entrance (admission) charge?

Quel est le prix d'entrée?

Khel eh ler pree delahngtreh?

218 **Is there a reduction for children/students/senior citizens?**
Y-a-til une réduction pour les enfants/les étudiants/les personnes du troisième âge?
Eeahteel ewn rehdewkssyawng poor lehzahngfahng/ lehzehtewdyahng/leh pehrson dew trwahzyehm ahzh?

219 **What time does the next guided tour start?**
A quelle heure commence la prochaine visite guidée?
Ah kehlur komahngs lah proshain vysyt gueedeh?

220 **One/two adults/children, please.**
Un/deux adulte(s)/enfant(s), s'il vous plaît.
Ewn/durzahdewlt/ahngfahng, seel voo play.

221 **May I take photographs here?**
Je peux prendre des photos ici?
Zher per prangdr deh phowtoh eessee?

ENTERTAINMENT

222 **Can you recommend a good bar/nightclub?**
Pouvez-vous me recommander un bar/une boîte de nuit?
Poovehvoo mer rerkomahngdeh ang bahr/ewn boaht der newee?

223 **Do you know what is on at the cinema (playing at the movies)/theatre at the moment?**
Savez-vous ce qu'il y a au cinéma/théâtre en ce moment?
Sahvehvoo ser keelyah o cinema/ tehahtr ahng ser momahng?

224 **I would like to book (purchase) . . . tickets for the matinée/evening performance on Monday.**
Je voudrais réserver . . . places pour la séance en matinée/ soirée lundi.
Zher voodray rehzehrveh . . . plass poor lah sehahngss ahng mahteeneh/swoiray lerndi.

225 **What time does the film/ performance start?**
A quelle heure commence la séance/la représentation?
Ah kehlur komahngss lah sehahngss/lah rerprehzahngtahssyawng?

MEETING PEOPLE

226 **Hello/Goodbye.**
Bonjour/Au revoir.
Bawngzhoor/oa revwahr.

227 **Good morning/good afternoon/good evening/ goodnight.**
Bonjour/bonjour/bonsoir/ bonne nuit.
Bawngzhoor/bawngzhoor/ bawngswahr/bun nwee.

228 **Pleased to meet you.**
Enchanté de faire votre connaissance.
Ahngsahngteh der fair votr konehssahngss.

F
R
E
N
C
H

229 **How are you?**
Comment allez-vous?
Komahng ahlehvoo?

230 **Fine, thank you. And you?**
Bien merci. Et vous?
Beeang mehrsee. Eh voo?

231 **My name is . . .**
Je m'appelle. . .
Zher mahpehl . . .

232 **This is my friend/boyfriend/
girlfriend/husband/wife/
brother/sister.**
C'est un ami/c'est mon ami/
mon amie/mon mari/ma
femme/mon frère/ma soeur.
*Saytangnahmee/say
mawngnahmee/mawngnahmee/
mawng mahree/mah fahm/
mawng frayr/mah surr.*

233 **Where are you travelling to?**
Où partez-vous en voyage?
Oo pahrtehvoo ahng vwahahzh?

234 **I am/we are going to . . .**
Je vais/nous allons à . . .
Zher vay/noozahlawng ah . . .

235 **How long are you travelling
for?**
Combien de temps partez-vous?
*Kawngbeeang der tahng
pahrtehvoo?*

236 **Where do you come from?**
D'où venez-vous?
Doo vernehvoo?

237 **I am/we are from . . .**
Je suis/nous sommes de . . .
Zher sewea/noo soam der . . .

238 **We're on holiday.**
Nous sommes en vacances.
Noo som ahng vahkahngss.

239 **This is our first visit here.**
C'est la première fois que nous
venons ici.
*Seh lah prermiair fwah ker noo
vernon eeesee.*

240 **Would you like/May I have a
cigarette?**
Voulez-vous/Puis-je avoir une
cigarette?
*Voolehvoo/pweezhahvwahr ewn
seegahrett?*

241 **I am sorry but I do not
understand.**
Je suis désolé(e) mais je ne
comprends pas.
*Zher sewee dehzoleh meh zher ner
kawngprahng pah.*

242 **Please speak slowly.**
Veuillez parler lentement.
Vuryeh pahrleh lahngtmahng.

243 **Do you mind if I smoke?**
Est-ce que cela vous ennuie si je
fume?
*Ehsker cerlah voo ahngnewee ssi
zher fewm?*

244 **Do you have a light?**
Avez-vous du feu?
Ahveh-voo dew fur?

245 **I am waiting for my husband/
wife/boyfriend/girlfriend.**
J'attends mon mari/ma femme/
mon ami/mon amie.
*Zhatahng mawng mahree/mah fahm/
mawngnahmee/mawngnahmee.*

TRAVELLING WITH CHILDREN

246 **Do you have a high chair/
baby-sitting service/cot?**

Avez-vous une chaise pour
bébé/un service de garde pour
enfants/un berceau?

*Ahvehvoo ewn shehz poor behbeh/
ang sehrvees der gahrd poor
ahngfahng/ang behrso?*

247 **Where is the nursery/
playroom?**

Où se trouve la chambre
d'enfants/la salle de jeux?

*Ooser troov lah shahngbr
dahngfahng/lah sall der zur?*

248 **Where can I warm the baby's
bottle?**

Où puis-je faire réchauffer le
biberon?

*Oo pweezh fair rehshoffeh ler
beebrawng?*

COMMUNICATIONS

Post

249 **How much will it cost to send
a letter/postcard/this
package to Britain/Ireland/
America/Australia/
New Zealand/Canada?**

Quel est le tarif pour envoyer
une lettre/carte postale/ce
paquet en Grande-Bretagne/
Irlande/Amérique/Australie/
Nouvelle-Zélande/au Canada?

*Kehl eh ler tariff poor
ahngvwahyeh ewn lettr/kahrt
postahl/ser pahkeh ahng grahngd-
brertahnya/irland/amehrick/
ostrahlee/noovel-zehland/oh
kahnahdah?*

250 **I would like one stamp/two
stamps.**

Je voudrais un timbre/deux
timbres.

*Zher voodray ang tangbr/der
tangbr.*

251 **I'd like . . . stamps for
postcards to send abroad,
please.**

Je voudrais . . . timbres pour
envoyer des cartes postales à
l'étranger sil vous plaît.

*Zher voodray . . . tangbr poor
ahngvwahyeh deh kahrt postahl
ah lehtrahngzhai seelvooplay*

Phones

252 **I would like to make a
telephone call/reverse the
charges to (make a collect
call to) . . .**

Je voudrais téléphoner/
téléphoner en PCV à . . .

*Zher voodray telephoneh/telephoneh
ahng PehCehVeh ah . . .*

253 **Which coins do I need for the
telephone?**

Quelles pièces me faut-il pour
téléphoner?

*Kehl peaehss mer foteel poor
tehlehphoneh?*

F R E N C H

254 ↑ 270

254 **The line is engaged (busy).**
La ligne est occupée.
Lah lyñ eh okewpeh.

255 **The number is . . .**
Le numéro est . . .
Ler newmehro eh . . .

256 **Hello, this is . . .**
Bonjour, c'est . . . à lappareil.
Bawngzhoor, seh . . . ahlahparay.

257 **May I speak to . . ?**
Je voudrais parler à . . .
Zher voodray pahrlay ah . . .

258 **He/She is not in at the moment. Can you call back?**
Il/elle n'est pas là. Pouvez-vous rappeler?
Eel/ehl nay pah lah. Voo poovay rahperlay?

MONEY

259 **I would like to change these travellers' cheques (travelers' checks)/this currency/this Eurocheque.**
J'aimerais changer ces chèques de voyage/ces devises/cet Eurochèque.
Zhaymray shahngzheh seh cheque der vwahahzh/seh derveez/seht eurocheque.

260 **How much commission do you charge? (What is the service charge?)**
Quelle commission prenez-vous?
Kehl komyssyawng prernehvoo?

261 **Can I obtain money with my**

MasterCard?
Puis-je avoir de l'argent avec ma MasterCard?
Pweezh ahvwahr der largaang ahvek mah mastercard?

SHOPPING

Names of Shops and Departments

262 **Librairie/Papeterie**
Leebrayree/pahpaytehree
Bookshop/Stationery

263 **Bijoutier/Cadeaux**
Beezhootehree/Kahdow
Jeweller's/Gifts

264 **Chaussures**
Showsewr
Shoes

265 **Quincaillerie**
Kahngkahyeree
Hardware

266 **Antiquaire**
Ahnteekair
Antiques

267 **Coiffeur (hommes)/(femmes)**
Cwafferr
Hairdresser's (men's)/(women's)

268 **Bureau de tabac**
Bewrow der tahbah
Tobacconist

269 **Boulangerie**
Boolahngzheree
Baker's

270 **Supermarché**
Sewpermahrshay

Supermarket

271 Photographe
Phohtowgraf
Photoshop

272 Jouets
Zhooay
Toys

273 Bureau de voyages
Bureoh der vwoyazh
Travel Agency

274 Articles de toilette
Ahrteekl der twahleht
Toiletries

275 Disques
Deesk
Records

In the Shop

276 What time do the shops open/close?
A quelle heure ouvrent/ferment les magasins?
Ah kehlur oovr/fehrm leh mahgazhang?

277 Where is the nearest market?
Où est le marché le plus proche?
Oo eh ler mahrshay ler plew prosh?

278 Can you show me the one in the window/this one?
Pouvez-vous me montrer celui/celle dans la vitrine/celui-ci/celle-ci?
Poovayvoo mer mohntray serlwee/sel dahng lah veetreen/serlweesi/selsi?

279 Can I try this on?

Puis-je essayer ceci?
Pweezh ehssayeh cerssee?

280 What size is this?
Quelle est cette taille?
Kehleh saytt tahye?

281 This is too large/too small/too expensive.
C'est trop grand/trop petit/trop cher.
Say trohw grahng/trohw pertee/trohw share.

282 Do you have any others?
Vous en avez d'autres?
Voozahngnahvay doatr?

283 My size is . . .
Ma taille (clothes)/ma pointure (shoes) est . . .
Mah tie (clothes)/mah pooahngtewr ay . . .

284 Where is the changing room/childrens/cosmetic/ladieswear/menswear/food department?
Où se trouve le salon d'essayage/le rayon enfants/le rayon produits de beauté/le rayon femmes/le rayon hommes /l'alimentation?
Oo ser troov ler sahlawng dehsayahzh/ler rehyawng ahngfahng/ler rehyawng prodewee der boteh/ler rehyawng fahm/ler rehyawng ohm/lahleemahng-tahsyawng?

285 I would like . . .
Je voudrais . . .
Zher voodray . . .

271
↕
285

83

286 I would like a quarter of a kilo/half a kilo/a kilo of bread/butter/cheese/ham/tomatoes.

Je voudrais deux cent cinquante grammes (250g)/un demi-kilo/un kilo de pain/beurre/fromage/jambon/tomates.

Zher voodray dur sahng sangkahngt gram/ahng dermeekilo/ang kilo der pang/burr/frohmahzh/zhahngbawng/tomaht.

287 How much is this?

C'est combien?

Cey combeean?

288 I'll take this one, thank you.

Je prends celui-ci/celle-ci merci.

Zher prahng serlweesi/sehlsee mehrsee.

289 Do you have a carrier (shopping) bag?

Avez-vous un sac?

Ahvehvoo ang sahk?

290 Do you have anything cheaper/larger/smaller/of better quality?

Avez-vous quelque chose de moins cher/plus petit/plus grand/de meilleure qualité?

Ahvehvoo kehlkershos der moang shehr/plew pertee/plew grohnd/der mehyur kaleeteh?

291 I would like a film for this camera.

Je voudrais une pellicule pour cet appareil photo.

Zher voodray ewn pehleekewl poor sayt ahpahrehye foto

292 I would like some batteries, the same size as this old one.

Je voudrais des piles, comme celle-ci.

Zher voodray deh peel, kom cehlsee.

293 Would you mind wrapping this for me, please?

Pourriez-vous m'envelopper ceci, s'il vous plaît?

Pooreeehvoo mahngverloppeh cersee, seelvooplay?

294 Sorry, but you seem to have given me the wrong change.

Excusez-moi, mais je crois que vous ne m'avez pas rendu le compte.

Excewsehmwah meh zher krwah ker voo ner mahveh pah rahngdew ler kawngt.

MOTORING

Car Hire (Rental)

295 I have ordered (rented) a car in the name of . . .

J'ai réservé une voiture au nom de . . .

Zhay rehzehrveh ewn vwahtewr o nawng der . . .

296 How much does it cost to hire (rent) a car for one day/two days/one week?

Quel est le prix de location d'une voiture pour un jour/deux jours/une semaine?

*Kehl eh ler pree der lokahsyawng
d'ewn vwahtewr poor ang zoor/
der zoor/ewn sermen?*

297 Is the tank already full of petrol (gas)?
Le plein est-il fait?
Ler plang ehtylfeh?

298 Is insurance and tax included? How much is the deposit?
Est-ce que l'assurance et les taxes sont comprises? Combien faut-il donner de caution?
Ehss ker lahsewrahngss eh leh tax sawng kawngpreezh? Kawngbyabg foteel doneh der kossyawng?

299 By what time must I return the car?
A quelle heure dois-je ramener la voiture?
Ah kehlur dwahzh rahmerneh lah vwahtewr?

300 I would like a small/family car with a radio/cassette player.
Je voudrais une petite voiture/
une grosse voiture avec radio/
lecteur de cassettes.
Zher voodray ewn perteet vwahtewr/ewn gross vwahtewr ahvehk rahdio/lecturr der kassaytt.

Asking the Way

301 Excuse me, can you help me please?
Excusez-moi, vous pouvez m'aider s'il vous plaît?

Ekskewzaymwah, voo poovay mahyday seelvooplay

302 How do I reach the motorway/main road?
Pour aller jusqu'à l'autoroute/la route principale?
Poor ahleh zhewskah lowtohroot/lah root prahngsipahl?

303 I think I have taken the wrong turning.
Je crois que je me suis trompé de chemin.
Zher krawh ker zhay mer trompay der sheman.

304 I am looking for this address.
Je cherche cette adresse.
Zher shaersh set adress.

305 I am looking for the . . . hotel.
Je cherche l'hôtel . . .
Zher shaersh lohtel . . .

306 How far is it to . . . from here?
. . . c'est loin d'ici?
. . . say looahng deesee?

307 Carry straight on for . . . kilometres.
Continuez tout droit pendant . . . kilomètres.
Kohnteeneway too drooah pahngdahng . . . kilomehtr.

308 Take the next turning on the right/left.
Prenez la prochaine rue/route à droite/à gauche.
Prernay lah proshen rew/root ah drwaht/ah goash.

F
R
E
N
C
H

309 **Turn right/left at the next crossroads/traffic lights.**
Tournez à droite/à gauche au prochain croisement/aux feux.
Toornay ah drwaht/ah goash oh prohshahng krowzmahng/oh phyer.

310 **You are going in the wrong direction.**
Vous allez dans la mauvaise direction.
Vooz ahleh dahng lah mowvehz deerekseeawng.

Parking

311 **How long can I park here?**
Combien de temps est-ce que je peux rester garé ici?
Kawngbeeang der tahng essker zher per restay gahray eessee?

309
↕
325

312 **Is there a car park near here?**
Y a-t-il un parking près d'ici?
Eeyahteel ahng parking preh deessee?

313 **At what time does this car park close?**
A quelle heure est-ce que le parking ferme?
Ah kehl urr essker ler parking fehrm?

Signs and Notices

314 **Sens unique**
Sahns uhneek
One way

315 **Sens interdit**
Sahns ahngterdee
No entry

316 **Stationnement interdit**
Stassionmahng ahngterdee
No parking

317 **Déviation**
Dehveeasseeawng
Detour (diversion)

318 **Stop**
Stop
Stop

319 **Cédez la**
Preeohreetay
Give way (yield)

320 **Chaussée glissante**
Showsay gleesahnt
Slippery road

321 **Dépassement interdit**
Daypassmahng ahngterdee
No overtaking

At the Filling Station

322 **Unleaded (lead-free)/ Standard/Premium**
Sans plomb/normal/super
Sahng plong/normall/sewpehr

323 **Fill the tank please.**
Le plein s'il vous plaît.
Ler plahng seelvooplay.

324 **Do you have a road map of this area?**
Vous avez une carte de la région?
Voozahvay ewn kahrt der lah rehzheeawng?

325 **How much is the car-wash?**

Le lavage automatique coûte
combien?
*Ler lahvahzh automateek koot
kawngbeeang?*

Breakdowns

326 I've had a breakdown at . . .
Je suis tombé(e) en panne à . . .
Zher sewee tombay ahng pan ah . . .

327 I am on the road from . . . to . . .
Je suis sur la route de . . . à . . .
*Zher sewee sewr lah root der . . .
ah . . .*

328 I can't move the car. Can you
send a tow-truck?
Je ne peux pas déplacer la
voiture. Vous pouvez envoyer
une dépanneuse?
*Zher ner purr pah dehplahsay lah
vwahtewr. Voo poovay
ahngvwahyeh ewn daypahnurze?*

329 I have a flat tyre.
J'ai un pneu crevé.
Zhai ang punerr krervay.

330 The windscreen (windshield)
has smashed/cracked.
Le pare-brise est cassé/fendu.
*Ler pahrbreez ay kahseh/
fahngdew.*

331 There is something wrong
with the engine/brakes/
lights/steering/gearbox/
clutch/exhaust.
Il y a un problème avec le
moteur/les freins/les feux/la
direction/la boîte à vitesses/
l'embrayage/le pot

d'échappement.
*Eeleeyah ang problairm ahvek ler
mowturr/leh frahng/leh fur/lah
deerehkseeaawng/lah
bwahtahveetess/lahngbrayyazh/
ler poh dehshahpmahng.*

332 It's overheating.
Le moteur chauffe.
Ler mohturr showf.

333 It won't start.
La voiture ne démarre pas.
Lah vwahtewr ner dehmahr pah.

334 Where can I get it repaired?
Où est-ce que je peux le/la faire
réparer?
*Oo essker zher purr ler/lah fair
rehpahray?*

335 Can you take me there?
Vous pouvez m'y emmener?
Voo poovay mee ahngmernay?

336 Will it take long to fix?
La réparation prendra
longtemps?
*Lah rehpahrasseeaawng prahngdrah
lohngtahng?*

337 How much will it cost?
Ça coûtera combien?
Sah kootrah kawngbeeang?

Accidents

338 Can you help me? There has
been an accident.
Vous pouvez m'aider? Il y a eu
un accident.
*Voo poovay mayday? Eelyaew ang
akseedahng.*

F
R
E
N
C
H

325
↕
338

339 Please call the police/an ambulance.
Vous pouvez appeler la police/ une ambulance s'il vous plaît.
Voo poovay ahperleh lah poleess/ ewn ahngbewlahngss seelvooplay.

340 Is anyone hurt?
Y a-t-il des blessés?
Eeahteel deh blaysay?

Traffic Offences

341 I'm sorry, I didn't see the sign.
Je suis désolé(e), je n'ai pas vu le panneau.
Zher sewee dehzoleh, zher nay pah vew ler panow.

342 Must I pay a fine? How much?
Est-ce que je dois payer une amende? Combien?
Ehsker zher dwah payeh ewn amahnd? Kawngbeeang?

343 Show me your documents.
Vos papiers s'il vous plaît.
Vow pahpyeh seelvooplay.

HEALTH

Pharmacy

344 Do you have anything for a stomachache/headache/sore throat/toothache?
Avez-vous quelque chose contre le mal à l'estomac/les maux de tête/le mal de gorge/le mal de dents?

Ahveh-voo kelhkshoz kawngtr ler mal ah lestoma/leh mo der teht/ler mal der gorzh/ler mal der dahng?

345 I need something for diarrhoea (diarrhea)/ constipation/a cold/a cough/ insect bites/sunburn/travel (motion) sickness.
J'ai besoin de quelque chose contre la diarrhée/la constipation/un rhume/la toux/ les piqûres d'insectes/les brûlures de soleil/le mal de la route (car)/de l'air (plane)/de mer (boat).
Zhai berzwoang der kehlkshoz kawngtr lah diarrhae/ang rhoom/ ewn tou/lers peakewr dangsect/leh koo der soleye/ler mal der lah root/der l'air/der mair.

346 How much/how many do I take?
Combien dois-je en prendre?
Kawngbeeang dwahzh ahng prahngdr?

347 How often do I take it/them?
Combien de fois dois-je en prendre?
Kawngbeeang der fwah dwahzh ahng prahngdr?

348 How much does it cost?
Quel est le prix?
Khel eh ler pree?

349 Can you recommend a good doctor/dentist?
Pouvez-vous me recommander un bon médecin/dentiste?

*Pooveh-voo mer rerkomahngdeh
ang bawng medeesang/dahngtist?*

350 Is it suitable for children?

Est-ce qu'on peut le donner aux
enfants?

*Esskawng pew ler doneh
ozahnfahn?*

Doctor

**351 I have a pain here/in my arm/
leg/chest/stomach.**

J'ai mal ici/au bras/à la jambe/à
la poitrine/à l'estomac.

*Zhai mal eessee/o brah/ah lah
zhahngb/ah lah pwahtryn/ah
lestomah.*

**352 Please call a doctor, this is an
emergency.**

Appelez un médecin, s'il vous
plaît, c'est urgent.

*Ahperleh ewn medeesang, seel voo
play, sehtewrzhahng.*

**353 I would like to make an
appointment to see a doctor.**

Je voudrais prendre rendez-
vous chez le médecin.

*Zher voodray prahngdr
rahngdehvoo sheh ler doctur.*

354 I am diabetic/pregnant.

Je suis diabétique/enceinte.

Zher sewee diabetic/ahngsang.

355 I need a prescription for . . .

J'ai besoin d'une ordonnance
pour . . .

*Zhai berzooang dewnordonahngss
poor . . .*

**356 Can you give me something
to ease the pain?**

Pouvez-vous me donner
quelque chose contre la
douleur?

*Poovayvoo mer doneh kehlkshoz
kawngtr lah doolur?*

**357 I am/he is/she is allergic to
penicillin.**

Je suis/il est/elle est allergique à
la pénicilline.

*Zher sewee/eel ay/ehl ay
allerzheek ah lah pehneeseeleen.*

358 Does this hurt?

Ça fait mal?

Sah fay mahl?

**359 You must/he must/she must
go to hospital.**

Vous devez/il doit/elle doit
aller à l'hôpital.

*Voo dervay/eel dwah/ehl dwah
ahleh ah lopeetahl.*

**360 Take these once/twice/three
times a day.**

Prenez ces médicaments une
fois/deux fois/trois fois par
jour.

*Prernay say medeekahmahng ewn
fwah/dur fwah/trwah fwah pahr
zhoor.*

**361 I am/he is/she is taking this
medication.**

Je prends/il prend/elle prend
ces médicaments.

*Zher prahng/eel prahng/ehl
prahng say medeekahmahng.*

**F
R
E
N
C
H**

362 I have medical insurance.
J'ai une assurance médicale.
Zhay ewn assurans mehdeekahl.

Dentist

363 I have toothache.
J'ai mal aux dents.
Zhai mahl o dahng.

364 My filling has come out.
Mon plombage est tombé.
Mawng plawngbahz eh tawngbeh.

365 I do/do not want to have an injection first.
Je veux/je ne veux pas qu'on me donne une piqûre avant.
Zher vur/zher nur vur pah ke orn mer don oon peakewr ahvehn.

EMERGENCIES

366 Help!
Au secours!
Ossercoor!

367 Call an ambulance/a doctor/the police!
Appelez une ambulance/un médicin/la police!
Ahperleh ewnahngbewlahngss/ang medeesang/lah poleess!

368 I have had my travellers' cheques (travelers' checks)/credit cards/purse/handbag/rucksack (knapsack)/luggage/wallet stolen.
On m'a volé mes chèques de voyage/mes cartes de crédits/mon porte-monnaie/mon sac à main/mon sac à dos/mes bagages/mon porte-feuille.
Awng mah voleh meh cheque der vwahahzh/meh carte der crehdite/mawng portemonneh/mawng sackamahn/mawng sackadoe/meh bahgagzh/mawng portfur-ye.

369 Can you help me, I have lost my daughter/son?
Pouvez-vous m'aider, j'ai perdu ma fille/mon fils?
Poovehvoo mehdeh, jeh pehrdew mah feeye/mawng feess?

370 Please go away/leave me alone.
Allez-vous en/Laissez-moi tranquille.
Ahlehvoozahng/lehssehmwah trahngkeel.

371 Fire!
Au feu!
Oh fur!

372 I want to contact the British/American/Canadian/Irish/Australian/New Zealand/South African consulate.
Je veux contacter le Consulat britannique/américain/canadien/irlandais/australien/néo-zélandais/sud-africain.
Zher vurr kontaktay ler kohnsewlah breetahneek/ahmehreekahng/kahnahdyahng/eerlahnday/austrahleeahng/nayozaylahngday/sewdafreekahng.

Introduction

German is the official language of both Germany and Austria, and is also spoken in regions of Switzerland, in the East Cantons area of Belgium, some areas of northern Italy and in Luxembourg. It is also used as a second language in Central European countries, such as Hungary and the Czech Republic. Considering this wide geographical extent, it is not surprising that considerable regional variation exists in accent, vocabulary and sometimes spelling.

**G
E
R
M
A
N**

Addresses for travel and tourist information

Australia: *German National Tourist Office,* Chamber of Commerce & Industry, PO Box A980, Sydney, NSW 1235; tel: (92) 678148
Canada: *German National Tourist Office,* PO Box 65162, Toronto, Ontario, M4K 3Z2; tel: (877) 3156237
South Africa: *German National Tourist Office,* 22 Girton Road, Parktown, Johannesburg; tel: (11) 643 1615.
UK: *German National Tourist Office,* Nightingale House, 65 Curzon St, London, W1Y 7PE; tel: (020) 7317 0908. *Austrian National Tourist Office,* 13–14 Cork Street, London, W1S 3NS; tel: (020) 7629 0461. *Swiss National Tourist Office,* Swiss Centre, 10 Wardour St, London, W1D 6QF; tel: (020) 7734 1921.
USA: *German National Tourist Office,* 122E 42nd Street, 52nd Floor, New York, NY 10168–0072; tel: (212) 661 7200. *Austrian National Tourist Office,* PO Box 1142, New York, NY 101018-1142; tel: (212) 944 6880. *Swiss National Tourist Office,* Swiss Center, 608 Fifth Avenue, New York, NY 10020; tel: (212) 757 5944.

ESSENTIALS

ESSENTIALS

Alphabet

A *ah*	Ä *ah oomlowt*
B *bey*	C *tsey*
D *dey*	E *ey*
F *ef*	G *gey*
H *hah*	I *ee*
J *yot*	K *kah*
L *el*	M *em*
N *en*	O *oh*
Ö *oh oomlowt*	P *pey*
Q *koo*	R *eyr*
S *es*	ß (= double S) *ess-tsett*
T *tey*	U *oo*
Ü *oo oomlowt*	V *fow*
W *vey*	X *iks*
Y *oopsilon*	Z *tset*

Basic Words and Phrases

1 **Yes**
Ja
Yah
   No
Nein
nine

2 **Please**
Bitte
Bitter
   Thank you
Danke
Danke

3 **That's O.K.**
Das stimmt
Das shtimt
   Perhaps
Vielleicht
Feellykht

4 **To**
Nach
Nakh
   From
Von
fon

5 **Here**
Hier
Here
   There
dort
dort

6 **None**
Kein
Kinee
   Also
Auch
Aukh

7 **How**
Wie
Vee
   When
Wann
Ven

8 **What**
Was
Vas
   Why
Warum
Varum

9 **I don't understand.**
Ich verstehe Sie nicht.
Ikh ferhstayher zee nikht.

10 **I don't speak German.**
Ich spreche kein Deutsch.
Ikh shprekher kine doitsh.

11 **Do you speak English?**
Sprechen Sie Englisch?
Shprekhen zee english?

G E R M A N

01 ↕ 11

¹² **Can you please write it down?**
Könnten Sie das bitte aufschreiben?
Kernten zee das bitter owfshryben?

¹³ **Can you please speak more slowly?**
Könnten Sie bitte langsamer sprechen?
Kernten zee bitter langzamer shprekhen?

¹⁴ **How much does it/this cost?**
Was kostet es/das?
Vas kostet es/das?

Days

¹⁵ **Monday** **Tuesday**
Montag Dienstag
Mohntagh *Deenstagh*

¹⁶ **Wednesday** **Thursday**
Mittwoch Donnerstag
Mitvokh *Donnerstagh*

¹⁷ **Friday** **Saturday**
Freitag Samstag
Frytagh *Samstagh*

¹⁸ **Sunday** **Morning**
Sonntag Morgen
Sontagh *Morgen*

¹⁹ **Afternoon** **Evening**
Nachmittag Abend
Naakhmittag *Aabend*

²⁰ **Night** **Week**
Nacht Woche
Naakht *Wokhe*

²¹ **Yesterday/Today/Tomorrow**
Gestern/Heute/Morgen
Gess-tern/Hoyter/Morgen

Numbers

²² **Zero** **One**
Null Eins
Nool *Ines*

²³ **Two** **Three**
Zwei Drei
Tsvy *Dry*

²⁴ **Four** **Five**
Vier Fünf
Feer *Foonf*

²⁵ **Six** **Seven**
Sechs Sieben
Zex *Zeeben*

²⁶ **Eight** **Nine**
Acht Neun
Akht *Noyn*

²⁷ **Ten** **Eleven**
Zehn Elf
Tseyn *Elf*

²⁸ **Twelve** **Thirteen**
Zwölf Dreizehn
Tsverlf *Drytseyn*

²⁹ **Fourteen** **Fifteen**
Vierzehn Fünfzehn
Feertseyn *Foonftseyn*

³⁰ **Sixteen** **Seventeen**
Sechzehn Siebzehn
Zekhtseyn *Zeeptseyn*

³¹ **Eighteen** **Nineteen**
Achtzehn Neunzehn
Akhttseyn *Noinetseyn*

G E R M A N

12 ↕ 31

ESSENTIALS

32 Twenty   **Twenty-one**
Zwanzig   Einundzwanzig
Tvantsig   *Ine-oont-tsvantsikh*

33 Twenty-two   **Thirty**
Zweiundzwanzig   Dreißig
Zvioonttvantsikh   *Drysikh*

34 Forty   **Fifty**
Vierzig   Fünfzig
Feertsikh   *Foonftsikh*

35 Sixty   **Seventy**
Sechzig   Siebzig
Zekhtsikh   *Zeebtsikh*

36 Eighty   **Ninety**
Achtzig   Neunzig
Akhtsikh   *Noyntsikh*

37 One hundred   **Five hundred**
Hundert   Fünfhundert
Hoondert   *Foonfhoondert*

38 One thousand   **One million**
Ein tausend   Eine Million
Ine towsend   *Iner millyohn*

Time

39 9.00
Neun Uhr
Noyn oor

40 9.05
Neun Uhr fünf
Noyn oor foonf

41 9.10
Neun Uhr zehn
Noyn oor tseyn

42 9.15
Neun Uhr fünfzehn
Noyn oor foonftseyn

43 9.20
Neun Uhr zwanzig
Noyn oor tvantsikh

44 9.25
Neun Uhr fünfundzwanzig
Noyn oor foonf-oont-tsvantsig

45 9.30
Neun Uhr dreißig
Noyn oor drytsig

46 9.35
Neun Uhr fünfunddreißig
Noyn oor foonf-oont-drysikh

47 9.40
Neun Uhr vierzig
Noyn oor feertsikh

48 9.45
Neun Uhr fünfunfvierzig
Noyn oor foonf-oont-feertsikh

49 9.50
Neun Uhr fünfzig
Noyn oor foonftsikh

50 9.55
Neun Uhr fünfundfünfzig
Noyn oor foonf-oont-foonftsikh

51 12.00/Midday/Midnight
Mittag/Mitternacht
Mittagh/mitternakht

52 What time is it?
Wie spät ist es?
Vee shpeyt is es?

53 It is . . .
Es ist . . .
Es ist . . .

ARRIVING AND DEPARTING

Airport

54 Excuse me, where is the check-in desk for . . . airline?
Entschuldigung, wo ist der Abfertigungsschalter für . . ?
Entshuldeegen, vo ist dair abfairtigoongs-shalter foor . . ?

55 What is the boarding gate/ time for my flight?
Von welchem Flugsteig geht mein Flug ab?/Wann muß ich einsteigen?
Fon velchem floogstyge geyht mine floog ab?/Vann moos ik eynstygen?

56 How long is the delay likely to be?
Wieviel Verspätung hat mein Flug?
Veefeel fershpeytung hat mine floog?

57 Where is the duty-free shop?
Wo ist der zollfreie Laden?
Vo ist dair tsollfryer larden?

58 Which way is the baggage reclaim?
Wo ist die Gepäckausgabe?
Vo ist dee gepekowsgarber?

59 Where can I get the bus to the city centre?
Wo fährt der Bus ins Stadtzentrum ab?
Vo fairt dair boos ins shtat-tsentrum ab?

Train Station

60 Where is the ticket office/ information desk?
Wo ist der Fahrkartenschalter/ das Informationszentrum?
Voh ist der faarkartenshalter/das informatsion tsentroom?

61 Which platform does the train to . . . depart from?
Von welchem Bahnsteig fährt der Zug nach . . . ab?
Fon velkhen baanshtykh fairt der tsook nakh . . . ab?

62 Where is platform . . ?
Wo ist Bahnsteig . . ?
Voh ist baanshtykh . . ?

63 When is the next train to . . ?
Wann fährt der nächste Zug nach . . ?
Vann fairt der nexter tsook nakh . . ?

64 Is there a later train to . . ?
Gibt es einen späteren Zug nach . . ?
Geebt es inen shpaeteren tsook nakh . . ?

Port

65 How do I get to the port?
Wie komme ich zum Hafen?
Vee kommer ikh zoom haafen?

66 When is the next sailing to . . ?
Wann fährt die nächste Fähre nach . . ?
Van fairt dee nexter fairer nakh . . ?

ARRIVING AND DEPARTING

67 Can I catch an earlier ferry
with this ticket?
Kann ich mit diesem Ticket eine
frühere Fähre nehmen?
*Can ikh mit deesem ticket iner
froohere fairer neymen?*

Notices and Signs

68 **Speisewagen**
shpyzevaagen
Buffet (Dining) Car

69 **Bus**
Bus
Bus

70 **Trinkwasser/kein
Trinkwasser**
treenkvasser/kine treenkvasser
Drinking/Non-drinking water

71 **Eingang**
Ine-gang
Entrance

72 **Ausgang**
Ows-gang
Exit

73 **Information**
Eenformatsion
Information

74 **Gepäckaufbewahrung**
gepeckowfbevaarung
Left Luggage (Baggage Claim)

75 **Schließfächer**
schleessfekher
Luggage Lockers

76 **Postamt**
postamt
Post Office

77 **Bahnsteig**
baanshtykh
Platform

78 **Bahnhof**
baanhof
Railway (Railroad) Station

79 **Flughafen**
Floogharfen
Airport

80 **Hafen**
Harfen
Port

81 **Restaurant**
restohrong
Restaurant

82 **Raucher/Nichtraucher**
raukher/nikhtraukher
Smoking/Non-smoking

83 **Telefon**
taylefohn
Telephone

84 **Fahrkartenschalter**
faarkartenshalter
Ticket Office

85 **Abfertigungsschalter**
Abfairtigoongs-shalter
Check-in Desk

86 **Fahrplan**
faarplaan
Timetable (Schedule)

87 **Toiletten**
toletten
Toilets (Restrooms)

88 Herren
Herren
Gentlemen

89 Damen
Daamen
Ladies'

90 Straßenbahn
Shtraasenbaan
Tram (Streetcar)

91 Die U-Bahn
Dee Oo-baan
Underground (Subway)

92 Warteraum
Varterowm
Waiting Room

Buying a Ticket

**93 I would like a first-class/
second-class/single (one-
way)/return (round-trip)
ticket to . . .**
Ich möchte bitte eine (einfache
Fahrkarte)/Rückfahrkarte
(Rundfahrkarte) erster Klasse/
zweiter Klasse nach . . .
*Eek merkhter bitter iner inefakhe
faarkaarte/rookfaarkaarte airster
classer/tsvyter classer nakh . . .*

**94 Is my rail pass valid on this
train/ferry/bus?**
Gilt mein Rail Pass für diesen
Zug/diese Fähre/diesen Bus?
*Guilt mine rail pass foor deesen
tsug/deese fairer/deesen boos?*

**95 I would like an aisle/window
seat.**
Bitte einen Sitzplatz am
Fenster/Durchgang.
*Bitter inen plaats am fenster/
doorkhgang.*

96 No smoking/smoking, please.
Raucher/Nichtraucher.
Raukher/nikhtraukher.

**97 We would like to sit
together.**
Wir möchten gerne zusammen
sitzen.
*Veer merkhten gairner
tsoozammen zitsen.*

**98 I would like to make a seat
reservation.**
Ich möchte gern einen Platz
reservieren.
*Ikh merkhter gairn inen plats
resairveeren.*

**99 I would like to reserve a
couchette/sleeper for one
person/two people/for my
family.**
Ich möchte eine Schlafwagen-/
Liegewagenreservierung für
eine Person/zwei Personen/
meine Familie.
*Ikh merkhter ine shlaafvaagen-/
leegevaagen-reserveerung foor iner
pairzohn/tsvy pairzohnen/miner
fameelyer.*

**100 I would like to reserve a
cabin.**
Ich möchte gern eine Kabine
reservieren.
*Ikh merkhther gairn iner cabeener
resairveeren.*

G
E
R
M
A
N

88
↑
100

97

ARRIVING AND DEPARTING

Timetables (Schedules)

101 Ankunft
Ankunft
Arrive

102 Hält in . . . an
Helt in . . . an
Calls (Stops) at

103 Mini bar
Minibar
Catering Service

104 In . . . umsteigen
In . . . oomshtygen
Change at . . .

105 Anschluß
Aanshluss
Connection

106 Täglich
Tayglikh
Daily

107 Alle . . . Minuten
Aller . . . minooten
Every 40 Minutes

108 Erste Klasse
Airster classer
First-class

109 Stündlich
Shtundlikh
Hourly

110 Sitzplatzreservierung
empfohlen
Zitsplats-reserveerung empvoolen
Seat reservations are
recommended

111 Zweite Klasse
Tsvyte classe
Second class

112 Zuschlagspflichtig
Tsooshlaags-pfleechteeg
Supplement Payable

113 über
Oober
Via

Luggage

114 How much will it cost to
send (ship) my luggage in
advance?
Wieviel kostet es mein Gepäck
vorauszuschicken?
*Veefeel kostet es mine gepeck
forowss-tsoosheeken?*

115 Where is the left luggage
(baggage claim) office?
Wo ist die
Gepäckaufbewahrung?
Voo ist dee gepeck-owfbevaarung?

116 What time do you open/
close?
Um wieviel Uhr machen Sie
auf/zu?
*Oom veefeel oor makhen zee owf/
tsoo?*

117 Where are the luggage
trolleys (carts)?
Wo finde ich die Gepäckwagen?
Voo feende ikh dee gepeckvaagen?

118 Where are the lockers?
Wo sind die Schließfächer?
Vo seent dee shlees-fekher?

119 I have lost my locker key.
Ich habe den Schlüssel für mein
Schließfach verloren.
*Ikh haaber den shlossel foor mine
shleesfakh ferlooren.*

On Board

120 Is this seat taken?
Ist dieser Platz besetzt?
Ist deezer plats bezetst?

121 Excuse me, you are sitting in
my reserved seat.
Entschuldigen Sie bitte, aber Sie
sitzen auf meinem reservierten
Platz.
*Entshuldigen zee bitter, aber zee
zitsen owf minem rezerveerten
plats.*

122 Which station is this?
Wie heißt dieser Bahnhof?
Vee hysst deezer baanhof?

123 What time is this train/bus/
ferry/flight due to arrive/
depart?
Wann kommt dieser Zug/dieser
Bus/diese Fähre/dieser Flug
an?/Wann geht dieser Zug/
dieser Bus/diese Fähre/dieser
Flug?
*Van kommt deeser tsug/deeser
boos/deeser fairer/deeser floog an?/
Van geyt deeser tsug/deeser boos/
deeser fairer/deeser floog?*

124 Will you wake me just before
we arrive?
Bitte wecken Sie mich kurz
bevor wir ankommen.
*Bitter vekken zee meekh koorts
before veer ankommen.*

Customs and Passports

125 Ihren Reisepass bitte!
Passports, please!
Eeren ryzerpass, bitter!

126 I have nothing/wine/spirits
(alcohol)/tobacco to declare.
Ich habe nichts/keinen Wein/
keinen Schnaps/keinen Tabak
zu verzollen.
*Ikh haabe neekhst/kinen vine/
kinen shnapps/kinen tabak tsoo
fertsollen.*

127 I shall be staying for . . .
days/weeks/months.
Ich werde für . . . Tage/
Wochen/Monate bleiben.
*Ikh verder foor . . . taager/
wokhen/mohnate blyben.*

AT THE TOURIST OFFICE

128 Do you have a map of the
town/area?
Haben Sie eine Stadtkarte/
Landkarte?
*Haaben zee iner shtatkaarter/
landkaarter?*

129 Can I reserve accommodation
here?
Kann ich hier eine Unterkunft
reservieren?
*Can ikh here iner oonterkoonft
reserveeren?*

**G
E
R
M
A
N**

¹³⁰ Do you have a list of
accommodation?
Haben Sie ein
Unterkunftsverzeichnis?
*Haben see ine unterkunfts-
fertsychnis?*

ACCOMMODATION

Hotels

¹³¹ I have a reservation in the
name of . . .
Ich habe eine Reservierung
foor . . .
*Ikh haabe iner reserveerung
foor . . .*

¹³² I wrote to/faxed/telephoned
you last month/last week in .
. .
Ich habe Ihnen letzten Monat/
die letzte Woche im . . .
geschrieben/ein Fax geschickt/
angerufen
*Ikh haber eenen letsten mohnat/dee
letste wokhe im . . . geshreeben/ine
fax gesheekt/angeroofen*

¹³³ Do you have any rooms free?
Haben Sie Zimmer frei?
Haben zee tsimmer fry?

¹³⁴ I would like to reserve a
single/double room with/
without bath/shower.
Ich möchte ein Einzelzimmer/
Doppelzimmer mit/ohne Bad/
Dusche reservieren.
*Ikh merkhter ine inetsel-tsimmer/
doppel-tsimmer meet/oohner baad/
doosher reserveeren.*

¹³⁵ I would like bed and
breakfast/(room and) half
board/(room and) full board.
Ich möchte Übernachtung mit
Frühstück/Halbpension/
Vollpension.
*Ikh merkhter oobernakhtung meet
frooshtook/halbpensiohn/
follpensiohn.*

¹³⁶ How much is it per night?
Wieviel kostet das pro Nacht?
Veefeel kostet das pro nakht?

¹³⁷ Is breakfast included?
Einschließlich Frühstück?
Ineshleesslykh frooshtook?

¹³⁸ May I see the room?
Kann ich das Zimmer bitte sehen?
Can ikh das tsimmer bitter sehen?

¹³⁹ Do you have any cheaper
rooms?
Haben Sie billigere Zimmer?
Haaben see beeligerer tsimmer?

¹⁴⁰ I would like to take the room
Ich nehme das Zimmer, bitte.
Ikh nehmer das tsimmer, bitter.

¹⁴¹ I would like to stay for . . .
nights.
Ich möchte für . . . Nächte
bleiben.
*Ikh merkhter foor . . . nekhte
blyben*

¹⁴² The shower/light/tap doesn't
work.
Die Dusche/das Licht/der
Wasserhahn funktioniert nicht.
*Dee doosher/das licht/dair
vasserharn foonktsioneert nikht.*

143 At what time/where is
breakfast served?
Um wieviel Uhr/wo wird
Frühstück serviert?
*Omm veefeel oor/vo veerd
frooshtook serveert?*

144 What time do I have to check
out?
Um wieviel Uhr müssen wir das
Zimmer verlassen?
*Oom veefeel oor moossen veer das
tsimmer ferlassen?*

145 Can I have the key to room
no . . ?
Könnten Sie mir bitte den
Schlüssel für Zimmer Nummer .
. . geben?
*Kernten zee mere bitter dayn
shloosel foor tsimmer noomer . . .
geyben?*

146 My room number is . . .
Meine Zimmernummer ist . . .
Miner tsimmer-noomer ist . . .

147 Do you accept travellers'
cheques/Eurocheques/credit
cards?
Nehmen Sie Reiseschecks/
Euroschecks/Kreditkarten an?
*Neymen zee ryzersheks/oirosheks/
credeetcarten an?*

148 May I have the bill please?
Die Rechnung, bitte?
Dee rekhnung, bitter?

149 Excuse me, I think there is a
mistake in this bill.
Entschuldigung, ich glaube auf
dieser Rechnung ist ein Fehler.

*Entshuldeegen, ikh glowbe owf
deeser rekhnoong ist ine feyler.*

Youth Hostels

150 How much is a dormitory bed
per night?
Wieviel kostet ein Bett im
Schlafsaal pro Nacht, bitte?
*Veefeel kostet ine bet eem
shlaafzaal pro nakht, bitter?*

151 I am/am not an HI member.
Ich bin ein/kein Mitglied des
internationaler
Jugendherbergsverbands.
*Ikh been ine/kine meetgleed des
internatsionaaler yoogent-
hairbairgs-ferbands.*

152 May I use my own sleeping bag?
Kann ich meinen eigenen
Schlafsack benutzen?
*Can ikh minen ygenen shlaafzack
benootsen?*

153 What time do you lock the
doors at night?
Um wieviel Uhr wird abends
abgeschlossen?
*Oom veefeel oor weerd abends
abgeshlossen?*

Camping

154 May I camp here for the
night/two nights?
Kann ich für eine Nacht/zwei
Nächte hier campen?
*Can ikh foor ine/tsvy nekhte here
campen?*

GERMAN

143
↑
154

ACCOMMODATION

155 Where can I pitch my tent?
Wo kann ich mein Zelt
aufstellen?
Voo can ikh mine tselt owfshtellen?

**156 How much does it cost for
one night/week?**
Wieviel kostet es für eine
Nacht/Woche?
*Veefeel kostet es foor iner nakht/
wokhe?*

**157 Where can we park our
caravan?**
Wo können wir unseren
Wohnwagen parken?
*Vo kernen veer oonseren
vohnvargen parken?*

**158 Where are the washing
facilities?**
Wo sind die Waschraüme?
Voo seent dee vashroyme?

**159 Is there a restaurant/
supermarket/swimming pool
on site/nearby?**
Gibt ein Restaurant/einen
Supermarkt/ein Schwimmbad in
der Nähe dieses
Campingplatzes?
*Geebt es ine restohrong/inen
zoopermarkt/ine shvimmbad in
der neyher deezes campingplatses?*

**160 Do you have a safety deposit
box?**
Haben Sie eine
Sicherheitsverwahrung?
*Haaben see iner zeekherhytes-
fervaarung?*

EATING AND DRINKING

Cafés and Bars

**161 I would like a cup of/two
cups of/another coffee/tea.**
Eine Tasse/Zwei Tassen/noch
eine Tasse Kaffee/Tee, bitte.
*Ikh merkhter iner tasser/tsvy
tassen kafey/tey, bitter.*

162 With/without milk/sugar
Mit/ohne Milch/Zucker.
Meet/ohner milkh/tsukker.

**163 I would like a bottle/glass/
two glasses of mineral water/
red wine/white wine, please**
Ich möchte eine Flasche/ein
Glas/zwei Gläser
Mineralwasser/Rotwein/
Weißwein, bitte.
*Ikh merkhter iner flasher/ine glas/
tsvy glayzer mineraalvasser/
rohtvine/vice-vine, bitter.*

**164 I would like a beer/two
beers, please.**
Ein Bier/Zwei Biere, bitte.
Ine beer/tsvy beerer, bitter.

165 May I have some ice?
Kannich etwas Eis haben?
Can ikh etvas ice haaben?

**166 Do you have any matches/
cigarettes/cigars?**
Haben Sie Streichhölzer/
Zigaretten/Zigarren?
*Haaben see shtrykhherltser/
tseegaretten/tseegarren?*

ACCOMMODATION/EATING AND DRINKING

Restaurants

167 Can you recommend a good/ inexpensive restaurant in this area?

Können Sie ein gutes/nicht zu teueres Restaurant in dieser Gegend empfehlen?

Kernen zee ine gootes/nikht tsoo toyeress restohrong in deezer geygent empfeylen?

168 I would like a table for . . . people.

Ein Tisch für . . . Personen, bitte.

Ine teesh foor . . . perzohnen, bitter.

169 Do you have a non-smoking area?

Haben Sie einen Bereich für Nichtraucher?

Haben zee inen berykh foor nikhtrowkher?

170 Waiter/Waitress!

Herr Ober/Fräulein, bitte!

Hair ohber/froyline, bitter!

171 Do you have a set menu/ children's menu/wine list?

Haben Sie eine Tageskarte/ Kinderspeisekarte/Weinkarte?

Haaben zee iner tahgeskaarter/ keender-shpyzekaarter/ vinekaarter?

172 Do you have any vegetarian dishes, please?

Gibt es bei Ihnen vegetarische Gerichte, bitte?

Geebt es by eehnen vegetareesher gereekhter, bitter?

173 Are there any local specialities?

Gibt es örtliche Spezialitäten?

Geebt es ortlikhe specialitayten?

174 Are vegetables included?

Ist Gemüse dabei?

Ist gemoose darbye?

175 Could I have it well-cooked/ medium/rare please?

Ich möchte es bitte durch/halb durch/englisch gebraten.

Ikh merkhter es bitter doorkh/halb doorkh/english gebrarten.

176 What does this dish consist of?

Was für ein Gericht ist es?

Vas foor ine gereekht ist es?

177 I would like the set menu, please.

Das Tageskarte, bitte.

Das tahgeskaarte, bitter.

178 We have not been served yet.

Wir warten noch auf Bedienung.

Veer varten nokh owf bedeenung.

179 Excuse me, this is not what I ordered.

Entschuldigung, das habe ich nicht bestellt.

Entshuldeegen, das haber ikh nikht beshtelt.

180 May I have some/some more bread/water/coffee/tea?

Kann ich noch etwas Brot, Wasser/Kaffee/Tee haben?

Can ikh etvas/nokh etvas broht/ vasser/kaffey/tey haaben?

181 **May I have the bill, please?**
Die Rechnung, bitte?
Dee rekhnung, bitter?

182 **Does this bill include service?**
Ist diese Rechnung einschließlich Bedienung?
Ist deeze rekhnung ine-shleessleekh bedeenung?

183 **Do you accept travellers' cheques (travelers' checks)/ Eurocheques/MasterCard/ US dollars?**
Nehmen sie Reisechecks/ Euroschecks/MasterCard/US Dollars?
Naymen zee Ryzersheks/ Eurosheks/MasterCard/US Dollars?

184 **Can I have a receipt, please?**
Könnte ich bitte eine Quittung haben?
Kernter ikh bitter ine kwitoong harben?

185 **Where is the toilet (restroom), please?**
Wo sind die Toiletten, bitte?
Voo zeent dee toletten, bitter?

On the Menu

186 **First courses**
Vorspeisen
Fore-shpysen

187 **Soups**
Suppen
Sooppen

188 **Main courses**
Hauptgerichte
Howpt-gerikhte

189 **Fish dishes**
Fischgerichte
Fish-gerikhte

190 **Meat dishes**
Fleischgerichte
Flyesh-gerikhte

191 **Vegetarian dishes**
Vegetarische Gerichte
Vegetairishe gerikhte

192 **Cheese**
Käse
Keyse

193 **Desserts**
Desserts
Desayrs

194 **Specialities**
Spezialitäten
Specialitayten

GETTING AROUND

Public Transport

195 **Where is the bus stop/coach station/nearest metro (subway) station?**
Wo ist die nächste Bushaltestelle/der nächste Busbahnhof/die U-Bahnhaltestelle, bitte?
Voo ist die nexter bushaltersteller/ der nexter busbaanhof/dee nexter Oo-baahn-halter-shteller?

196 When is the next/last bus
to . . ?
Wann fährt der nächste/letzte
Bus nach . . ?
*Vann fairt der nexter/letster bus
nakh . . ?*

197 How much is the fare to the
city centre (downtown)/
railway (railroad) station/
airport?
Wieviel kostet es zur
Stadtmitte/zum Bahnhof/
Flughafen?
*Veefeel kostet es tsoor shtatmitte/
tsoom baanhof/flooghaafen?*

198 Will you tell me when to
get off?
Sagen Sie mir bitte wann ich
aussteigen muß?
*Zaagen zee meer bitter vann ikh
owsstygen moos?*

199 Does this bus go to . . ?
Fährt dieser Bus nach . . ?
Fairt deezer bus nakh . . ?

200 Which number bus goes to
. . ?
Welcher Bus fährt nach . . ?
Velkher bus fairt nakh . . ?

201 May I have a single (one-
way)/return (round-trip)/
day ticket/book of tickets?
Ich möchte eine einfache
Fahrkarte/Rückfahrkarte/
Rundfahrkarte/Tageskarte/ein
Fahrkartenheft?
*Ikh merkhter iner inefakher
faarkaarter/ruekfaarkaarter/*

*tagheskaarter/iner
faarkaartenheft?*

Taxis

202 I would like to go to . . .
How much will it cost?
Ich möchte nach . . . fahren,
wieviel kostet das?
*Ikh merkhter nakh . . . faaren,
veefeel kostet das?*

203 Please stop here.
Bitte anhalten.
Bitter anhalten.

204 I would like to order a taxi
today/tomorrow/at 2pm to
go from . . . to . . .
Ich möchte gerne ein Taxi für
heute/morgen/zwei Uhr
bestellen um von . . . nach . . . zu
fahren.
*Ikh merkhter gairner ine Taxi foor
hoyter/morgen/tsvy oor bestellen
oom fon . . . nakh . . . zu faaren.*

Asking the Way

205 Excuse me, do you speak
English?
Entschuldigen Sie, sprechen Sie
Englisch?
*Entshuldigen zee, shprekhen zee
english?*

206 Excuse me, is this the right
way to . . ?
Entschuldigung, bin ich hier
richtig für . . ?
*Entshuldeegen, bin ikh here rikhtig
foor . . ?*

GERMAN

196
↑
206

G E R M A N

207 ... the cathedral/the tourist information office/the castle/the old town
... den Dom/die Touristeninformation/das Schloß/die Altstadt?
... den dorm, dee tooristeninformatsion/das shloss/dee altshtat?

208 Can you tell me the way to the railway station/bus station/taxi rank (stand)/city centre (downtown)/beach?
Können sie mir bitte sagen wie ich zum Bahnhof/zum Busbahnhof/zum TaxiRank/zur Stadtmitte/zum Strand komme?
Kernen zee meer bitter zaagen, vee ikh tsoom baanhof/tsoom busbaanhof/tsoom taxirank/tsoor shtatmitter/tsoom shtrant kommer?

209 First/second left/right/straight ahead.
Die erste Straße links/rechts/geradeaus.
Dee airste shtraasser leenks/rekhts/geraader-ows.

210 Where is the nearest police station/post office/doctor/hospital/pharmacy?
Wo ist die nächste Polizeiwache/das nächste Postamt/das nächste arzt/das nächste krankenhaus/das nächste apotheke?

Voo ist dee nexter politsywakhe/das nexter postamt/das nexter artst/das nexter krankenhouse/das nexter apoteyker?

211 Is it far?
Ist es weit?
Ist es vyte?

212 Do I need to take a taxi/a bus?
Muß ich eine Taxi/einen Bus nehmen?
Moos ikh iner taxi/inen bus nayhmen?

213 Can you point to it on my map?
Können Sie es mir bitte auf der Karte zeigen?
Kernen see es meer bitter owf der kaarte tsygen?

214 Thank you for your help.
Vielen Dank für Ihre Hilfe.
Feelen dank foor eehrer heelfe.

SIGHTSEEING

215 Where is the Tourist Information office?
Wo ist das TouristenInformationsbüro?
Voo ist das touristen-informatisons-booro?

216 Where is the cathedral/church/museum?
Wo ist der Dom/die Kirche/das Museum?
Voh ist der dohm/dee keerkhe/das moozeyum?

217 How much is the entrance (admission) charge?
Was kostet der Eintritt?
Vas kostet der inetreet?

218 Is there a reduction for children/students/senior citizens?
Gibt es eine Ermäßigung für Kinder/Studenten/Rentner?
Geebt es iner ermeyssigung foor kinder/shtudenten/rentner?

219 What time does the next guided tour start?
Um wieviel Uhr ist die nächste Führung?
Oom veefeel oor ist dee nexter foohrung?

220 One/two adults/children, please.
Ein Erwachsener/zwei Erwachsene/Kinder, bitte.
Ine ervaxener/tsvy ervaxener/ kinder, bitter.

221 May I take photographs here?
Darf man hier fotografieren?
Darf man here fotografeeren?

ENTERTAINMENT

222 Can you recommend a good bar/nightclub?
Können Sie eine gute Bar/einen guten Nachtklub empfehlen?
Kernen zee iner gooter bar/inen gooten nakhtklub empfehlen?

223 Do you know what is on at the cinema (playing at the movies)/ theatre at the moment?

Was spielt im Augenblick im Kino/Theater?
Vass shpeelt im augenbleek im keeno/teyaater?

224 I would like to book (purchase) . . . tickets for the matinée/evening performance on Monday.
Ich möchte gerne Eintrittskarten für die Frühvorstellung am Montag bestellen.
Ikh merkhter gairner inetreetskaarten foor dee frooforshtellung am mohntagh beshtellen.

225 What time does the film/ performance start?
Um wieviel Uhr fängt der Film/ die Vorstellung an?
Oom veefeel oor fengt der film/dee forshtellung an?

MEETING PEOPLE

226 Hello/Goodbye.
Hallo/Auf Wiedersehen.
Hallo/Owf Veederzeyhen.

227 Good morning/good afternoon/good evening/ goodnight.
Guten Morgen/guten Tag/ guten Abend/gute Nacht.
Gooten morgen/gooten targ/ gooten arbent/goote nakht.

228 Pleased to meet you.
Es freut mich Sie kennenzulernen.
Es froyt mikh zee kennen-tsoo-lernen.

G E R M A N

217
↑
228

ENTERTAINMENT/MEETING PEOPLE

229 How are you?
Wie geht es Ihnen?
Vee gayht es eehnen?

230 Fine, thank you. And you?
Gut danke, und Ihnen?
Goot, danker, oond eenen?

231 My name is . . .
Mein Name ist . . .
Mine naamer ist . . .

**232 This is my friend/boyfriend/
girlfriend/husband/wife/
brother/sister.**
Dies ist mein Freund/mein
Freund/meine Freundin/mein
Mann/meine Frau/mein Bruder/
meine Schwester.
*Dees ist mine froynd/mine froynd/
miner froindeen/mine man/miner
frow/mine brooder/miner shvester.*

233 Where are you travelling to?
Wohin reisen Sie?
Voheen ryzen zee?

234 I am/we are going to . . .
Ich fahre/wir fahren nach . . .
Ikh faare/weer faaren nakh . . .

**235 How long are you travelling
for?**
Wie lange reisen Sie?
Vee lange ryzen zee?

236 Where do you come from?
Woher kommen Sie?
Vohair kommen zee?

237 I am/we are from . . .
Ich komme/wir kommen aus . . .
Ikh kommer/veer kommen aus . . .

238 We're on holiday.
Wir machen Urlaub.
Veer makhen oorlowb.

239 This is our first visit here.
Wir sind zum ersten Mal hier.
Veer sind tsum airsten marl here.

**240 Would you like a cigarette?/
May I have a cigarette?**
Möchten Sie eine Zigarette/
Kann ich bitte eine Zigarette
haben?
*Merkhten zee iner tsigaretter/Can
ikh bitter iner tsigaretter haaben?*

**241 I am sorry but I do not
understand.**
Es tut mir leid, aber ich verstehe
es nicht.
*Es toot meer lite, aaber ikh
ferstayher es nikht.*

242 Please speak slowly.
Sprechen Sie bitte langsam.
Sprekhen zee bitter langzam.

243 Do you mind if I smoke?
Darf ich rauchen?
Darf ikh raukhen?

244 Do you have a light?
Haben Sie Feuer bitte?
Haaben see foyer bitter?

**245 I am waiting for my husband/
wife/boyfriend/girlfriend.**
Ich warte auf meinen Mann/
meine Frau/meinen Freund/
meine Freundin.
*Ikh varter owf minen mann/miner
frow/minen froind/miner froindin.*

TRAVELLING WITH CHILDREN

246 Do you have a high chair/ babysitting service/cot?
Haben Sie einen Kinderstuhl/ Babysitter/ein Kinderbett?
Haaben zee inen kindershtool/ Babysittier/ine kinderbet?

247 Where is the nursery/ playroom?
Wo ist das Kinderzimmer/ Spielzimmer?
Voh ist das kindertsimmer/ speeltsimmer?

248 Where can I warm the baby's bottle?
Wo kann ich die Milchflasche für das Baby aufwärmen?
Voh can ikh die Milkflasher foor das Baby owf-vairmen?

COMMUNICATIONS

Post

249 How much will it cost to send a letter/postcard/this package to Britain/Ireland/ America/Canada/Australia/ New Zealand?
Wieviel kostet ein Brief/eine Postkarte/dieses Paket nach England/Irland/Amerika/ Kanada/Australien/Neuseeland?
Veefeel kostet ine breef/iner postkaarter/deezes pakayt nakh England/Eerland/America/ Canada/Owstralee-en/ Noyzeyland.

250 I would like one stamp/two stamps.
Ich möchte eine/zwei Briefmarke(n).
Ikh merkhter iner/tsvy breefmarke(n).

251 I'd like . . . stamps for postcards to send abroad, please.
Ich möchte . . . Briefmarken für Postkarten ins Ausland bitte.
Ikh merkhter . . . breefmarken foor postkarten ins owslund bitter.

Phones

252 I would like to make a telephone call/reverse the charges to (make a collect call to) . . .
Ich möchte einen Anruf/ein RGespräch nakh . . . machen
Ikh merkhter inen aanroof/ine eyr-geshprekh nakh . . . makhen

253 Which coins do I need for the telephone?
Welche Münzen brauche ich für dieses Telefon?
Velkhe moontsen browkhe ikh foor deezes teylefohn?

254 The line is engaged (busy).
Die Nummer ist besetzt.
Dee noommer ist bezetst.

255 The number is . . .
Die Nummer ist . . .
Dee noommer ist . . .

G
E
R
M
A
N

246
↕
255

109

256 Hello, this is . . .
Hallo, hier spricht . . .
Hallo, here shprikht . . .

257 May I speak to . . ?
Kann ich bitte mit . . .sprechen?
Can ikh bitter mit . . .shprekhen?

258 He/She is not in at the
moment. Can you call back?
Er/Sie ist im Moment nicht da.
Könnten Sie später noch einmal
anrufen?
Air/Zee ist im morment nikht dar.
Kernten zee shpeter nokh inemarl
anroofen?

MONEY

259 I would like to change these
travellers' cheques (travelers'
checks)/this currency/this
Eurocheque.
Ich möchte gerne diese
Reisescheks/dieses Geld/
diesen Euroscheck wechseln.
Ikh merkhter gairner deezer
ryzersheks/deezes gelt/deezen
Euroshek vexseln.

260 How much commission do
you charge (What is the
service charge)?
Wie hoch ist Ihre Provision?
Vee hokh ist eere provizion?

261 Can I obtain money with my
MasterCard?
Kann ich mit meiner
MasterCard Geld bekommen?
Can ikh meet miner MasterCard
gelt bekommen?

SHOPPING

Names of Shops and
Departments

262 Buchgeschäft/Schreibwaren
Bookhgesheft/Shribevahren
Bookshop/Stationery

263 Schmuckgeschäft/Geschenke
Shmookgesheft/Geshenker
Jeweller's/Gifts

264 Schuhe
Shooher
Shoes

265 Eisenwaren
Eyesenvahren
Hardware

266 Antiquitäten
Anteekweeteyten
Antiques

267 Friseur (Herren)/(Damen)
Freesoor (hairren)/(darmen)
Hairdresser's (men's)/(women's)

268 Tabakwarengeschäft
Tabakvahrengesheft
Tobacconist

269 Bäckerei
Bekkereye
Baker's

270 Supermarkt
Soopermarkt
Supermarket

271 Fotogeschäft
Fotogesheft
Photoshop

272 Spielwaren
Speelvahren
Toys

273 Reisebüro
Ryesebooro
Travel Agent

274 Toilettenartikel
Toiletenarteekel
Toiletries

275 Schallplatten
Shallplatten
Records

In the Shop

276 What time do the shops open/close?
Um wieviel Uhr öffnen/ schließen die Geschäfte?
Oom veefeel oor erffnen/shleessen dee geshefter?

277 Where is the nearest market?
Wo ist der nächste Markt?
Vo ist dair nekster markt?

278 Can you show me the one in the window/this one?
Zeigen Sie mir bitte den im Fenster/diesen da?
Tsyegen zee mere bitter den im fenster/deezen dar?

279 Can I try this on?
Kann ich das anprobieren?
Can ikh das anprobeeren?

280 What size is this?
Welche Größe ist dieses Stück?
Velkhe grersser ist deezes shtook?

281 This is too large/too small/ too expensive.
Es ist zu groß/zu klein/zu teuer.
Es ist tsu gross/tsu kline/tsu toyer.

282 Do you have any others?
Haben Sie noch andere?
Haben zee nokh anderer?

283 My size is . . .
Ich habe Größe . . .
Ikh haber grerser . . .

284 Where is the changing room/ children's/cosmetic/ ladieswear/menswear/food department?
Wo ist der Umkleideraum/ Kinder- /Damen- / Herrenkleidungs- / Lebensmittel-abteilung?
Voh ist der oomklyderowm/dee kinder/daamen/herenklydungs/ leybensmittel abtylung?

285 I would like . . .
Ich hätte gern . . .
Ikh hetter gairn . . .

286 I would like a quarter of a kilo/half a kilo/a kilo of bread/butter/cheese/ham/ tomatoes.
Ich möchte gerne ein viertel Kilo/halbes Kilo/ein Kilo Brot/ Butter/Käse/Schinken/ Tomaten.
Ikh merkhter gairner ine feertel keelo/halbes keelo/ine keelo broht/ booter/kayzer/sheenken/tomaten.

G
E
R
M
A
N

272
↕
286

111

287 How much is this?
Wieviel kostet das?
Veefeel kostet das?

288 I'll take this one, thank you.
Ich nehme das, dankeschön.
Ikh neymer das, dankershern.

289 Do you have a carrier
(shopping) bag?
Haben Sie eine Tragetasche?
Haaben zee iner traager-tasher?

290 Do you have anything
cheaper/larger/smaller/of
better quality?
Haben Sie etwas billigeres/
größeres/kleineres/Haben Sie
eine bessere Qualität?
*Haaben zee etvas billigeress/
grersseress/klineress/Haaben zee
iner bessere qualitaet?*

291 I would like a film for my
camera.
Ich möchte einen Film für
meinen Fotoapparat.
*Ikh merkhter inen film foor minen
fotoaparat.*

292 I would like some batteries,
the same size as this old one.
Ich möchte einige Batterien, die
gleiche Größe wie die alten.
*Ikh merkhter iyniger batteree-en,
dee glykhe grersser vee dee alten.*

293 Would you mind wrapping
this for me, please?
Können Sie es bitte einpacken?
Kernen zee es bitter ine-pakken?

294 Sorry, but you seem to have
given me the wrong change.
Entschuldigung, aber Sie
scheinen einen Fehler mit dem
Wechselgeld gemacht zu haben.
*Entshuldigung, aber zee shinern
inen fayler mit dem vekhselgeld
gemahkt tsoo haaben.*

MOTORING

Car Hire (Rental)

295 I have ordered (rented) a car
in the name of . .
Ich habe einen Wagen für . . .
bestellt.
*Ikh haaber inen vaagen foor . . .
beshtellt.*

296 How much does it cost to
hire (rent) a car for one day/
two days/one week?
Was kostet es einen Wagen für
einen Tag/zwei Tage/eine
Woche zu mieten?
*Vas kostet es inen vaagen foor inen
taagh/tsvy taager/iner wokher
tsoo meeten?*

297 Is the tank already full of
petrol (gas)?
Ist der Tank voll?
Ist der tank foll?

298 Is insurance and tax
included? How much is the
deposit?
Ist die Versicherung und Steuer
inbegriffen? Wieviel muß man
anzahlen?
*Ist dee ferzeekherung oont shtoyer
inbegreeffen? Veefeel moos man
aantsahlen?*

299 By what time must I return the car?

Um wieviel Uhr muß ich den Wagen zurückbringen?

Oom veefeel oor moos ikh den vaagen tsoo-rookh bringen?

300 I would like a small/family car with a radio/cassette player.

Ich möchte einen kleinen/ Familienwagen mit Radio und Kassettenspieler.

Ikh merkhter inen klinen/fameelien vaagen mit radio oont cassettenshpeeler.

Asking the Way

301 Excuse me, can you help me please?

Entschuldigung, könnten Sie mir bitte helfen?

Entshuldeegn, kernten zee mere bitter helfen?

302 How do I reach the motorway/main road?

Wie komme ich zur Autobahn/ zur Hauptstraße?

Vee kommer ikh tsur owtobarn/ tsur howpt-shtrarser?

303 I think I have taken the wrong turning.

Ich glaube, ich bin falsch abgebogen.

Ikh glowber, ikh bin falsh abgeborgen.

304 I am looking for this address.

Ich suche diese Adresse.

Ikh sookher deeser ardresse.

305 I am looking for the . . . hotel.

Ich suche das . . . Hotel.

Ikh sookher das . . . hotel.

306 How far is it to . . . from here?

Wie weit ist es bis . . . von hier?

Vee vite ist es bees . . . fon here?

307 Carry straight on for . . . kilometres.

Fahren Sie . . . Kilometer geradeaus.

Faren zee . . . keelometer gerarde ows.

308 Take the next turning on the right/left.

Biegen Sie die nächste Straße rechts/links ab.

Beegen zee dee nekste shtrarser rekhts/links ab.

309 Turn right/left at the next crossroads/traffic lights.

Biegen Sie an der nächsten Kreuzung/Ampel rechts/links ab.

Beegen zee un dair neksten kroitsung/ampel rekhts/links ab.

310 You are going in the wrong direction.

Sie fahren in die falsche Richtung.

Zee faren in dee falsher richtung.

MOTORING

Parking

311 How long can I park here?
Wie lange darf man hier parken?
Vee langer darf man here parken?

312 Is there a car park near here?
Gibt es einen Parkplatz in der Nähe?
Geebt es inen parkplats in dair neher?

313 At what time does this car park close?
Wann schließt dieser Parkplatz?
Van shleest deeser parkplats?

Signs and Notices

314 Einbahnstraße.
Ine-barn-shtraser.
One way.

315 Zutritt/Einfahrt verboten.
Tsutreet/Inefart ferbohten.
No entry.

316 Parkverbot.
Park-ferboht.
No parking.

317 Umweg (Umleitung)
Oomweyg (oomlytung)
Detour (diversion)

318 Halt.
Halt.
Stop.

319 Vorfahrt beachten.
Forfart beakhten.
Give way (yield).

320 Straßenglätte.
Shtrasen-gletter.
Slippery road.

321 Überholen verboten.
Ooberhohlen ferbohten.
No overtaking.

At the Filling Station

322 Unleaded (lead-free)/ Standard/Premium
Bleifrei/Normal/Super
Blye-frye/normahl/super

323 Fill the tank please.
Volltanken, bitte.
Foll-tanken, bitter.

324 Do you have a road map of this area?
Haben Sie eine Straßenkarte für diese Gegend?
Haben zee iner shtrasen-karte foor deeser gegent?

325 How much is the car-wash?
Was kostet die Autowäsche?
Vas kostet dee owtowesher?

Breakdowns

326 I've had a breakdown at . . .
Ich habe eine Panne bei . . .
Ikh haber ine panner bye . . .

327 I am on the road from . . . to . . .
Ich bin auf der Straße von . . . nach . . .
Ikh bin owf dair shtrase fon . . . nakh . . .

328 I can't move the car. Can you send a tow-truck?
Mein Auto ist kaputt. Können Sie einen Abschleppwagen schicken?
Mine owto ist kapoot. Kernnen zee inen Abshlep-vagen shiken?

329 I have a flat tyre.
Mein Reifen ist platt.
Mine ryefen ist platt.

330 The windscreen (windshield) has smashed/cracked.
Die Windschutzscheibe ist kaputt/gesprungen.
Dee vindshoots-shyeber ist kapoot/ geshprungen.

331 There is something wrong with the engine/brakes/ lights/steering/gearbox/ clutch/exhaust.
Ich habe Probleme mit dem Motor/der Bremse/dem Licht/ der Steuerung/dem Getriebe/ der Kupplung/dem Auspuff.
Ikh haber probleyme mit dem motor/dair bremser/dem licht/dair shtoyerung/dem getreeber/dair koopploong/dem owspooff.

332 It's overheating.
Der Motor ist überhitzt.
Dair motor ist ooberhitst.

333 It won't start.
Es springt nicht an.
Es shpringt nikht an.

334 Where can I get it repaired?
Wo kann ich es reparieren lassen?

Vo can ikh es repareeren lassen?

335 Can you take me there?
Können Sie mich dort hinbringen?
Kernen zee mikh dort hinbringen?

336 Will it take long to fix?
Dauert die Reparatur lange?
Dowert dee reparatoor languer?

337 How much will it cost?
Was wird es kosten?
Vas veerd es kosten?

Accidents

338 Can you help me? There has been an accident.
Können Sie mir helfen? Es ist ein Unfall passiert.
Kernen zee mere helfen? Es ist ine oonfal paseert.

339 Please call the police/an ambulance.
Bitte rufen Sie die Polizei/einen Krankenwagen.
Bitter roofen zee dee politsye/inen krankenvagen.

340 Is anyone hurt?
Ist jemand verletzt?
Ist yemant fairletst?

Traffic Offences

341 I'm sorry, I didn't see the sign.
Tut mir leid, ich habe das Schild nicht gesehen.
Toot mere lyed, ikh haber das shilt nikht gesayhen.

G
E
R
M
A
N

328
↑
341

115

G E R M A N

342 **Must I pay a fine? How much?**
Gibt das einen Strafzettel? Wieviel?
Geebt das inen shtraf-tsettel? Veefeel?

343 **Show me your documents.**
Zeigen Sie mir Ihre Papiere.
Tsyegen zee mere eere papeerer.

HEALTH

Pharmacy

344 **Do you have anything for a stomachache/headache/sore throat/toothache?**
Haben Sie etwas für Magen-schmerzen/Kopfschmerzen/ Halsschmerzen/Zahn-schmerzen?
Haaben zee etvas foor maagenshmertsen/kopfshmertsen/ hals-shmertsen/tsahnschmertsen?

345 **I need something for diarrhoea (diarrhea)/ constipation/a cold/a cough/ insect bites/sunburn/travel (motion) sickness.**
Ich benötige etwas für Durchfall/Verstopfung/eine Erkältung/einen Husten/ Insektenstiche/Sonnenbrand/ Reisekrankheit.
Ikh benertiger etvas foor doorkhfall/fershtopfung/iner erkeltung/inen hoosten/ insektenshteekhe/zonnenbrand/ ryzerkrankhite.

346 **How much/how many do I take?**
Wieviel/wieviele soll ich nehmen?
Veefeel/veefeeler soll ikh neymen?

347 **How often do I take it/them?**
Wie oft soll ich es/sie nehmen?
Vee oft soll ikh es/zee neymen?

348 **How much does it cost?**
Wieviel kostet das?
Veefeel kostet das?

349 **Can you recommend a good doctor/dentist?**
Können Sie einen guten Arzt/ Zahnarzt empfehlen?
Kernen see meer inen gooten artst/ tsaanartst empfehlen?

350 **Is it suitable for children?**
Ist es gut mit Kindern?
Ist es goot mit kindern?

Doctor

351 **I have a pain here/in my arm/ leg/chest/stomach.**
Ich habe hier Schmerzen/an meinem Arm/Bein/an meiner Brust/an meinem Magen.
Ikh haaber shmertsen here/an minem arm/bine/an miner broost/ an minem maagen.

352 **Please call a doctor, this is an emergency.**
Rufen Sie bitte einen Arzt, es ist ein Notfall.
Roofen zee bitter inen artst, es ist ine nohtfall.

342
↑
352

³⁵³ I would like to make an
appointment to see a doctor.
Ich möchte einen Arzttermin
vereinbaren.
*Ikh merkhter inen artst-termeen
ferinebaaren.*

³⁵⁴ I am diabetic/pregnant.
Ich bin ein Diabetiker/ich bin
schwanger.
*Ikh been ine deeabetiker/ikh been
shvanger.*

³⁵⁵ I need a prescription for . . .
Ich benötige ein Rezept foor . . .
Ikh benertiger ine retsept foor . . .

³⁵⁶ Can you give me something
to ease the pain?
Können Sie mir etwas gegen die
Schmerzen geben?
*Kernen zee meer etvas geygen dee
shmertsen geyben?*

³⁵⁷ I am/he is/she is allergic to
penicillin.
Ich bin/er ist/sie ist allergisch
auf Penizillin.
*Ikh bin/air ist/zee ist allergish owf
penitsileen.*

³⁵⁸ Does this hurt?
Tut das weh?
Toot das way?

³⁵⁹ You must/he must/she must
go to hospital.
Sie müssen/er muß/sie muß ins
Krankenhaus.
*Zee moossen/air mousse/zee mous
ins krankenhouse.*

³⁶⁰ Take these once/twice /three
times a day.
Nehmen Sie diese einmal/
zweimal/dreimal täglich.
*Naymen zee deeser inemal/
tsvyemal/drymal teyglikh.*

³⁶¹ I am/he is/she is taking this
medication.
Ich nehme/er nimmt/sie nimmt
diese Medikamente.
*Ikh naymer/air nimmt/zee nimmt
deeser medikamenter.*

³⁶² I have medical insurance.
Ich habe eine
Krankenversicherung.
*Ikh haber ine kranken-
fersikheroong.*

Dentist

³⁶³ I have toothache.
Ich habe Zahnschmerzen.
Ikh haabe tsahn-shmertsen.

³⁶⁴ My filling has come out.
Eine Füllung ist herausgefallen.
Iner fooloong ist herowsgefallen.

³⁶⁵ I do/do not want to have an
injection first.
Ich will eine/keine Spritze haben.
*Ikh vill iner/kiner shpreetse
haaben.*

EMERGENCIES

³⁶⁶ Help!
Hilfe!
Heelfe!

353
↑
366

367 Call an ambulance/a doctor/ the police!

Rufen Sie bitte einen Krankenwagen/einen Arzt/die Polizei!

Roofen zee bitter inen krankenvaagen/inen artst/dee politsye!

368 I have had my travellers' cheques (travelers' checks)/ credit cards/purse/handbag/ rucksack (knapsack)/ luggage/wallet stolen.

Man hat mir meine Reiseschecks/Kreditkarten/ meinen Geldbeutel/meine Handtasche/meinen Rucksack/ mein Gepäck/meine Brieftasche gestolen.

Man hat meer miner ryzersheks/ creditkaarten/minen geldboytel/ miner handtasher/miner ruckzack/mine gepeck/miner breeftasher geshtohlen.

369 Can you help me, I have lost my daughter/son?

Können Sie mir bitte helfen, ich habe meine Tochter/meinen Sohn verloren?

Kernen zee meer bitter helfen, ikh haabe miner tokhter/minen zohn ferloren?

370 Please go away/leave me alone.

Lassen Sie mich bitte in Ruhe!

Lassen see meekh bitter in roohe!

371 Fire!

Feuer!

Foyer!

372 I want to contact the British/ American/Canadian/Irish/ Australian/New Zealand/ South African consulate.

Ich möchte mich mit dem britischen/amerikanischen/ kanadischen/irischen/ australischen/neuseeländischen/ südafrikanischen Konsulat in Verbindung setzen.

Ikh merkhter mikh mit dem britishen/amerikanishen/ karnardishen/eereeshen/ owstralishen/noysaylendishen/ soodafrikanishen konsoolat in ferbeendoong setsen.

Introduction

Greek is a language with a 3000-year history, and modern written Greek would be readable, and probably to a large degree comprehensible, by an ancient Athenian. The non-roman script is the most difficult aspect of the language for the visitor, although many street signs and notices have both the Greek characters and a transliteration into the roman alphabet. This is in itself a source of potential confusion, however, as there is no one accepted way of writing a Greek word in roman script, so any Greek text can have a variety of spellings in the roman alphabet.

The spoken language has fewer pitfalls, although beware that the word for 'yes' sounds like English 'nay', whereas a Greek who nods his head up and down is probably saying 'no', this being the equivalent of shaking the head. English is widely spoken in tourist areas, and French is an official second language, but be prepared to speak Greek when off the beaten track.

Addresses for travel and tourist information

Australia: *Greek National Tourist Office,* 51–7 Pitt St, Sydney, NSW 2000; tel: (2) 9241 1663-5.
Canada: *Greek National Tourist Office,* 1300 Bay St, Main Level, Toronto, Ontario, M5R 3K8; tel: (416) 968 2220.
UK: *National Tourist Organisation of Greece,* 4 Conduit St, London, W1S 2DJ; tel: (020) 7734 5997.
USA: *National Tourist Organisation of Greece,* Olympic Tower, 645 Fifth Ave (5th Floor), New York, NY 10022; tel: (212) 421 5777.

ESSENTIALS

ESSENTIALS

Alphabet

A, α *alpha*	B, β *vita*
Γ, γ *gamma*	Δ, δ *delta*
E, ε *epsilon*	Z, ζ *zeeta*
H, η *eeta*	Θ, θ *theeta*
I, ι *iota*	K, κ *kappa*
Λ, λ *lamda*	M, μ *mi*
N, ν *ni*	Ξ, ξ *xi*
O, o *omikron*	Π, π *pi*
P, ρ *ro*	Σ, σ *sigma*
T, τ *taf*	Y, υ *ipsilon*
Φ, φ *fi*	X, χ *hi*
Ψ, ψ *psi*	Ω, ω *omega*

Basic Words and Phrases

1 **Yes**　　　　　**No**
Ναι　　　　　　Οχι
Ne　　　　　　*Ohi*

2 **Please**　　　**Thank you**
Παρακαλώ　Ευχαριστώ
Parakalo　*Efharisto*

3 **That's O.K.**　**Perhaps**
Εντάξει　　　Ισως
Entaxi　　　*Isos*

4 **To**　　　　　**From**
Προς　　　　　Από
Pros　　　　　*Apo*

5 **Here**　　　　**There**
Εδώ　　　　　Εκεί
Edo　　　　　*Eki*

6 **None**　　　　**Also**
Τίποτα　　　Επίσης
Tipota　　　*Episis*

7 **How**　　　　**When**
Πώς　　　　　Πότε
Pos　　　　　*Pote*

8 **What**　　　　**Why**
Τι　　　　　　Πού;
Ti　　　　　　*Pu?*

9 **I don't understand.**
Δεν καταλαβαίνω.
Den katalaveno

10 **I don't speak Greek.**
Δεν μιλώ Ελληνικά.
Den milo Ellinika

11 **Do you speak English?**
Μιλάτε Αγγλικά;
Milate Anglika?

12 **Can you please write it down?**
Μπορείτε σας παρακαλώ να το γράψετε;
Borite sas parakalo na to grapsete?

13 **Can you please speak more slowly?**

Μπορείτε σας παρακαλώ να
μιλάτε πιο αργά;
*Borite sas parakalo na milate pio
arga?*

14 How much does it/this cost?
Πόσο κοστίζει αυτό;
Poso kostizi afto?

Days

15 Monday   **Tuesday**
Δευτέρα   Τρίτη
Deftera   *Triti*

16 Wednesday   **Thursday**
Τετάρτη   Πέμπτη
Tetarti   *Pembti*

17 Friday   **Saturday**
Παρασκευή   Σάββατο
Paraskevi   *Savvato*

18 Sunday   **Morning**
Κυριακή   Πρωί
Kiriaki   *Proi*

19 Afternoon   **Evening**
Απόγευμα   Βράδυ
Apoyevma   *Vradi*

20 Night   **Week**
Νύχτα   Εβδομάδα
Nihta   *Evdomada*

21 Yesterday/Today/Tomorrow
Χτες /σήμερα/Αύριο
Htes/Simera/Avrio

Numbers

22 Zero   **One**
Μηδέν   Ένα
Miden   *Ena*

23 Two   **Three**
Δύο   Τρία
Dio   *Tria*

24 Four   **Five**
Τέσσερα   Πέντε
Tessera   *Pente*

25 Six   **Seven**
Έξι   Επτά
Exi   *Epta*

26 Eight   **Nine**
Οκτώ   Εννέα
Okto   *Ennea*

27 Ten   **Eleven**
Δέκα   Εντεκα
Deka   *Endeka*

28 Twelve   **Thirteen**
Δώδεκα   Δεκατρία
Dodeka   *Dekatria*

29 Fourteen   **Fifteen**
Δεκατέσσερα   Δεκαπέντε
Dekatessera   *Dekapente*

30 Sixteen   **Seventeen**
Δεκαέξι   Δεκαεπτά
Dekaexi   *Dekaepta*

31 Eighteen   **Nineteen**
Δεκαοχτώ   Δεκαεννέα
Dekaokto   *Dekaennea*

32 Twenty   **Twenty-one**
Είκοσι   Είκοσι ένα
Ikosi   *Ikosi ena*

33 Twenty-two   **Thirty**
Είκοσι δύο   Τριάντα
Ikosi dio   *Trianta*

**G
R
E
E
K**

**14
↕
33**

**G
R
E
E
K**

**34
↕
54**

³⁴ **Forty**   **Fifty**
Σαράντα   Πενήντα
Saranta   *Peninta*

³⁵ **Sixty**   **Seventy**
Εξήντα   Εβδομήντα
Exinta   *Evdominta*

³⁶ **Eighty**   **Ninety**
Ογδόντα   Ενενήντα
Ogdonta   *Eneninta*

³⁷ **One hundred** **Five hundred**
Εκατό   Πεντακόσια
Ekato   *Pentakosia*

³⁸ **One thousand** **One million**
Χίλια   Ενα εκατομμύριο
Hilia   *Ena ekatommirio*

Time

³⁹ **9.00**
Εννέα
Ennea

⁴⁰ **9.05**
Εννέα και πέντε
Ennea ke pente

⁴¹ **9.10**
Εννέα και δέκα
Ennea ke deka

⁴² **9.15**
Εννέα και τέταρτο
Ennea ke tetarto

⁴³ **9.20**
Εννέα και είκοσι
Ennea ke ikosi

⁴⁴ **9.25**
Εννέα και είκοσι πέντε
Ennea ke ikosi pente

⁴⁵ **9.30**
Εννέα και μισή
Ennea ke misi

⁴⁶ **9.35**
Δέκα πάρα είκοσι πέντε
Deka para ikosi pente

⁴⁷ **9.40**
Δέκα πάρα είκοσι
Deka para ikosi

⁴⁸ **9.45**
Δέκα πάρα τέταρτο
Deka para tetarto

⁴⁹ **9.50**
Δέκα πάρα δέκα
Deka para deka

⁵⁰ **9.55**
Δέκα πάρα πέντε
Deka para pente

⁵¹ **12.00/Midday/Midnight**
Δώδεκα/Μεσημέρι/
Μεσάνυχτα
Dodeka/Mesimeri/Mesanihta

⁵² **What time is it?**
Τί ώρα είναι;
Ti ora ine?

⁵³ **It is . . .**
Είναι . . .
Ine . . .

ARRIVING AND DEPARTING

Airport

⁵⁴ **Excuse me, where is the
check-in desk for . . . airline?**
Με συγχωρείτε, πού είναι ο
έλεγχος αποσκευών και

εισιτηρίων για την
αερογραμμή . . ;
*Me sinhorite, pu ine o elenhos
aposkevon kai isitirion ya tin
aerogrammi . . ?*

55 **What is the boarding gate/
time for my flight?**
Ποια είναι η θύρα/ώρα
επιβίβασης για την πτήση μου;
*Pia ine i thira/ora epivivasis ya tin
ptisi mu?*

56 **How long is the delay likely
to be?**
Πόσο προβλέπεται να
διαρκέσει η καθυστέρηση;
*Poso provlepete na diarkesi i
kathisterisi?*

57 **Where is the duty-free shop?**
Πού είναι το κατάστημα
αφορολόγητων;
Pu ine to katastima aforoloyiton?

58 **Which way is the baggage
reclaim?**
Πού είναι η αίθουσα
αποσκευών;
Pu ine i ethusa aposkevon?

59 **Where can I get the bus to
the city centre?**
Από πού μπορώ να πάρω το
λεωφορείο για το κέντρο
της πόλης;
*Apo pu boro na paro to leoforio ya
to kentro tis polis?*

Train Station

60 **Where is the ticket office/
information desk?**

Πού είναι το γραφείο
εισιτηρίων/το γραφείο
πληροφοριών;
*Pu ine to grafio isitirion/to grafio
pliroforion?*

61 **Which platform does the
train to . . . depart from?**
Από ποια πλατφόρμα
αναχωρεί το τραίνο για
την . . ;
*Apo pia platforma anahori to
treno ya tin . . ?*

62 **Where is platform . . ?**
Πού είναι η πλατφόρμα . . ;
Pu ine i platforma . . ?

63 **When is the next train to . . ?**
Πότε είναι το επόμενο
τραίνο για την . . ;
Pote ine to epomeno treno ya tin . . ?

64 **Is there a later train to . . ?**
Υπάρχει αργότερα τραίνο
για την . . ;
Iparhi argotera treno ya tin . . ?

Port

65 **How do I get to the port?**
Πώς μπορώ να πάω στο
λιμάνι;
Pos boro na pao sto limani?

66 **When is the next sailing
to . . ?**
Ποια είναι η επόμενη
πλεύση για την . . ;
Pia ine i epomeni plefsi ya tin . . ?

**G
R
E
E
K**

**55
↕
66**

ARRIVING AND DEPARTING

67 Can I catch an earlier ferry with this ticket?
Με αυτό το εισιτήριο μπορώ να επιβιβαστώ σε φέρρυ που φεύγει νωρίτερα;
Me avto to isitirio boro na epivivasto se ferry pu fevyi noritera?

Notices and Signs

68 Αμαξοστοιχία με μπουφέ
Amaxostihia me Buffet
Buffet (Dining) Car

69 Λεωφορείο
Leoforio
Bus

70 Πόσιμο/μη πόσιμο νερό
Posimo/mi posimo nero
Drinking/Non-drinking water

71 Είσοδος
Isodos
Entrance

72 Εξοδος
Exodos
Exit

73 Πληροφορίες
Plirofories
Information

74 Χώρος Αποσκευών
Horos Aposkevon
Left Luggage

75 Θυρίδες Αποσκευών
Thirides Aposkevon
Luggage Lockers

76 Ταχυδρομείο
Tahidromio
Post Office

77 Πλατφόρμα/Εξέδρα
Platforma/Exedra
Platform

78 Σιδηροδρομικός Σταθμός
Sidirodromikos Stathmos
Railway (Railroad) Station

79 Αεροδρόμιο
Aerodromio
Airport

80 Λιμάνι
Limani
Port

81 Εστιατόριο
Estiatorio
Restaurant

82 Για Καπνιστές/Για μη καπνιστές
Ya kapnistes/ya mi kapnistes
Smoking/Non-smoking

83 Τηλέφωνο
Tilephono
Telephone

84 Γραφείο Εισιτηρίων
Grafio Isitirion
Ticket Office

85 Ελεγχος Αποσκευών & Εισιτηρίων
Elenhos Aposkevon ke Isitirion
Check-in Desk

86 Δρομολόγιο
Dromologio
Timetable (Schedule)

87 Αποχωρητήρια
Apohoritiria

124

Toilets (Restrooms)

88 Ανδρών
Andron
Gentlemen

89 Γυναικών
Yinekon
Ladies'

90 Τραμ
Tram
Tram (Streetcar)

91 Υπόγειος Σιδηρόδρομος
Ipoyios Sidirodromos
Underground (Subway)

92 Αίθουσα Αναμονής
Ethusa Anamonis
Waiting Room

Buying a Ticket

93 I would like a first-class/
second-class single (one-
way)/return (round-trip)
ticket to . . .
Θα ήθελα πρώτης θέσεως/
δευτέρας θέσεως απλό/μετ'
επιστροφής εισιτήριο για
την . . .
*Tha ithela protis theseos/defteras
theseos/aplo/met epistrofis isitirio
ya tin . . .*

94 Is my rail pass valid on this
train/ferry/bus?
Το σιδηροδρομικό
εισιτήριο που έχω ισχύει
για αυτό το τραίνο/φέρρυ/
λεωφορείο;

*To sidirodromiko isitirio pu eho
ishii ya afto to treno/ferry/
leoforio?*

95 I would like an aisle/window
seat.
Θα ήθελα μια θέση δίπλα
στο διάδρομο/παράθυρο.
*Tha ithela mia thesi dipla sto
diadromo/parathiro.*

96 No smoking/smoking, please.
Απαγορεύεται το
κάπνισμα/επιτρέπεται το
κάπνισμα, παρακαλώ.
*Apagorevete to kapnisma/
epitrepete to kapnisma, parakalo.*

97 We would like to sit
together.
Θα θέλαμε να καθίσουμε
μαζί.
Tha thelame na kathisoume mazi.

98 I would like to make a seat
reservation.
Θα ήθελα να κρατήσω μία
θέση.
Tha ithela na kratiso mia thesi.

99 I would like to reserve a
couchette/sleeper for one
person/two people/my
family.
Θα ήθελα να κρατήσω
κουκέτα/κλινάμαξα για ένα
άτομο/δύο άτομα/την
οικογένειά μου.
*Tha ithela na kratiso kuketa/
klinamaxa ya ena atomo/dio
atoma/tin ikoyenia mu.*

G R E E K

88 ↕ 99

ARRIVING AND DEPARTING

100 I would like to reserve a cabin.
Θα ήθελα να κρατήσω μία
καμπίνα.
Tha ithela na kratiso mia kabina.

Timetables (Schedules)

101 Αφίξεις
Afixis
Arrive

102 Σταματά στο
Stamata sto
Calls (Stops) at

103 Υπηρεσία Εστίασης
Ipiresia estiasis
Catering Service

104 Αλλάζει στο
Allazi sto
Change at

105 Σύνδεση
Sindesi
Connection

106 Καθημερινά
Kathimerina
Daily

107 Κάθε σαράντα (40) λεπτά
Kathe saranta (40) lepta
Every 40 minutes

108 Πρώτης θέσεως
Protis Theseos
First-class

109 Κάθε ώρα
Kathe ora
Hourly

110 Συστήνονται κρατήσεις
θέσεων

Sistinonte kratisis theseon
Seat reservations are
recommended

111 Δευτέρας Θέσεως
Defteras Theseos
Second-class

112 Συμπληρωματικό Ποσό
Simpliromatiko Poso
Supplement Payable

113 Μέσω
Meso
Via

Luggage

114 How much will it cost to send
(ship) my luggage in
advance?
Πόσο θα μου στοιχίσει να
στείλω εκ των προτέρων τις
αποσκευές μου;
*Poso tha mu stihisi na stilo ek ton
proteron tis aposkeves mu?*

115 Where is the left luggage
(baggage claim) office?
Πού είναι το γραφείο
αποσκευών;
Pu ine to grafio aposkevon?

116 What time do you open/
close?
Τί ώρα ανοίγετε/κλείνετε;
Ti ora aniyete/klinete?

117 Where are the luggage
trolleys (carts)?
Πού είναι τα τρόλλεϋ των
αποσκευών;
Pu ine ta trolley ton aposkevon?

118 **Where are the lockers?**
Πού είναι οι θυρίδες;
Pu ine i thirides?

119 **I have lost my locker key.**
Εχασα το κλειδί της
θυρίδας μου.
Ehasa to klidi tis thiridas mu.

On Board

120 **Is this seat taken?**
Μήπως αυτή η θέση είναι
ελεύθερη;
Mipos afti i thesi ine eleftheri?

121 **Excuse me, you are sitting in
my reserved seat.**
Με συγχωρείτε, αλλά
κάθεστε στην κρατημένη
μου θέση.
*Me sinhorite, alla katheste stin
kratimeni mu thesi.*

122 **Which station is this?**
Ποιος σταθμός είναι αυτός;
Pios stathmos ine aftos?

123 **What time is this train/bus/
ferry/flight due to arrive/
depart?**
Τι ώρα αναμένεται να
φθάσει/αναχωρήσει το
τραίνο/λεωφορείο/φέρρυ/
πτήση;
*Ti ora anamenete na fthasi/
anahorisi to treno/leoforio/ferry/
ptisi?*

124 **Will you wake me just before
we arrive?**
Μπορείτε να με ξυπνήσετε
προτού φτάσουμε;

*Borite na me xipnisete protu
ftasume?*

Customs and Passports

125 **Τα διαβατήριά σας,
παρακαλώ!**
Ta diavatiria sas, parakalo!
Passports, please!

126 **I have nothing/wine/spirits
(alcohol)/tobacco to declare.**
Δεν έχω τίποτα να δηλώσω/
κρασί/οινοπνευματώδη/
καπνό.
*Den eho tipota na diloso/krasi/
inopnevmatodi/kapno.*

127 **I shall be staying for . . .
days/weeks/months.**
Θα μείνω για . . . ημέρες/
εβδομάδες/μήνες.
*Tha mino ya . . . imeres/
evdomades/mines.*

128 **Do you have a map of the
town/area?**
Μήπως έχετε χάρτη της
πόλης/περιοχής;
*Mipos ehete harti tis polis/
periohis?*

129 **Can I reserve accommodation
here?**
Μπορώ να κρατήσω
δωμάτια εδώ;
Boro na kratiso domatia edo?

G
R
E
E
K

118
↕
129

ACCOMMODATION

¹³⁰ Do you have a list of accommodation?
Εχετε κάποια λίστα δωματίων που νοικιάζονται;
Ehete kapia lista domation pu nikiazonte?

ACCOMMODATION

Hotels

¹³¹ I have a reservation in the name of . . .
Εχω κρατήση στο όνομα . . .
Eho kratisi sto onoma . . .

¹³² I wrote to/faxed/telephoned you last month/last week in . . .
Σας έγραψα/έστειλα φαξ/τηλεφώνησα τον/την περασμένο(η) μήνα/εβδομάδα . . .
Sas egrapsa/estila fax/tilephonisa ton/tin perasmeno(i) mina/evdomada . . .

¹³³ Do you have any rooms free?
Εχετε ελεύθερα δωμάτια;
Ehete elefthera domatia?

¹³⁴ I would like to reserve a single/double room with/without bath/shower.
Θα ήθελα να κρατήσω ένα μονό/διπλό δωμάτιο με/χωρίς μπάνιο/ντους.
Tha ithela na kratiso ena mono/diplo domatio me/horis banio/dush.

¹³⁵ I would like bed and breakfast/(room and) half board/(room and) full board.
Θα ήθελα δωμάτιο με πρόγευμα/δωμάτιο με δύο φαγητά/δωμάτιο με φαγητά.
Tha ithela domatio me proyevma/domatio me dio fayita/domatio me fayita.

¹³⁶ How much is it per night?
Πόσο στοιχίζει τη νύχτα;
Poso stihizi ti nihta?

¹³⁷ Is breakfast included?
Περιλαμβάνει και πρόγευμα;
Perilamvani ke proyevma?

¹³⁸ May I see the room?
Μπορώ να δω το δωμάτιο;
Boro na do to domatio?

¹³⁹ Do you have any cheaper rooms?
Μήπως έχετε φτηνότερα δωμάτια;
Mipos ehete ftinotera domatia?

¹⁴⁰ I would like to take the room.
Θα ήθελα να πάρω αυτό το δωμάτιο.
Tha ithela na paro afto to domatio.

¹⁴¹ I would like to stay for . . . nights.
Θα ήθελα να μείνω για . . . νύχτες.
Tha ithela na mino ya . . . nihtes.

¹⁴² The shower/light/tap doesn't work.
Το ντους/ηλεκτρικό/βρύση δεν λειτουργεί.
To dush/ilektriko/vrisi den lituryi.

¹⁴³ At what time/where is breakfast served?

Τι ώρα/πού σερβίρεται το πρόγευμα;

Ti ora/pu servirete to proyevma?

¹⁴⁴ What time do I have to check-out?

Τι ώρα πρέπει να αδειάσω το δωμάτιο;

Ti ora prepi na adiaso to domatio?

¹⁴⁵ Can I have the key to room no . . ?

Μπορείτε να μου δώσετε το κλειδί για το δωμάτιο αριθ. . . ;

Borite na mu dosete to klidi ya to domatio arithmos . . ?

¹⁴⁶ My room number is . . .

Ο αριθμός του δωματίου μου είναι . . .

O arithmos tu domatiu mu ine . . .

¹⁴⁷ Do you accept travellers' cheques/Eurocheques/credit cards?

Δέχεστε ταξιδιωτικές επιταγές/Ευρωεπιταγές/ πιστωτικές κάρτες;

Deheste taxidiotikes epitayes/ Evroepitayes/pistotikes kartes?

¹⁴⁸ May I have the bill, please?

Μπορώ να έχω το λογαριασμό, παρακαλώ;

Boro na eho to logariasmo, parakalo?

¹⁴⁹ Excuse me, I think there is a mistake in this bill.

Με συγχωρείτε, νομίζω πως υπάρχει κάποιο λάθος στο λογαριασμό.

Me sinhorite, nomizo pos iparhi kapio lathos sto logariasmo.

Youth Hostels

¹⁵⁰ How much is a dormitory bed per night?

Πόσο κάνει ένα κρεβάτι κοιτώνα τη νύχτα;

Poso kani ena krevati kitona ti nihta?

¹⁵¹ I am/am not an HI member.

Είμαι/δεν είμαι μέλος της HI.

Ime/den ime melos tis HI.

¹⁵² May I use my own sleeping bag?

Μπορώ να χρησιμοποιήσω το δικό μου σλήπιγκ μπαγκ;

Boro na hrisimopiiso to diko mu sleeping bag?

¹⁵³ What time do you lock the doors at night?

Τί ώρα κλείνετε τις πόρτες τα βράδια;

Ti ora klinete tis portes ta vradia?

Camping

¹⁵⁴ May I camp here for the night/two nights?

Μπορώ να κάνω κάμπιγκ εδώ για τη νύχτα/δύο νύχτες;

Boro na kano camping edo ya ti nihta/dio nihtes?

G
R
E
E
K

143
↕
154

¹⁵⁵ Where can I pitch my tent?
Πού μπορώ να στήσω την
τέντα μου;
Pu boro na stiso tin tenta mu?

¹⁵⁶ How much does it cost for
one night/one week?
Πόσο στοιχίζει για μία
νύχτα/μία εβδομάδα;
*Poso stihizi ya mia nihta/mia
evdomada?*

¹⁵⁷ Where can we park our
caravan?
Πού μπορούμε να
παρκάρουμε το τροχόσπιτό
μας;
*Pu borume na parkarume to
trochospito mas?*

¹⁵⁸ Where are the washing
facilities?
Πού είναι οι ευκολίες
πλυσίματος;
Pu ine i efkolies plisimatos?

¹⁵⁹ Is there a restaurant/
supermarket/swimming pool
on site/nearby?
Υπάρχει μήπως
εστιατόριο/υπεραγορά/
πισίνα εδώ/εδώ κοντά;
*Iparhi mipos estiatorio/iperagora/
pisina edo/edo konta?*

¹⁶⁰ Do you have a safety deposit
box?
Μήπως έχετε θυρίδα
ασφαλείας αντικειμένων;
*Mipos ehete thirida asfalias
antikimenon?*

EATING AND DRINKING

Cafés and Bars

¹⁶¹ I would like a cup of/two
cups of/another coffee/tea.
Θα ήθελα ένα φλιτζάνι/δύο
φλιτζάνια/ακόμη ένα καφέ/
τσάι.
*Tha ithela ena flitzani/dio
flitzania/akomi ena kafe/tsai.*

¹⁶² With/without milk/sugar.
Με/χωρίς γάλα/ζάχαρη.
Me/horis gala/zahari.

¹⁶³ I would like a bottle/glass/
two glasses of mineral water/
red wine/white wine, please.
Θα ήθελα ένα μπουκάλι/
ποτήρι/δύο ποτήρια
μεταλλικό νερό/κόκκινο
κρασί/άσπρο κρασί,
παρακαλώ.
*Tha ithela ena bukali/potiri/dio
potiria metalliko nero/kokkino
krasi/aspro krasi, parakalo.*

¹⁶⁴ I would like a beer/two
beers, please.
Θα ήθελα μια μπύρα/δύο
μπύρες, παρακαλώ.
*Tha ithela mia bira/dio bires,
parakalo.*

¹⁶⁵ May I have some ice?
Μπορώ να έχω λίγο πάγο;
Boro na eho ligo pago?

¹⁶⁶ Do you have any matches/
cigarettes/cigars?
Μήπως έχετε σπίρτα/
τσιγάρα/πούρα;

Mipos ehete spirta/tsigara/pura?

Restaurants

167 **Can you recommend a good/inexpensive restaurant in this area?**
Μπορείτε να μου συστήσετε ένα καλό/φτηνό εστιατόριο σε αυτή την περιοχή;
Borite na mu sistisete ena kalo/ftino estiatorio se afti tin periohi?

168 **I would like a table for . . . people.**
Θα ήθελα ένα τραπεζάκι για . . . άτομα.
Tha ithela ena trapezaki gia . . . atoma.

169 **Do you have a non-smoking area?**
Εχετε ορισμένη περιοχή για αυτούς που δεν καπνίζουν;
Ehete orismeni periohi ya aftus pu den kapnizun?

170 **Waiter/Waitress!**
Γκαρσόν/Σερβιτόρα!
Garson/Servitora!

171 **Do you have a set menu/children's menu/wine list?**
Εχετε σετ μενού/παιδικό μενού/κατάλογο κρασιών;
Ehete set menu/pediko menu/katalogo krasion?

172 **Do you have any vegetarian dishes, please?**
Μήπως έχετε πιάτα για χορτοφάγους, παρακαλώ;
Mipos ehete piata ya hortofagous, parakalo?

173 **Are there any local specialities?**
Εχετε κάτι το ειδικό που συνηθίζεται τοπικά;
Ehete kati to idiko pu sinithizete topika?

174 **Are vegetables included?**
Χορταρικά και λαχανικά συμπεριλαμβάνονται;
Hortarika ke lahanika simperilamvanonte?

175 **Could I have it well-cooked/medium/rare please?**
Μπορώ να το έχω καλά/μέτρια/ελάχιστα ψημένο, παρακαλώ;
Boro na to eho kala/metria/elahista psimeno, parakalo?

176 **What does this dish consist of?**
Από τι αποτελείται αυτό το πιάτο;
Apo ti apotelite afto to piato?

177 **I would like the set menu, please.**
Θα ήθελα το σετ μενού, παρακαλώ.
Tha ithela to set menu, parakalo.

178 **We have not been served yet.**
Δεν σερβιριστήκαμε ακόμη.
Den serviristikame akomi.

G
R
E
E
K

167
↕
178

EATING AND DRINKING

179 Excuse me, this is not what I ordered.
Με συγχωρείτε, δεν είναι αυτό που παράγγειλα.
Me sinhorite, den ine afto pu paragila.

180 May I have some/some more bread/water/coffee/tea?
Μπορώ να έχω λίγο/ακόμη λίγο ψωμί/νερό/καφέ/τσάι;
Boro na eho ligo/akomi ligo psomi/nero/kafe/tsai?

181 May I have the bill, please?
Μπορώ να έχω το λογαριασμό, παρακαλώ;
Boro na eho to logariasmo, parakalo?

182 Does this bill include service?
Ο λογαριασμός περιλαμβάνει και σέρβις;
O logariasmos perilamvani ke service?

183 Do you accept travellers' cheques (travelers' checks)/Eurocheques/MasterCard/US dollars?
Μήπως παίρνετε ταξιδιωτικές επιταγές/Ευρωεπιταγές/Μάστερ Καρτς/Αμερικανικά Δολλάρια;
Mipos pernete taxidiotikes epitayes/Evroepitayes/MasterCard/Amerikanika dollaria?

184 Can I have a receipt, please?
Μπορώ να έχω την απόδειξη, παρακαλώ;
Boro na eho tin apodixi, parakalo?

185 Where is the toilet (restroom), please?
Πού είναι η τουαλέτα, παρακαλώ;
Pu ine i tualeta, parakalo?

On the Menu

186 First courses
Πρώτα φαγητά
Prota fayita

187 Soups
Σούπες
Supes

188 Main courses
Κύρια φαγητά
Kiria fayita

189 Fish dishes
Φαγητά με ψάρι
Fayita me psari

190 Meat dishes
Φαγητά με κρέας
Fayita me kreas

191 Vegetarian dishes
Είδη χορτοφαγίας
Idi hortofayias

192 Cheese
Τυριά
Tiria

193 Desserts
Επιδόρπιο
Epidorpio

194 Specialities
Πιάτο της ημέρας
Piato tis imeras

GETTING AROUND

Public Transport

195 **Where is the bus stop/coach station/nearest metro (subway) station?**
Πού είναι η στάση λεωφορείων/ο σταθμός των πούλμαν/το πλησιέστερο μετρό;
Pu ine i stasi leoforion/o stathmos ton pullman/to plisiestero metro?

196 **When is the next/last bus to . . ?**
Πότε είναι το επόμενο/ τελευταίο λεωφορείο για την . . ;
Pote ine to epomeno/teleteo leoforio ya tin . . ?

197 **How much is the fare to the city centre (downtown)/ railway (railroad) station/ airport?**
Πόσο κάνει το εισιτήριο για το κέντρο της πόλης/το σιδηροδρομικό σταθμό/το αεροδρόμιο;
Poso kani to isitirio ya to kentro tis polis/to sidirodromiko stathmo/to aerodromio?

198 **Will you tell me when to get off?**
Μου λέτε πού να κατέβω;
Mu lete pu na katevo?

199 **Does this bus go to . . ?**
Αυτό το λεωφορείο πάει στο . . ;
Afto to leoforio pai sto . . ?

200 **Which number bus goes to . . ?**
Ποιο λεωφορείο πηγαίνει στο . . ;
Pio leoforio piyeni sto . . ?

201 **May I have a single (one-way)/return (round-trip)/day ticket/book of tickets?**
Μπορώ να έχω μονό/μετ' επιστροφής/ημερήσιο εισιτήριο/βιβλίο εισιτηρίων;
Boro na eho mono/met epistrofis/ imerisio isitirio/vivlio isitirion?

Taxis

202 **I would like to go to . . . How much will it cost?**
Θα ήθελα να πάω στο . . ., πόσο θα μου στοιχίσει;
Tha ithela na pao sto . . ., poso tha mu stihisi?

203 **Please stop here.**
Παρακαλώ σταματάυε εδώ.
Parakalo stamatate edo.

204 **I would like to order a taxi today/tomorrow/at 2pm to go from . . . to . . .**
Θα ήθελα να παραγγείλω ταξί σήμερα/αύριο/στις 2 μ.μ. να με πάρει από το . . . στο . . .
Tha ithela na parangilo taxi simera/avrio/stis 2 to apoyevma na me pari apo to . . . sto . . .

133

GETTING AROUND/SIGHTSEEING

Asking the Way

205 Excuse me, do you speak English?
Με συγχωρείτε, μήπως μιλάτε Αγγλικά;
Me sinhorite, mipos milate Anglika?

206 Excuse me, is this the right way to . . ?
Με συγχωρείτε, μπορείτε να μου πείτε πώς θα πάω στο/στη . . ;
Me sinhorite, borite na mu pite pos tha pao sto/sti . . ?

207 . . . the cathedral/the tourist information office/the castle/the old town
. . . καθεδρικό ναό/ τουριστικό γραφείο πληροφοριών/κάστρο/ παλιά πόλη
. . . kathedriko nao/turistiko grafio pliroforion/kastro/palia poli

208 Can you tell me the way to the railway (railroad) station/bus station/taxi rank (stand)/city centre (downtown)/beach?
Μπορείτε να μου πείτε το δρόμο προς τον σιδηροδρομικό σταθμό/ σταθμό λεωφορείων/στάση ταξί/το κέντρο της πόλεως/ την πλαζ;
Borite na mu pite ton dromo pros ton sidirodromiko stathmo/ stathmo leoforion/stasi taxi/to kentro tis poleos/tin plaz?

209 First/second/left/right/

205 ↕ 215

straight ahead.
Πρώτη/δεύτερη στροφή/ αριστερά/δεξιά/ευθεία.
Proti/defteri strofi/aristera/dexia/ efthia.

210 Where is the nearest police station/post office/doctor/ hospital/pharmacy?
Πού είναι ο πλησιέστερος αστυνομικός σταθμός/το ταχυδρομείο/ γιατρο/νοσοκομείο/ Φαρμρχειο
Pu ine o plisiesteros astinomikos stathmos/to tahidromio/yatro/ nosokomio/farmakio?

211 Is it far?
Είναι μακριά;
Ine makria?

212 Do I need to take a taxi/catch a bus?
Χρειάζομαι να πάρω ταξί/ λεωφορείο;
Hriazome na paro taxi/leoforio?

213 Can you point to it on my map?
Μπορείτε να μου το υποδείξετε στο χάρτη;
Borite na mu to ipodixete sto harti?

214 Thank you for your help.
Σας ευχαριστώ για τη βοήθειά σας.
Sas efharisto ya ti voithia sas.

SIGHTSEEING

215 Where is the Tourist Information office?

134

Πού είναι το Γραφείο
Τουρισμού;
Pu ine to grafio Turismu?

**216 Where is the cathedral/
church/museum?**
Πού είναι η Μητρόπολη/
Εκκλησία/το Μουσείο;
*Pu ine i mitropoli/ekklisia/to
musio?*

**217 How much is the entrance
(admission) charge?**
Πόσο κάνει η είσοδος;
Poso kani i isodos?

**218 Is there a reduction for
children/students/senior
citizens?**
Μήπως υπάρχει έκπτωση
για παιδιά/φοιτητές/
ηλικιωμένους;
*Mipos iparhi ekptosi ya pedia/
fitites/ilikiomenus?*

**219 What time does the next
guided tour start?**
Τί ώρα αρχίζει η επόμενη
περιοδεία με ξεναγό;
*Ti ora arhizi i epomeni periodia me
xenago?*

**220 One/two adults/children,
please.**
Ενα/δυό ενήλικες/παιδιά,
παρακαλώ.
Ena/dio enilikes/pedia, parakalo.

**221 May I take photographs
here?**
Επιτρέπεται η λήψη
φωτογραφιών εδώ;
Epitrepete i lipsi photographion edo?

ENTERTAINMENT

**222 Can you recommend a good
bar/nightclub?**
Μπορείτε να μου
συστήσετε ένα καλό μπαρ/
νυχτερινό κέντρο;
*Borite na mu sistisete ena kalo
bar/nihterino kentro?*

**223 Do you know what is on at
the cinema (playing at the
movies)/theatre at the
moment?**
Ξέρετε τι παίζεται τώρα στο
σινεμά/στο θέατρο;
*Xerete ti pezete tora sto cinema/sto
theatro?*

**224 I would like to book
(purchase) . . . tickets for the
matinée/evening
performance on Monday.**
Θα ήθελα να κρατήσω . . .
εισιτήρια για
απογευματινή/βραδινή
παράσταση τη Δευτέρα.
*Tha ithela na kratiso . . . isitiria ya
apoyevmatini/vradini parastasi ti
Deftera.*

**225 What time does the film/
performance start?**
Τί ώρα αρχίζει το φιλμ/η
παράσταση;
Ti ora arhizi to film/i parastasi?

MEETING PEOPLE

226 Hello/Goodbye.
Γειά σας/Χαίρετε.
Ya sas/Herete.

G
R
E
E
K

216
↕
226

G
R
E
E
K

227 **Good morning/good afternoon/good evening/goodnight.**
Καλημέρα/χαίρετε/
καλησπέρα/καληνύχτα.
*Kalimera/herete/kalispera/
kalinihta.*

228 **Pleased to meet you.**
Χαίρω πολύ.
Hero poli.

229 **How are you?**
Τι κάνετε;
Ti kanete?

230 **Fine, thank you. And you?**
Πολύ καλά, ευχαριστώ. Κι
εσείς;
Poli kala, efharisto. Ki esis?

231 **My name is . . .**
Ονομάζομαι . . .
Onomazome . . .

232 **This is my friend/boyfriend/
girlfriend/husband/wife/
brother/sister.**
Σας συστήνω το φίλο μου/
το φίλο μου/τη φίλη μου/το
σύζυγό μου/τη σύζυγό μου/
τον αδελφό μου/την αδελφή
μου.
*Sas sistino to filo mu/to filo mu/ti
fili mu/to sizigo mu/ti sizigo mu/
ton adelfo mu/tin adelfi mu.*

233 **Where are you travelling to?**
Για πού ταξιδεύετε;
Ya pu taxidevete?

234 **I am/we are going to . . .**
Πάω/πάμε στο . . .
Pao/pame sto . . .

235 **How long are you travelling
for?**
Για πόσο καιρό θα
ταξιδέψετε;
Ya poso kero tha taxidepsete?

236 **Where do you come from?**
Από πού είστε;
Apo pu iste?

237 **I am/we are from . . .**
Είμαι/είμαστε από την . . .
Ime/imaste apo tin . . .

238 **We're on holiday.**
Είμαστε σε διακοπές.
Imaste se diakopes.

239 **This is our first visit here.**
Είναι η πρώτη μας
επίσκεψη εδώ.
Ine i proti mas episkepsi edo.

240 **Would you like/May I have a
cigarette?**
Θα θέλατε/Μπορώ να έχω
ένα τσιγάρο;
Tha thelate/Boro na eho ena tsigaro?

241 **I am sorry, but I do not
understand.**
Λυπάμαι, μα δεν καταλαβαίνω.
Lipame, ma den katalaveno.

242 **Please speak slowly.**
Παρακαλώ, μιλάτε αργά.
Parakalo, milate arga.

243 **Do you mind if I smoke?**
Θα σας πείραζε αν κάπνιζα;
Tha sas piraze an kapniza?

244 **Do you have a light?**
Μήπως έχετε φωτιά;
Mipos ehete fotia?

245 I am waiting for my husband/
wife/boyfriend/girlfriend.
Περιμένω τον/την/το/τη
άντρα/γυναίκα/φίλο/φίλη
μου.
*Perimeno ton/tin/to/ti/antra/
gineka/filo/fili mu.*

TRAVELLING WITH CHILDREN

246 Do you have a high chair/
baby-sitting service/cot?
Μήπως έχετε καρέκλα
μωρού/υπηρεσία μπέιμπυ
σίττιγκ/παιδικό κρεβάτι;
*Mipos ehete karekla moru/ipiresia
baby-sitting/pediko krevati?*

247 Where is the nursery/
playroom?
Πού είναι το νηπιαγωγείο/
η αίθουσα παιχνιδιών;
*Pu ine to nipiagoyio/i ethusa
pehnidion?*

248 Where can I warm the baby's
bottle?
Πού μπορώ να ζεστάνω το
μπουκάλι του μωρού;
*Pu boro na zestano to bukali tu
moru?*

COMMUNICATIONS

Post

249 How much will it cost to send
a letter/postcard/this
package to Britain/Ireland/
America/Canada/Australia/
New Zealand?

Πόσο θα στοιχίσει να
στείλω μια επιστολή/καρτ
ποστάλ/αυτό το πακέτο στη
Βρετανία/Ιρλανδία/
Αμερική/Καναδά/Νέα
Ζηλανδία;
*Poso tha stihisi na stilo mia
epistoli/card postale/afto to paketo
sti Vretania/Irlandia/Ameriki/
Canada/Nea Zilandia?*

250 I would like one stamp/two
stamps.
Θα ήθελα ένα
γραμματόσημο/δύο
γραμματόσημα.
*Tha ithela ena grammatosimo/dio
grammatosima.*

251 I'd like . . . stamps for
postcards to send abroad,
please.
Θα ήθελα . . .
γραμματόσημα για
καρτποστάλ να τις στείλω
στο εξωτερικό, παρακαλώ.
*Tha ithela . . . gramatosima ya
card postale na tis stilo sto
exoteriko, parakalo.*

Phones

252 I would like to make a
telephone call/reverse the
charges to (make a collect call
to) . . .
Θα ήθελα να τηλεφωνήσω/
να αντιστρέψω το κόστος
στο . . .
*Tha ithela na tilefoniso/na
antistrepso to kostos . . .*

GREEK

245
↕
252

G
R
E
E
K

²⁵³ **Which coins do I need for the telephone?**
Ποια κέρματα χρειάζομαι για το τηλέφωνο;
Pia kermata hriazome ya to tilefono?

²⁵⁴ **The line is engaged (busy).**
Η γραμμή είναι κατειλημμένη.
I grami ine katilimeni.

²⁵⁵ **The number is . . .**
Ο αριθμός είναι . . .
O arithmos ine . . .

²⁵⁶ **Hello, this is . . .**
Επρός, είμαι . . .
Empros, ime . . .

²⁵⁷ **May I speak to . . ?**
Μπορώ να μιλήσω στον/στην . . ;
Boro na miliso ston/stin . . ?

²⁵⁸ **He/She is not in at the moment. Can you call back?**
Δεν είναι εδώ αυτή τη στιγμή. Μπορείτε να ξανακαλέσετε;
Den ine edo avti ti stigmi. Borite na xanakalesete?

MONEY

²⁵⁹ **I would like to change these travellers' cheques (travelers' checks)/this currency/this Eurocheque.**
Θα ήθελα να εξαργυρώσω αυτές τις ταξιδιωτικές επιταγές/αυτό το συνάλλαγμα/αυτή την Ευρωεπιταγή.
Tha ithela na exaryiroso aftes tis taxidiotikes epitayes/afto to sinallagma/afti tin Evroepitayi.

²⁶⁰ **How much commission do you charge? (What is the service charge?)**
Τί προμήθεια επιβάλλετε;
Ti promithia epivallete?

²⁶¹ **Can I obtain money with my MasterCard?**
Μπορώ να τραβήξω λεφτά με την Μάστερκαρτ μου;
Boro na travixo lefta me tin MasterCard mu?

SHOPPING

Names of Shops and Departments

²⁶² **Βιβλιοπωλείο/Χαρτοπωλείο**
Vivliopolio/Hartopolio
Bookshop/Stationery

²⁶³ **Κατάστημα Κοσμημάτων/Δώρων**
Katastima Kosmimaton/Thoron
Jeweller's/Gifts

²⁶⁴ **Υποδήματα**
Ipodimata
Shoes

²⁶⁵ **Είδη Κιγκαλερίας**
Idi Kingalerias
Hardware

²⁶⁶ **Αντίκες**
Antiques
Antiques

267 Κομμωτήριο (ανδρών)/
(γυναικών)
Komotirio (andron)/(ginekon)
Hairdresser's (men's)/(women's)

268 Καπνοπωλείο
Kapnopolio
Tobacconist

269 Αρτοποιείο
Artopiio
Baker's

270 Σουπερμάρκετ
Supermaket
Supermarket

271 Φωτογραφείο
Photographio
Photoshop

272 Παιχνίδια
Pehnidia
Toys

273 Ταξιδιωτικός Πράκτορας
Taxidiotikos Praktoras
Travel Agent

274 Είδη Τουαλέτας
Idi Tualetas
Toiletries

275 Δίσκοι
Diski
Records

In the Shop

276 What time do the shops
open/close?
Τι ώρα ανοίγουν/κλείνουν
τα καταστήματα;
*Ti ora anigun/klinun ta
katastimata?*

277 Where is the nearest
market?
Πού είναι η κοντινότερη
αγορά;
Pu ine i kontinoteri agora?

278 Can you show me the one
in the window/this one?
Μπορείτε να μου δείξετε
κάτι που είδα στη βιτρίνα/
αυτό εδώ;
*Borite na mu dixete kati pu ida
sti vitrina/afto edo?*

279 Can I try this on?
Μπορώ να το
δοκιμάσω;
Boro na to dokimaso?

280 What size is this?
Τι μέγεθος είναι;
Ti meyethos ine?

281 This is too large/too small/
too expensive.
Είναι πολύ μεγάλο/μικρό/
ακριβό.
*Ine poli megalo/mikro/
akrivo.*

282 Do you have any others?
Εχετε άλλα;
Ehete ala?

283 My size is . . .
Το νούμερό μου
είναι . . .
To numero mu ine . . .

G
R
E
E
K

267
↕
283

284 Where is the changing room/
childrens'/cosmetic/
ladieswear/menswear/food
department?
Πού είναι το
δοκιμαστήριο/το παιδικό
τμήμα/το τμήμα
καλλυντικών/γυναικείων/
ανδρικών/τροφίμων.
*Pu ine to dokimastirio/to pediko
tmima/to tmima kalintikon/
ginekion/andrikon/trofimon?*

285 I would like . . .
Θα ήθελα . . .
Tha ithela . . .

286 I would like a quarter of a
kilo/half a kilo/a kilo of
bread/butter/cheese/ham/
tomatoes.
Θα ήθελα ένα τέταρτο κιλό/
μισό κιλό/ένα κιλό ψωμί/
βούτυρο/τυρί/ζαμπόν/
τομάτες.
*Tha ithela ena tetarto kilo/miso
kilo/ena kilo psomi/vutiro/tiri/
zambon/tomates.*

287 How much is this?
Πόσο κάνει αυτό;
Poso kani afto?

288 I'll take this one, thank you.
Θα πάρω αυτό εδώ,
ευχαριστώ.
Tha paro afto edo, efharisto.

289 Do you have a carrier
(shopping) bag?
Έχετε μία σακούλα;
Ehete mia sakula?

290 Do you have anything
cheaper/larger/smaller/of
better quality?
Έχετε τίποτα φτηνότερο/
μεγαλύτερο/μικρότερο/
καλύτερης ποιότητας;
*Ehete tipota ftinotero/megalitero/
mikrotero/kaliteris piotitas?*

291 I would like a film for this
camera.
Θα ήθελα ένα φιλμ για αυτή
την φωτογραφική μηχανή.
*Tha ithela ena film ya afti tin
fotografiki mihani.*

292 I would like some batteries,
the same size as this old one.
Θα ήθελα μερικές
μπαταρίες, του ίδιου
μεγέθους, όπως αυτή η
παλιά.
*Tha ithela merikes bataries, tu idiu
meyethus, opos afti i palia.*

293 Would you mind wrapping
this for me, please?
Θα μπορούσατε να μου το
τυλίξετε, παρακαλώ;
*Tha borusate na mu to tilixete,
parakalo?*

294 Sorry, but you seem to have
given me the wrong change.
Συγνώμη, αλλά φαίνεται ότι
μου δώσατε λάθος ρέστα.
*Signomi, alla fenete oti mu dosate
lathos resta.*

MOTORING

Car Hire (Rental)

295 I have ordered (rented) a car in the name of . . .
Παράγγειλα αυτοκίνητο στο όνομα . . .
Parangila aftokinito sto onoma . . .

296 How much does it cost to hire (rent) a car for one day/ two days/one week?
Πόσο στοιχίζει να ενοικιάσω αυτοκίνητο για μία μέρα/δύο μέρες/μία εβδομάδα;
Poso stihizi na enikiaso aftokinito ya mia mera/dio meres/mia evdomada?

297 Is the tank already full of petrol (gas)?
Μήπως το ντεπόζιτο είναι ήδη γεμάτο με βενζίνη;
Mipos to deposito ine idi yemato me venzini?

298 Is insurance and tax included? How much is the deposit?
Περιλαμβάνει ασφάλεια και φόρο; Πόσα είναι η προκαταβολή;
Perilamvani asfalia ke foro? Posa ine prokatavoli?

299 By what time must I return the car?
Μέχρι πότε πρέπει να επιστρέψω το αυτοκίνητο;
Mehri pote prepi na epistrepso to aftokinito?

300 I would like a small/family car with a radio/cassette player.
Θα ήθελα ένα μικρό/ οικογενειακό αυτοκίνητο με ράδιο/κασετόφωνο.
Tha ithela ena mikro/ikoyeniako aftokinito me radio/kassetofono.

Asking the Way

301 Excuse me, can you help me please?
Με συγχωρείτε, μπορείτε σας παρακαλώ να με βοηθήσετε;
Me sinchorite, borite sas parakalo na me voithisete?

302 How do I reach the motorway/main road?
Από πού μπορώ να πάω στον αυτοκινητόδρομο/ κύριο δρόμο;
Apo pu boro na pao ston aftokinitodromo/kirio dromo?

303 I think I have taken the wrong turning.
Νομίζω πως πήρα λάθος στροφή.
Nomizo pos pira lathos strofi.

304 I am looking for this address.
Ψάχνω για αυτή τη διεύθυνση.
Psachno ya afti ti diefthinsi.

305 I am looking for the . . . hotel.
Ψάχνω για το ξενοδοχείο . . .
Psachno ya to xenodohio . . .

G
R
E
E
K

295
↕
305

306 How far is it to . . . from here?
Πόσο μακριά είναι από εδώ
το . . .
Poso makria ine apo edo to . . .

307 Carry straight on for . . .
kilometres.
Προχωρήστε κατευθείαν
για . . . χιλιόμετρα.
*Prohoriste katefthia ya . . .
hiliometra.*

308 Take the next turning on the
right/left.
Στρίψετε στην επόμενη
στροφή δεξιά/αριστερά.
*Stripsete stin epomeni strofi dexia/
aristera.*

309 Turn right/left at the next
crossroads/traffic lights.
Στρίψετε δεξιά/αριστερά
στο(α) επόμενο(α)
σταυροδρόμι/φανάρια
κυκλοφορίας.
*Stripsete dexia/aristera sto(a)
epomeno(a) stavrodromi/fanaria
kikloforias.*

310 You are going in the wrong
direction.
Εχετε πάρει την αντίθετη
κατεύθυνση.
Ehete pari tin antitheti katefthinsi.

Parking

311 How long can I park here?
Για πόσο διάστημα μπορώ
να παρκάρω εδώ;
*Ya poso diastima boro na parkaro
edo?*

312 Is there a car park near here?
Υπάρχει χώρος
σταθμεύσεως κάπου εδώ;
*Iparhi horos stathmefseos kapu
edo?*

313 At what time does this car
park close?
Τι ώρα κλείνει ο χώρος
σταθμεύσεως;
Ti ora klini o horos stathmefseos?

Signs and Notices

314 Μονόδρομος
Monodromos
One way

315 Απαγορεύεται η είσοδος
Apagorevete i isodos
No entry

316 Απαγορεύεται η
στάθμευση
Apagorevete i stathmefsi
No parking

317 Παρακαμπτήριος
Parakamptirios
Detour (diversion)

318 Σταμάτημα/Stop
Stamatima/Stop
Stop

319 Δώσε προτεραιότητα
Dose protereotita
Give way (yield)

320 Ολισθηρός δρόμος
Olisthiros dromos
Slippery road

321 Απαγορεύεται η
υπέρβαση

306
↕
321

Apagorevete i ipervasi
No overtaking

At the Filling Station

322 Unleaded (lead-free)/
Standard/Premium
Αμόλυβδη/Απλή (Regular)/
Σούπερ (Super).
Amolivdi/Apli/Super.

323 Fill the tank please.
Γεμίστε το ντεπόζιτο
παρακαλώ.
Gemiste to depozito parakalo.

324 Do you have a road map of
this area?
Εχετε χάρτη οδικού δικτύου
αυτής της περιοχής;
Ehete harti odiku diktiu aftis tis periohis?

325 How much is the car-wash?
Πόσο κοστίζει το πλύσιμο
αυτοκινήτου;
Poso kostizi to plisimo aftokinitu?

Breakdowns

326 I've had a breakdown at . . .
Το αυτοκίνητο χάλασε
στη . . .
To aftokinito halase sti . . .

327 I am on the road from . . . to . . .
Είμαι στο δρόμο από . . .
στο/στη . . .
Ime sto dromo apo . . . sto/sti . . .

328 I can't move the car. Can you
send a tow-truck?
Δεν μπορώ να κινήσω το

αυτοκίνητο. Μπορείτε να
στείλετε ρυμουλκό;
Den boro na kiniso to aftokinito.
Borite na stilete rimulko?

329 I have a flat tyre.
Εχω ξεφουσκωμένο
λάστιχο.
Eho xefuskomeno lastiho.

330 The windscreen (windshield)
has smashed/cracked.
Το παρμπρίζ έσπασε/
ράγισε.
To parbriz espase/ragise.

331 There is something wrong
with the engine/brakes/
lights/steering/gearbox/
clutch/exhaust.
Κάτι δεν πάει καλά με τη/
τα μηχανή/φρένα/φώτα/
τιμόνι/ταχύτητες/
συμπλέκτη/εξάτμιση.
Kati den pai kala me ti/ta mihani/
frena/fota/timoni/tahitites/
siblekti/exatmisi.

332 It's overheating.
Υπερθερμαίνεται.
Iperthermenete.

333 It won't start.
Δεν ξεκινά.
Den xekina.

334 Where can I get it repaired?
Πού μπορώ να το
επισκευάσω;
Pu boro na to episkevaso?

335 Can you take me there?
Μπορείτε να με πάτε εκεί;
Borite na me pate eki?

336 Will it take long to fix?
Πόση ώρα θα κάνετε να το
επισκευάσετε;
*Posi ora tha kanete na to
episkevasete?*

337 How much will it cost?
Πόσο θα κοστίσει;
Poso tha kostisi?

Accidents

338 Can you help me? There has
been an accident.
Μπορείτε να με βοηθήσετε;
Έχει συμβεί κάποιο ατύχημα.
*Borite na me voithisete? Ehi simvi
kapio atihima.*

339 Please call the police/an
ambulance.
Παρακαλώ καλέσετε την
αστυνομία/ασθενοφόρο.
*Parakalo kalesete tin astinomia/
asthenoforo.*

340 Is anyone hurt?
Έχει τραυματιστεί κανείς;
Ehi travmatisti kanis?

Traffic Offences

341 I'm sorry, I didn't see the
sign.
Συγγνώμη, δεν πρόσεξα την
πινακίδα.
Signomi, den prosexa tin pinakida.

342 Must I pay a fine? How
much?
Πρέπει να πληρώσω
πρόστιμο; Πόσα;
Prepi na pliroso prostimo? Posa?

343 Show me your documents.
Δείξτε μου τα χαρτιά σας.
Dixte mu ta hartia sas.

HEALTH

Pharmacy

344 Do you have anything for a
stomachache/headache/sore
throat/toothache?
Έχετε κάτι για
στομαχόπονο/πονοκέφαλο/
ερεθισμένο λαιμό/
πονόδοντο;
*Ehete kati ya stomahopono/
ponokefalo/erethismeno lemo/
ponodonto?*

345 I need something for
diarrhoea (diarrhea)/
constipation/a cold/a cough/
insect bites/sunburn/travel
(motion) sickness.
Χρειάζομαι κάτι για τη
διάρροια/δυσκοιλιότητα/
κρύο/βήχα/δαγκώματα
εντόμων/ηλιοκαύματα/
ναυτία.
*Hriazome kati ya ti diarria/
dispepsia/krio/vinha/dangomata
entomon/iliokavmata/naftia.*

346 How much/how many do I
take?
Πόσο/Πόσα να παίρνω;
Poso/posa na perno?

347 How often do I take it/them?
Κάθε πόση ώρα να το/τα
παίρνω;
Kathe posi ora na to/ta perno?

348 How much does it cost?
Πόσο κοστίζει;
Poso kostizi?

349 Can you recommend a good doctor/dentist?
Μπορείτε να μου συστήσετε ένα καλό γιατρό/οδοντογιατρό;
Borite na mu sistisete ena kalo yatro/odontoyatro?

350 Is it suitable for children?
Είναι κατάλληλο για παιδιά;
Ine katallilo ya pedia?

Doctor

351 I have a pain here/in my arm/leg/chest/stomach.
Πονάω εδώ/στο βραχιόνα μου/στη γάμπα/στο στήθος/στο στομάχι.
Ponao edo/sto vrahiona mu/sti gamba/sto stithos/sto stomahi.

352 Please call a doctor, this is an emergency.
Παρακαλώ τηλεφωνήστε ένα γιατρό, είναι επείγουσα κατάσταση.
Parakalo tilefoniste ena yatro, ine epigusa katastasi.

353 I would like to make an appointment to see a doctor.
Θα ήθελα να κλείσω ραντεβού για να δω τον γιατρό.
Tha ithela na kliso rantevou ya na tho ton yatro.

354 I am diabetic/pregnant.
Είμαι διαβητικός/έγκυος.
Ime diavitikos/engios.

355 I need a prescription for . . .
Θέλω συνταγή για . . .
Thelo sintayi ya . . .

356 Can you give me something to ease the pain?
Μπορείτε να μου δώσετε κάτι για να καταπραύνει τον πόνο;
Borite na mu dosete kati gia na katapraini ton pono?

357 I am/he is/she is allergic to penicillin.
Είμαι/είναι/αλλεργικός(ή) στην πενικιλίνη.
Ime/ine/alergikos(i) stin penicilini.

358 Does this hurt?
Πονάει;
Ponai?

359 You must/he must/she must go to hospital.
Πρέπει να πάτε/πάει στο νοσοκομείο.
Prepi na pate/pai sto nosokomio.

360 Take these once/twice /three times a day.
Παίρνετε αυτά μία φορά/δύο/τρεις φορές την ημέρα.
Pernete afta mia fora/dio/tris fores tin imera.

361 I am/he is/she is taking this medication.
Παίρνω/παίρνει αυτό το φάρμακο.
Perno/perni afto to pharmako.

GREEK

348
↕
361

145

HEALTH/EMERGENCIES

³⁶² I have medical insurance.
Εχω ασφάλεια
νοσοκομειακής
περίθαλψης.
*Echo asfalia nosokomiakis
perithalpsis.*

Dentist

³⁶³ I have toothache.
Νοιώθω πονόδοντο.
Niotho ponodonto.

³⁶⁴ My filling has come out.
Βγήκε το σφράγισμα.
Vgike to sfrayisma.

³⁶⁵ I do/do not want to have an
injection first.
Θέλω/δεν θέλω να έχω
πρώτα ένεση.
Thelo/den thelo na eho prota enesi.

EMERGENCIES

³⁶⁶ Help!
Βοήθεια!
Voithia!

³⁶⁷ Call an ambulance/a doctor/
the police!
Τηλεφωνήστε για
ασθενοφόρο/γιατρό/
αστυνομία !
*Tilefoniste yia asthenoforo/yatro/
astinomia!*

³⁶⁸ I have had my travellers'
cheques (travelers' checks)/
credit cards/purse/handbag/
rucksack (knapsack)/
luggage/wallet stolen.
Μου κλέψανε τις
ταχυδρομικές μου επιταγές/τις
πιστωτικές μου κάρτες/το
τσαντάκι μου/τη τσάντα μου/
τον εκδρομικό σάκο/τις
αποσκευές/το πορτοφόλι μου.
*Mu klepsane tis tahidromikes mu
epitayes/tis pistotikes mu kartes/to
portofoli mu/tin tsanta mu/ton
ekdromiko sako/tis aposkeves/to
portofoli mu.*

³⁶⁹ Can you help me, I have lost
my daughter/son?
Μπορείτε να με βοηθήσετε,
έχασα τη θυγατέρα μου/τον
γιο μου;
*Borite na me voithisete, ehasa ti
thigatera mu/ton yo mu?*

³⁷⁰ Please go away/leave me
alone.
Παρακαλώ φύγετε/αφήστε
με μόνη.
Parakalo fiyete/afiste me moni.

³⁷¹ Fire!
Πυρκαγιά!
Pirkaya!

³⁷² I want to contact the British/
American/Canadian/Irish/
Australian/New Zealand/
South African consulate.
Θέλω να επικοινωνήσω με το
Βρετανικό/Αμερικανικό/
Καναδικό/Ιρλανδικό/
Αυστραλιανό/Νέας Ζηλανδίας/
Νοτίου Αφρικής Προξενείο.
*Thelo na epikioniso me to
Vretaniko/Amerikaniko/Kanadiko/
Irlandiko/Avstraliano/Neas
Zilandias/Notiu Afrikis Proxenio.*

146

Introduction

Hungarian, or Magyar, is distantly related to Finnish and Estonian, but is utterly unlike the languages of the other main linguistic groups of Europe. German is widespread as a second language.

Hungarian is undoubtedly a difficult language to master, and Hungarians are well aware of this, but you should nevertheless try to learn a few greetings, as silence when entering a shop, for instance, is considered rude.

Prepositions are replaced by suffixes. Each suffix has two forms, choose one that sounds harmonious with the noun/place name. There is no specific gender in the Hungarian language, therefore there is no difference in the words for 'he/she/it'.

H U N G A R I A N

Addresses for travel and tourist information

New Zealand: *Embassy,* 17 Beale Crescent, Deakin; tel: (6) 282 3226, *Commercial Counsellor,* 17 Upland Rd, Kelburn, Wellington; tel: (4) 471 2456.
UK: *IBUSZ (Hungarian National Tourist Office),* 46 Eaton Place, London, SW1X 8AL; tel: (020) 7823 1032/1055
USA: *IBUSZ (Hungarian Travel North American Division),* 1 Parker Plaza, Suite 1104, Fort Lee, NJ 07024; tel: (201) 592 8585.

ESSENTIALS

ESSENTIALS

Letters

A	Á
O	*ah*
B	C
bay	*tsay*
CS	D
chay	*day*
E	É
eh	*ay*
F	G
eff	*gay*
GY	H
dj	*hah*
I	J
ee	*yay*
K	L
kah	*el*
LY	M
yeu	*em*
N	NY
en	*nee-uh*
O	Ó
o	*aw*
Ö	Ő
uh	*ur*
P	Q
pay	*q*
R	S
air	*esh*
SZ	T
ess	*tay*
TY	U

tch	oo
Ú	Ü
ooh	*ew*
Ű	V
eew	*vay*
W	X
doop-lo vay	*ex*
Y	Z
eep-see-lon	*zat*
ZS	
zhay	

Basic Words and Phrases

1. **Yes**   **No**
   Igen   Nem
   Igen   *Nem*

2. **Please**   **Thank you**
   Kérem szépen   Köszönöm
   Kay-rem say-pan   *Kuh-suh-nuhn*

3. **That's O.K.**   **Perhaps**
   Rendben van.   Esetleg
   Rhend-ben von   *Eh-shet-leg*

4. **To**   **From**
   Fele   Onnan
   Fah-lah   *On-non*

5. **Here**   **There**
   Itt   Ott
   It   *Ot*

6. **None**   **Also**
   Semelyik   Szintén
   Sheh-may-yeek   *Seen-tayn*

7. **How**   **When**
   Hogyan   Mikor
   Ho-djon   *Mee-kor*

8 What
Mit
Mit

Why
Miért
Mee-ayrt

9 I don't understand.
Nem értem.
Nem ayr-tehm.

10 I don't speak Hungarian.
Nem tudok magyarul.
Nem too-dok mo-djo-rool.

11 Do you speak English?
Beszél angolul?
Beh-sayl on-go-lool?

12 Can you please write it down?
Kérem le tudná ezt írni?
Kay-rehm leh tood-nay ehz eeyr-ni?

13 Can you please speak more slowly?
Kérem beszéljen lassabban?
Kay-rehm beh-sayl-yen losh-shob-bon?

14 How much does it/this cost?
Ez mennyibe kerül?
Ehz mehnn-yee-beh keh-rewl?

Days

15 Monday
Hétfő
Heyt-fur

Tuesday
Kedd
Kehdd

16 Wednesday
Szerda
Sehr-dah

Thursday
Csütörtök
Chew-tohr-tuhk

17 Friday
Péntek
Payn-tehk

Saturday
Szombat
Soom-bot

18 Sunday
Vasárnap

Morning
Délelőtt

Vo-shahr-nop *Dayl-eh-lurtt*

19 Afternoon
Délután
Dayl-oo-tahn

Evening
Este
Esh-teh

20 Night
Éjjel
Eey-yehl

Week
Hét
Hayt

21 Yesterday/Today/Tomorrow
Tegnap/Mára/Holnap
Tehg-nop/Mah-ro/Hol-nop

Numbers

22 Zero
Nulla
Nool-lo

One
Egy
Edj

23 Two
Kettő
Keht-tur

Three
Három
Hah-rom

24 Four
Négy
Naydj

Five
Öt
Uht

25 Six
Hat
Hot

Seven
Hét
Hayt

26 Eight
Nyolc
Nn-yolts

Nine
Kilenc
Kee-lehnts

27 Ten
Tíz
Teez

Eleven
Tizenegy
Tee-zehn-edj

28 Twelve
Tizenkettő
Tee-zehn-keht-tur

Thirteen
Tizenhárom
Tee-zehn-hah-rom

29 Fourteen
Tizennégy
Tee-zehn-naydj

Fifteen
Tizenöt
Tee-zehn-uht

HUNGARIAN

08 ↑ 29

30 **Sixteen** **Seventeen**
Tizenhat Tizenhét
Tee-zehn-hot *Tee-zehn-hayt*

31 **Eighteen** **Nineteen**
Tizennyolc Tizenkilenc
Tee-zehn-n-yolts *Tee-zehn-kee-lehnts*

32 **Twenty** **Twenty-one**
Húsz Huszonegy
Hoos *Hoo-son-edj*

33 **Twenty-two** **Thirty**
Huszonkettő Harminc
Hoo-son-keht-tur *Hor-mints*

34 **Forty** **Fifty**
Negyven Ötven
Nehdj-vehn *Uht-vehn*

35 **Sixty** **Seventy**
Hatvan Hetven
Hot-von *Heht-vehn*

36 **Eighty** **Ninety**
Nyolcvan Kilencven
N-yolts-von *Kee-lehnts-vehn*

37 **One hundred** **Five hundred**
Egyszáz Ötszáz
Edj-sahz *Oht-sahz*

38 **One thousand** **One million**
Egyezer Egy millió
Edj-eh-zehr *Edj meel-li-aw*

Time

39 **9.00**
Kilenc óra
Kee-lehnts aw-ro

40 **9.05**
Kilenc óra öt perc
Kee-lehnts aw-ro uht pertz

41 **9.10**
Kilenc óra tíz perc
Kee-lehnts aw-ro teez pertz

42 **9.15**
Negyed tíz
Neh-djehd teez

43 **9.20**
Kilenc óra húsz perc
Kee-lehntz aw-ro hoos pertz

44 **9.25**
Kilenc óra huszonöt perc
Kee-lehntz aw-ro hoo-son-uht pertz

45 **9.30**
Fél tíz
Fayl teez

46 **9.35**
Kilenc óra harmincöt perc
Kee-lehntz aw-ro hor-mints-uht pertz

47 **9.40**
Kilenc óra negyven perc
Kee-lehntz aw-ro nehdj-vehn pertz

48 **9.45**
Háromnegyed tíz
Hah-rom-neh-djehd teez

49 **9.50**
Kilenc óra ötven perc
Kee-lehntz aw-ro uht-ven pertz

50 **9.55**
Kilenc óra ötvenöt perc
Kee-lehntz aw-ro uht-vehn-uht pertz

51 **12.00/Midday/Midnight**
Tizenkét óra/Dél/Éjfél
Tee-zen-kayt aw-ro/dayl/ay-fayl

52 What time is it?
Hány óra van?
Hahnn-y aw-ro von?

53 It is . . .
. . . óra van.
. . . *aw-ro von.*

ARRIVING AND DEPARTING

Airport

54 Excuse me, where is the
check-in desk for . . . airline?
Bocsánat, hol találom a . . .
légitársaság utaskezelő pultját?
*Bo-chah-not, hol to-lah-lom o . . .
lay-gee-tahr-sho-shahg oo-tosh-
keh-zeh-lur poolt-yaht?*

55 What is the boarding gate/
time for my flight?
Melyik az én gépem beszálló
kapuja?/Mikor indul a gépem?
*Meh-yeek oz ayn gay-pehm beh-
sahl-law ko-poo-ya?/Mee-kor in-
dool o gay-pehm?*

56 How long is the delay likely
to be?
Mennyi a várható késés?
*Mehnn-y-ee o vahr-ho-taw kay-
shaysh?*

57 Where is the duty-free shop?
Hol van a Duty-Free üzlet?
Hol von o duty-free ewz-leht?

58 Which way is the baggage
reclaim?
Merre van a poggyász kiváltó?
*Mehr-rheh von o podj-djahs ki-
vahl-taw?*

59 Where can I get the bus to
the city centre?
Honnan indul a busz a
városközpontba?
*Hon-non in-dool o bus o vah-rosh-
kuhz-pont-bo?*

Train Station

60 Where is the ticket office/
information desk?
Hol van a jegypénztár/
információ?
*Hol von o yedj-pehnz-tahr/in-for-
mah-tsi-aw?*

61 Which platform does the
train to . . . depart from?
Melyik vágányról indul a vonat
. . . -ba/-be?
*Meh-yeek vah-gahn-yrawl in-dool
o vo-not . . . -bo/-beh?*

62 Where is platform . . . ?
Hol van a . . . -os/es vágány?
Hol von o . . . -osh/ash vah-gahn?

63 When is the next train to . . ?
Mikor indul a következő vonat .
. .-ba/-be?
*Mee-kor in-dool o kuh-veht-keh-
zur vo-not . . . -bo/-beh?*

64 Is there a later train to . . ?
Van egy későbbi vonat is . . . -
ba/-be?
*Von edj kay-shurb-bi vo-not eesh .
. .-bo/-beh?*

H
U
N
G
A
R
I
A
N

52
↕
64

151

ARRIVING AND DEPARTING

Port

65 How do I get to the port?
Hogy jutok el a kikötőbe?
Hodj yoo-tok ehl o kee-kuh-tur-beh?

66 When is the next sailing to . . ?
Mikor indul a következő hajó . .
. -ba/-be?
Mee-kor in-dool o kuh-veht-keh-zur ho-yaw . . . -bo/-beh?

67 Can I catch an earlier ferry with this ticket?
Ezzel a jeggyel egy korábbi kompra is felszállhatok?
Ehz-zehl o yehdj-ehl edj ko-rahb-bee komp-ro ish fehl-sahl-ho-tok?

Notices and Signs

68 Büfé
Buh-fay
Buffet (Dining Car)

69 Autóbusz
O-oo-taw-boos
Bus

70 Ivóvíz/Nem ivóvíz
Ee-vaw-veez/nem ee-vaw-veez
Drinking/Non-drinking water

71 Bejárat
Beh-yah-rot
Entrance

72 Kijárat
Kee-yah-rot
Exit

73 Információ
In-for-mah-tsee-aw
Information

74 Poggyász Kiváltó
Podj-djahs kee-vahl-taw
Left Luggage (Baggage Claim)

75 Kulcsra zárható csomagmegőrző szekrény
Koolch-ro zahr-ho-taw cho-mog-mehg-ur-zur sehk-raynn-y
Luggage Lockers

76 Posta/Postahivatal
Posh-to/posh-to-hee-vo-tol
Post Office

77 Peron/Vágány
Peh-ron/vah-gahn-y
Platform

78 Vasútállomás/Vonatállomás
Vo-shoot-ahl-lo-mahsh/vo-not-ahl-lo-mahsh
Railway (Railroad Station)

79 Repülőtér
Re-pew-lur-tayr
Airport

80 Hajókikötő/Hajóállomás
Ho-yaw-kee-kuh-tur/ho-yaw-ahl-lo-mahsh
Port

81 Étterem/Vendéglő
Ayt-teh-rehm/vehn-dayg-lur
Restaurant

82 Dohányzó/Nem-Dohányzó
Do-hahnn-yzaw/nem do-hahnn-yzaw
Smoking/Non-Smoking

83 Telefon
Teh-leh-fon
Telephone

84 **Jegypénztár**
Yedj-paynz-tahr
Ticket Office

85 **Utaskezelő Pult**
Oo-tosh-keh-zeh-lur poolt
Check-in Desk

86 **Menetrend**
Meh-neht-rehnd
Timetable (Schedule)

87 **WC**
Vay-tsay
Toilets (Restrooms)

88 **Férfiak**
Fayr-fee-ok
Gentlemen

89 **Nők**
Nurk
Ladies'

90 **Villamos**
Veel-lo-mosh
Tram (Streetcar)

91 **Metro**
Meht-raw
Underground (Subway)

92 **Váróterem**
Vah-raw-teh-rehm
Waiting-Room

Buying a Ticket

93 **I would like a first-class/
second-class single (one-
way)/return (round-trip)
ticket to . . .**
Kérek egy elsőosztályú/
másodosztályú egyszeri
utazásra szóló/retúr jegyet . . . -
ba/-be.

*Kay-rehk edj ehl-shur-os-tah-
yooh/mah-shod-os-tah-yooh edj-
seh-ree oo-to-zahsh-ro saw-law/
reh-toohr yeh-djeht . . . -bo/-beh*

94 **Is my rail pass valid on this
train/ferry/bus?**
A jegyem erre a vonatra/
kompra/buszra is érvényes?
*O yeh-djehm er-reh o vo-not-ro/
komp-ro/boos-ro eesh ayr-vayn-
yehsh*

95 **I would like an aisle/window
seat.**
A közlekedő folyosó/ablak
melletti ülést kérném.
*O kuhz-leh-keh-dur fo-yo-shaw/
oblok mehl-leht-tee ew-laysht
kehr-nehm*

96 **No smoking/smoking, please.**
Kérem ne dohányozzanak/
Dohányozni szabad.
*Kay-rehm neh do-hahnn-yoz-zo-
nok/do-hahnn-yoz-ni so-bod.*

97 **We would like to sit
together.**
Szeretnénk egymás mellett ülni.
*Seh-reht-naynk edj-mahsh mehl-
lehtt ewl-ni.*

98 **I would like to make a seat
reservation.**
Szeretnék ülőhelyet foglalni.
*Seh-reht-nayk ew-lur-heh-yeht
fog-lol-ni.*

H
U
N
G
A
R
I
A
N

84
↑
98

99 I would like to reserve a couchette/sleeper for one person/two people/for my family.
Szeretnék egy couchettet/hálókocsit foglalni egy személyre/két személyre/a családomnak.
Seh-reht-nayk edj coo-shehtt-eht/hah-law-ko-cheet fog-lol-ni edj seh-may-reh/kayt seh-may-reh/o cho-lah-dom-nok.

100 I would like to reserve a cabin.
Egy kabint szeretnék foglalni.
Edj co-beent seh-reht-nayk fog-lolni.

Timetables (Schedules)

101 Érkezés
Ayr-keh-zaysh
Arrive

102 Megáll . . . -ban/-ben
Mehg-ahll . . . -bon/-behn
Calls (Stops at . . .)

103 Étkezési Lehetőség
Ayt-keh-zay-shee le-heh-tur-shayg
Catering Service

104 Átszállás . . . -ban/-ben
Aht-sahl-lahsh . . . -bon/-behn
Change at . . .

105 Csatlakozás
Chot-lo-ko-zahsh
Connection

106 Napi
No-pee
Daily

107 Negyven percenként
Nehdj-vehn pert-zehn-kaynt
Every 40 Minutes

108 Első-osztály
El-shur os-tahy
First-Class

109 óránként
Aw-rahn-kaynt
Hourly

110 Ajánlott a helyfoglalás
O-yahn-lott o hehy-fog-lo-lahsh
Seat reservations are recommended

111 Másodosztály
Mah-shod-os-tahy
Second-class

112 Fizetendő Pótdíj
Fee-zeh-tehn-dur pawt-deey
Supplement Payable

113 útvonalon
Ooht-vo-no-lon
Via

Luggage

114 How much will it cost to send (ship) my luggage in advance?
Mennyibe kerül előreküldeni a poggyászomat?
Mehnn-yee-beh keh-rewl eh-lur-re-kewl-deh-nee o podj-djah-so-mot?

115 Where is the left luggage (baggage claim) office?
Merre van a talált csomagok irodája?
Mehr-reh von o to-lahlt cho-mo-gok eero-dah-yah?

116 What time do you open/ close?
Mikor nyitnak/zárnak?
Mee-kor nn-yeet-nok/zahr-nok?

117 Where are the luggage trolleys (carts?)
Hol találom a poggyász trolikat?
Hol to-lah-lom o podj-djahs tro-lee-kot?

118 Where are the lockers?
Hol találom a kulcsra zárható csomagmegőrző szekrényeket?
Hol to-lah-lom o koolch-ro zahr-ho-taw cho-mog-mehg-ur-zur sehk-raynn-yeh-keht?

119 I have lost my locker key.
Elvesztettem a csomagmegőrző kulcsát.
El-vehs-teht-tehm o cho-mog-mehg-ur-zur kool-chaht.

On Board

120 Is this seat taken?
Foglalt ez a hely?
Fog-lolt ehz o hehy?

121 Excuse me, you are sitting in my reserved seat.
Bocsánatot kérek, de ön az én foglalt helyemen ül.
Bo-chah-no-tot kay-rehk, deh uhn oz ayn fog-lolt heh-yeh-mehn ewl

122 Which station is this?
Ez melyik állomás?
Ehz meh-yeek ahl-lo-mahsh?

123 What time is this train/bus/ ferry/flight due to arrive/ depart?
Ez a vonat/busz/komp/repülő mikor érkezik/indul ?
Ehz o vonot/boos/komp/reh-pew-lur mee-kor ayr-keh-zeek/in-dool?

124 Will you wake me just before we arrive?
Felébresztene közvetlenül a megérkezésünk előtt?
Fehl-ayb-rehs-teh-neh kuhz-veht-leh-newl o mehg-ayr-keh-zay-shewnk eh-lurtt?

Customs and Passports

125 Passports, please!
Kérjük az útleveleket!
Kayr-yewk oz ooht-leh-veh-leh-keht!

126 I have nothing to declare. I have wine/spirits (alcohol)/ tobacco to declare.
Semmi elvámolni valóm sincs.
Bor/szesz/dohányárú elvámolni valóm van.
Shehm-mee ehl-vah-mol-ni vo-lawm sheench. bor/sehs/do-hahnn-y-ah-rooh ehl-vah-mol-ni vo-lawm von.

127 I shall be staying for . . . days/weeks/months.
. . . napig/hétig/hónapig maradok.
. . . no-pig/hay-tig/haw-nopig morodok.

AT THE TOURIST OFFICE/ACCOMMODATION

AT THE TOURIST OFFICE

128 **Do you have a map of the town/area?**
Van egy városi/helyi térképe?
Von edj vah-ro-shee/heh-yee tayr-kay-peh

129 **Can I reserve accommodation here?**
Lehet itt szállást foglalni?
Leh-heht itt sahl-lahsht fog-lol-ni?

130 **Do you have a list of accommodation?**
Van önnek egy szállás listája?
Von uhn-nehk edj sahl-lahsh lish-tah-yo?

ACCOMMODATION

Hotels

131 **I have a reservation in the name of . . .**
Szobát foglaltam . . . néven.
So-baht fog-lol-tom . . . nay-vehn

132 **I wrote to/faxed/telephoned you last month/last week in . . .**
Irtam/faxot küldtem/telefonáltam önnek a múlt hónapban/héten . . . -án/-én
Eer-tom/fox-ot kewld-tehm/teh-leh-fo-nahl-tom uhn-nehk o moolt haw-nop-bon/hay-tehn . . ahn/ehn

133 **Do you have any rooms free?**
Van szabad szobájuk?
Von so-bod so-bah-yook?

134 **I would like to reserve a single/double room with/without bath/with/without shower.**

Szeretnék foglalni egy egyágyas/kétágyas szobát fürdőszobával/fürdőszoba nélkül/zuhanyozóval/zuhanyozó nélkül.
Seh-reht-naynk fog-lolni edj edj-ah-djos/kayt-ahd-jos so-baht fewr-dur-so-bahvol/fewr-dur-so-bah nayl-kewl/zoo-honn-yozaw-vol/zoo-honn-yozaw nayl-kewl.

135 **I would like bed and breakfast/room and half board/room and full board.**
Szeretnék egy szobát reggelivel/Szeretnék egy szobát reggelivel és vacsorával/Szeretnék egy szobát teljes ellátással.
Seh-reht-nayk edj so-baht rehg-gehlee-vehl/seh-reht-nayk edj so-baht rehg-geh-lee-vehl aysh vo-cho-rah-vol/seh-reht-nayk edj so-baht tehl-yehsh ehl-lah-tahsh-shol.

136 **How much is it per night?**
Mennyibe kerül egy éjjelre?
Mehnn-yee-beh keh-rewl edj ay-yehl-reh?

137 **Is breakfast included?**
Az árban a reggeli is benne van?
Oz ahr-bon o rehg-geh-li ish behn-neh von?

138 **May I see the room?**
Megnézhetem a szobát?
Mehg-nayz-hehtehm o so-baht?

139 **Do you have any cheaper rooms?**
Van olcsóbb szobájuk?
Von ol-chawbb so-bah-yook?

¹⁴⁰ I would like to take the room.
Szeretném kivenni a szobát.
Seh-reht-naym ki-vehn-ni o so-baht.

¹⁴¹ I would like to stay for . . .
nights.
Szeretnék . . . éjjelt maradni.
Seh-reht-nayk . . . ay-yehlt mo-rod-ni.

¹⁴² The shower/light/tap doesn't
work.
A zuhany/villany/csap nem
működik.
*O zoo-honn-y/veel-lonn-y/chop
nem meew-kuh-dik.*

¹⁴³ At what time/where is
breakfast served?
Hány órakor/hol lehet
reggelizni?
*Hahnn-y aw-rokor/hol leh-eht
rehg-geh-leez-ni?*

¹⁴⁴ What time do I have to
check-out?
Hány órakor kell átadnom a
szobát?
Hahnn-y aw-ro-kor kehll aht-od-nom o so-baht?

¹⁴⁵ Can I have the key to room
no . . ?
Megkaphatnám a . . . -os szάmu
szoba kulcsát.
*Meg-kop-hot-nahm o . . . -osh
sah-moo so-bah kool-chaht.*

¹⁴⁶ My room number is . . .
A szobaszámom . . .
O so-bo-sah-mom . . .

¹⁴⁷ Do you accept travellers'
cheques/Eurocheques/credit
cards?
Elfogadnak Traveller's csekket/
Euro-csekket/hitelkártyát?
El-fo-god-nok travellers chehk-keht/euro-chehk-keht/hee-tehl-kahrt-yaht?

¹⁴⁸ May I have the bill please?
Megkaphatnám a számlát?
Meg-kop-hot-nahm o sahm-laht

¹⁴⁹ Excuse me, I think there is a
mistake in this bill.
Elnézést kérek, de azt hiszem
hiba van a számlában.
*Ehl-nay-zay-sht kay-rehk, deh ozt
hee-sehm hee-bo von o sahm-lah-bon.*

Youth Hostels

¹⁵⁰ How much is a dormitory bed
per night?
Mennyibe kerül a hálóteremben
egy ágy egy éjjelre?
*Mehnn-yee-beh keh-rewr o hah-law-teh-rehm-behn edj ahdj ehdj
ay-yehl-reh?*

¹⁵¹ I am/am not an HI member.
HI tag vagyok/Nem vagyok HI
tag.
*HI tog vo-djok/nem vo-djok HI
tog.*

¹⁵² May I use my own sleeping
bag?
Használhatom a saját
hálózsákomat?
Hos-nahl-ho-tom o sho-yaht hah-law-zhah-ko-mot?

HUNGARIAN

140
↕
152

ACCOMMODATION/EATING AND DRINKING

153 What time do you lock the doors at night?
Hány órakor zárják be a kaput éjjelre?
Hahnn-y aw-rokor zahr-yahk beh o ko-poot ay-yehl-reh?

Camping

154 May I camp here for the night/two nights?
Campingezhetünk itt egy éjjelre/két éjjelre?
Com-pin-gehz-heh-tuhnk itt edj ay-yehl-reh/kayt ay-yehl-reh?

155 Where can I pitch my tent?
Hol verhetem fel a sátramat?
Hol vehr-heh-tehm fehl o saht-ro-mot?

156 How much does it cost for one night/week?
Mennyibe kerül egy éjjelre/egy hétre?
Mehnn-yee-beh keh-rewr edj ay-yehl-reh/edj hayt-reh?

157 Where can we park our caravan?
Hol állíthatjuk le a lakókocsinkat?
Hol ahl-leet-hot-yook leh o lo-kaw-ko-cheen-kot

158 Where are the ?washing facilities?
Hol van a mosakodási lehetőség?
Hol von o mo-sho-ko-dah-shi leh-heh-tur-shayg?

159 Is there a restaurant/supermarket/swimming pool on site/nearby?

Van étterem/szupermarket/uszoda a területen/környéken?
von ayt-teh-rehm/soo-pehr-mor-keht/oo-sodo o teh-rew-leh-tehn/kuhr-nn-yay-kehn?

160 Do you have a safety deposit box?
Van önöknek értékmegőrzőjük?
Von uh-nuhk-nehk ayr-tayk-meg-ur-zur-yewk

EATING AND DRINKING

Cafés and Bars

161 I would like a cup of/two cups of/another coffee/tea.
Szeretnék kérni egy csésze/két csésze/mégegy kávét/teát.
Seh-reht-nayk kayr-ni edj chay-seh/kayt chay-seh/mayg-edj kah-vayt/teh-aht

162 With milk/sugar. Without milk/sugar.
Tejjel/Cukorral. Tej nélkül/Cukor nélkül.
Tehy-yehl/tsoo-kor-rol. tehy nayl-kewl/tsoo-kor nayl-kewl.

163 I would like a bottle/glass/two glasses of mineral water/red wine/white wine, please.
Szeretnék kérni egy üveg/egy pohár/két pohár ásvány vizet/vörös bort/fehér bort.
Seh-reht-nayk kayr-ni edj ew-vehg/edj po-hahr/kayt po-hahr ahsh-vahnn-y vee-zeht/vuh-ruhsh bort/feh-hayr bort.

158

164 I would like a beer/two beers, please.
Szeretnék kérni egy sört/két sört.
Seh-reht-nayk kayr-ni edj sh-uhrt/ kayt sh-uhrt.

165 May I have some ice?
Kaphatok jeget?
Kop-ho-tok yeh-geht

166 Do you have any matches/ cigarettes/cigars?
Van gyufája/cigarettája/szivarja?
Von djoo-fah-yo/tsee-go-reht-tahyo/see-vor-yo?

Restaurants

167 Can you recommend a good/ inexpensive restaurant in this area?
Tud egy jó/olcsó éttermet ajánlani ezen a környéken?
Tood edj yaw/ol-chaw ayt-tehr-meht o-yahn-loni eh-zehn o kuhr-nn-yay-kehn?

168 I would like a table for . . . people.
Szeretnék egy asztalt . . . főre.
Seh-reht-nayk edj os-tolt . . . fur-reh.

169 Do you have a non-smoking area?
Van itt nem dohányzó rész?
Von itt nem do-hahnn-yzaw rays?

170 Waiter/Waitress!
Pincér/Pincérnő!
Pin-cayr/pin-cayr-nur!

171 Do you have a set menu/ children's menu/wine list?
Van komplett menüjük/ gyermek menüjük/itallapjuk?
Von komp-lett meh-new-yewk/ djehr-mehk meh-new-yewk/ee-tol-lop-yook?

172 Do you have any vegetarian dishes, please?
Van vegetariánus ételük?
Von veh-geh-to-ri-ah-noosh ay-teh-lewk?

173 Are there any local specialities?
Van valamilyen helyi specialitásuk?
Von volo-mee-yehn heh-yi shpe-tsi-o-lee-tah-shook?

174 Are vegetables included?
A zöldségek is benne vannak az árban?
O zuhld-shay-gehk ish behn-neh von-nok oz ahr-bon?

175 Could I have it well-cooked/ medium/rare please?
Kérhetem a húst jól átsülten/ közepesen sülten/angolosan sülten?
Kayr-heh-tehm o hoosht yawl aht-shewl-tehn/kuh-zeh-peh-shehn shewl-tehn/on-golo-shon shewl-tehn?

176 What does this dish consist of?
Miből készült ez az étel?
Mee-bur kay-sewlt ehz oz ay-tehl

H
U
N
G
A
R
I
A
N

164
↕
176

177 I would like the set menu, please.
Szeretném kérni a komplett menüt.
Seh-reht-naym kayr-ni o komp-lett meh-neewt.

178 We have not been served yet.
Még nem szolgáltak ki minket.
Mayg nem sol-gahl-tok kee meen keht.

179 Excuse me, this is not what I ordered.
Elnézést kérek, de nem ezt rendeltem.
Ehl-nay-zaysht kay-rehk, deh nem ehzt rehn-dehl-tem.

180 May I have some/some more bread/water/coffee/tea?
Kérhetek kenyeret/még kenyeret/vizet/kávét/teát?
Kayr-heh-tehk kehnn-yeh-reht/ mayg kehnn-yeh-reht/vee-zeht/ kah-vayt/teh-aht?

181 May I have the bill, please?
Szeretném kérni a számlát.
Seh-reht-naym kayr-ni o sahm-laht?

182 Does this bill include service?
A számla a felszolgálási díjat is tartalmazza?
O sahm-lah o fehl-sol-gah-lah-shi dee-yot ish tor-tol-moz-zo?

183 Do you accept travellers' cheques (travelers' checks)/ Eurocheques/MasterCard/US dollars?
Elfogadnak travellers'csekket/ Euro-csekket/Master Cardot/ Amerikai Dollárt?
El-fo-god-nok travellers chehk-keht/euro-chehk-keht/master card-ot/a-meh-ree-koi dol-lahrt

184 Can I have a receipt, please?
Kérhetek nyugtát erről?
Kayr-heh-tehk nn-yoog-taht ehr-rurl

185 Where is the toilet (restroom), please?
Megmondaná hol találom a WC-t?
Mehg-mon-do-nah hol to-lah-lom o vay-tsayt

On the Menu

186 First courses
Előételek
Eh-lur-ay-teh-lehk

187 Soups
Levesek
Leh-veh-shehk

188 Main courses
Főételek
Fur-ay-teh-lehk

189 Fish dishes
Halételek
Hol-ay-teh-lehk

190 Meat dishes
Húsételek
Hoosh-ay-teh-lehk

191 Vegetarian dishes
Vegetariánus ételek
Veh-geh-to-ree-ah-noosh ay-teh-lehk

192 Cheese
Sajtok
Shoy-tok

193 Desserts
Édességek
Ay-dehsh-shay-gehk

194 Specialities
Specialitások
Shpeh-tzi-o-li-tah-shok

GETTING AROUND

Public Transport

195 Where is the bus stop/coach station/nearest metro (subway) station?
Hol van a buszmegálló/ autóbusz állomás/legközelebbi metro állomás?
Hol von o boos-mehg-ahl-law/o-oo-taw-boos ahl-lo-mahsh/leg-kuh-zeh-lehb-bi meht-raw ahl-lo-mahsh.

196 When is the next/last bus to. . .?
Mikor indul a következő/utolsó busz . . . -ba/-be?
Mee-kor in-dool o kuh-veht-keh-zur boos . . . -bo/-beh

197 How much is the fare to the city centre (downtown)/ railway (railroad station/ airport?
Mennyibe kerül a menetjegy a városközpontba/ Vasútállomáshoz/repülőtérre?
mehnn-yee-beh keh-rewl o meh-neht-yehdj o vah-rosh-kuhz-pont-bah/vo-shoot-ahl-lo-mahsh-hoz/reh-pew-lur-tayr-reh

198 Will you tell me when to get off?
Szólna, mikor kell leszállnom?
Sawl-no mee-kor kehll leh-sahll-nom?

199 Does this bus go to . . ?
Ez a busz megy . . . -ba/-be?
Ehz o boos mehdj . . . -bo/-beh

200 Which number bus goes to . . ?
Hányas busz megy . . . -ba/-be?
Hahnn-yos boos mehdj . . . -bo/-beh

201 May I have a single (one-way)/return (round-trip)/day ticket/book of tickets?
Szeretnék kéni egy egyszeri utazásra szóló/retúr/napi jegyet/jegycsomagot.
Seh-reht-nayk kayr-ni edj edj-seh-ree oo-to-zahsh-ro saw-law/reh-toor/nopi ye-djeht/yedj-cho-mo-got

Taxis

202 I would like to go to . . . How much will it cost?
Szeretnék eljutni . . . -ba/-be. Mibe fog ez kerülni?
Seh-reht-nayk ehl-yoot-ni . . . -bo/-beh Mee-beh fog ehz keh-rewl-ni

203 Please stop here.
Kérem itt álljon meg.
Kay-rehm itt ahll-yon mehg

204 I would like to order a taxi today/tomorrow/at 2pm to go from . . . to . . .
Szeretnék rendelni egy taxit mára/holnapra/délután 2 órára hogy elvigyen . . . -ból/-ből . . . -ba/-be.
Seh-reht-nayk rehn-dehl-ni ehdj toxit mah-ro/hol-nop-ro/dayl-oo-tahn kayt aw-rah-ro hodj ehl-vee-djehn . . . -bawl/burl . . . -bo/-beh

H
U
N
G
A
R
I
A
N

193
↑
204

Asking the Way

205 Excuse me, do you speak English?
Bocsánat, beszél angolul?
Bo-chah-not, beh-sayl on-go-lool

206 Excuse me, is this the right way to . . ?
Bocsánat, erre kell menni . . . -ba/-be?
Bo-chah-not, ehr-reh kehll mehn-ni . . . -bo/-beh

207 . . . the cathedral/the tourist information office/the castle/the old town
. . . a katedrális/a turista információs iroda/a kastély/az óváros
. . . .o ko-tehd-rah-leesh/o too-rish-to in-for-mah-tsi-awsh ee-ro-do/o kosh-tay/oz aw-vah-rosh

208 Can you tell me the way to the railway (railroad station)/bus station/taxi rank (stand)/city centre (downtown)/beach?
Meg tudná mondani hogy jutok el a vasútállomáshoz/buszmegállóhoz/taxiállomáshoz/városközpontba/tengerpartra?
Mehg tood-nah mon-doni hodj yoo-tok ehl o vo-shoot-ahl-lo-mahsh-hoz/boos-mehg-ahl-law-hoz/toxi-ahl-lo-mahsh-hoz/vah-rosh-kuhz-pont-bo/tehn-gehr-port-ra

209 First/second left/right/straight ahead.
Első/második balra/jobbra/egyenesen előre.
Eehl-sur/mah-sho-dik bol-ro/yobb-ro/edj-eh-neh-shen eh-lur-re

210 Where is the nearest police station/post office/doctor/hospital/pharmacy?
Hol van a legközelebbi rendőrőrs/postahivatal/orvost/mennie/patika?
Hol von o lehg-kuh-zeh-lehb-bi rehn-dur-uhrsh/posh-to-hee-vo-to/or-vost/mehn-ni-eh /patika?

211 Is it far?
Messze van?
Mehs-seh von?

212 Do I need to take a taxi/catch a bus?
Taxival/Busszal kell mennem?
Toxi-vol/boos-sol kehll mehn-nehm?

213 Can you point to it on my map?
Megmutatná ezt a térképen?
Mehg-moo-tot-nah ehzt o tayr-kay-pehn?

214 Thank you for your help.
Köszönöm a segítségét.
Kuh-suh-nuhm o sheh-geet-shay-gayt.

SIGHTSEEING

215 Where is the Tourist Information office?
Hol van a Turista Információs Iroda?
Hol von o too-reesh-to in-for-mah-tsee-awsh ee-ro-do?

216 Where is the cathedral/
church/museum?
Hol van a katedrális/templom/
múzeum?
*Hol von o ko-tehd-rah-leesh/
tehmp-lom/mooh-zeh-oom?*

217 How much is the entrance
(admission) charge?
Mennyibe kerül a belépődíj?
*Mehnn-yee-beh keh-rewl o beh-
lay-pur-deey?*

218 Is there a discount for children/
students/senior citizens?
Adnak árengedményt
gyermekeknek/
egyetemistáknak/
nyugdíjasoknak?
*Od-nok ahr-ehn-gehd-maynn-yt
djehr-meh-kehk-nehk/e-djeh-teh-
meesh-tahk-nok/nn-yoog-dee-yo-
shok-nok?*

219 What time does the next
guided tour start?
Mikor indul a következő csoport
idegennyelvű vezetővel?
*Mee-kor in-dool o kuh-veht-keh-
zur cho-port ee-deh-gehn-nn-yel-
veew veh-zeh-tur-vehl?*

220 One/two adults/children,
please.
Egy/Két felnőtt/gyermek
jegyet kérek.
*Edj/kayt fehl-nurtt/djehr-mehk ye-
djeht kay-rehk.*

221 May I take photographs
here?
Lehet itt fényképezni?
Leh-heht itt faynn-y-kay-pehz-ni?

ENTERTAINMENT

222 Can you recommend a good
bar/nightclub?
Tudna ajánlani egy jó bárt/éjjeli
szórakozóhelyet?
*Tood-no o-yahn-loni edj yaw
bahrt/ay-yeli saw-ro-ko-zaw-heh-
yeht?*

223 Do you know what is on at
the cinema (playing at the
movies)/theatre at the
moment?
Meg tudná mondani, most mit
játszanak a moziban/szinházban?
*Mehg tood-nah mon-doni, mosht
mit yaht-sonok o mo-zee-bon/seen-
hahz-bon?*

224 I would like to book
(purchase) . . . tickets for the
matinée/evening
performance on Monday.
Szeretnék . . . jegyet foglalni
venni a hétfő délutáni/esti
előadásra.
*Seh-reht-nayk . . . yeh-djeht fog-
lolni o hayt-fur dayl-oo-tah-ni/
ehsh-tee eh-lur-o-dahsh-ro.*

225 What time does the film/
performance start?
Mikor kezdődik a film/az
előadás ?
*Mee-kor kehz-dur-dik o film/oz
eh-lur-o-dahsh?*

MEETING PEOPLE

226 Hello/Goodbye.
Helló/Viszontlátásra
Hehl-law/vee-sont-lah-tahsh-ro.

HUNGARIAN

216
↑
226

MEETING PEOPLE

227 Good morning/good afternoon/good evening/goodnight.
Jó reggelt/jó napot/jó estét/jó éjszakát.
Yaw rehg-gehlt/yaw no-pot/yaw ehsh-tayt/yaw ay-y-so-kaht.

228 Pleased to meet you.
Örülök hogy találkoztunk.
Uh-rew-luhk hodj to-lahl-koz-toonk.

229 How are you?
Hogy van?
Hodj von?

230 Fine, thank you. And you?
Köszönöm, jól. És ön?
Kuh-suh-nuym yawl. aysh uhn?

231 My name is . . .
A nevem . . .
O neh-vehm . . .

232 This is my friend/boyfriend/girlfriend/husband/wife/older brother/younger brother/older sister/younger sister.
Ez a barátom/udvarlóm/barátnőm/férjem/feleségem/bátyám/öcsém/nővérem/hugom.
Ehz o bo-rah-tom/ood-vor-lawm/bo-raht-nurm/fayr-yehm/feh-leh-shay-gehm/baht-yahm/uh-chaym/nur-vay-rehm/hoo-gom.

233 Where are you travelling to?
Hova utazik?
Ho-vo oo-to-zik

234 I am going to . . . /we are going to . . .
Én . . . -ba/-be utazom/Mi . . . -ba/-be utazunk.

Ayn . . . -bo/-beh oo-to-zom/mee . . . -bo/-beh oo-to-zoonk

235 How long are you travelling for?
Meddig utazik?
Mehd-deeg oo-to-zik

236 Where do you come from?
Honnan jött?
Hon-non yuhtt

237 I am from . . ./we are from . . .
Én . . . -ból/-ből jöttem/Mi . . . -ból/-ből jöttünk.
Ayn . . . -bawl/-burl yuht-tehm/mee . . . -bawl/-burl yuht-tewnk

238 We're on holiday.
Szabadságon vagyunk.
So-bod-shah-gon vo-djoonk

239 This is our first visit here.
Most vagyunk itt először.
Mosht vo-djoonk itt eh-lur-suhr

240 Would you like a cigarette?/May I have a cigarette?
Kér egy cigarettát?/ Kérhetek egy cigarettát?
Kayr edj tsee-go-reht-taht//kayr-heh-tehk edj tsee-go-reht-taht

241 I am sorry but I do not understand.
Sajnálom, de nem értem.
Soj-nah-lom, deh nem ayr-tehm

242 Please speak slowly.
Kérem, beszéljen lassabban.
Kay-rehm, beh-sayl-yehn losh-shob-bon.

243 Do you mind if I smoke?
Zavarja ha dohányzom?
Zo-vor-yo ho do-hahnn-y-zom?

164

²⁴⁴ **Do you have a light?**
Kérhetek tüzet?
Kayr-heh-tehk tew-zeht?

²⁴⁵ **I am waiting for my husband/ wife/boyfriend/girlfriend.**
A férjemre/feleségemre/ udvarlómra/barátnőmre várok.
O fayr-yehm-reh/feh-leh-shay-gehm-reh/ood-vor-lawm-ro/bo-raht-nurm-reh vah-rok.

TRAVELLING WITH CHILDREN

²⁴⁶ **Do you have a high chair/ baby-sitting service/cot?**
Van önöknek etetőszékük/ gyermek-vigyázó szolgálatuk/ gyermekágyuk?
Von uh-nuhk-nehk eh-teh-tur-say-kewk/djehr-mehk-vee-djah-zaw sol-gah-lo-took/djehr-mehk-ah-djook?

²⁴⁷ **Where is the nursery/ playroom?**
Hol van az ovoda/játékszoba?
Hol von oz o-vo-do/yah-tayk-so-bo?

²⁴⁸ **Where can I warm the baby's bottle?**
Hol tudom megmelegíteni a baby cumis-üvegét?
Hol too-dom mehg-meh-leh-gee-teh-ni o baby coo-meesh-ew-veh-gayt?

COMMUNICATIONS

Post

²⁴⁹ **How much will it cost to send**

a letter/postcard/this package to Britain/Ireland/ America/Canada/Australia/ New Zealand?
Mennyibe kerül egy levél/ képeslap/ez a csomag Angliába/Írországba/ Amerikába/Kanadába/ Ausztráliába/Új Zélandba?
Mehnn-yee-be keh-rewl edj leh-vayl/kay-pehsh-lop/ehz o cho-mog ong-li-ahba/eer-or-sahg-bo/o-meh-ri-kah-bo/ko-no-dah-bo/oust-rah-liah-bo/ooy zay-londbo?

²⁵⁰ **I would like one stamp/two stamps.**
Szeretnék egy bélyeget/két bélyeget.
Seh-reht-nayk edj bay-yeh-geht/ kayt bay-yeh-geht.

²⁵¹ **I'd like . . . stamps for postcards to send abroad, please.**
Külföldre küldendő képeslapra szeretnék . . . bélyeget kérni.
Kewl-fuhld-reh kewl-dehn-dur kay-pehsh-lopro seh-reht-nayk . . . bay-yeh-geht kayr-ni.

Phones

²⁵² **I would like to make a telephone call/reverse the charges (make a collect call) to . . .**
Szeretnék telefonálni/R beszélgetést kérni . . . -ba/-be.
Sehreht-nayk teh-leh-fo-nahl-ni/ ehrr beh-sayl-geh-taysht kayr-ni . . . -bo/-beh.

²⁵³ **Which coins do I need for the telephone?**
Milyen érmével működik a telefon?
Mee-yehn ayr-may-vehl meew-kuh-dik o teh-leh-fon.

²⁵⁴ **The line is engaged (busy).**
Foglalt a vonal.
Fog-lolt o vo-nol.

²⁵⁵ **The number is . . .**
A szám . . .
A sahm . . .

²⁵⁶ **Hello, this is . . .**
Halló, itt . . . beszél.
Hol-law, itt . . . beh-sayl

²⁵⁷ **May I speak to . . ?**
Beszélhetnék . . . . . . -val/-vel?
be-sayl-heht-nayk . . . -vol/-vehl

²⁵⁸ **He/She is not in at the moment. Can you call back?**
Pillanatnyilag nincs a helyén. Visszaszólna később?
Peel-lo-not-nn-yee-log neench o heh-yayn. vees-so-sawl-no kay-shurbb?

MONEY

²⁵⁹ **I would like to change these travellers' cheques (travelers' checks)/this currency/this Eurocheque.**
Szeretném beváltani ezeket a Travellers csekkeket/ezt a valutát/ezt az Euro csekket.
Seh-reht-naym beh-vahl-toni eh-zeh keht o travellers chehk-keh-keht/ehzt o vo-loo-taht/ehzt oz euro chehk-keht

²⁶⁰ **How much commission do you charge? (What is the service charge?)**
Mennyit számolnak fel jutalékként?
Mehnn-yeet sah-mol-nok fehl yoo-to-layk-kaynt?

²⁶¹ **Can I obtain money with my MasterCard?**
Válthatok ki pénzt a MasterCard-ommal?
Vahlt-ho-tok ki paynzt o mastercard-om-mol

SHOPPING

Names of Shops and Departments

²⁶² **Könyvüzlet/Irószerbolt**
Kuhnn-yv-ewz-leht/ee-raw-sehr-bolt
Bookshop/Stationery

²⁶³ **Ékszerész/Ajándéküzlet**
Ayk-seh-rays/o-jahn-dayk-ewz-leht
Jeweller's/Gifts

²⁶⁴ **Cipők**
Tsee-purk
Shoes

²⁶⁵ **Vaskereskedés**
Vosh-keh-rehsh-keh-daysh
Hardware

²⁶⁶ **Antikvárium**
On-teek-vah-ree-oom
Antiques

²⁶⁷ **Férfi/Női Fodrász**
Fayr-fi/nur-i fod-rahs
Hairdresser's (men's)/(women's)

SHOPPING

268 Dohányáruda/Dohányüzlet
Do-hahnn-y-ah-roo-do/do-hahnn-y-ewz-leht
Tobacconist

269 Pékség/Kenyérüzlet
Payk-shayg/keh-nn-yayr-ewz-leht
Baker's

270 Szupermarket
Supermarket
Supermarket

271 Ofotért/Fotóüzlet
O-fo-tayrt/fo-taw-ewz-leht
Photoshop

272 Játéküzlet/Játékbolt
Yah-tayk-ewz-leht/Yah-tayk-bolt
Toys

273 Utazási Iroda/IBUSZ
Oo-to-zah-shi ee-rodo/Ee-boos
Travel Agent

274 Illatszerek
Eel-lot-seh-rehk
Toiletries

275 Lemezek
Leh-meh-zehk
Records

In the Shop

276 What time do the shops open/close?
Mikor nyitnak/zárnak az üzletek?
Mee-kor nn-y-eet-nok/zahr-nok oz ewz-leh-tehk?

277 Where is the nearest market?
Hol van a legközelebbi piac?
Hol von o lehg-kuh-zeh-lehb-bi pee-ots?

278 Can you show me the one in the window/this one?
Megmutatná nekem az ablakban levőt/ezt?
Mehg-moo-tot-nah neh-kehm oz ob-lok-bon leh-vurt/ehzt?

279 Can I try this on?
Felpróbálhatom?
Fehl-praw-bahl-ho-tom?

280 What size is this?
Mekkora méret ez?
Mehk-koro may-reht ehz?

281 This is too large/too small/too expensive.
Ez túl nagy/túl kicsi/túl drága.
Ehz tool nodj/tool kee-chi/tool drah-go.

282 Do you have any others?
Van még más is?
Von mayg máhsh eesh

283 My size is . . .
. . . -os/-es a méretem.
. . . -osh/-ehsh o may-reh-tehm.

284 Where is the changing room/childrens/cosmetic/ladieswear/menswear/food department?
Hol van a próbafülke/a gyermek osztály/a kozmetikai osztály/a nőiruha osztály/a férfiruha orszály/az élemiszer osztály?
Hol von o praw-bo-fewl-keh/o djehr-mehk os-tahy/o koz-meh-tee-koi os-tahy/o nur-y-roo-ho os-tahy/o fayr-fee-roo-ho os-tahy/oz ay-lehl-mee-sehr os-tahy?

H U N G A R I A N

268
↑
284

167

SHOPPING/MOTORING

²⁸⁵ I would like . . .
Szeretnék egy . . . -t.
Seh-reht-nayk edj . . . -t

²⁸⁶ I would like a quarter of a
kilo/half a kilo/a kilo of
bread/butter/cheese/ham/
tomatoes.
Kérek egy negyed kiló/fél kiló/
kiló kenyeret/vajat/sajtot/
sonkát/paradicsomot.
*Kay-rehk edj neh-djehd kee-law/
fayl kee-law/kee-law keh-nn-yeh-
reht/vo-jot/soy-tot/son-kaht/poro-
dee-cho-mot.*

²⁸⁷ How much is this?
Ez mennyibe kerül?
Ehz mehnn-yee-beh keh-rewl?

²⁸⁸ I'll take this one, thank you.
Ezt megveszem, köszönöm.
Ehzt mehg-veh-sehm, kuh-suh-nuhm.

²⁸⁹ Do you have a carrier
(shopping) bag?
Kérhetek egy nylonzacskót?
Kayr-heh-tehk edj nehy-lon-zoch kawt?

²⁹⁰ Do you have anything
cheaper/larger/smaller/of
better quality?
Van önnek olcsóbb/nagyobb
méretű/kissebb méretű/jobb
minőségű áruja?
*Von uhn-nehk ol-chawbb/nod-
jobb may-reh-teew/kee-shehbb
may-reh-teew/yobb mee-nur-shay-
geew ah-roo-yo?*

²⁹¹ I would like a film for this
camera.
Ehhez a fényképezőgéphez
szeretnék filmet venni.
*Eh-hehz o faynn-y-kay-peh-zur-
gayp-hehz seh-reht-nayk feel-meht
vehn-ni.*

²⁹² I would like some batteries,
the same size as this old one.
Ugyanolyan méretű elemet
szeretnék venni, mint ez a régi.
*Oodjon-ol-yon may-reh-teew eh-
leh-meht seh-reht-nayk vehn-ni,
meent ehz o ray-gi.*

²⁹³ Would you mind wrapping
this for me, please?
Becsomagolná nekem ezt, kérem?
*Beh-cho-mogol-nah neh-kehm
ehzt, kay-rehm?*

²⁹⁴ Sorry, but you seem to have
given me the wrong change.
Elnézést kérek, de azt hiszem
rosszul adott vissza.
*Ehl-nay-zaysht kay-rehk, deh ozt
hee-sehm ros-sool o-dott vees-so.*

MOTORING

Car Hire (Rental)

²⁹⁵ I have ordered (rented) a car
in the name of . . .
Egy autót béreltem . . . néven.
*Ejd o-oo-tawt bay-rehl-tehm . . .
nay-vehn.*

²⁹⁶ How much does it cost to
hire (rent) a car for one day/
two days/one week?
Mennyibe kerül egy autó bérlése
egy napra/két napra/egy hétre?
*Mehnn-yee-beh keh-rewl edj o-oo-
taw bayr-lay-sheh edj nop-ro/kayt
nop-ro/edj hayt-reh?*

297 Is the tank already full of petrol (gas)?

Az autó fel van már tankolva?

Oz o-oo-taw fehl von mahr ton-kol-vo?

298 Is insurance and tax included? How much is the deposit?

A biztosítás és az adó is az árban benne van? Mennyi letétet kérnek?

O beez-to-shee-tahsh ays oz o-daw eesh oz ahr-bon behn-neh von? mehnn-yee leh-tay-teht kayr-nehk

299 By what time must I return the car?

Mikorra kell visszahoznom az autót?

Mee-kor-rah kehll vees-so-hoz-nom oz o-oo-tawt?

300 I would like a small/family car with a radio/cassette player.

Szeretnék egy kisméretű/családi autót rádióval/magnóval.

Seh-reht-nayk edj keesh-may-reh-teew o-oo-tawt rah-dee-aw-vol/mog-naw-vol.

Asking the Way

301 Excuse me, can you help me please?

Bocsánatot kérek, segítene nekem?

Bo-chah-no-tot kay-rehk, sheh-gee-teh-neh neh-kehm?

302 How do I reach the motorway/main road?

Hogy jutok el az autópályára/a főútvonalra?

Hodj yoo-tok ehl oz o-oo-taw-pah-yah-ro/o fur-oot-vo-nol-ro?

303 I think I have taken the wrong turning.

Azt hiszem rossz helyen fordultam be.

Ozt hee-sehm ross heh-yehn for-dool-tom beh.

304 I am looking for this address.

Ezt a címet keresem.

ehzt o cee-meht keh-reh-shem

305 I am looking for the . . . hotel.

A . . . szállót keresem.

O . . . sahl-lawt keh-reh-shem.

306 How far is it to . . . from here?

Milyen messze van a . . . innen?

Mee-yehn mehs seh von o . . in-nehn?

307 Carry straight on for . . . kilometres.

Menjen egyenesen . . . kilométert.

Mehn-yehn eh-djeh-neh-shehn . . . kee-lo-may-tehrt.

308 Take the next turning on the right/left.

Forduljon be a következő sarkon jobbra/balra.

Ford-ool-jon beh o kuh-veht-keh-zur shor-kon yobb-ro/bol-ro.

309 Turn right/left at the next crossroads/traffic lights.

Forduljon jobbra/balra a következő útkereszteződésnél/közlekedési lámpánál.

For-dool-yon yobb-ro/bol-ro o kuh-veht-keh-zur ooht-keh-rehs-Teh-zur-daysh-nayl/kuhz-leh-keh-day-shi lahm-pah-nahl.

MOTORING

³¹⁰ You are going in the wrong
direction.
Ön rossz fele megy.
Uhn ross feh-leh mehdj.

Parking

³¹¹ How long can I park here?
Meddig parkolhatok itt?
Mehd-dig por-kol-ho-tok itt?

³¹² Is there a car park near here?
Van itt a közelben egy parkoló?
Von itt o kuh-zehl-behn edj por-ko-law?

³¹³ At what time does this car
park close?
Mikor zár be ez a parkoló?
Mee-kor zahr beh ehz o por-ko-law?

Signs and Notices

³¹⁴ Egyirányú utca
Edj-ee-rahnn-y-ooh oot-tzo
One way

³¹⁵ Behajtani tilos
Be-hoj-toni tee-losh
No entry.

³¹⁶ Parkolni tilos.
Por-kol-ni tee-losh
No parking

³¹⁷ Útelterelés
Oot-ehl-teh-reh-laysh
Detour (diversion)

³¹⁸ Állj
Ahlly
Stop.

³¹⁹ Elsőbbségadás kötelező
Ehl-shurbb-shayg-o-dahsh kuh-teh-leh-zur
Give way (yield).

³²⁰ Csúszós út
Choo-sawsh oot
Slippery road

³²¹ Előzni tilos
Eh-lurz-ni tee-losh
No overtaking.

At the Filling Station

³²² Unleaded (lead-free)/
Standard/Premium
Ólommentes benzin/
Normálbenzin/Szuperbenzin
Aw-lom-mehn-tehsh behn-zeen normahl-behn-zeen/soo-pehr-behn-zeen

³²³ Fill the tank please.
Kérem töltse tele a tankot.
Kay-rehm tuhlt-sheh teh-leh o ton-kot?

³²⁴ Do you have a road map of
this area?
Van önnek erről a környékről
autótérképe?
Von uhn-nehk ehr-rurl o kuhr-nn-y-ayk-rurl o-oo-taw-tayr-kay-peh?

³²⁵ How much is the car-wash?
Mennyibe kerül az autómosás?
Mehnn-yee-beh keh-rewl oz o-oo-taw-mo-shah-sh?

Breakdowns

³²⁶ I've had a breakdown at . . .
Meghibásodott az autónk . . -nál nél.

170

Mehg-hee-bah-sho-dott oz o-oo-tawnk . . . -nahl/-nayl.

327 I am on the road from . . to . .
A . . -tól . . -ig vezető úton vagyok.
O . . -tawl . . -ig veh-zeh-tur ooh-ton vod-jok.

328 I can't move the car. Can you send a tow-truck?
Lerobbant az autóm. Tudna küldeni egy autómentőt?
Leh-rob-bont oz o-oo-tawm. tood-no kewl-deh-ni edj o-oo-taw-mehn-turt?

329 I have a flat tyre.
Defektet kaptam.
Deh-fehk-teht kop-tom.

330 The windscreen (windshield) has smashed/cracked.
A szélvédő széttörött/megrepedt.
O sayl-vay-dur sayt-tuh-ruhtt/mehg-reh-pehdt.

331 There is something wrong with the engine/brakes/lights/steering/gearbox/clutch/exhaust.
Valami baj van a motorral/fékekkel/lámpákkal/kormánnyal/sebességváltóval/kipuffogó csővel.
Vo-lomi boy von o motor-rol/fay-kehk-kehl/lahm-pahk-kol/kor-mahnn-y-ol/sheh-behsh-shayg-vahl-taw-vol/kee-poof-fo-gaw chur-vehl.

332 It's overheating.
A kocsi túlmelegszik.
O ko-chi tool-meh-lehg-sik.

333 It won't start.
Az autó nem indul be.
Oz o-oo-taw nem in-dool beh.

334 Where can I get it repaired?
Hol tudom megjavíttatni?
Hol too-dom mehg-yo-veet-tot-ni?

335 Can you take me there?
El tudna vinni engem odáig?
el tood-no veen-ni ehn-gehm o-dah-eeg?

336 Will it take long to fix?
Sokáig tart míg megjavítják ?
Sho-kah-ig tort meeg mehg-yo-veet-jahk?

337 How much will it cost?
Mennyibe fog kerülni?
Mehnn-yee-beh fog keh-rewl-ni

Accidents

338 Can you help me? There has been an accident.
Tudna segíteni? Baleset történt.
Tood-no sheh-gee-teh-ni? bol-eh-sheht tuhr-taynt.

339 Please call the police/an ambulance.
Kérem hívja a rendőrséget/mentőket.
Kay-rehm heev-yo o rehn-dur-shay-geht/mehn-tur-keht.

340 Is anyone hurt?
Megsebesült valaki?
Meg-she-beh-shewlt vo-loki?

HEALTH

Traffic Offences

341 I'm sorry, I didn't see the sign.
Bocsánatot kérek, de nem
láttam a táblát.
*Bo-chah-notot kay-rehk, deh nem
laht-tom o tahb-laht.*

342 Must I pay a fine? How much?
Kell büntetés fizetnem?
Mennyit?
*Kehll bewn-teh-taysht fee-zeht-
nehm? mehnn-yeet?*

343 Show me your documents.
Mutassa az okmányait.
Moo-tosh-sho oz ok-mah-nn-y-oit.

HEALTH

At the Pharmacy

344 Do you have anything for a
stomachache/headache/sore
throat/toothache?
Tudna adni valamit
gyomorfájásra/fejfájásra/
torokfájásra/fogfájásra?
*Tood-no odni vo-lo-meet djo-mor-fah-
yahsh-ro/fehy-fah-yahsh-ro/torok-
fah-yah-shro/fog-fah-yash-ro?*

345 I need something for
diarrhoea (diarrhea)/
constipation/a cold/a cough/
insect bites/sunburn/travel
(motion) sickness.
Kérek valamit hasmenésre/
székrekedésre/megfázásra/
köhögés ellen/rovarcsípésre/
leégés ellen/utazás közbeni
hányinger ellen.

*Kay-rehk vo-lo-mit hosh-meh-
naysh-reh/sayk-reh-keh-daysh-
reh/meg-fah-zahsh-ro/kuh-huh-
gays el-lehn/ro-vor-chee-paysh-
reh/le-ay-gaysh el-lehn/oo-to-
zahsh kuhz-beh-ni hahnn-y-in-
gehr el-lehn?*

346 How much/how many do I
take?
Mennyit/hány darabot kell
bevennem?
*Mehnn-yeet/hahnn-y do-ro-bot
kehll beh-vehn-nehm?*

347 How often do I take it/them?
Milyen gyakran kell ezt/ezeket
bevennem?
*Mee-yehn djok-ron kehll ehzt/eh-
zeh-keht beh-vehn-nehm?*

348 How much does it cost?
Mennyibe kerül?
Mehnn-yee-beh keh-ruhl?

349 Can you recommend a good
doctor/dentist?
Tud ajánlani egy jó doktort/
fogorvost?
*Tood o-yahn-loni edj jaw dok-
tort/fog-or-vosht?*

350 Is it suitable for children?
Gyermekeknek is való?
Djer-meh-kehk-nehk ish volaw?

Doctor

351 I have a pain here/in my arm/
leg/chest/stomach.
Fájdalmat érzek itt/a karomban/
a lábamban/a mellkasomban/a
gyomromban.

Fahy-dolmot ayr-zehk itt/o ko-rom-bon/o lah-bom-bon/a mehll-ko-shom-bon/a djom-rom-bon.

352 Please call a doctor, this is an emergency.
Kérem azonnal hívjon orvost, sürgősségi esetről van szó.
Kay-rehm o-zon-nol heev-yon or-vosht, shewr-gur-sh-shay-gi eh-shet-rurl von saw.

353 I would like to make an appointment to see a doctor.
Szeretnék bejelentkezni az orvoshoz.
Seh-reht-nayk beh-yeh-lehnt-kehz-ni oz or-vosh-hoz

354 I am diabetic/pregnant.
Cukorbeteg/terhes vagyok.
Tsoo-kor-beh-tehg/tehr-hesh vod-yok.

355 I need a prescription for . . .
Egy receptre van szükségem . . . -ra/-re.
Edj reh-tzehpt-reh von sewk-shay-gehm . . . -ro/-reh.

356 Can you give me something to ease the pain?
Tudna valami fájdalomcsillapítót adni?
Tood-no vo-lo-mee fahy-do-lom-chil-lo-pee-taw odni?

357 I am allergic to penicillin.
He/she is allergic to penicillin.
Allergiás vagyok a penicillinre.
Ő allergiás a penicillinre.
Ol-lehr-gee-ahsh vod-yok o peh-ni-tzi-lin-reh. Ur ol-lehr-gee-ahsh o peh-ni-tzi-lin-reh.

358 Does this hurt?
Ez fáj?
Ehz fahy?

359 You must go to hospital.
He/she must go to hospital.
önnek kórházba kell mennie.
Neki kórházba kell mennie.
Uhn-nehk kawr-hahz-bo kehll mehn-ni-eh. Neh-ki kawr-hahz-bo kehll mehn-ni-eh.

360 Take these once/twice/three times a day.
Ezt naponta egyszer/kétszer/háromszor kell bevenni.
Ehzt no-pon-to edj-sehr/kayt-sehr/hah-rom-sor kehll beh-ven-ni.

361 I am taking this medication.
He is/she is taking this medication.
Én ezt a gyógyszert szedem.
Ő ezt a gyógyszert szedi.
Ayn ehzt o djawdj-sehrt seh-dehm Ur ehzt o djawdj-sehrt seh-dee

362 I have medical insurance.
Van betegbiztosításom.
Von beh-tehg-beez-to-shee-tah-shom.

Dentists

363 I have toothache.
Fáj a fogam.
Fahy o fo-gom

364 My filling has come out.
Kiesett a tömés a fogamból.
Kee-eh-shehtt o toh-maysh o fo-gom-bawl

³⁶⁵ I do/do not want to have an
injection first.
Először kérek/nem kérek injekciót.
*Eh-lur-suhr kay-rehk/nem kay-
rehk ee-nyehk-tzee-awt.*

EMERGENCIES

³⁶⁶ Help!
Segítség!
Sheh-geet-shayg!

³⁶⁷ Call an ambulance/a doctor/
the police!
Hívja azonnal a mentőket/az
orvost/a rendőrséget!
*Heev-jo ozon-nol o mehn-tur-keht/
oz or-vosht/o rehn-dur-shay-geht!*

³⁶⁸ I have had my travellers'
cheques (travelers' checks)/
credit cards/purse/handbag/
rucksack (knapsack)/
luggage/wallet stolen.
Ellopták a Travellers
csekkjeimet/a hitelkártyáimat/a
pénztárcámat/a táskámat/a
hátizsákomat/a poggyászomat/
az irattárcámat.
*El-lop-tahk o travellers chehk-ye-
hee-meht/o hee-tehl-kahrt-yah-ee-
mot/o paynz-tahr-tzah-mot/o
tahsh-kah-mot/o hah-tee-zhah-ko-*

mot/o podj-djah-so-mot/oz ee-rot-
tahr-tzah-mot.

³⁶⁹ Can you help me, I have lost
my daughter/son?
Tudna segíteni, nem találom a
lányomat/fiamat?
*Tood-no sheh-gee-teh-ni, nem to-lah-
lom o lah-nn-y-omot/fee-o-mot?*

³⁷⁰ Please go away/leave me
alone.
Kérem menjen innen/hagyjon
békében.
*Kay-rehm mehn-yehn in-nehn/
hod-jon bay-kay-behn.*

³⁷¹ Fire!
Tűz van!
Teewz von!

³⁷² I want to contact the British/
American/Canadian/Irish/
Australian/New Zealand/
South African consulate.
Fel akarom hívni a Brit/
Amerikai/Kanadai/ír/
Ausztráliai/Új Zélandi/Dél
Afrikai konzulátust.
*Fehl o-korom heev-ni o brit/o-
meh-ree-koi/ko-nodoi/eer/o-oost-
rah-lee-o-i/ooy zay-lon-di/dayl of-
ree-koi kon-zoo-lah-toosht.*

Introduction

Italian, the closest to the original Latin of all the 'Romance' languages, is spoken in the southern cantons of Switzerland as well as the Italian peninsula and surrounding islands. Local dialects vary greatly from standard Italian: this is to be expected in a country that consisted of a large number of small independent states for most of its history. The pure form of the language, derived from the dialect of Tuscany, is understood and spoken everywhere. It is not a difficult language to pick up because its spelling is entirely regular, there are no unexpected quirks of pronunciation, and accented characters are few.

**I
T
A
L
I
A
N**

Addresses for travel and tourist information

Australia: *Embassy,* 12 Grey St, Deakin 2601, PO Box 360 Canberra; tel: (2) 73 3333.
Canada: *Italian Gvmt Travel Office,* 17 Bloor Street, East Suite 907, South Tower M4W3R8 Toronto, Ontario; tel: (416) 9254882/9253725.
UK: *Italian State Tourist Board,* 1 Princess St, London, W1R 9AY; tel: (020) 7355 1557/7355 1439.
USA: *Italian Government Travel Office,* 630 Fifth Ave (Suite 1565), New York, NY 10111; tel: (212) 2455095/2454822.

ESSENTIALS

ESSENTIALS

Alphabet

The letters J (i lungo), K (cappa), W (vu doppia), X (ics) and Y (ipsilon) are used only to spell foreign words and names.

A	B
a	*bee*
C	D
chi	*dee*
E	F
eyy	*effe*
G	H
gee	*acca*
I	L
ee	*elle*
M	N
emme	*enne*
O	P
o	*pea*
Q	R
ku	*erre*
S	T
esse	*tee*
U	V
oo	*voo*
Z	
zeta	

Basic Words and Phrases

1 **Yes**   **No**
Sì   No
See   *Noh*

2 **Please**   **Thank you**

    Per favore   Grazie
    Perr fahvawreh Grahtsyeh

3 **That's O.K.**   **Perhaps**
Va bene   Forse
Vah behneh   *Forrseh*

4 **To**   **From**
A   da
ah   *dah*

5 **Here**   **There**
Qui   là
Kwee   *lah*

6 **None**   **Also**
Nessuno   Anche
Nessoonaw   *Ahnkeh*

7 **How**   **When**
Come   quando
Cawme   *kwahndaw*

8 **What**   **Why**
che   perché
keh   *perrkeh*

9 **I don't understand.**
Non capisco.
Nawn kahpeescaw

10 **I don't speak Italian.**
Non parlo italiano.
Nawn parrlaw itahlyahnaw

11 **Do you speak English?**
Parla inglese?
Parrla eenglehzeh?

12 **Can you please write it down?**
Potrebbe scriverlo, per favore?
Pawtrebbeh screevehrrlaw, perr fahvawreh?

13 **Can you please speak more slowly?**

Potrebbe parlare più
lentamente, per favore?
*Pawtrebbeh pahrrlahrreh pyoo
lehntahmehnteh, perr fahvawreh?*

14 How much does it/this cost?
Quant'è/quanto costa?
Kwahntèh/kwahntah kawstah?

Days

15 Monday **Tuesday**
Lunedì Martedì
Loonehdee *Marrtehdee*

16 Wednesday **Thursday**
Mercoledì Giovedì
Merrcawlehdee *Jawvehdee*

17 Friday **Saturday**
Venerdì Sabato
Venerrdee *Sàbahtaw*

18 Sunday **Morning**
Domenica Mattino
Dawméhneeca *Mahtteenaw*

19 Afternoon **Evening**
Pomeriggio Sera
Pawmehreedjaw *Sehra*

20 Night **Week**
Notte Settimana
Notteh *Setteemahna*

21 Yesterday/Today/Tomorrow
Ieri/Oggi/Domani
Yeree/Odjee/Dawmahnee

Numbers

22 Zero **One**
Zero Uno
Tsehraw *Oonaw*

23 Two **Three**
Due Tre
Dweh *Treh*

24 Four **Five**
Quattro Cinque
Kwahttraw *Cheenkweh*

25 Six **Seven**
Sey Sette
Say *Setteh*

26 Eight **Nine**
Otto Nove
Ottaw *Noveh*

27 Ten **Eleven**
Dieci Undici
Dyehchee *Oondeechee*

28 Twelve **Thirteen**
Dodici Tredici
Dawdeechee *Tréhdeechee*

29 Fourteen **Fifteen**
Quattordici Quindici
Kwahttòrrdeechee *Kweendeechee*

30 Sixteen **Seventeen**
Sedici Diciassette
Sédeechee *Deechassetteh*

31 Eighteen **Nineteen**
Diciotto Diciannove
Deechottaw *Deechannoveh*

32 Twenty **Twenty-one**
Venti Ventuno
Ventee *Ventoonaw*

33 Twenty-two **Thirty**
Ventidue Trenta
Venteedweh *Trenta*

34 Forty **Fifty**
Quaranta Cinquanta
Kwahrahnta *Cheenkwahnta*

ITALIAN

14
↕
34

35 **Sixty** **Seventy**
Sessanta Settanta
Sessahnta *Settahnta*

36 **Eighty** **Ninety**
Ottanta Novanta
Ottahnta *Novahnta*

37 **One hundred** **Five hundred**
Cento Cinquecento
Chentaw
Cheenkwechentaw

38 **One thousand** **One million**
Mille Un milione
Meelleh *Oon meellyawneh*

Time

39 **9.00**
Nove
Noveh

40 **9.05**
Nove e cinque
Noveh eh cheenkweh

41 **9.10**
Nove e dieci
Noveh eh dyehchee

42 **9.15**
Nove e quindici
oveh eh kweendechee

43 **9.20**
Nove e venti
Noveh eh ventee

44 **9.25**
Nove e venticinque
Noveh eh venteecheenkweh

45 **9.30**
Nove e trenta
Noveh eh trenta

46 **9.35**
Nove e trentacinque
Noveh eh trentacheenkweh

47 **9.40**
Nove e quaranta
Noveh eh kwahranta

48 **9.45**
Nove e quarantacinque
Noveh eh kwahrantacheenkweh

49 **9.50**
Nove e cinquanta
Noveh eh cheenkwahnta

50 **9.55**
Nove e cinquantacinque
Noveh eh cheenkwahntacheenkweh

51 **12.00/Midday/Midnight**
Dodici/Mezzogiorno/
mezzanotte
Dohdychee/metsawjorrnaw/
metsanotteh

52 **What time is it?**
Che ore sono?
Keh awreh sawnaw?

53 **It is . . .**
Sono le . . .
Sawnaw leh . . .

ARRIVING AND DEPARTING

Airport

54 **Excuse me, where is the**
check-in desk for . . . airline?
Mi scusi, dov'è il banco
accettazioni per la linea aerea . . ?
Mee scoozee, dawvèh eel bahnkaw
ahchettatsyawnee perr lah
leenayah ah-aerrhayah . . ?

55 **What is the boarding gate/
time for my flight?**
Qual'è il cancello di imbarco/
orario del mio volo?
*Kwaalèh eel kahnchehlaw dee
ihmbahrcaw/awrahreeaw deel
meeoh vawloh?*

56 **How long is the delay likely
to be?**
Qual'è il ritardo previsto?
*Kwaalhè eel rreehtahrdaw
prehveestaw?*

57 **Where is the duty-free shop?**
Dov'è il duty-free?
Dawvèh eel duty-free?

58 **Which way is the baggage
reclaim?**
Dove si trova il recupero bagagli?
*Dawveh see trawvah eel
rehkupehrraw bahgahlyee?*

59 **Where can I get the bus to
the city centre?**
Dove posso prendere l'autobus
per il centro?
*Dawveh pawssaw prendereh
lahutobhuss perr eel chentraw?*

Train Station

60 **Where is the ticket office/
information desk?**
Dov'è la biglietteria/l'ufficio
informazioni?
*Dawvèh lah beelyetteryha/
looffeechaw eenformahtseeawnee?*

61 **Which platform does the
train to . . . depart from?**
Da quale marciapiede parte il
treno per . . ?

*Dah kwahleh marchyahpyedeh
parteh eel trehnaw perr . . ?*

62 **Where is platform . . ?**
Dov'è il marciapiede . . ?
Dawvèh eel marchyahpyedeh . . ?

63 **When is the next train to . . ?**
A che ora arriva il prossimo
treno per . . ?
*Ah keh awrah arreevah eel
prosseemaw trehnaw perr . . ?*

64 **Is there a later train to . . ?**
C'è un altro treno per . . ?
Chèh oon ahltraw trehnaw perr . . ?

Port

65 **How do I get to the port?**
Come arrivo al porto?
Cawmeh arrevaw ahl pawrrtaw?

66 **When is the next sailing to . . ?**
Quand'è la prossma partenza
per . . ?
*Kwandèh lah prawssema
parrtentsa perr . . ?*

67 **Can I catch an earlier ferry
with this ticket?**
Posso prendere un traghetto
che parta prima con questo
biglietto?
*Pawssaw prendereh oon
trahgettaw keh pahrrtah preemah
kawn kwestaw beelyettaw?*

Notices and Signs

68 **Carrozza rinfreschi**
Carrotsa reenfreskee
Buffet (Dining) Car

ITALIAN

**55
↕
68**

ARRIVING AND DEPARTING

69 **Autobus**
Ahootawboos
Bus

70 **Acqua potabile/non potabile**
Aqua pawtahbeeleh/non pawtahbeeleh
Drinking/Non-drinking water

71 **Entrata**
Entrahta
Entrance

72 **Uscita**
Oosheeta
Exit

73 **Informazioni**
Eenformahtsyawnee
Information

74 **Bagaglio depositato**
Bahgalyaw depawseetahtaw
Left Luggage (Baggage Claim)

75 **Armadietti per bagagli**
Armahdyettee perr baghgalee
Luggage Lockers

76 **Ufficio postale**
Ooffeechaw pawstahleh
Post Office

77 **Marciapiede**
Marchyahpyedeh
Platform

78 **Stazione ferroviaria**
Stahtsyawneh ferrawvyarya
Railway (Railroad) Station

79 **Aeroporto**
Ahaerrhawpawrrtaw
Airport

80 **Porto**
Pawrrtaw
Port

81 **Ristorante**
Reestawrahnteh
Restaurant

82 **Per fumatori/non fumatori**
Perr foomahtawree/non foomahtawree
Smoking/Non-Smoking

83 **Telefono**
Telèfawnaw
Telephone

84 **Biglietteria**
Beelyetterya
Ticket Office

85 **Banco accettazioni**
Bahnkaw ahchettahtsyawnee
Check-in Desk

86 **Orario**
Awraryaw
Timetable (Schedule)

87 **Tolette**
Tawletteh
Toilets (Restrooms)

88 **Signori**
Seenyawree
Gentlemen

89 **Signore**
Seenyawreh
Ladies'

90 **Tram**
Trahm
Tram (Streetcar)

91 **Metropolitana**
Metrawpawleetahna
Underground (Subway)

92 Sala d'attesa
Sahla dahttehsa
Waiting Room

Buying a Ticket

93 I would like a first-class/
second-class single (one-
way)/return (round-trip)
ticket to . . .
Vorrei un biglietto di sola
andata/andata e ritorno di
prima classe/di seconda classe
per . . .
*Vawrray oon beelyettaw dee
sawlah ahndahta/ahndahta eh
reetawrnaw dee preema classeh/
dee seconda classeh perr . . .*

94 Is my rail pass valid on this
train/ferry/bus?
Il mio abbonamento è valido su
questo treno/traghetto/
autobus?
*Eel meeoh abhawnahmentaw èh
vahleedhaw soo kwestaw
trehnaw/trahgehtaw/
ahootawboos?*

95 I would like an
aisle/window seat.
Vorrei un posto vicino al
corridoio/al finestrino.
*Vawrray oon pawstaw
veecheenaw ahl correedoyaw/ahl
feenestreenaw.*

96 No smoking/smoking,
please.
Per favore nello
scompartimento per fumatori/
non fumatori.

*Perr fahvawreh nehllo
scomparteementaw peer
foomahtawree /non foomahtawree.*

97 We would like to sit
together.
Vorremmo sedere accanto.
*Vawrremmaw sehdehreh
ahckahntaw.*

98 I would like to make a seat
reservation.
Vorrei prenotare un posto.
*Vawrray prehnawtahrreh oon
pawstaw.*

99 I would like to reserve a
couchette/sleeper for one
person/two people/for my
family.
Vorrei prenotare una cuccetta/
una cabina per una persona/due
persone/per la mia famiglia.
*Vawrray prehnawtareh oona
coocchetta/oona cahbeena perr
oona perrsawna/dweh
perrsawneh/perr lah myah
fahmeelya.*

100 I would like to reserve a
cabin.
Vorrei prenotare una cabina.
*Vawrray prehnawtahrreh oonah
kahbeenah.*

Timetables (Schedules)

101 Arrivare
Arreevahreh
Arrive

102 Ferma a
Ferrma ah
Calls (Stops) at

I
T
A
L
I
A
N

92
↑
102

ARRIVING AND DEPARTING

I T A L I A N

103
↕
119

103 **Servizio d'approvvigionamento**
Serveetsyaw dahpprawvveejawnahmentaw
Catering Service

104 **Cambiare a**
Cahmbyareh ah
Change at

105 **Coincidenza**
Coincheedentsa
Connection

106 **Giornaliero**
Jawrnahlyeraw
Daily

107 **Ogni quaranta minuti**
Awnee kwahrahnta meenootee
Every 40 Minutes

108 **Prima classe**
Preema classeh
First Class

109 **Ogni ora**
Awnee awra
Hourly

110 **Si raccomanda la prenotazione dei posti**
See rahckawmahnda la prehnawtatsyawneh day pawstee
Seat reservations are recommended

111 **Seconda classe**
Secawnda classeh
Second Class

112 **Supplemento esigibile**
Soopplehmentaw eseejeebeeleh
Supplement Payable

113 **Via**
Veeha
Via

Luggage

114 **How much will it cost to send (ship) my luggage in advance?**
Quanto costa la spedizione anticipata del mio bagaglio?
Kwahntaw cawstah la spehdeetsyawneh ahnteecheepahta del myaw bahgalyaw?

115 **Where is the left luggage (baggage claim) office?**
Dov'è il deposito bagagli?
Dawvèh eel dehpawseetaw bahgahlee?

116 **What time do you open/close?**
A che ora aprite/chiudete?
Ah keh awra ahpreeteh/kewdehteh?

117 **Where are the luggage trolleys (carts)?**
Dove sono i carrelli portabagagli?
Dawveh sawnaw ee carrellee porrtahbahgalee?

118 **Where are the lockers?**
Dove sono gli armadietti?
Dawveh sawnaw lyee ahrmahdyettee?

119 **I have lost my locker key.**
Ho perso la chiave del mio armadietto.
Aw perrsaw lah kyahveh del myaw armahdyettaw.

On Board

120 **Is this seat taken?**
È libero questo posto?
Èh leebehraw kwestaw pawstaw?

121 **Excuse me, you are sitting in my reserved seat.**
Scusi, Lei siede nel mio posto riservato.
Scoozee, Lay syedeh nel myaw pawstaw reeservahtaw.

122 **Which station is this?**
Che stazione è?
Keh stahtsyawneh èh?

123 **What time is this train/bus/ ferry/flight due to arrive/ depart?**
A che ora è previsto l'arrivo/ partenza di questo treno/ autobus/volo?
Ah keh awrah èh prehveestaw lahrreevaw/pahrrtehntsah dee kwestaw trehnaw/ ahootawboos/ vawlaw?

124 **Will you wake me just before we arrive?**
Mi sveglia poco prima dell'arrivo?
Mee svelyah pawcaw preema dellarreevaw?

Customs and Passports

125 **Passaporti per favore!**
Passaporrtee perr fahvawreh!
Passports, please!

126 **I have nothing/wine/spirits (alcohol)/tobacco to declare.**
Non ho nulla da dichiarare/ho

vino/alcolici/tabacco da dichiarare.
Non aw noollah dah deekyarareh/ aw veenaw/ahlcoleechee/ tahbahckaw dah deekyarareh.

127 **I shall be staying for . . . days/weeks/months.**
Mi tratterrò per . . . giorni/ settimane/mesi.
Mee trahtterraw perr . . . jawrnee/ setteemahneh/mehzee.

AT THE TOURIST OFFICE

128 **Do you have a map of the town/area?**
Ha una mappa della città/della zona?
Ah oona mahppa della cheettàh/ della zawna?

129 **Can I reserve accommodation here?**
Posso prenotare qui l'alloggio?
Pawssaw prenotahre kwee lallodjaw?

130 **Do you have a list of accommodation?**
Ha un elenco di alloggi?
Ah oon ehlehnkaw dee ahlawdjee?

ACCOMMODATION

Hotels

131 **I have a reservation in the name of . . .**
Ho una prenotazione per . . .
Aw oona prehnawtahtsyawneh perr . . .

I
T
A
L
I
A
N

120
↑
131

132 I wrote to/faxed/telephoned you last month/last week in . . .
Vi ho scritto/inviato un fax/telefonato il mese scorso/la settimana scorsa a . . .
Vee haw skreehtaw/eenveeahtaw oon fax/tehlehfonahtaw eel mehseh skawhrsaw/lah sehteemahnah skawrsah ah . . .

133 Do you have any rooms free?
Avete camere libere?
Ahvehteh kahmehreh leebehreh?

134 I would like to reserve a single/double room with/without bath/shower.
Vorrei prenotare una camera singola/matrimoniale con/senza bagno/doccia.
Vawrray prehnawtahreh oona cahmehra seengawlah/mahtreemawnyahleh con/sentsa bahnyaw/doccha

135 I would like bed and breakfast/(room and) half board/(room and) full board.
Vorrei una camera con colazione/con mezza pensione/pensione completa.
Vawrray oona cahmehra con cawlahtsyawneh/con metsa pensyawneh/pensyawneh complehta.

136 How much is it per night?
Quant'è per notte?
Kwahntèh perr notteh?

137 Is breakfast included?
È compresa la colazione?
Èh comprehsa lah cawlatsyawneh?

138 May I see the room?
Posso vedere la camera?
Pawssaw vehdehreh lah cahmehra?

139 Do you have any cheaper rooms?
Ha delle camere più economiche?
Ah delleh cahmehreh pyoo ehcawnohmikeh?

140 I would like to take the room
Vorrei la camera.
Vawrray lah cahmehra.

141 I would like to stay for . . . nights.
Vorrei alloggiare per . . . notti.
Vawrray allawdjahreh perr . . . nottee.

142 The shower/light/tap doesn't work.
La doccia/luce/rubinetto non funziona.
Lah dawcheeah/loocheh/roobeenehttaw nawn foontsyawnah.

143 At what time/where is breakfast served?
A che ora/dove viene servita la colazione?
Ah keh awra/dawveh vyeneh serrveeta lah cawlahtsyawneh?

144 What time do I have to check-out?
A che ora devo lasciare libera la camera?
Ah keh awra dehvaw lahshareh leebehra lah cahmehra?

145 Can I have the key to room no . . ?
Posso avere la chiave della camera numero . . ?

*Payssaw ahvehreh lah keeyahveh
dehlah noohmehraw . . ?*

146 **My room number is . . .**
La mia camera ha il numero . . .
*Lah myah cahmehra ah eel
noomehraw . . .*

147 **Do you accept travellers'
cheques/Eurocheques/credit
cards?**
Accettate assegni turistici/
euroassegni/carte di credito?
*Achetahteh asehnyee
tooreesteechee/ehooraw-ahsehnyee/
kahrrteh dee krehdeehtaw?*

148 **May I have the bill please?**
Mi dà il conto per favore?
*Mee dah eel cawntaw perr
fahvawreh?*

149 **Excuse me, I think there is a
mistake in this bill.**
Mi scusi, credo ci sia un errore
nel conto.
*Mee scozee, kredaw chee syah oon
errawreh nel cawntaw.*

Youth Hostels

150 **How much is a dormitory bed
per night?**
Quant'è un letto in dormitorio
per notte?
*Kwahntèh oon lettaw een
dormeetawryaw perr notteh?*

151 **I am/am not an HI member.**
Sono/non sono membro
dell'Associazione Internazionale
Ostelli della Gioventù.
*Sawnaw/non sawnaw membraw
dell Assawchahtsyawne*

*Eenterrnahtsyawnahleh ostelee
della Jovehntoo.*

152 **May I use my own sleeping
bag?**
Posso usare il mio sacco a pelo?
*Pawssaw oozahreh eel myaw
saccaw ah pehlaw?*

153 **What time do you lock the
doors at night?**
A che ora chiudete le porta la
notte?
*Ah keh awra kewdehte leh porrteh
lah notteh?*

Camping

154 **May I camp here for the
night/two nights?**
Posso accamparmi qui per la
notte/due notti?
*Pawssaw accahmparmee kwee perr
lah notteh/dweh nottee?*

155 **Where can I pitch my tent?**
Dove posso piantare la tenda?
*Dawveh pawssaw pyahntareh lah
tenda?*

156 **How much does it cost for
one night/week?**
Qual'è la tariffa per una notte/
una settimana?
*Kwalèh lah tahreeffa perr oona
notteh/oona setteemahna?*

157 **Where can we park our
caravan?**
Dove possiamo parcheggiare la
roulotte?
*Dawveh pawseeyahmaw
pahrkehdjyahreh lah roolhawt?*

ITALIAN

146
↕
157

185

¹⁵⁸**Where are the washing facilities?**
Dove sono le lavanderie?
Dawveh sawnaw leh lavahndehryeh?

¹⁵⁹**Is there a restaurant/supermarket/swimming pool on site/nearby?**
C'è un ristorante/un supermercato/una piscina al campeggio/nelle vicinanze?
Chèh oon reestawrahnteh/oon sooperrmerrcahtaw/oona peesheena ahl cahmpedjaw/nelleh veecheenahntseh?

¹⁶⁰**Do you have a safety deposit box?**
Ha una cassaforte?
Ah oona cassahforrteh?

EATING AND DRINKING

Cafés and Bars

¹⁶¹**I would like a cup of/two cups of/another coffee/tea.**
Vorrei una tazza di/due tazze di/un altro caffè/tè.
Vawrray oona tatsa dee/dweh tatseh dee/oon ahltraw caffèh/teh.

¹⁶²**With/without milk/sugar.**
Con/senza latte/zucchero.
Con/sentsa latteh/tsoockehraw.

¹⁶³**I would like a bottle/glass/two glasses of mineral water/red wine/white wine, please.**
Per cortesia, vorrei una bottiglia/un bicchiere/due bicchieri d'acqua minerale/vino rosso/vino bianco.

Peer corrtehzya, vawrray oona botteelya/oon beeckyereh/dweh beeckyeree daqua meenehrahleh/veenaw rawssaw/veenaw byahncaw.

¹⁶⁴**I would like a beer/two beers, please.**
Per cortesia, vorrei una birra, due birre.
Perr corrteshzya, vawrray oona beerra, dweh beerreh.

¹⁶⁵**May I have some ice?**
Può darmi del ghiaccio?
Poohòh darrmee del ghyacchaw?

¹⁶⁶**Do you have any matches/cigarettes/cigars?**
Vendete fiammiferi, sigarette/sigari?
Vendehteh fyammeefehree, seegahretteh, séegaree?

Restaurants

¹⁶⁷**Can you recommend a good/inexpensive restaurant in this area?**
Può raccomandarmi un buon ristorante/un ristorante economico in questa zona?
Poohòh raccomahndarmee oon boohòn reestawrahnteh/oon reestawrahnteh ehcawnawmeecaw een kwesta zawna?

¹⁶⁸**I would like a table for . . . people.**
Vorrei un tavolo per . . . persone.
Vawrray oon tahvawlaw perr . . . perrsawneh.

ITALIAN

158
↕
168

169 Do you have a non-smoking area?
Avete un'area non fumatori?
Ahvehteh oonahrreyah nawn foomahttawree?

170 Waiter/Waitress!
Cameriere/cameriera!
Cahmehryereh/cahmehryera!

171 Do you have a set menu/children's menu/wine list?
Ha un menù fisso/un menù per bambini/una lista dei vini?
Ah oon mehnoo feessaw/oon mehnoo perr bambeenee/oona leesta day veenee?

172 Do you have any vegetarian dishes, please?
Per favore, ha dei piatti vegetariani?
Perr fahvawreh, ah day pyattee vehgehtahryanee?

173 Are there any local specialities?
Avete qualche specialità locale?
Ahvehteh kwalkeh spehchiahleehtah lawkahleh?

174 Are vegetables included?
Sono incluse anche le verdure?
Sawnaw eenclooseh ahnkeh leh vehrdooreh?

175 Could I have it well-cooked/medium/rare please?
Potrei averlo ben cotto/mediamente cotto/poco cotto, per favore?
Pawtray ahvehrlaw behn cawtaw/mehdeeyahmehnteh cawtaw/

pawcaw cawtaw perr fahvawreh?

176 What does this dish consist of?
Quali sono gli ingredienti di questo piatto?
Kwahlee sawnaw lee eengrehdyehntee dee kwestaw pyattaw?

177 I would like the set menu, please.
Vorrei il menù fisso.
Vawrray eel mehnoo feessaw.

178 We have not been served yet.
Non ci hanno ancora serviti.
Non chee annaw ahncawra serrveetee.

179 Excuse me, this is not what I ordered.
Mi scusi, questo non è quello che ho ordinato.
Mee scozee, kwehstaw nawn eh kwellaw keh haw awrdeehnahtaw.

180 May I have some/some more bread/water/coffee/tea?
Può darmi del/dell'altro pane/caffè/tè?
Puuòh darrmee del/dellahltraw pahneh/caffèh/tèh?

181 May I have the bill, please?
Mi dà il conto, per favore?
Mee dah eel cawntaw, perr fahvawreh?

182 Does this bill include service?
Il conto include il servizio?
Eel cawntaw eencloodeh eel serrveetsyaw?

I
T
A
L
I
A
N

169
↕
182

¹⁸³ **Do you accept travellers' cheques (travelers' checks)/ Eurocheques/MasterCard/US dollars?**
Accettate assegni turistici/ euroassegni/MasterCard/dollari USA?
Acchettahteh assenee tooreesteechee/ ehoorawassenee/MasterCard/ dollahree OO EZ AY?

¹⁸⁴ **Can I have a receipt, please?**
Potrei avere la ricetta, per favore?
Pawtray ahvehreh lah reechettah, perr fahvawreh?

¹⁸⁵ **Where is the toilet (restroom), please?**
Dov'è la toletta, per cortesia?
Dawvèh lah tawletta, perr corrtehzya?

On the Menu

¹⁸⁶ **First courses**
Primi piatti
Preemee pyattee

¹⁸⁷ **Soups**
Zuppe
Zooppeh

¹⁸⁸ **Main courses**
Piatti principali
Pyattee preencheepahlee

¹⁸⁹ **Fish dishes**
Piatti di pesce
Pyattee dee pesheh

¹⁹⁰ **Meat dishes**
Piatti di carne
Pyattee dee kahrneh

¹⁹¹ **Vegetarian dishes**
Piatti vegetariani
Pyattee vehjehtaryanee

¹⁹² **Cheese**
Formaggio
Fawrmahdyiaw

¹⁹³ **Desserts**
Dessert
Dehssehrt

¹⁹⁴ **Specialities**
Specialità
Spehcheeyahleehtàh

GETTING AROUND

Public Transport

¹⁹⁵ **Where is the bus stop/coach station/nearest metro (subway) station?**
Dov'è la fermata degli autobus/ la stazione delle corriere/la più vicina stazione della metropolitana?
Dawvèh lah ferrmahta delee ahootawboos/lah stahtsyawneh delleh corryereh/lah pyoo veecheena stahtsyawneh della metropawleetahna?

¹⁹⁶ **When is the next/last bus to . . ?**
A che ora è il prossimo/l'ultimo autobus per . . ?
Ah keh awra èh eel prawssemaw/ loolteemaw ahootawboos perr . . ?

¹⁹⁷ **How much is the fare to the city centre (downtown)/ railway (railroad) station/ airport?**

Qual'è la tariffa per il centro
città/la stazione ferroviaria/
l'aeroporto?
*Kwahlèh lah tahreeffa perr eel
chentraw cheettàh/lah
stahtsyawone ferrawvyarya/
l'aheraoporrtaw?*

198 Will you tell me when to get
off?
Può dirmi quando devo
scendere?
*Poohòh deerrmee kwahndaw
dehvaw shendehreh?*

199 Does this bus go to . . ?
Quest'autobus va a . . ?
Kwest ahootawboos vah ah . . ?

200 Which number bus goes to . . ?
Qual'è il numero dell'autobus
per . . ?
*Kwahlèh eel noomehraw dell
ahootawboos perr . . ?*

201 May I have a single (one-
way)/return (round-trip)/day
ticket/book of tickets?
Vorrei un biglietto di sola
andata/di andata e ritorno
valido per un giorno/un
blocchetto di biglietti.
*Vawrray oon beelyettaw dee sawla
ahndahta/dee ahndahta eh
reetorrnaw vahleedaw perr oon
jawrrnaw/oon blawckettaw dee
beelyettee.*

Taxis

202 I would like to go to . . . How
much will it cost?
Vorrei andare a . . . , quant'è?

*Vawrray ahnahre ah . . .
kwahntèh?*

203 Please stop here.
Fermi qui, per cortesia.
Fermee koohee perr corrtehzya.

204 I would like to order a taxi
today/tomorrow/at 2pm to
go from . . . to . . .
Vorrei prenotare un tassì per
oggi/per domani/per le
quattordici che mi porti
da . . . a . . .
*Vawrray prehnawtahreh oon
tassee perr odjee/perrdawmahnee/
perr leh kwahttorrdeechee keh mee
porrtee
dah . . . ah . . .*

Asking the Way

205 Excuse me, do you speak
English?
Mi scusi, parla inglese?
Mee scoozee, parrla eenglehzeh?

206 Excuse me, is this the right
way to . . ?
Mi scusi, è questa la strada per . . ?
*Mee scoozee, eh kwehstah lah
strahda perr . . ?*

207 . . . the cathedral/the tourist
information office/the castle/
the old town.
. . . la cattedrale/l'ufficio
informazioni turistiche/il
castello/la città vecchia.
*. . . lah kahttehdrahleh/
looffeechaw eenforrmahtsyawnee
tooreesteekeh/eel kahstehllaw/lah
cheettàh vehkyah.*

I T A L I A N

208 ↕ 218

208 Can you tell me the way to the railway (railroad) station/bus station/taxi rank (stand)/city centre (downtown)/beach?
Sa indicarmmi la strada per andare alla stazione ferroviaria/alla stazione degli autobus/al posteggio di auto pubbliche/al centro città/alla spiaggia?
Sah eendeecarrmee lah strahda perr ahndareh ahlla stahtsyawneh ferrawvyarya/ahlla stahtsyawneh delee ahootawboos/ahl pawstedjaw dee ahootaw poobbleekeh/ahl chentraw cheettàh/ahlla spyadjya?

209 First/second left/right/straight ahead.
Prenda la prossima/la seconda a sinistra/a destra/Vada sempre diritto.
Prehnda lah prawsseema/lah secawnda ah seeneestra/ah destra/vahda sempreh deereettaw.

210 Where is the nearest police station/post office/doctor/hospital/pharmacy?
Dov'è il più vicino posto di polizia/ufficio postale/medico/ospedale/farmacia?
Dawvèh eel pyoo veecheenaw pawstaw dee pawleetsya/ooffechaw pawstahle/medeekoo/ohspeetahl/farmaseea?

211 Is it far?
È lontano
Èh lawntahnaw?

212 Do I need to take a taxi/catch a bus?
Devo prendere un tassì/l'autobus?
Dehvaw prendehreh oon tassee/lahootawboos?

213 Can you point to it on my map?
Può indicarmelo sulla mappa?
Poohòh eendeecarrmehlaw soolla mappa?

214 Thank you for your help.
Grazie dell'aiuto.
Grahtsyeh dell ahyootaw.

SIGHTSEEING

215 Where is the Tourist Information office?
Dov'è l'Ufficio informazioni turistiche?
Dawvèh l'ooffeechaw eenforrmahtsyawnee tooreesteekeh?

216 Where is the cathedral/church/museum?
Dov'è la cattedrale/la chiesa/il museo?
Dawvèh lah cattehdrahleh/lah kyehza/eel moozehaw?

217 How much is the entrance (admission) charge?
Qual'è la tariffa d'ingresso?
Kwahlèh lah tahreeffa deengressaw?

218 Is there a reduction for children/students/senior citizens?
I bambini/gli studenti/i pensionati hanno diritto a una

riduzione?
Ee bahmbeenee/lee stoodentee/ee pensyawnahtee annaw deereettaw ah oona reedootsyawneh?

219 What time does the next guided tour start?
A che ora ha inizio la prossima visita guidata?
Ah keh awra ah eeneetsyaw lah prosseemah veeseeta goohedahta?

220 One/two adults/children, please.
Un adulto/due adulti/due bambini, per favore
Oon ahdooltaw/dweh ahdooltee/dweh bahmbeenee, perr fahvawreh

221 May I take photographs here?
Posso fare fotografie qui?
Payssaw fahreh fotografyeh kwee?

ENTERTAINMENT

222 Can you recommend a good bar/nightclub?
Può raccomandarmi un buon bar/locale notturno?
Poohòh rahccawmahdarrmee oon bwòn barr/lawcahleh nawttoornaw?

223 Do you know what is on at the cinema (playing at the movies)/theatre at the moment?
Conosce il programma del cinema/teatro?
Cawnawsheh eel prawgramma del ceenema/tehatraw?

224 I would like to book

(purchase) . . . tickets for the matinee/evening performance on Monday.
Vorrei prenotare . . . posti per la matinée/lo spettacolo serale di lunedì.
Vawrray prehnawtahre . . . pawstee perr lah mateenéh/law spettahcawlaw sehrahleh dee loonehdee.

225 What time does the film/ performance start?
A che ora incomincia il film/lo spettacolo?
Ah keh awra eencawmeencha eel film/law spettahcawlaw?

MEETING PEOPLE

226 Hello/Goodbye.
Salve/arrivederci
Sahlveh/arreevehderrchee

227 Good morning/good afternoon/good evening/ goodnight.
Buon giorno/buon pomeriggio/ buona sera/buona notte.
Booawn geeyawrnaw/booawn pawmehreehdjaw/booawnah sehrah/booawnah nawtteh

228 Pleased to meet you.
Piacere
Pyahchehreh

229 How are you?
Come sta?
Cawmeh stah?

230 Fine, thank you. And you?
Bene, grazie. E lei?
Behneh grahtsyeh. Eh ley?

I
T
A
L
I
A
N

219
↕
230

231 My name is . . .
Mi chiamo . . .
Mee kyahmaw . . .

232 This is my friend/
boyfriend/girlfriend/
husband/wife/brother/
sister.
Le presento il mio amico/il mio
ragazzo/la mia ragazza/mio
marito/mia moglie/mio fratello/
mia sorella.
*Leh prehsentaw eel myaw
ahmeecaw/eel myaw rahgatsaw/
lah myah rahgatsa/myaw
mahreetaw/myah mawlyeh/
myaw frahtèllaw/myah sawrella.*

233 Where are you travelling to?
Dov'è diretto?
Dawvèh deerettaw?

234 I am/we are going to . . .
Vado/andiamo a . . .
Vahdaw/ahndyahmaw ah . . .

235 How long are you travelling
for?
Per quanto tempo sarà in
viaggio?
*Perr kwahntaw tempaw sahràh
een veehadjaw?*

236 Where do you come from?
Da dove viene?
Dah dawveh vyehneh?

237 I am/we are from . . .
Vengo/veniamo da . . .
Vehngaw/vehnyahmaw dah . . .

238 We're on holiday.
Siamo in vacanza.
Seeyahmaw een vahkahntsah.

239 This is our first visit here.
Questa è la nostra prima visita
qui.
*Kwehstah eh lah nawstrah
preemah veeseetah kwee.*

240 Would you like/May I have a
cigarette?
Vuole una sigaretta?/Potrebbe
darmi una sigaretta?
*Voohòleh oona seegahretta?/
Pawtrebbeh darrmee oona
seegahretta?*

241 I am sorry but I do not
understand.
Mi scusi, non capisco.
Mee scoozee, non cahpeescaw.

242 Please speak slowly.
La prego di parlare lentamente.
*Lah prehgaw dee parrlahreh
lentahmenteh.*

243 Do you mind if I smoke?
Le spiace se fumo?
Leh speehacheh seh foomaw?

244 Do you have a light?
Mi fa accendere?
Me fah acchendereh?

245 I am waiting for my
husband/wife/boyfriend/
girlfriend.
Sto aspettando mio marito/
moglie/fidanzato/fidanzata.
*Staw ahspehtahndaw meeaw
mahreetaw/mawiyeh/
feedahntsahtaw/feedahntsahtah.*

I
T
A
L
I
A
N

231
↕
245

TRAVELLING WITH CHILDREN

**246 Do you have a high chair/
baby-sitting service/cot?**
Ha un seggiolone/dei baby-
sitter/un lettino?
*Ah oon sedjawlawneh/day baby-
sitter/oon letteenaw?*

**247 Where is the nursery/
playroom?**
Dov'è la camera dei bambini/la
stanza dei giochi?
*Dawvèh lah cahmera day
bahmbeenee/las stantsa day
jawkee?*

**248 Where can I warm the baby's
bottle?**
Dove posso riscaldare il biberon?
*Dawveh pawssaw reescahldareh
eel beebehròn?*

COMMUNICATIONS

Post

**249 How much will it cost to send
a letter/postcard/this
package to Britain/Ireland/
America/Canada/Australia/
New Zealand?**
Qual'è la tariffa per l'invio di
una lettera/cartolina postale/di
questo pacco in Gran Bretagna/
Irlanda/America/Canada/
Australia/Nuova Zelanda?
*Kwahlèh lah tahreeffa perr
l'eenvyaw dee oona lettehra/
carrtawleena pawstahle/dee
kwehstaw pahccaw een Grahn
Brehtanya/Eerrlahnda/*

*Ahmehreeca/Cahnada/
Ahoostrahlia/Noohawva
Tsehlahnda?*

**250 I would like one stamp/two
stamps.**
Vorrei un francobollo/due
francobolli.
*Vawrray oon frahncawbawllaw/
dweh francawbawllee.*

**251 I'd like . . . stamps for
postcards to send abroad,
please.**
Vorrei . . . dei francobolli per
delle cartoline da inviare
all'estero, per favore.
*Vawrray . . . dey frahnkawbawlee
perr dehleh kahrtawleeneh dah
eenveeyahreh ahlehstehraw, perr
fahvawreh.*

Phones

**252 I would like to make a
telephone call/reverse the
charges to (make a collect call
to) . . .**
Vorrei fare una telefonata/a
carico del destinatario a . . .
*(Vawrray fahreh oona telefawnahta/
ah càhreecaw del desteenahtahryaw ah*

**253 Which coins do I need for
the telephone?**
Che monete devo usare con
quest'apparecchio?
*Keh mawnehteh dehvaw oozahreh
con kwestaw apparecckyaw?*

254 The line is engaged (busy).
La linea è occupata.
Lah leeneha èh occoopahta.

²⁵⁵ The number is . . .
Il numero è . . .
Eel noomehraw èh . . .

²⁵⁶ Hello, this is . . .
Pronto, sono . . .
Prawntaw, sawnaw . . .

²⁵⁷ May I speak to . . ?
Potrei parlare con . . . ?
Pawtray pahrlahreh kon . . ?

²⁵⁸ He/She is not in at the moment. Can you call back?
Ora non c'è. Può richiamare?
Awrrah nawn cheh. Poohòh reekyahmahreh?

MONEY

²⁵⁹ I would like to change these travellers' cheques (travelers' checks)/this currency/this Eurocheque.
Vorrei cambiare questi assegni turistici/questa valuta/questo euroassegno.
Vawrray cahmbyahreh kwestee assenee tooreesteechee/kwesta vahloota/kwestaw ehoorawassenyaw.

²⁶⁰ How much commission do you charge (What is the service charge)?
Qual'è la vostraprovvigione?
Kwalèh lah vostra prawvveejawneh?

²⁶¹ Can I obtain money with my MasterCard?
Posso incassare contanti con il Mastercard?
Pawssaw eencassahreh cawntahntee con eel Mastercard?

SHOPPING

Names of Shops and Departments

²⁶² Libreria/Cartoleria
Leebrehreeyah/Kahrtawlehreeyah
Bookshop/Stationery

²⁶³ Gioielleria/Articoli da regalo
Djaweeyehllehreeyah/Ahrteekawleedah rehgahlaw
Jeweller's/Gifts

²⁶⁴ Scarpe
Skahrpeh
Shoes

²⁶⁵ Ferramenta
Fehrrahmehntah
Hardware

²⁶⁶ Antiquario
Ahnteehkwahryaw
Antiques

²⁶⁷ Parrucchiere (per uomini)/(per donne)
Pahrrookyehreh (perr ooawmeenee) (perr dawneh)
Hairdressers (men's)/(women's)

²⁶⁸ Tabaccaio
Tahbahkaiyaw
Tobacconist

²⁶⁹ Panificio
Pahneefeechyaw
Baker's

²⁷⁰ Supermercato
Soopehrmehrkahtaw
Supermarket

ITALIAN

255
↑
270

271 Fotografo
Fotografaw
Photoshop

272 Giocattoli
Djawkahttawlee
Toys

273 Agenzia di viaggi
Ahjehntsyah dee veeyahdjee
Travel Agent

274 Articoli da toletta
Ahrteekawlee dah tawlettah
Toiletries

275 Dischi
Deeskee
Records

In the Shop

276 What time do the shops open/close?
A che ora aprono/chiudono i negozi?
Ah keh awra àhprawnaw/ kewdawnaw ee nehgotsee?

277 Where is the nearest market?
Dov'è il mercato più vicino?
Dawvèh eel mehrkahtaw pyoo veecheehnaw?

278 Can you show me the one in the window/this one?
Può mostrarmi quello in vetrina/questo?
Poohòh mawstrahrmee kwehllaw een vehtreenah/kwehstaw?

279 Can I try this on?
Posso provarlo?
Pawssaw prawvarrlaw?

280 What size is this?
Di che misura è?
Dee keh meezoora eh?

281 This is too large/too small/ too expensive.
Questo è troppo grande/troppo piccolo/troppo caro.
Kwestaw eh trawpaw grahndeh/ trawpaw peekawlaw/trawpaw kahraw.

282 Do you have any others?
Ne avete degli altri?
Neh ahvehteh delyee ahltree?

283 My size is . . .
La mia taglia è . . .
Lah meeyah tahlyah eh . . .

284 Where is the changing room/ childrens/cosmetic/ ladieswear/menswear/food department?
Dov'è lo spogliatoio/il reparto bambini/cosmetici/ abbigliamento femminile/ abbigliamento maschile/ alimentari?
Dawvèh law spawlyahtoyaw/eel rehparrtaw bahmbeenee/ cosmeteechee abbeelyahmentaw femmeeneeleh/ abbeelyahmentaw maskeeleh/ahleemehntahree?

285 I would like . . .
Vorrei . . .
Vawrray . . .

286 I would like a quarter of a kilo/half a kilo/a kilo of bread/butter/cheese/ham/tomatoes.

Vorrei due etti e mezzo/mezzo chilo/un chilo di pane/burro/formaggio/prosciutto/pomodori.

Vawrray dweh ehttee eh metsaw/metsaw keelaw/oon keelaw dee pahneh/boorraw/forrmahdjaw/prawshoottaw/pawmawdoree.

287 How much is this?

Quant'è?

Kuahntèh?

288 I'll take this one, thank you.

Prenderò questo, grazie.

Prehndehròh kwestaw, grahtsyeh.

289 Do you have a carrier (shopping) bag?

Ha un sacchetto di plastica?

Ah oon sahckettaw dee plahsteeca?

290 Do you have anything cheaper/larger/smaller/of better quality?

Ha un articolo meno caro/più grande/più piccolo/di migliore qualità?

Ah oon arrteecawlaw mehnaw cahraw/pyoo grahndeh/pyoo peeckawlaw/dee meelyawreh kwahleetàh?

291 I would like a film for this camera.

Vorrei una pellicola per questa macchina fotografica.

Vawrray oona pelleecawla perr kwesta màckeena fawtawgràhfeeca.

292 I would like some batteries, the same size as this old one.

Vorrei delle pile della stessa grandezza di quella vecchia.

Vawrray delleh peeleh della stehssah grahndetsa dee kwella veckya.

293 Would you mind wrapping this for me, please?

Le dispiacerebbe impacchett-armele?

Leh deespyahcherebbeh eempahckett-arrmehleh?

294 Sorry, but you seem to have given me the wrong change.

Scusi, si è sbagliato nel darmi il resto se non erro.

Scoozee, se eh sbahlyahtaw nel darrmee eel restaw seh non erraw.

MOTORING

Car Hire (Rental)

295 I have ordered (rented) a car in the name of . . .

Ho ordinato una vettura per . . .

Aw orrdeenahtaw oona vettoora perr . . .

296 How much does it cost to hire (rent) a car for one day/two days/one week?

Quant'è il nolo di una vettura per un giorno/due giorni/una settimana?

Kwahntèh eel nawlaw dee oona vettoora perr oon jornaw/dweh joornee/oona setteemahna?

297 Is the tank already full of petrol (gas)?

Il serbatoio è pieno di benzina?

Eel serbahtoyaw èh pyehnaw dee bentseena?

298 Is insurance and tax included? How much is the deposit?

L'assicurazione e l'imposta sono comprese? Quant'è la caparra?

Lasseecoorahtsyawne eh leempawsta sawnaw cawmprehseh? Kwahnteh lah cahparra?

299 By what time must I return the car?

A che ora devo ritornare la vettura?

Ah keh awra devaw reetornnahreh lah vettoora?

300 I would like a small/family car with a radio/cassette player.

Vorrei una piccola vettura/una familiare con radio/mangianastri.

Vawrray oona peeccawla vettoora/ oona fahmeelyareh con rahdyaw/ mahnjanastree.

Asking the Way

301 Excuse me, can you help me please?

Mi scusi, può aiutarmi per favore?

Mee scoozee, poohòh ahyiootahrmee, perr fahvawreh?

302 How do I reach the motorway/main road?

Come si arriva all'autostrada/

strada principale?

Cawmeh see ahrreevah alahootawstrahdah/strahdah preencheepahleh?

303 I think I have taken the wrong turning.

Penso di aver preso la svolta sbagliata.

Pehnsaw dee avehr prehsaw lah svawltah sbahlyahtah.

304 I am looking for this address.

Sto cercando questo indirizzo.

Staw cherkahndaw kwestaw eendeereetsaw.

305 I am looking for the . . . hotel.

Sto cercando l'hotel . . .

Staw cherkahndaw lotehl . . .

306 How far is it to . . . from here?

Quanto dista . . . da qui?

Kwantaw deestah . . . dah kwee?

307 Carry straight on for . . . kilometres.

Vada dritto per . . . chilometri.

Vahdah dreetaw perr . . . .keehlawmehtree.

308 Take the next turning on the right/left.

Prenda la prossima svolta a destra/sinistra.

Prehndah lah prawseehmah svawltah ah dehstrah/seeneestrah.

309 Turn right/left at the next crossroads/traffic lights.

Giri a destra/sinistra al prossimo incrocio/semaforo.

Djyree ah dehstrah/seeneestrah ahl prawseemaw eencrawchyaw/ sehmahfawraw.

I
T
A
L
I
A
N

297
↕
309

MOTORING

³¹⁰ You are going in the wrong
direction.
Sta andando nella direzione
sbagliata.
*Stah ahndahndaw nehllah
deerehtsyawneh sbahlyahtah.*

Parking

³¹¹ How long can I park here?
Per quanto tempo posso
parcheggiare qui?
*Pehr kwantaw tehmpaw payssaw
pahrkehdjahreh kwee?*

³¹² Is there a car park near here?
C'è un parcheggio da queste
parti?
*Cheh oon pahrkehdjaw dah
kwesteh pahrtee?*

³¹³ At what time does this car
park close?
A che ora chiude il parcheggio?
*Ah keh awrah keeyoodeh eel
pahrkehdjaw?*

Signs and Notices

³¹⁴ Senso unico.
Sehnsaw ooneekaw.
One way.

³¹⁵ Divieto di accesso.
Deeveeyehtaw dee ahchehssaw.
No entry.

³¹⁶ Divieto di sosta.
Deeveeyehtaw dee sawstah.
No parking.

³¹⁷ Deviazione
Dehveeyahtsyawneh.
Detour (diversion

³¹⁸ Stop.
Stop.
Stop.

³¹⁹ Dare precedenza.
Dahreh prehchehdehntsah.
Give way (yield).

³²⁰ Strada sdrucciolevole.
Strahdah sdroocheeyawlehvawleh.
Slippery road.

³²¹ Divieto di sorpasso.
Deeveeyehtaw áee sawrpahssaw.
No overtaking.

At the Filling Station

³²² Unleaded (lead-free)/
Standard/Premium
Carburante senza piombo/
normale/super
*Kahrboorahnteh sehntsah
peeyawmbaw/nawrmahleh/soopehrr*

³²³ Fill the tank please.
Il pieno, per favore.
Eel peeyehnaw perr fahvawreh.

³²⁴ Do you have a road map of
this area?
Avete una carta stradale di
quest'area?
*Ahvehteh oonah kahrtah
strahdahleh dee kwestahreyah?*

³²⁵ How much is the car-wash?
Quanto costa l'autolavaggio?
*Kwahntaw kawstah
lahootawlahvahdjyoh.*

Breakdowns

³²⁶ I've had a breakdown at . . .
Ho avuto un guasto a . . .

Haw ahvootaw oon gwastaw
ah . . .

327 I am on the road from . . . to . . .
Sono sulla strada da . . . a . . .
*Sawnaw soollah strahdah
dah . . . ah . . .*

328 I can't move the car. Can
you send a tow-truck?
Non posso spostare l'auto.
Potrebbe mandare un carro
attrezzi?
*Nawn pawssaw spawstahreh
lahootaw. Pawtrebbeh
mahndahreh oon kahrraw
ahtretzee?*

329 I have a flat tyre.
Ho una ruota a terra.
Haw oonah rooawtah ah tehrrah.

330 The windscreen (windshield)
has smashed/cracked.
Il parabrezza si è sfondato/
incrinato.
*Eel pahrahbretzah see eh
sfawndahtaw/eenkreenahtaw.*

331 There is something wrong
with the engine/brakes/
lights/steering/gearbox/
clutch/exhaust.
C'è qualcosa che non va con il
motore/i freni/le luci/lo sterzo/
il cambio/la frizione/lo scarico.
*Cheh kwahlkawsah keh nawn vah
kawn eel mawtawreh/ee frehnee/
leh loochee/law stehrtsaw/eel
kahmbeeyaw/lah freetsyawneh/
law skahreehkaw.*

332 It's overheating.
E' surriscaldato.

Eh soorreeskahldhataw.

333 It won't start.
Non parte.
Nawn pahrteh.

334 Where can I get it repaired?
Dove posso ripararla?
Dawveh pawssaw reepahrarlah?

335 Can you take me there?
Mi ci potrebbe accompagnare?
*Mee chee pawtrebbeh
ahkawmpahnyareh?*

336 Will it take long to fix?
Ci vorrà molto tempo per
ripararla?
*Chee vawrràh mawltaw
tehmpaw perr reepahrahrlah?*

337 How much will it cost?
Quanto mi costerà?
Kwantaw mee kawstehràh?

Accidents

338 Can you help me? There has
been an accident.
Potrebbe aiutarmi? C'è stato un
incidente.
*Pawtrebbeh ahyiootahrmee? Cheh
stahtaw oon eencheedehnteh.*

339 Please call the police/an
ambulance.
Per favore, chiami la polizia/
un'ambulanza.
*Perr fahvawreh keeyahmee lah
pawleetseeyah/oonamboolahntsah.*

340 Is anyone hurt?
Ci sono feriti?
Chee sawnaw fehreetee?

ITALIAN

327
↕
340

MOTORING/HEALTH

Traffic Offences

³⁴¹ I'm sorry, I didn't see the sign.
Mi scusi, non ho visto il cartello.
Mee scoozee, nawn haw veestaw eel kahrtehllaw.

³⁴² Must I pay a fine? How much?
Devo pagare una multa? Quant'è?
Dehvaw pahgareh oonah mooltah? Kwantèh?

³⁴³ Show me your documents.
Mi mostri i documenti.
Mee mawstree ee dawcoomehntee.

HEALTH

Pharmacy

³⁴⁴ Do you have anything for a stomachache/headache/sore throat/toothache?
Ha un preparato per il mal di stomaco/mal di testa/mal di gola/mal di denti?
Ah oon prehpahrahtaw perr eel mahl dee stohmahcaw/mahl dee testa/mahl dee gawla/mahl dee dehntee?

³⁴⁵ I need something for diarrhoea (diarrhea)/constipation/a cold/a cough/insect bites/sunburn/travel (motion) sickness.
Ho bisogno di un rimedio per la diarrea/la stitichezza/il raffreddore/la tosse/le punture di insetti/l'eritema solare/il mal di viaggio.
Aw beesawnyaw dee oon reemehdyaw perr lah dyahrreha/lah steeteeketsa/eel rahffredawreh/lah tawsseh/leh poontooreh dee eensehttee/lehreetehma sawlahreh/eel mahl dee vyahdjaw.

³⁴⁶ How much/how many do I take?
Quanto/quanti ne devo prendere?
Kwahntaw/kwahntee neh dehvaw préndereh?

³⁴⁷ How often do I take it/them?
Ogni quanto devo prenderlo/prenderli?
Awnee kwahntaw dehvaw prenderrlaw/prenderrlee?

³⁴⁸ How much does it cost?
Quanto costa?
Kwahntaw cawsta?

³⁴⁹ Can you recommend a good doctor/dentist?
Può raccomandarmi un buon medico/dentista?
Poohò rhaccawmahndarrmee oon boohòn méhdeecaw/denteesta?

³⁵⁰ Is it suitable for children?
È adatto per i bambini?
Èh ahdahttaw perr ee bahmbeenee?

Doctor

³⁵¹ I have a pain here/in my arm/leg/chest/stomach.
Ho un dolore qui/nel braccio/

nella gamba/nel petto/nello stamco.

Aw oon dawlawreh kwee/nel bracchaw/nella gahmba/nel pettaw/nellaw stohmahcaw.

352 Please call a doctor, this is an emergency.

La prego di chiamare un medico. È un'emergenza.

Lah prehgaw dee kyahmahreh oon mèdeecaw. Èh oonemerrgentsa.

353 I would like to make an appointment to see a doctor.

Vorrei prendere un appuntamento con un medico.

Vawrray prendehre oon ahppoontahmentaw con oon mèdeecaw.

354 I am diabetic/pregnant.

Sono diabetica/incinta.

Sawnaw dyahbèhteeca/eencheenta.

355 I need a prescription for . . .

Ho bisogno di una ricetta per . . .

Aw beesohnyaw dee oona reechetta perr . . .

356 Can you give me something to ease the pain.

Può prescrivermi qualcosa che allevii il dolore?

Poohòh prehscreeverrmee kwahlcawsa keh allevee eel dawlawreh?

357 I am/he is/she is allergic to penicillin.

Sono/egli è/ella è allergico (masc.)/allergica (fem.) alla penicillina.

Sawnaw/ehlyee eh/ehlah eh

allehrjeekaw/allehrjeekah ahlah pehneecheeleenah.

358 Does this hurt?

Questo fa male?

Kwestaw fah mahleh?

359 You must/he must/she must go to hospital.

Lei deve/egli deve/ella deve andare in ospedale.

Ley dehveh/ehlyee dehveh/ehlah dehveh ahndahreh een awspehdahleh.

360 Take these once/twice/three times a day.

Prenda queste una volta/due volte/tre volte al giorno.

Prehndah kwesteh oonah vawltah/dooweh vawlteh/treh vawlteh ahl djeeyawrnaw.

361 I am/he is/she is taking this medication.

Sto/egli sta/ella sta prendendo questa medicina.

Staw/ehlyee stah/ehlah stah prehndehndaw kwestah mehdeecheenah.

362 I have medical insurance.

Ho un'assicurazione medica.

Haw oonahseekoorahtsyawneh mehdeekah.

Dentist

363 I have toothache.

Ho mal di denti.

Aw mahl dee dentee.

HEALTH/EMERGENCIES

364 **My filling has come out.**
È uscita l'otturazione.
Èh oosheeta lawttoorahtsyawneh.

365 **I do/do not want to have an injection first.**
Voglio/non voglio l'anestetico.
Vawlyaw/non vawlyaw lahnestehteecaw.

EMERGENCIES

366 **Help!**
Aiuto!
Ahyootaw!

367 **Call an ambulance/a doctor/ the police!**
Chiamate un'ambulanza/un medico/la polizia!
Kyahmahteh oon ahmboolahntsa/ oon mehdeecaw/la pawleetsya!

368 **I have had my travellers' cheques (travelers' checks)/ credit cards/purse/handbag/ rucksack (knapsack)/ luggage/wallet stolen.**
Mi hanno rubato gli assegni turistici/le carte di credito/il borsellino/la borsetta/lo zaino/ il bagaglio/il portafoglio.
Mee annaw roobahtaw lee assenee tooreesteechee/leh carrteh dee crédeetaw/eel borrsellenaw/lah borrsetta/law tsaheenaw/eel bahgalyaw/eel porrtafawlyaw.

369 **Can you help me, I have lost my daughter/son?**
Può aiutarmi? Ho perduto mia figlia/mio figlio.
Poohòh ahyootarrmee? Aw perrdootaw myah feelya/myaw feelyaw.

370 **Please go away/leave me alone.**
Se ne vada/mi lasci in pace!
Seh neh vahda/me lahshee een pahcheh!

371 **Fire!**
Al fuoco!
Ahl fooawcaw!

372 **I want to contact the British/American/ Canadian/Irish/Australian/ New Zealand/South African consulate.**
Voglio contattare il consolato britannico/americano/canadese/ irlandese/australiano/ neozelandese/sudafricano.
Vawlyaw kawn!attahreh eel kawnsawlahtaw breetahnneekaw/ ahmehreekahnaw/kahnahdehseh/ eerlahndehseh/ ahoostrahleeyahnaw/ nehawzehlahndehseh/ soodahfrikahnaw.

Introduction

Polish is a Slavic tongue and therefore related to Russian, Czech and many other Eastern European languages. English is spoken to some extent in larger cities, particularly by younger people, though older inhabitants are more likely to speak German or French as a second language. Russian is understood but unpopular.

P
O
L
I
S
H

Addresses for travel and tourist information

Australia: *Embassy,* 7 Turrana St, Yarrahumla ACT, 2600 Canberra; tel: (6) 273 1208/11.
Canada: *Embassy,* 443 Daly Ave, Ontario, K1N 6H3; tel: (613) 789 1468.
New Zealand: *Commercial Counsellor,* 17 Upland Rd, Kelburn, Wellington; tel: (4) 471 2456.
South Africa: *Embassy,* 14 Amos St, Colbyn, Pretoria 0083; tel: (12) 432 631.
UK: *Polish Tourism Centre,* POSK Building, 238–246 King Street, London, W6 ORF; tel: (020) 8741 5541.
USA: *AMTA Americans Travel Abroad,* Apt 1120, 250 West 57th Street, Broadway, New York, 10107; tel: (212) 586 5230.

ESSENTIALS

ESSENTIALS

Alphabet

A	B
ah	*bey*
C	D
tsey	*dey*
E	F
ey	*ef*
G	H
gye	*hah*
I	J
ea	*yot*
K	L
kah	*el*
M	N
em	*en*
O	P
oh	*pey*
Q	R
koo	*air*
S	T
es	*tey*
U	V
oo	*fow*
W	X
voo	*iks*
Y	Z
eegrec	*zet*

Basic Words and Phrases

1 **Yes**   **No**
Tak   nie
Tak   *nye*

2 **Please**   **Thank you**
Proszę   Dziękuję
Proshem   *Jenkooyem*

3 **That's O.K.**   **Perhaps**
To jest O.K.   Może
Toe yest O.K.   *Mozhe*

4 **To**   **From**
Do   Z
Doe   Z

5 **Here**   **There**
Tu   Tam
Too   *Tam*

6 **None**   **Also**
Nic   Także
Neets   *Takzhe*

7 **How**   **When**
Jak   Kiedy
Yak   *Kyedy*

8 **What**   **Why**
Co   Dlaczego
Tso   *Dlachego*

9 **I don't understand.**
Nie rozumiem
Nye rhozoomyem

10 **I don't speak Polish.**
Nie mówię po polsku.
Nye movyem po polsku.

11 **Do you speak English?**
Czy pan (pani) mówi po
angielsku?

01
↑
11

Chi pan (pani) movee po angielskoo?

12 **Can you please write it down?**
Proszę napisać.
Proshem napisach.

13 **Can you please speak more slowly?**
Proszę mówić wolniej.
Proshem moveech volnyey.

14 **How much does it/this cost?**
Ile to kosztuje?
Eele to koshtooye?

Days

15 **Monday** / **Tuesday**
Poniedziałek / Wtorek
Poniejawek / *Vtorek*

16 **Wednesday** / **Thursday**
Środa / Czwartek
Shroda / *Chvartek*

17 **Friday** / **Saturday**
Piątek / Sobota
Pyontek / *Sobota*

18 **Sunday** / **Morning**
Niedziela / Rano
Niejela / *Rano*

19 **Afternoon** / **Evening**
Po południu / Wieczór
Po powoodnyoo / *Vyechoor*

20 **Night** / **Week**
Noc / Tydzień
Nots / *Tyjen*

21 **Yesterday/Today/Tomorrow**
Wczoraj/Dzisiaj/Jutro
Vchoray/Jishyay/Yootro

Numbers

22 **Zero** / **One**
Zero / Jeden
Zero / *Yeden*

23 **Two** / **Three**
Dwa / Trzy
Dva / *Tshee*

24 **Four** / **Five**
Cztery / Pięć
Chteree / *Pyench*

25 **Six** / **Seven**
Sześć / Siedem
Sheshch / *Siedem*

26 **Eight** / **Nine**
Osiem / Dziewięć
Oshem / *Dzieviench*

27 **Ten** / **Eleven**
Dziesięć / Jedenaście
Jeshench / *Yedenashchiem*

28 **Twelve** / **Thirteen**
Dwanaście / Trzynaście
Dvanashchiem / *Tsheenashchiem*

29 **Fourteen** / **Fifteen**
Czternaście / Piętnaście
Chternashchiem / *Pyentnashchiem*

30 **Sixteen** / **Seventeen**
Szesnaście / Siedemnaście
Shesnasschiem / *Shiedemnashchiem*

31 **Eighteen** / **Nineteen**
Osiemnaście / Dziewiętnaście
Oshemnashchiem / *Jevietnashchiem*

P
O
L
I
S
H

12
↑
31

ESSENTIALS

32 Twenty
Dwadzieścia
Dvajeshshchia

Twenty-one
Dwadzieścia jeden
Dvajeshchia yeden

33 Twenty-two
Dwadzieścia dwa
Dvajeshchia dva

Thirty
Trzydzieści
Tsheejeshchee

34 Forty
Czterdzieści
Chterjeshchee

Fifty
Pięćdziesiąt
Pyenjeshiont

35 Sixty
Sześćdziesiąt
Sheshjeshiont

Seventy
Siedemdziesiąt
Shiedemjesiont

36 Eighty
Osiemdziesiąt
Osiemjeshiont

Ninety
Dziewięćdziesiąt
Jevienjeshiont

37 One hundred
Sto
Sto

Five hundred
Pięćset
Pyenchset

38 One thousand
Tysiąc
Tyshionc

One million
Milion
Million

Time

39 9.00
Dziewiąta
Jevionta

40 9.05
Dziewiąta pięć
Jevionta pyench

41 9.10
Dziewiąta dziesięć
Jevionta jeshench

42 9.15
Dziewiąta piętnaście
Jevionta pyentnashchiem

43 9.20
Dziewiąta dwadzieścia
Jevionta dvajeshchia

44 9.25
Dziewiąta dwadzieścia pięć
Jevionta dvajeshchia piench

45 9.30
Dziewiąta trzydzieści
Jevionta tsheejeshchee

46 9.35
Dziewiąta trzydzieści pięć
Jevionta tsheejeshchee pyench.

47 9.40
Dziewiąta czterdzieści
Jevionta chterjeshchee

48 9.45
Dziewiąta czterdzieści pięć
Jevionta chterjeshchee pyench.

49 9.50
Dziewiąta pięćdziesiąt
Jevionta pyenjeshiont

50 9.55
Dziewiąta pięćdziesiąt pięć
Jevionta pyenjeshiont pyench

51 12.00/Midday/Midnight
Dwunasta/Południe/Północ
Dvoonasta/Powoodnye/Poownots

52 What time is it?
Która godzina?
Ktoora gojeena?

53 It is . . .
Jest . . .
Yest . . .

ARRIVING AND DEPARTING

Airport

54 **Excuse me, where is the check-in desk for . . . airline?**
Przepraszam, gdzie jest stanowisko linii . . ?
Psheyprasham, gje yest stanovizko leenyi . . ?

55 **What is the boarding gate/ time for my flight?**
Gdzie jest wyjście na/O której jest . . . mój lot?
Gje yest veeyshche na/o ktoorey yest . . . mooy lot?

56 **How long is the delay likely to be?**
Jakie będzie opóźnienie?
Yakhe benjeh opoozhnyenye?

57 **Where is the duty-free shop?**
Gdzie jest sklep wolno-cłowy
Gje yest sklep volnoh-tzlovy?

58 **Which way is the baggage reclaim?**
Gdzie jest odbiór bagażu?
Gje yest odbyoor bagazhoo?

59 **Where can I get the bus to the city centre?**
Gdzie jest autobus do centrum?
Gje yest owtohbus do tzentrum?

Train Station

60 **Where is the ticket office/ information desk?**
Gdzie jest kasa/informacja?

Gje yest kasa/informatsya?

61 **Which platform does the train to . . . depart from?**
Z którego peronu odchodzi pociąg do . . ?
Z ktoorego peronu odhojee pochiong do . . ?

62 **Where is platform . . ?**
Gdzie jest peron . . ?
Gje yest peron . . ?

63 **When is the next train to . . ?**
Kiedy odchodzi następny pociąg do . . ?
Kyedy odhojee nastempny pociong do . . ?

64 **Is there a later train to . . ?**
Czy jest późniejszy pociąg do . . ?
Chi jest poozhnieyshee pociong do . . ?

Port

65 **How do I get to the port?**
Jak się dostać do portu?
Yak siem dostach doh portoo?

66 **When is the next sailing to . . ?**
Kiedy odchodzi następny prom do . . ?
Kyedy odhojee nastempny prom doh . . ?

67 **Can I catch an earlier ferry with this ticket?**
Czy ten bilet jest ważny na wcześniejszy prom?
Chi ten beelet yest vazhnee na wchesnyeyshi prom?

P
O
L
I
S
H

54
↑
67

207

ARRIVING AND DEPARTING

Notices and Signs

68 Wagon restauracyjny
Vagon restauratsiny
Buffet (Dining) Car

69 Autobus
Owtoboos
Bus

70 Woda pitna/nie do picia
Voda pitna/nye do pitcha
Drinking/Non-drinking water

71 Wejście
Veishchye
Entrance

72 Wyjście
Veeyshchye
Exit

73 Informacja
Informatsya
Information

74 Przechowalnia bagażu
Pshehovalnya bagazhoo
Left Luggage (Baggage Claim)

75 Schowki na bagaż
S'hovky na bagazh
Luggage Lockers

76 Poczta
Pochta
Post Office

77 Peron
Peron
Platform

78 Dworzec kolejowy
Dvozhets koleyovy
Railway (Railroad) Station

79 Port lotniczy
Port lotneechi
Airport

80 Port
Port
Port

81 Restauracja
Restauratsya
Restaurant

82 Dla palących/niepalących
Dla palontsyh/nyepalontsych
Smoking/Non-Smoking

83 Telefon
Telefon
Telephone

84 Kasa biletowa
Kasa biletova
Ticket Office

85 Odprawa
Odprava
Check-in Desk

86 Rozkład jazdy
Rozkwad yazdy
Timetable (Schedule)

87 Toalety
Toalety
Toilets (Restrooms)

88 Mężczyźni
Menzhtchyzni
Gentlemen

89 Dla kobiet
Dla kobyet
Ladies'

90 Tramwaj
Tramvay
Tram (Streetcar)

91 Metro
Metro
Underground (Subway)

92 Poczekalnia
Potchekalnya
Waiting room

Buying a Ticket

93 I would like a first-class/
second-class single (one-
way)/return (round-trip)
ticket to . . .
Proszę o bilet pierwszej klasy/
drugiej klasy w jedną stronę/
powrotny do . . .
*Proshe o bilet pyervshey/droogyey
klasy v yednom strone/povrotny
doh . . .*

94 Is my rail pass valid on this
train/ferry/bus?
Czy ten bilet ważny jest na ten
pociąg/prom/autobus?
*Chi ten beelet yest vazhnee nah ten
pochong/prom/owtohbus?*

95 I would like an aisle/window
seat.
Proszę o miejsce przy przejściu/
oknie.
*Proshe o mieystse pshee
psheyshchu/oknye.*

96 No smoking/smoking, please.
Palenie wzbronione/
dozwolone.

Palenye vzbronione/dozvolone.

97 We would like to sit
together.
Chcemy siedzieć razem.
Htsemy shiejech razem.

98 I would like to make a seat
reservation.
Chcę zamówić miejscówkę
*Htsem zahmooveech myeys-
tsoovkeh.*

99 I would like to reserve a
couchette/sleeper for one
person/two people/for my
family.
Chcę zarezerwować kuszetkę/
miejsce sypialne dla jednej
osoby/dwóch osób/rodziny.
*Hcem zarezervovach kooshetkem/
mieystse sipyalne dla yedney
osoby/dvooh osoob/rojiny.*

100 I would like to reserve a
cabin.
Chcę zamówić kabinę.
Htsem zahmooveech cabin-eh.

Timetables (Schedules)

101 Przyjazd
Pshiyazd
Arrive

102 Zatrzymuje się w
Zatzhimuye shiem v
Calls (Stops) at

103 Usługi gastronomiczne
Uswoogy gastronomichne
Catering Service

POLISH

90
↑
103

ARRIVING AND DEPARTING

104 Przesiadka w
Psheshadka v
Change at

105 Połączenie
Powonchenye
Connection

106 Codziennie
Tsojennye
Daily

107 Co 40 minut
Tso 40 minut
Every 40 Minutes

108 Pierwsza klasa
Pyervsha klasa
First-class

109 Co godzinę
Tso gojinem
Hourly

110 Zaleca się rezerwację miejsc
Zaletsa shiem rezervatsye mieysts
Seat reservations are recommended

111 Druga klasa
Drooga klasa
Second-class

112 Dodatkowa opłata
Dodatkova opwata
Supplement Payable

113 Przez
Pshez
Via

Luggage

114 How much will it cost to send (ship) my luggage in advance?
Ile kosztuje nadanie rzeczy na bagaż?
Eele koshtooye nadanye zhechi na bagazh?

115 Where is the left luggage (baggage claim) office?
Gdzie jest przechowalnia bagażu?
Gje jest pshehovalnya bagazhoo?

116 What time do you open/close?
O której otwieracie/zamykacie?
O ktoorey otvyerachie/zamykachie?

117 Where are the luggage trolleys (carts)?
Gdzie są wózki bagażowe?
Gje som voozky bagazhove?

118 Where are the lockers?
Gdzie są schowki?
Gje som s-hovkee?

119 I have lost my locker key.
Zgubiłem klucz do schowka.
Zgoobiwem klooch do s'hovka.

On Board

120 Is this seat taken?
Czy to miejsce jest wolne?
Chi to mieystse yest volne?

121 Excuse me, you are sitting in my reserved seat.
Przepraszam, to jest moje

zarezerwowane miejsce.
*Psheprasham, toe yest moye
zarezervovane mieystse.*

122 Which station is this?
Jaka to stacja?
Yaka to statsya?

**123 What time is this train/bus/
ferry/flight due to arrive/
depart?**
O której przyjeżdża/odjeżdża
pociąg/autobus/prom? (O
której jest przylot/odlot?)
*O ktoorey pshijezdzha/odyezdzha
pochong/owtohbus/prom? (O
ktoorey yest pshillot/odlot?)*

**124 Will you wake me just before
we arrive?**
Proszę mnie zbudzić przed
przyjazdem.
*Proshem mnye zbujeech pshed
pshyiazdem.*

Customs and Passports

125 Proszę o paszporty!
Proshem o pashporty!
Passports, please!

**126 I have nothing/wine/spirits
(alcohol)/tobacco to declare.**
Nie mam do zgłoszenia
niczego/wina/alkoholu/tytoniu.
*Nye mam doe zgwoshenya
nichego/vina/alkoholu/titonyoo.*

**127 I shall be staying for . . .
days/weeks/months.**
Będę tu . . . dni/tygodni/
miesięcy.

*Bendem too . . . dnee/tygodnee/
miesyentsy.*

AT THE TOURIST OFFICE

**128 Do you have a map of the
town/area?**
Czy macie plan miasta/rejonu?
Chi matsie plan miasta/reyonoo?

**129 Can I reserve accommodation
here?**
Czy mogę tutaj zarezerwować
zakwaterowanie?
*Chi mogem tutay zarezerovovach
zakvaterovanye?*

**130 Do you have a list of
accommodation?**
Gdzie można się zatrzymać?
Gje mozhna sheh zahtcheemach?

ACCOMMODATION

Hotels

**131 I have a reservation in the
name of . . .**
Mam rezerwację na
nazwisko . . .
Mam rezervatsyem na nazvisko . . .

**132 I wrote to/faxed/telephoned
you last month/last week in . . .**
Pisałem(am)/faxowałem(am)/
telefonowałem(am) w zeszłym
miesiącu/zeszłego tygodnia/w . . .
*Peesawem(am)/faxovawem(am)/
telefonovawem(am) v zeshweem
myeshontzoo/zeshwego teegodnya/
v . . .*

**P
O
L
I
S
H**

122
↑
132

211

ACCOMMODATION

133 Do you have any rooms free?
Czy są wolne pokoje?
Chi som wolneh pokoye?

134 I would like to reserve a single/double room with/ without bath/shower.
Chcę zarezerwować pokój pojedynczy/podwójny, z łazienką/prysznicem, bez łazienki/prysznicu.
Htsem zarezervovach pokooy poyedynchy/podvooyny, z wazienkom/pryshnitsem/bez wazienki/pryshnicoo.

135 I would like bed and breakfast/(room and) half board/(room and) full board.
Chcę pokój ze śniadaniem/z dwoma posiłkami/zpełnym wyżywieniem.
Hcem pokooy ze sniadanyem/z dvoma poshiwkamy/z pewnym vizhivyenyem.

136 How much is it per night?
Ile kosztuje jedna noc?
Eele koshtooye yedna nots?

137 Is breakfast included?
Czy jest w to wliczone śniadanie?
Chi yest v to vlichoney shniadanye?

138 May I see the room?
Czy mogę zobaczyć ten pokój?
Chi mogem zobachich ten pokooy?

139 Do you have any cheaper rooms?

Czy macie tańsze pokoje?
Chi machie tanishe pokoje?

140 I would like to take the room
Wezmę ten pokój.
Vezmem ten pokooy.

141 I would like to stay for . . . nights.
Chcę się zatrzymać na . . . nocy.
Htsem shiem zatzhimach na . . . notsy.

142 The shower/light/tap doesn't work.
Prysznic/światło/kran nie działa.
Prishnitz/shvyawo/kran nye dzhawa.

143 At what time/where is breakfast served?
O której godzinie/gdzie jest śniadanie?
O ktoorey gojeenye/gje yest shnyadanye?

144 What time do I have to check-out?
O której godzinie mam opróżnić pokój?
O ktoorey gojeenye mam oproozhnich pokooy?

145 Can I have the key to room no . . ?
Proszę o klucz do pokoju numer . . .
Proshem o klooch doh pokoyoo noomer . . .

146 My room number is . . .
Numer mojego pokoju jest . . .

212

Noomer moyego pokoyoo yest . . .

147 Do you accept travellers' cheques/Eurocheques/credit cards?

Czy przyjmujecie czeki podróżne/Euroczeki/karty kredytowe?

Chi pshiymuyecheh chekee podroozhne/Eurochekee/karti kreditoveh?

148 May I have the bill please.

Proszę o rachunek.

Proshem o rahoonek.

149 Excuse me, I think there is a mistake in this bill.

Przepraszam, wydaje mi się, że jest pomyłka w rachunku.

Psheprasham, veedayeh me sheh, zhe yest pomiwka w rahoonkoo.

Youth Hostels

150 How much is a dormitory bed per night?

Ile kosztuje łóżko we wspólnej sypialni, na jedną noc?

Eele koshtooye woozhko ve vspoolney sypyalnee, na yednom nots?

151 I am/am not an HI member.

Należę/nie należę do HI.

Nalezhem/nye nalezhem do hah, ea.

152 May I use my own sleeping bag?

Czy mogę używać własny śpiwór?

Chi mogem uzhivach vwasny shpivoor?

153 What time do you lock the doors at night?

O której zamykacie drzwi na noc?

O ktoorey zamykatsye djvee na nots?

Camping

154 May I camp here for the night/two nights?

Czy mogę się tu kampingować przez jedną noc/dwie noce?

Chi mogem too kampingovach pshes jednom nots/dvye notse?

155 Where can I pitch my tent?

Gdzie mogę rozbić namiot?

Gje mogem rozbich namyot?

156 How much does it cost for one night/week?

Ile wynosi opłata za jedną noc/za tydzień?

Eele vynoshi opwata za yednom nots/za tyjyen?

157 Where can we park our caravan?

Gdzie możemy postawić przyczepę?

Gje mozhemi postaveech pshichepeh?

158 Where are the washing facilities?

Gdzie można się umyć?

Gje mozhna shem oomych?

P
O
L
I
S
H

147
↕
158

159 Is there a restaurant/ supermarket/swimming pool on site/nearby?

Czy jest na miejscu/w pobliżu restauracja/supersam/basen kąpielowy?

Chi yest na mieystsu/v poblizhoo restauratsya/supersam/basen kompielovy?

160 Do you have a safety deposit box?

Czy jest tu sejf?

Chi yest too seyf?

Cafés and Bars

161 I would like a cup of/two cups of/another coffee/tea.

Proszę o jedną/dwie/jeszcze jedną kawę/herbatę.

Proshem o yednom/dvye/yeshche yednom kavem/herbatem.

162 With/without milk/sugar.

Z mlekiem/bez mleka/z cukrem/bez cukru.

Z mlekyem/bez mleka/z tsukrem/ bez tsookroo.

163 I would like a bottle/glass/ two glasses of mineral water/ red wine/white wine, please.

Proszę o butelkę/szklankę/dwie szklanki wody mineralnej/ czerwonego wina/białego wina.

Proshem o bootelkem/shklankem/ dvye shklankee vody mineralney/ chervonego vina/biawego vina.

164 I would like a beer/two beers, please.

Proszę o piwo/dwa piwa.

Proshem o pivo/dva piva.

165 May I have some ice?

Proszę o lód.

Proshem o lood.

166 Do you have any matches/ cigarettes/cigars?

Czy są zapałki/papierosy/ cygara?

Chi som zapawki/papyerosy/ tsygara?

Restaurants

167 Can you recommend a good/ inexpensive restaurant in this area?

Czy możecie mi polecić dobrą/ niedrogą restaurację w pobliżu?

Chi mozheche me polechich dobrom/nyedrogom restauratsye v poblizhoo?

168 I would like a table for . . . people.

Proszę o stolik dla . . . osób.

Proshem o stolik dla . . . osoob.

169 Do you have a non-smoking area?

Czy są miejsca dla niepalących?

Chi som myeystsa dla nyepalontzeeh?

170 Waiter/Waitress!

Kelner/Kelnerka!

Kelner/Kelnerka!

171 Do you have a set menu/
children's menu/wine list?

Czy mogę prosić o zestaw potraw/
menu dla dzieci/listę win?

*Chi mogem proshich o zestav
potrav/menu dla jechee/listem vin?*

172 Do you have any vegetarian
dishes, please?

Czy są dania jarskie?

Chi som danya yarskye?

173 Are there any local
specialities?

Czy są jakieś specjalności lokalne?

*Chi som jakyesh
spetzyahlnoshchee lokalneh?*

174 Are vegetables included?

Czy to razem z jarzynami?

Chi toh razem z yazhinyamee?

175 Could I have it well-cooked/
medium/rare please?

Poproszę wysmażone dobrze/
średnio/czerwone.

*Poproshem vysmazhoneh dobzeh/
shrednyo/chervoneh.*

176 What does this dish consist of?

Co to za potrawa?

Tso toe za potrava?

177 I would like the set menu,
please.

Proszę o zestaw potraw.

Proshem o zestav potrav.

178 We have not been served yet.

Nie obsłużono nas jeszcze.

Nye obswoozhono nas yeshche.

179 Excuse me, this is not what I
ordered.

Przeparaszam, nie to
zamówiłem(am).

*Pshephrasham, nye to
zamooviwem(am).*

180 May I have some bread/
water/coffee/tea?

May I have some more
bread/water/coffee/tea?

Proszę o chleb/wodę/kawę/
herbatę?

Proszę o więcej chleba/wody/
kawy/herbaty?

*Proshem o hleb/vodem/kavem/
herbatem?*

*Proshem o vyentzey hleba/vodee/
kavee/herbatee?*

181 May I have the bill, please?

Proszę o rachunek.

Proshem o rahoonek.

182 Does this bill include service?

Czy jest w to wliczona obsługa?

Chi yest v toe vlichona obswooga?

183 Do you accept travellers'
cheques (travelers' checks)/
Eurocheques/MasterCard/US
dollars?

Czy przyjmujecie czeki
podróżne/Euroczeki/
MasterCard/dolary USA?

*Chi pshiymooyechie cheky
podroozhne/Eurocheky/
MasterCard/ dolary USA?*

184 Can I have a receipt, please?

Pokwitowanie poproszę

Pokveetovanye poproshem.

GETTING AROUND

185 Where is the toilet
(restroom), please?
Gdzie jest toaleta?
Gje yest toaleta?

On the Menu

186 First courses
Pierwsze dania
Pyerwshe danya

187 Soups
Zupy
Zoopi

188 Main courses
Główne dania
Gwoowneh danyah

189 Fish dishes
Dania rybne
Danya ribneh

190 Meat dishes
Dania mięsne
Danya myensneh

191 Vegetarian dishes
Dania jarskie
Danya yarskye

192 Cheese
Ser
Ser

193 Desserts
Desery
Desseree

194 Specialities
Specjalności
Specyalnoshchee

GETTING AROUND

Public Transport

195 Where is the bus stop/coach
station/nearest metro
(subway) station?
Gdzie jest przystanek
autobusowy/dworzec
autobusowy/najbliższa stacja
metra?
*Gje yest pshystanek autoboosovy/
dworzec autobusowy/najblizhsha
statsya metra?*

196 When is the next/last bus
to . . ?
Kiedy odchodzi następny/
ostatni autobus do . . ?
*Kyedy odhojee ostatnee autoboos
doh . . ?*

197 How much is the fare to the
city centre (downtown)/
railway (railroad) station/
airport?
Ile kosztuje przejazd do
centrum/na dworzec kolejowy/
na lotnisko?
*Eele koshtooye psheyazd do
centroom/na dvozhets koleyovy/
na lotnisko?*

198 Will you tell me when to get
off?
Proszę mi powiedzieć kiedy
mam wysiąść.
*Proshem mi povyejech kyedy mam
vyshonshch.*

P O L I S H

185 ↕ 198

199 Does this bus go to . . ?
Czy ten autobus jedzie
do . . ?
Chi ten autoboos yejee doh . . ?

200 Which number bus goes
to . . ?
Który numer jedzie do . . ?
Ktoory numer yedzhye doh . . ?

201 May I have a single (one-
way)/return (round-trip)/day
ticket/book of tickets?
Proszę o bilet w jedną stronę/
powrotny/całodzienny/karnet
biletowy?
*Proshem o bilet v yednom
stronem/povrotny/tzawojennee/
karnet biletovy?*

Taxis

202 I would like to go to . . .
How much will it cost?
Chcę jechać do . . . , ile to
będzie kosztować?
*Htsem yehach doh . . . , ile toe
benjey koshtovach?*

203 Please stop here.
Proszę się tu zatrzymać.
Proshem shiem too zatzhimach.

204 I would like to order a taxi
today/tomorrow/at 2pm to
go from . . . to . . .
Chę zamówić taksówkę na
dzisiaj/jutro/na drugą po
południu, na przejazd z . . .
do . . .
Htsem zamoovich taxoovkem na

*jishyay/na yootro/na droogom po
powoodnyoo, na psheyazd z . . .
doh . . .*

Asking the Way

205 Excuse me, do you speak
English?
Przepraszam, czy mówi Pan/
Pani (*woman*) po angielsku?
*Psheprasham, chi moovi pan/
panee po angyelskoo?*

206 Excuse me, is this the right
way to . . ?
Przepraszam, czy to jest droga
do . . ?
*Psheprasham, chi to yest drogah
doh . . ?*

207 . . . the cathedral/the tourist
information office/the castle/
the old town
. . . katedry/biura turystycznego/
zamku/starego miasta
*katedree/byura tooristichnego/
zamkoo/stahrego myasta*

208 Can you tell me the way to
the railway (railroad) station/
bus station/taxi rank (stand)/
city centre (downtown)/
beach?
Jak dojść do dworca
kolejowego/autobusowego/
postoju taksówek/centrum/na
plażę?
*Yak doyshch do dwortsa
koleyovego/autoboosovego/
postoyoo taxovek/centroom/na
plazhem?*

209 First/second left/right/
straight ahead.
Pierwsza/druga w lewo/w
prawo/prosto.
*Pyervsha/drooga v levo/v prawo/
prosto.*

210 Where is the nearest police
station/post office/doctor/
hospital/pharmacy?
Gdzie jest najbliższy posterunek
policji/poczta/karza/szpitala/
apteka?
*Gje yest nayblizhshy posteroonek
politsyee/pochta/lekazha/
shpitalah/ahptehkah?*

211 Is it far?
Czy to daleko?
Chi to daleko?

212 Do I need to take a taxi/
catch a bus?
Czy muszę wziąć taksówkę/
jechać autobusem?
*Chi mooshem wzionshch
taksoovkem/jehach autoboosem?*

213 Can you point to it on my map?
Czy może mi Pan/Pani (woman)
pokazać na mapie?
*Chi mozhe mi pan/pany pokazach
na mapye?*

214 Thank you for your help.
Dziękuję za pomoc.
Jenkooyem za pomots.

SIGHTSEEING

215 Where is the Tourist
Information office?

Gdzie jest Informacja
Turystyczna?
Gje yest informatsya tooristichna?

216 Where is the cathedral/
church/museum?
Gdzie jest katedra/kościół/
muzeum?
*Gje yest katedra/koshchoow/
mooseum?*

217 How much is the entrance
(admission) charge?
Ile wynosi opłata za wstęp?
Eele vynoshee opwata za vstemp?

218 Is there a reduction for
children/students/senior
citizens?
Czy jest zniżka dla dzieci/
studentów/emerytów?
*Chi yest znizhka dla jechee/
studentoof/emeritoof?*

219 What time does the next
guided tour start?
O której zaczyna się następny
obchód z przewodnikiem?
*O ktoorey zachina shiem
nastempny obhood z
pshevodnikyem?*

220 One/two adults/children,
please.
Jeden/dwa bilety dla
dorosłych/dzieci.
*Yeden/dva bilety dla doroswyh/
jechee.*

221 May I take photographs here?
Czy można tu fotografować?
Chi mozhna tu fotografovach?

ENTERTAINMENT

222 Can you recommend a good bar/nightclub?
Czy możecie mi polecić dobry bar/nocny lokal?
Chi mozhechie me polechich dobry bar/notsny lokal?

223 Do you know what is on at the cinema (playing at the movies)/theatre at the moment?
Co grają teraz w kinach/teatrach?
Tso grayom teraz w kinakh/teatrakh?

224 I would like to book (purchase) . . . tickets for the matinee/evening performance on Monday
Chcę zamówić . . . biletów na popołudniowe/wieczorne przedstawienie, w poniedziałek.
Khtsem zamoovich . . . biletoov na popowoodnyove/vyechorney pshedsytavyenye, v ponyedzyawek.

225 What time does the film/performance start?
O której zaczyna się spektakl?
O ktoorey zachina shiem spektakl?

MEETING PEOPLE

226 Hello/Goodbye.
Hallo/Do widzenia.
Hallo/Do vidzenia.

227 Good morning/good afternoon/good evening/goodnight.

Dzień dobry/dzień dobry/dobry wieczór/dobranoc
Djen dobri/ djen dobri/dobri vyechoor/dohbranotz

228 Pleased to meet you.
Miło mi poznać.
Miwo me poznach.

229 How are you?
Jak się Pan (Pani) ma?
Yak shem Pan (Panee) mah?

230 Fine, thank you. And you?
Bardzo dobrze, dziękuję. A Pan(Pani)?
Bardzho dobrzhe, djenkooye. Ah Pan (Panee)?

231 My name is . . .
Nazywam się . . .
Nazyvam shiem . . .

232 This is my friend/boyfriend/girlfriend/husband/wife/brother/sister.
To mój przyjaciel/moja sympatia/moja sympatia/mój mąż/moja żona/mój brat/moja siostra.
Toe mooy psheyatsyel/moya psheyatsyoovka/moya simpatya/mooy monj/moya zhona/moy brat/moya syostra.

233 Where are you travelling to?
Gdzie jedziesz?
Gje yejesh?

234 I am/we are going to . . .
Jadę/jedziemy do . . .
Yadem/yejemy doh . . .

235 How long are you travelling for?
Na jak długo jesteś w podrbży?
Na yak dwoogo yestesh v podroozhee?

236 Where do you come from?
Skąd jesteś?
Skond yestesh?

237 I am/we are from . . .
Jestem/jesteśmy z . . .
Yestem/yesteshme z . . .

238 We're on holiday.
Jesteśmy na wakacjach.
Yesteshme na vakatzyah.

239 This is our first visit here.
To jest nasz pierwszy pobyt.
To yest nash pyerwshee pobeet.

240 Would you like/May I have a cigarette?
Czy chcesz/Czy mogę prosić o papierosa?
Chi khcesh/Chi mogem proshich o papyerosa?

241 I am sorry but I do not understand.
Przykro mi, ale nie rozumiem.
Pshikro me, aly nye rozoomiem.

242 Please speak slowly.
Proszę mówić powoli.
Proshem moovich povolee.

243 Do you mind if I smoke?
Czy mogę zapalić?
Chi mogem zapalich?

244 Do you have a light?
Czy mogę prosić o ogień?

Chi mogem prosheech o ogien?

245 I am waiting for my husband/ wife/boyfriend/girlfriend.
Czekam na mego męża/moją żonę/mego chłopca/moją dziewczynę.
Chekam na megoh menzha/ moyom zhoneh/megoh hwoptza/ moyom dzhevchineh.

TRAVELLING WITH CHILDREN

246 Do you have a high chair/ baby-sitting service/cot?
Czy macie krzesło dla dziecka/ usługi czuwania nad dzieckiem/ łóżeczko dziecinne?
Chi matsye ksheswo dla jetska/ uswoogi choovanya nad jetskiem/ woozhechko jechinney?

247 Where is the nursery/ playroom?
Gdzie jest pokój dziecinny/ pokój zabaw dla dzieci?
Gje yest pokooy jechinny/pokooy zabav dla jechee?

248 Where can I warm the baby's bottle?
Gdzie mogę zagrzać butelkę dla dziecka?
Gje mogem zagzhach bootelkem dla jetska?

COMMUNICATIONS

Post

249 How much will it cost to send a letter/postcard/this

package to Britain/Ireland/ America/Canada/Australia/ New Zealand?

Ile kosztuje wysyłka listu/ pocztówki/tej paczki do Anglii/ Irlandii/Ameryki/Kanady/ Australii/Nowej Zelandii?

Eele koshtooye vysywka listoo/ poochtoovky/tey pachki do Anglee/Yrlandee/Amerykee/ Kanady/Australee/Novey Zelandee?

²⁵⁰ **I would like one stamp/two stamps.**

Proszę o jeden znaczek/dwa znaczki.

Proshem o yeden znachek/dva znachkee.

²⁵¹ **I'd like . . . stamps for postcards to send abroad, please.**

Proszę o . . . znaczków na karty pocztowe na zagranicę.

Proshem o . . . znachkoov na kartee pochtove na zagranitzheh.

Phones

²⁵² **I would like to make a telephone call/reverse the charges to (make a collect call to) . . .**

Chcę zadzwonić/na koszt abonenta do . . .

Ktsem zadzvonich/na kosht abonenta, doh . . .

²⁵³ **Which coins do I need for the telephone?**

Jakie muszę mieć monety do tego telefonu?

Yakye mushem miech monety doh tego telephonoo?

²⁵⁴ **The line is engaged (busy).**

Linia jest zajęta.

Linya yest zayenta.

²⁵⁵ **The number is . . .**

Numer jest . . .

Noomer yest . . .

²⁵⁶ **Hello, this is . . ?**

Halo, tu mówi . . .

Hello, tu moovee . . .

²⁵⁷ **May I speak to . . ?**

Czy mogę mówić z . . .

Chi mogem mooveech z . . .

²⁵⁸ **He/She is not in at the moment. Can you call back?**

Jego/jej niema w tej chwili. Proszę zadzwonić jeszcze raz.

Yego/yey nyema v tey hveelee. Proshem zadhzvoneech yeshche raz.

MONEY

²⁵⁹ **I would like to change these travellers' cheques (travelers' checks)/this currency/this Eurocheque.**

Chcę wymienić te czeki podróżne/tą walutę/ten Euroczek.

Khcem vymienich te chekee podroozhne/tom valootem/ten Eurochek.

P
O
L
I
S
H

250
↑
259

²⁶⁰ How much commission do you charge (What is the service charge)?
Ile liczycie za wymianę?
Eele lichytsye za vymianem?

²⁶¹ Can I obtain money with my MasterCard?
Czy mogę dostać pieniądze na MasterCard?
Chi mogem dostach pyenyondze na MasterCard?

SHOPPING

Names of shops and Departments

²⁶² Księgarnia/Materiały papiernicze
Kshengarnya/materyawee papyerneecheh
Bookshop/Stationery

²⁶³ Jubiler/Upominki
Yoobiler/Oopominkee
Jeweller's/Gifts

²⁶⁴ Sklep z obuwiem
Sklep z oboovyem
Shoes

²⁶⁵ Artykuły gospodarstwa domowego
Artikoowe gospodarstva domovego
Hardware

²⁶⁶ Antykwariat
Anticvaryat
Antiques

²⁶⁷ Fryzjer (męski)/(damski)
Frizyer (menskee)/(damskee

Hairdressers (men's)/(women's)

²⁶⁸ Kiosk z papierosami
Kiosk z papyerohsammy
Tobacconist

²⁶⁹ Piekarnia
Pyekarnya
Baker's

²⁷⁰ Supermarket
Soopermarkyet
Supermarket

²⁷¹ Foto Optyk
Photo-optic
Photoshop

²⁷² Zabawki
Zabavkee
Toys

²⁷³ Biuro podróży
Bureau podroozhi
Travel Agent

²⁷⁴ Perfumeria/Drogeria
Perfoomerya/Drogerya
Toiletries

²⁷⁵ Sklep muzyczny
Sklep moozichnee
Records

In the Shop

²⁷⁶ What time do the shops open/close?
O której otwierają/zamykają sklepy?
O ktoorey otvyerayom/zamykayom sklepy?

²⁷⁷ Where is the nearest market?
Gdzie jest najbliższy targ?

Gje yest nayblizhshi targ?

278 Can you show me the one in the window/this one?
Proszę pokazać mi ten z wystawy/ten.
Proshem pokazach me ten z vistavee/ten.

279 Can I try this on?
Czy mogę to przymierzyć?
Chi mogem to pshimiezhich?

280 What size is this?
Jaki to rozmiar?
Yakee toe rozmyar?

281 This is too large/too small/ too expensive.
To jest za duże/za małe/za drogie.
Toh yest za doozhe/za mawe/za drogye.

282 Do you have any others?
Czy są inne?
Chi som inneh?

283 My size is . . .
Noszę numer . . . .
Noshem noomer . . .

284 Where is the changing room/ childrens/cosmetic/ ladieswear/menswear/food department?
Gdzie jest szatnia/ubrania dla dzieci/kosmetyki/ubrania damskie/ ubrania męskie/żywność?
Gje yest shatnia/ubrania dla jechee/kosmetyki/ubrania damskiey/ubrania menskiey/ zhyvnoshch?

285 I would like . . .
Chciałbym (chciałabym)
Htzchawbim (htzchawabim) . . .

286 I would like a quarter of a kilo/half a kilo/a kilo of bread/butter/cheese/ham/ tomatoes.
Proszę o ćwierć kilo/pół kilo/ kilo chleba/masła/sera/szynki/ pomidorów.
Proshem o chvyerch kilo/poow kilo/kilo hleba/maswa/sera/ shinky/pomidoroov.

287 How much is this?
Ile to kosztuje?
Eele toe koshtooye?

288 I'll take this one, thank you.
Poproszę ten. Dziękuję.
Poproshem ten. Dzhenkooyeh.

289 Do you have a carrier (shopping) bag?
Czy mogę prosić o torbę?
Chi mogem proshich o torbem?

290 Do you have anything cheaper/larger/smaller/of better quality?
Czy macie coś tańszego/ większego/mniejszego/w lepszej jakości?
Chi machye tsosh tanshego/ vienkshego/mneyshego/v lepshey yakoshchee?

291 I would like a film for this camera.
Potrzebuję film do aparatu.
Potshebooyem film doe aparatoo.

P
O
L
I
S
H

278
↑
291

SHOPPING/MOTORING

292 I would like some batteries,
the same size as this old one.
Potrzebuję baterie, takie same
jak te stare.
*Potsheebooyem baterye, takye same
yak te starey.*

293 Would you mind wrapping
this for me, please?
Proszę mi to zapakować.
Proshem me toe zapakovac.

294 Sorry, but you seem to have
given me the wrong change.
Przepraszam, ale źle mi Pan
wydał.
*Psheprasham, aley zlye me Pan
vydaw.*

MOTORING

Car Hire (Rental)

295 I have ordered (rented) a car
in the name of . .
Zamówiłem samochód na
nazwisko . . .
*Zamooviwem samohood na
nazvisko . . .*

296 How much does it cost to
hire (rent) a car for one day/
two days/one week?
Ile kosztuje wynajęcie
samochodu na jeden dzień/dwa
dni/tydzień?
*Eele koshtooye vynayenchye
samohodoo na yeden jen/dva
dnyee/tyjen?*

297 Is the tank already full of
petrol (gas)?
Czy zbiornik jest pełny?
Chi zbyornik yest pewny?

298 Is insurance and tax
included? How much is the
deposit?
Czy to obejmuje ubezpieczenie
i podatek? Ile wynosi depozyt?
*Chi toe obeymooye ubezpyechenye
ee podatek? Eele koshtooye
depozyt?*

299 By what time must I return
the car?
Do której godziny mam
zwrócić samochód?
*Doe ktoorey gojeeny mam
zvroochich samohood?*

300 I would like a small/family
car with a radio/cassette
player.
Chcę mały/większy samochód z
radiem/magnetofonem
kasetowym.
*Ktsem mawy/vienkshy samohood
z radyem/magnetophonem
kasetovym.*

Asking the Way

301 Excuse me, can you help me
please?
Przepraszam, czy może mi
Pan(Pani) pomoc?
*Psheprasham, chi mozeh me
Pan(Pani) pomotz?*

302 How do I reach the
motorway/main road?
Którędy do autostrady/głównej
drogi?
*Ktoorendy do autostrady/
gwoovney drogi?*

303 I think I have taken the
wrong turning.
Chyba źle skręciłem(am)
Heeba zhle skrencheewem(am).

304 I am looking for this address.
Szukam tego adresu.
Shookam tego adresoo.

305 I am looking for the . . . hotel.
Szukam hotelu . . .
Shookam hoteloo . . .

306 How far is it to . . .
from here?
Jak daleko stąd do . . .
Yak dalekoh stond doh . . .

307 Carry straight on for . . .
kilometres.
. . . kilometrów prostą drogą.
. . . kilomtroov prostom drogom.

308 Take the next turning on the
right/left.
Następna przecznica w prawo/
w lewo
*Nastempna pshechneetzha v
pravo/v levo*

309 Turn right/left at the next
crossroads/traffic lights.
Trzeba skręcić w prawo/w lewo
na następnym skrzyżowaniu/
przy następnych światłach

*Tcheba skrenchich v pravo/v levo
na nastempneem
sksheezhovanyoo/pshee
nastempneeh shvyatwah.*

310 You are going in the wrong
direction.
Pan(Pani) jedzie w złym
kierunku.
*Pan(Pani) yedzhe v zweem
kyeroonkoo.*

Parking

311 How long can I park here?
Jak długo można tu parkować?
*Yak dwoogo mozhna tu
parkovach?*

312 Is there a car park near here?
Czy jest parking w pobliżu?
Chi yest parking v pobleezhoo?

313 At what time does this car
park close?
O której zamyka się parking?
O ktoorey zameeka shem parking?

Signs and Notices

314 Jeden kierunek
Yeden kyeroonek
One way

315 Zakaz wjazdu
Zakaz vyazdoo
No entry

316 Nie parkować
Nye parkovach
No parking

MOTORING

P
O
L
I
S
H

317 Objazd
Obyahzd
Detour (diversion)

318 Stop
Stop
Stop

319 Pierwszeństwo ruchu
Pyervshenstvo roohoo
Give way (yield)

320 Śliska nawierzchnia
Shleeska navyerzhnya
Slippery road

321 Zakaz wymijania
Zakaz vimeeyanya
No overtaking

At the Filling Station

322 Unleaded (lead-free)/ Standard/Premium
Bez-ołowiowa (bez ołowiu)/ Normalna/wysoko oktanowa
Bez-owoviova(bez owovyou)/ Normalna/visokoh oktanova

323 Fill the tank please.
Do pełna, poproszę.
Do pewna, poproshem.

324 Do you have a road map of this area?
Czy jest mapa drogowa tej okolicy?
Chi yest mapa drogova tey okolitzee?

325 How much is the car-wash?
Ile kosztuje auto-myjnia?
Eele koshtooye awtoh-meeynya?

Breakdowns

326 I've had a breakdown at . . .
Samochód mi się zepsuł na . . .
Samohood me shem zepsoow na . . .

327 I am on the road from . . . to . . .
Jestem w drodze z . . . do . . .
Yestem v drodzhe z . . . doh . . .

328 I can't move the car. Can you send a tow-truck?
Nie mogę ruszyć samochodu. Proszę przysłać pomoc drogową
Nye mogem rooshich samohodoo. Proshem pshiswach pomotz drogovom.

329 I have a flat tyre.
Mam płaską oponę.
Mam pwaskom oponeh.

330 The windscreen (windshield) has smashed/cracked.
Szyba się stłukła/pękła.
Sheba shem stwookwah/penkhwa.

331 There is something wrong with the engine/brakes/ lights/steering/gearbox/ clutch/exhaust.
Mam problem z silnikiem/ hamulcami/światłami/układem kierowniczym/skrzynią biegów/sprzęgłem/tłumikiem.
Mam problem z shilneekyem/ hamooltzame/shvyatwamee/

ookwadem kyerovneechem/
skhshinyom byegoow/
spshengwem/twoomikyem.

332 It's overheating.
Przegrzewa się.
Pshegzheva sheh.

333 It won't start.
Nie chce ruszyć.
Nye htse rooshich.

334 Where can I get it repaired?
Gdzie mogę naprawić?
Gje mogem napraveech?

335 Can you take me there?
Czy może mnie Pan(Pani) tam
zaprowadzić?
*Chi mozhe mnye Pan(Pani) tam
zaprovadzheech?*

336 Will it take long to fix?
Jak długo potrwa naprawa?
Yak dwoogoh potrva naprava?

337 How much will it cost?
Ile będzie kosztowało?
Eele bendzhe koshtovawoh?

Accidents

**338 Can you help me? There has
been an accident.**
Proszę mi pomoc. Chodzi o
wypadek.
*Proshem mi pomotz. Hodzhi o
vipadek.*

**339 Please call the police/an
ambulance.**
Proszę zawezwać policję/
pogotowie.

Proshem zavezvach policyem/
pogotohvye.

340 Is anyone hurt?
Czy ktoś jest ranny?
Chi ktosh yest rannee?

Traffic Offences

**341 I'm sorry, I didn't see the
sign.**
Przepraszam, nie widziałem(am)
znaku.
*Psheprasham, nye
vidzhyawem(am) znakoo.*

**342 Must I pay a fine? How
much?**
Czy muszę zapłacić mandat?
Ile?
*Chi mushem zapwacheech
mandat? Eele?*

343 Show me your documents.
Dokumenty poproszę.
Dokumenti poproshem.

HEALTH

Pharmacy

**344 Do you have anything for a
stomachache/headache/sore
throat/toothache?**
Czy jest coś na ból żołądka/ból
głowy/ból gardła/ból zęba?
*Chi yest tzosh na bool zholondka/
bool gwovy/bool gardwa/bool
zemba?*

P
O
L
I
S
H

332
↕
344

HEALTH

345 I need something for
diarrhoea (diarrhea)/
constipation/a cold/a cough/
insect bites/sunburn/travel
(motion) sickness.
Potrzebuję czegoś na biegunkę/
zaparcie/przeziębienie/kaszel/
ukąszenie owada/opaleniznę/
morską chorobę.
*Potshebooyem tsosh na
biegoonkew/zaparchee/
pshezyembyenye/kashel/
ukonshenye ovada/opaleniznem/
morskom horobem.*

346 How much/how many do I
take?
Ile mam zażyć?
Eele mam zazhych?

347 How often do I take it/them?
Jak często mam to brać?
Yak chensto mam toe brach?

348 How much does it cost?
Ile to kosztuje?
Eele toe koshtooye?

349 Can you recommend a good
doctor/dentist?
Czy możecie mi polecić
dobrego lekarza/dentystę?
*Chi mozhetsye me polechich
dobrego lekaja/dentystem?*

350 Is it suitable for children?
Czy nadaje się dla dzieci?
Chi nadaye shye dla jechee?

Doctor

351 I have a pain here/in my
arm/leg/chest/stomach.
Boli mnie tu/w ramieniu/
nodze/piersiach/żołądku.
*Bolee mnye too/v ramyenew/
nodzey/piershiah/zhowondkoo.*

352 Please call a doctor, this is an
emergency.
Proszę wezwać lekarza, to jest
nagły wypadek.
*Proshem wezvch lekazha, toe yest
nagwy vypadek.*

353 I would like to make an
appointment to see a doctor.
Chcę zamówić wizytę lekarską.
*Khcem zamoovich vizytem
lekarskom.*

354 I am diabetic/pregnant.
Jestem cukrzykiem/w ciąży.
Yestem tsukshykiem/v tsionjy.

355 I need a prescription for . . .
Potrzebuję receptę na . . .
Potshebooyem retseptem na . . .

356 Can you give me something
to ease the pain?
Czy może mi Pan/Pani (woman)
dać jakiś środek
przeciwbólowy?
*Chi mozhe me Pan/Pany dach
yakish shrodek pshechivboolovy?*

357 I am/he is/she is allergic to
penicillin.
Ja jestem/on jest/ona jest
uczulony/a na penicylinę.

Ya yestem/on yest/ona yest
uchoolonee/a na penitzileenem.

358 Does this hurt?
Czy to boli?
Chi to bolee?

**359 You must/he must/she must
go to hospital.**
Pan(Pani)/on/ona musi pójść do
szpitala.
*Pan(Pani)/on/ona mooshe
pooyshch doh shpitalah.*

**360 Take these once/twice /three
times a day.**
Proszę zażywać to raz/dwa/
trzy razy dziennie.
*Proshem zazhivach toh raz/dwa/
tshee razee djenye.*

**361 I am/he is/she is taking this
medication.**
Ja zażywam/on zażywa/ona
zażywa to lekarstwo.
*Ya zazheevam/on zazheeva/ona
zazheeva toh lekarstvoh.*

362 I have medical insurance.
Mam ubezpieczenie lekarskie.
Mam oobezpyechenye lekarskye.

Dentist

363 I have toothache.
Boli mnie ząb.
Boly mnie zomb.

364 My filling has come out.
Wyleciała mi plomba.
Vyletsyawa me plomba.

**365 I do/do not want to have an
injection first.**
Proszę najpierw o zastrzyk/nie
chcę zastrzyku.
*Proshem naipyerv o zastsheek/nye
khcem zastsheekoo.*

EMERGENCIES

366 Help!
Pomocy!
Pomotsy!

**367 Call an ambulance/a doctor/
the police!**
Prosze wezwać karetkę
pogotowia/lekarza/policję!
*Proshem zavezwach karetkem
pogotovya/lekazha/politsyem!*

**368 I have had my travellers'
cheques (travelers' checks)/
credit cards/purse/handbag/
rucksack (knapsack)/
luggage/wallet stolen.**
Skradziono mi czeki podróżne/
karty kredytowe/portmonetkę/
torebkę/plecak/bagaż/portfel.
*Skrajono me chekee podroozhne/
karty kreditovey/pormonetkem/
torebkem/pletsak/bagazh/portfel.*

**369 Can you help me, I have lost
my daughter/son?**
Czy może mi Pan (Pani) pomóc,
Zgubiłam córkę/syna?
*Chi mozheh me Pan (Panee),
Zgoobiwam tsoorkem/syna?*

P
O
L
I
S
H

358
↕
369

370 Please go away/leave me alone.

Proszę odejść/zostawić mnie w spokoju.

Proshem odeyshch/zostavich mnye v spokoyoo.

371 Fire!

Pożar!

Pozhar!

372 I want to contact the British/ American/Canadian/Irish/ Australian/New Zealand/

South African consulate.

Chcę się skontaktować z konsulatem brytyjskim/ amerykańskim/kanadyjskim/ irlandzkim/australijskim/nowo-zelandzkim/RPA.

Htsem shem skontaktovach z konsulatem britiyskeem/ americanskeem/canadeeyskeem/ irlandzkhim/awstraleeyskim/ novo-zelandzhkhim/er-pe-ah.

Introduction

Portuguese is a descendant of Latin, like Italian, Spanish and French, and a knowledge of any of these other languages will help you to understand a lot of written Portuguese. Spoken Portuguese, however, can be quite difficult for a beginner to comprehend and to speak, and you may need to ask to have things written down for you more often than in other Western European countries. If you have to resort to speaking a second language, try English or even French rather than Spanish.

**P
O
R
T
U
G
U
E
S
E**

Addresses for travel and tourist information

Australia: *Embassy,* 23 Culgoa Court, O'Malley Deakin, PO Box 9092; tel: (2) 901733.
UK: *Portuguese National Trade & Tourist Office,* 22/25A Sackville St (2nd Flr), London, W1X 1DE; tel: (020) 7494 1441.
USA: *Portuguese National Trade & Tourist Office,* 590 Fifth Ave (4th Flr), New York, NY 10036 4785; tel: (212) 354 4403/04.

ESSENTIALS

Alphabet

A *ah*	B *bay*
C *say*	D *day*
E *e*	F *efi*
G *jay*	H *agah*
I *ee*	J *jota*
K *kahpa*	L *eli*
M *emi*	N *eni*
O *o*	P *pay*
Q *kay*	R *erre*
S *esi*	T *tay*
U *oo*	V *vay*
W *vay dooplo*	X *sheesh*
Y *eepselohn*	Z *zay*

Basic Words and Phrases

1 Yes
Sim
Seem

No
Não
Nown

2 Please
Por favor
Poor favohr

Thank you
Obrigado/a
Ohbreegahdoo/a

3 That's O.K.
Está bem
Istah bayng

Perhaps
Talvez
Tahlvaysh

4 To
Para
Para

From
De
Di

5 Here
Aqui
Akee

There
Ali
Alee

6 None
Nenhum (a)
Nenyoom (a)

Also
Também
Tangbayng

7 How
Como
Kohmoo

When
Quando
Kkwahndoo

8 What
O que
Oo ki

Why
Porquê
Poorkay

9 I don't understand.
Não entendo
Nown ayngtayngdoo

10 I don't speak Portuguese.
Não sei falar [nome da linguagem]
Nown say falahr . . .

11 Do you speak English?
Fala Inglês?
Fahla eenglaysh?

12 Can you please write it down?
Por favor, pode escrever isso?
Poor favohr pohd ishkrivayr eessoo?

13 **Can you please speak more slowly?**
Por favor, pode falar mais devagar?
Poor favohr, pohd falahr myish devagahr?

14 **How much does it/this cost?**
Quanto custa isto?
Kwantoo kooshta ishtoo?

Days

15 **Monday**   **Tuesday**
Segunda-feira   Terça-feira
Sigoongda-fayra *Tayrsa-fayra*

16 **Wednesday**   **Thursday**
Quarta-feira   Quinta-feira
Kwahrta-fayra *Keengta-fayra*

17 **Friday**   **Saturday**
Sexta-feira   Sábado
Sayshta-fayra *Sahbadoo*

18 **Sunday**   **Morning**
Domingo   Manhã
Doomeengoo   *Manyang*

19 **Afternoon**   **Evening**
Tarde   Noite
Tahrd   *Noyt*

20 **Night**   **Week**
Noite   Semana
Noyt   *Simana*

21 **Yesterday/Today/Tomorrow**
Ontem/Hoje/Amanhã
Ohngtayng/Ohzhay/Ahmanyang

Numbers

22 **Zero**   **One**
Zero   Um
Zeroo   *Oong*

23 **Two**   **Three**
Dois   Três
Doysh   *Traysh*

24 **Four**   **Five**
Quatro   Cinco
Kwahtroo   *Seengkoo*

25 **Six**   **Seven**
Seis   Sete
Saysh   *Set*

26 **Eight**   **Nine**
Oito   Nove
Oytoo   *Nov*

27 **Ten**   **Eleven**
Dez   Onze
Desh   *Ohngz*

28 **Twelve**   **Thirteen**
Doze   Treze
Dohz   *Trayz*

29 **Fourteen**   **Fifteen**
Catorze   Quinze
Katohrz   *Keengz*

30 **Sixteen**   **Seventeen**
Dezasseis   Dezassete
Dizasaysh   *Dizaset*

31 **Eighteen**   **Nineteen**
Dezoito   Dezanove
Dizoytoo   *Dizanov*

32 **Twenty**   **Twenty-one**
Vinte   Vinte e um
Veengt   *Veengt ee oong*

ESSENTIALS/ARRIVING AND DEPARTING

33 Twenty-two Thirty
Vinte e dois Trinta
Veengt ee doysh Treengta

34 Forty Fifty
Quarenta Cinquenta
Kwarayngta Seengkwayngta

35 Sixty Seventy
Sessenta Setenta
Sisayngta Sitayngta

36 Eighty Ninety
Oitenta Noventa
Oytayngta Noovayngta

37 One hundred Five hundred
Cem Quinhentos
sayng Keenyengtoos

38 One thousand One million
Mil Um milhão
Meel Oong meelyowng

Time

39 9.00
Nove horas
Nov orash

40 9.05
Nove e cinco
Nov ee seengkoo

41 9.10
Nove e dez
Nov ee desh

42 9.15
Nove e um quarto
Nov ee oong kwahrtoo

43 9.20
Nove e vinte
Nov ee veengt

44 9.25
Nove e vinte e cinco
Nov ee veengt ee seengkoo

45 9.30
Nove e meia
Nov ee maya

46 9.35
Nove e trinta e cinco
Nov ee treengta ee seengkoo

47 9.40
Nove e quarenta
Nov ee kwarayngta

48 9.45
Nove e quarenta e cinco
Nov ee kwarayngta ee seengkoo

49 9.50
Nove e cinquenta
Nov ee seengkwayngta

50 9.55
Nove e cinquenta e cinco
Nov ee seengkwaynta ee seengkoo

51 12.00/Midday/Midnight
Doze horas/Meio dia/Meia noite
Dohzi orash/mayoo-deea/maya-noyt

52 What time is it?
Que horas são?
Ki orash sowng?

53 It is . . .
É/São . . .
Eh/sowng . . .

ARRIVING AND DEPARTING

Airport

**54 Excuse me, where is the
check-in desk for . . . airline?**

Desculpe, onde é o balcão de
check-in da . . . (companhia
aérea)?
*Dishkoolp, ohngdee eh oo
bahlkowngdi check-een da . . ?*

55 **What is the boarding gate/
time for my flight?**
Qual é a porta/hora para o meu
voo?
*Kwal e a porta/ora para oo mayo
vo'oo ?*

56 **How long is the delay likely
to be?**
De quanto será o atraso?
Di kwanto sirah oo atrahzoo?

57 **Where is the duty-free shop?**
Onde é a loja duty-free?
Ohngdee eh a lohzha duty-free?

58 **Which way is the baggage
reclaim?**
Onde é a recolha de bagagem?
*Ohngdee eh a rrecohlya di
bagahzhayng*

59 **Where can I get the bus to
the city centre?**
Onde posso tomar o autocarro
para o centro da cidade?
*Ohngd possoo toomahr oo
owtohkahrroo para o sayngtroo da
seedahdi?*

Train Station

60 **Where is the ticket office/
information desk?**
Onde é a bilheteira/o balcão de
informações?
Ohngdee eh a beelyaytayra/oo

bahlkowng di eenfoormasoyesh?

61 **Which platform does the
train to . . . depart from?**
De que linha parte o comboio
para . . . ?
*Di ke leenya pahrt oo kohmboyoo
para . . . ?*

62 **Where is platform . . ?**
Onde é a linha . . ?
ohngdee eh a leenya . . .

63 **When is the next train to . . ?**
Quando é o próximo combóio
para . . ?
*Kwandoo eh oo prohseemoo
kohngboyo para . . . ?*

64 **Is there a later train to . . ?**
Há um combóio mais tarde
para . . ?
*Ah oong kohngboyo myish tahrd
para . . . ?*

Port

65 **How do I get to the port?**
Como posso ir para o porto?
Kohmoo possoo eer para oo pohrto

66 **When is the next sailing to . . ?**
Quando é o próximo barco
para . . ?
*Kwandoo eh oo prohseemoo
bahrkoo para . . ?*

67 **Can I catch an earlier ferry
with this ticket?**
Posso apanhar um barco mais
cedo com este bilhete?
*Possoo apanyahr oong bahrkoo
myish saidoo kohm ayste beelyait?*

ARRIVING AND DEPARTING

Notices and Signs

68 Carruagem-Restaurante
Karrooahzhayng rishtowrahnt
Buffet (Dining) Car

69 Autocarro
Owtokahrroo
Bus

70 Água potável /não potável
Ahgwa pootahvel/nown pootahvel
Drinking/Non-drinking water

71 Entrada
Entrahda
Entrance

72 Saída
Saihda
Exit

73 Informações
Eemfoormasoyesh
Information

74 Recolha de Bagagem
Rrecohliya do bagahzhayng
Left Luggage (Baggage Claim)

75 Cacifos de bagagem
Kaseefoosh di bagahzhayng
Luggage Lockers

76 Correio
Koorrayoo
Post Office

77 Linha
Leenya
Platform

78 Estação de Caminho de Ferro
Ishtasowng di kamihnyo di fehrroo
Railway (Railroad) Station

79 Aeroporto
Aehrohportoo
Airport

80 Porto
Porto
Port

81 Restaurante
Ristowrangt
Restaurant

82 Fumadores/Não fumadores
Foomadohrsh/nown-foomadohrsh
Smoking/Non-Smoking

83 Telefone
Tilifohne
Telephone

84 Bilheteira
Beelyaytayra
Ticket Office

85 Balcão de check-in
Bahlkowng di check-een
Check-in Desk

86 Horário
Orahreoo
Timetable (Schedule)

87 Lavabos
Lavahboosh
Toilets (Restrooms)

88 Homens/Cavalheiros
Omayngsh/kavalyayroosh
Gentlemen

89 Senhoras
Sinyohrash
Ladies'

90 Carro eléctrico
Kahrroo elehtreekoo

Tram (Streetcar)

91 Metropolitano
Metropooleetahnoo
Underground (Subway)

92 Sala de espera
Sahla di ishpehra
Waiting-Room

Buying a Ticket

**93 I would like a first-class/
second-class single (one-
way)/return (round-trip)
ticket to . . .**
Queria um bilhete de primeira
classe/segunda classe/simples/
ida e volta para . . .
*Kireea oong beelyayt di
preemayra/sigoonda klahs/
seemplish/eeda ee vohlta para* . . .

**94 Is my rail pass valid on this
train/ferry/bus?**
A minha assinatura é válida para
este combóio/barco/autocarro?
*A meenya aseenatoora eh vahleeda
para eshte lohmboyoo/bahrkoo/
owtohkahrroo?*

**95 I would like an aisle/window
seat.**
Queria um lugar no corredor/na
janela.
*Kireea oong loogahr noo
korridohr/na zhanehla.*

96 No smoking/smoking, please.
Por favor, fumador/não
fumador.
*Poor favohr, foomadohr/nown
foomadohr.*

**97 We would like to sit
together.**
Queríamos lugares juntos.
*Kireeamoosh loogahrsh
zhoongtoosh.*

**98 I would like to make a seat
reservation.**
Queria marcar um lugar.
Kireea marcahr oong loogahr.

**99 I would like to reserve a
couchette/sleeper for one
person/two people/for my
family.**
Queria marcar uma couchette/
cama para uma pessoa/duas
pessoas/para a minha família.
*Kireea marcahr ooma koooshet/
kama para ooma pesoha/dooash
pesohash/para a meenya
fameehleea.*

**100 I would like to reserve a
cabin.**
Queria marcar uma cabina.
Kireea markahr ooma kahbeena

Timetables (Schedules)

101 Chegada
Shigahda
Arrive

102 Com paragem em . . .
Kohng parahzhayng ayng. . .
Calls (Stops) at. . .

103 Serviço de Restaurante
Serveehsoo di rishtowrangt
Catering Service

ARRIVING AND DEPARTING

104 Mudar em . . .
Moodahr ayng . . .
Change at . . .

105 Ligação
Leegasowng
Connection

106 Todos os dias
Tohdoosh oosh deeash
Daily

107 De 40 em 40 minutos
Di kwarayngta ayng kwarayngta meenootoosh
Every 40 Minutes

108 Primeira Classe
Preemayra klahs
First-Class

109 De hora a hora
Di ora a ora
Hourly

110 Recomenda-se marcação de lugares
Rrikoomaynda-si markasowng si loogahrsh
Seat reservations are recommended

111 Segunda classe
Sigoonda klahs
Second-class

112 Suplemento Pagável
Sooplimayngtoo pagahvel
Supplement Payable

113 Via
Veeah
Via

Luggage

114 How much will it cost to send (ship) my luggage in advance?
Quanto custa mandar a minha bagagem primeiro?
Kwantoo kooshta mandahr a meenya bagahzhayng preemayuroo?

115 Where is the left luggage (baggage claim) office?
Onde é o escritório de recolha de bagagem?
Ohngdee eh oo ishkreetohreeoo di rricohliyadi bagahzhayng

116 What time do you open/close?
A que horas abre/fecha?
A ke orash ahbre/fesha

117 Where are the luggage trolleys (carts)?
Onde estão os carrinhos (trolleys)
Ohngdee ishtowng oos karreenyoosh (trolleysh)

118 Where are the lockers?
Onde são os cacifos?
Ohngd sowng oos kaseefoosh?

119 I have lost my locker key.
Perdi a chave do meu cacifo.
Perdee a shahve doo mayo kaseefoo

On Board

120 Is this seat taken?
Este lugar está ocupado?
Aysht loogahr istah ohkoopahdoo?

121 Excuse me, you are sitting in my reserved seat.

Desculpe, está sentado no meu lugar marcado.

Dishkoolp, istah sayntahdoo noo mayo loogahr markahdoo

122 Which station is this?

Que estação é esta?

Ki ishtasowng eh ehshta?

123 What time is this train/bus/ ferry/flight due to arrive/ depart?

A que horas deve chegar/partir este combóio/autocarro/barco/ voo?

A ke orash dehv shigahr/parteer aysht kohngboyoo/owtohkahrro/ bahrkoo/vo'oo

124 Will you wake me just before we arrive?

Acorda-me antes de chegarmos?

Akohrda-mi antishdi shegahrmoosh?

Customs and Passports

125 Os passaportes, por favor!

Oosh pahsaportsh poor favohr!

Passports, please!

126 I have nothing to declare.I have wine/spirits (alcohol)/ tobacco to declare.

Não tenho nada a declarar. Tenho/vinho/bebidas alcoólicas/tabaco a declarar.

Nown taynyoo nahda a deklarahr. Taynyoo nahda/veenyo/bibeedash ahlcohleecash/tabahkoo a deklarahr

127 I shall be staying for . . . days/weeks/months.

Vou ficar durante . . . dias/ semanas/meses.

Voh feecahr doorangt . . . deeash/ simahnash/mehzesh.

AT THE TOURIST OFFICE

128 Do you have a map of the town/area?

Tem um mapa da cidade/zona?

Tayng oong mahpa da seedahde/ zohna?

129 Can I reserve accommodation here?

Posso fazer marcação de alojamento aqui?

Possoo fazayr markasowng de aloozhamayntoo akee?

130 Do you have a list of accommodation?

Tem uma lista de alojamentos?

Tayng ooma leeshta di aloozhamayntoosh?

ACCOMMODATION

Hotels

131 I have a reservation in the name of . . .

Tenho uma marcação em nome de . . .

Taynyo ooma markasowng ayng nohmi di . . .

P
O
R
T
U
G
U
E
S
E

121
↑
131

ACCOMMODATION

132 I wrote to/faxed/telephoned you last month/last week in . . .
Escrevi/mandei um fax/ telefonei no mês passado/na semana passada . . .
Ishkrevee/manday oong fahks/ tilifoonay noo mays pasahdoo/na simahna pasahda . . .

133 Do you have any rooms free?
Tem quartos vagos?
Tayng kwahrtoosh vahgoosh?

134 I would like to reserve a single/double room with/ without bath/shower.
Queria marcar um quarto para uma pessoa/para duas pessoas com/sem banho/chuveiro.
Kireea marcahr oong kwahrtoo para ooma pesoha/ para dooash pesoash.

135 I would like bed and breakfast/(room and) half board/(room and) full board.
Queria cama e pequeno almoço/meia pensão/pensão completa.
Kireea kam ee pikayno ahlmohso/ maya pengsowng/pengsowng komplehta.

136 How much is it per night?
Quanto custa por noite?
Kwantoo koosta poor noyt?

137 Is breakfast included?
O pequeno almoço está incluído?
Oo pikaynoo ahlmohsoo istah eenklooeedoo?

138 May I see the room?
Posso ver o quarto?
Possoo vayr oo kwartoo?

139 Do you have any cheaper rooms?
Tem quartos mais baratos?
Tayng kwartoosh myish barahtoosh?

140 I would like to take the room.
Queria ficar com o quarto.
Kireea feecahr kohm oo kwartoo

141 I would like to stay for . . . nights.
Queria ficar por . . . noites.
Kireea ficahr poor . . . noytish

142 The shower/light/tap doesn't work.
O chuveiro/a luz/a torneira não funciona.
Oo shoovayroo/er loosh/er toornayra nown foongsyona.

143 At what time/where is breakfast served?
A que horas/onde é servido o pequeno almoço?
Er ke orash eh sirveedo oo pikaynoo ahlmossoo?

144 What time do I have to check-out?
A que horas tenho de deixar o quarto?
A ke orash taynyo di dayshahr oo kwahrto?

145 Can I have the key to room no . . ?
Pode-me dar a chave do quarto número . . ?

Pohdi-mi dahr er shahv doo
kwahrtoo noomiroo . . ?

146 My room number is . . .
O número do meu quarto é . . .
*Oo noomiroo doo mayo kwahrto
eh . . .*

147 Do you accept travellers'
cheques/Eurocheques/credit
cards?
Aceita cheques de viagem/
Eurocheques/cartões de crédito?
*Asayta shehkiesh di veeahzhayng/
ayooorosheksh/kartoyesh di
kredeetoo*

148 May I have the bill please?
Pode-me dar a conta, por favor?
*Pohd-mi dahr er kohngta, poor
favohr?*

149 Excuse me, I think there is a
mistake in this bill.
Desculpe, acho que há um erro
nesta conta.
*Dishkoolp, ahshoo ke ah oong
ayrroo na kohngta*

Youth Hostels

150 How much is a dormitory bed
per night?
Quanto é uma cama num
dormitório por noite?
*Kwantoo eh ooma kama noong
dormeetohreeoo poor noyt?*

151 I am/am not an HI member.
Sou/não sou membro do HI
*Soh/nown soh mayngbroo doo
agah ee*

152 May I use my own sleeping
bag?
Posso usar o meu saco de
dormir?
*Possoo oozahr oo mayu sahkoo di
dormeer?*

153 What time do you lock the
doors at night?
A que horas fecham as portas à
noite?
*Er ki orash fayshowm as pportash
ah noyt?*

Camping

154 May I camp here for the
night/two nights?
Posso acampar aqui esta noite/
por duas noites?
*Posso akampahr akee eshta noyt/
poor dooash noytsh?*

155 Where can I pitch my tent?
Onde posso armar a minha
tenda?
*Ohngd possoo ahrmahr er meenya
tayngda?*

156 How much does it cost for
one night/week?
Quanto custa por uma noite/
uma semana?
*Kwantoo kooshta poor ooma noyt/
ooma simana?*

157 Where can we park our
caravan?
Onde podemos estacionar a
nossa roulotte?
*Ohngd podaymosh ishtaseeoonahr
er nossa roolohte?*

EATING AND DRINKING

[158] **Where are the washing facilities?**
Onde são as casas de banho?
Ohngd sowng ash kahzash di banyoo?

[159] **Is there a restaurant/ supermarket/swimming pool on site/nearby?**
Há aqui/perto um restaurante/ supermercado/uma piscina?
Ah akee pehrtoo oong ristowrangt/ soopermercahdoo/ooma peeshseena?

[160] **Do you have a safety deposit box?**
Tem cofre para guardar valores?
Tayng kohfr para gwardahr valohrsh?

EATING AND DRINKING

Cafés and Bars

[161] **I would like a cup of/two cups of/another coffee/tea.**
Queria uma chávena de/duas chávenas de/outro café/chá.
Kireea ooma shahvna di/dooash shahvnash di ohtroo kafeh/shah.

[162] **With/without milk/sugar.**
Com/sem leite/açúcar.
Kohng/sayng layt/asookar.

[163] **I would like a bottle/glass/ two glasses of mineral water/ red wine/white wine, please.**
Queria uma garrafa/um copo/ dois copos/ de água mineral/ vinho tinto/vinho branco, por

favor.
Kireea ooma garrahfa/oong kohpoo/doysh kopoosh/ di ahgwa meenirahl/veenyo teengto/ veenyo brahngkoo poor favohr

[164] **I would like a beer/two beers, please.**
Queria uma cerveja/duas cervejas, por favor.
Kireea ooma servayzha/dooash servaizhash, poor favohr.

[165] **May I have some ice?**
Pode-me dar gelo?
Pohd-mi dahr zhayloo?

[166] **Do you have any matches/ cigarettes/cigars?**
Tem fósforos/cigarros/ charutos?
Tayng fohshfooroosh/ seegahrroosh/sharootoosh?

Restaurants

[167] **Can you recommend a good/ inexpensive restaurant in this area?**
Pode recomendar um restaurante bom/económico nesta área?
Pohd rrikoomayndahr oong ristowrangt bohm/eekinohmeekoo nehshta ahreea?

[168] **I would like a table for . . . people.**
Queria uma mesa para . . . pessoas.
Kireea ooma mehza para . . . pesoash.

242

169 Do you have a non-smoking area?

Tem uma área de não fumadores?

Tayng ooma ahreea di nown foomadohrsh?

170 Waiter/Waitress!

Faz favor!

Fash favohr!

171 Do you have a set menu/ children's menu/wine list?

Tem uma ementa turística/ ementa para crianças/carta de vinhos?

Tayng oom eemaynta tooreehshteeka para kreeangsash/ kahrta di veenyoosh?

172 Do you have any vegetarian dishes, please?

Tem pratos vegetarianos, por favor?

Tayng prahtoosh vezhetareeahnoosh, poor favohr?

173 Are there any local specialities?

Há algumas especialidades locais?

Ah ahlgoomash ishpiseealeedahdsh lookeyish?

174 Are vegetables included?

Os legumes estão incluídos?

Oosh ligoomish ishtowng eenklooihdoosh?

175 Could I have it well-cooked/ medium/rare please?

Posso escolher bem passado/ médio/mal passado, por favor?

Possoo ishkoolyer bayng pasahdoo/mahl pasahdoo, poor favohr?

176 What does this dish consist of?

De que consiste este prato?

Di ki konseesht aysht prahtoo?

177 I would like the set menu, please.

Queria a ementa turística, por favor.

Kireea er eemengta toorihshteeca, poor favohr.

178 We have not been served yet.

Ainda não fomos servidos.

Aeehnda nown fohmoosh serveedosh.

179 Excuse me, this is not what I ordered.

Desculpe, não foi isto que encomendei.

Dishkoolp, nown fohee eeshtoo ki inkoomaynday.

180 May I have some/some more bread/water/coffee/tea?

Pode-me dar pão/mais pão/ água/café/chá?

Pohde-mi dahr myish powng/ ahgwa/cafeh/shah

181 May I have the bill, please?

Pode-me dar a conta, por favor?

Pohd-mi dahr er kohngta, poor favohr?

182 Does this bill include service?

A conta inclui serviço?

Er kohngta eengklooee sirveesso?

P
O
R
T
U
G
U
E
S
E

169
↕
182

243

[183] Do you accept travellers'
cheques (travelers' checks)/
Eurocheques/MasterCard/US
dollars?
Aceita cheques de viagem/
Eurocheques/MasterCard/
Dólares americanos?
*Asayta shehkish di veeahzhayng/
ayoorohsheksh/mahshtehrkahrd/
dohlarsh amireekahnoosh?*

[184] Can I have a receipt, please?
Pode-me dar um recibo, por
favor?
*Pohd-mi dahr oong rriseeboo, poor
favohr?*

[185] Where is the toilet
(restroom), please?
Por favor, onde são os lavabos?
*Poor favohr, ohngdee sowng oos
lavahboosh?*

On the Menu

[186] First courses
Entradas
Intrahdash

[187] Soups
Sopas
Sohpash

[188] Main courses
Pratos principais
Prahtoosh preengseepaheesh

[189] Fish dishes
Pratos de peixe
Prahtoosh di paysh

[190] Meat dishes
Pratos de carne
Prahtoosh di kahrni

[191] Vegetarian dishes
Pratos vegetarianos
Prahtoosh vizhitareeanoosh

[192] Cheese
Queijo
Kayzhoo

[193] Desserts
Sobremesas
Kohbrimehzash

[194] Specialities
Especialidades
Ishpiseealeedahdsh

GETTING AROUND

Public Transport

[195] Where is the bus stop/coach
station/nearest metro
(subway) station?
Onde é a paragem do autocarro/
garagem das camionetas/a
estação de metro mais próxima?
*âgdee eh er parahzhayng doo
owtohkahrroo/garahzhayng das
kameeonehtash/er ishtasowng di
mehtroo myish prohseema?*

[196] When is the next/last bus
to . . ?
Quando sai o próximo/último
autocarro para . . ?
*Kwandoo sahee oo prohseemoo
owtohkahrroo para . . ?*

[197] How much is the fare to the
city centre (downtown)/
railway (railroad) station/
airport?

P
O
R
T
U
G
U
E
S
E

183
↕
197

244

Quanto é o bilhete para o centro da cidade/estação de caminho de ferro/ aeroporto?
Ântoo eh oo beelyayte para oo sengtroo da seedahdi/ishtasowng di kaminyoo di fehrroo/ aehrohportoo?

198 **Will you tell me when to get off?**
Diz-me quando devo sair?
Deesh-mi kwandoo dehvoo saeehr?

199 **Does this bus go to . . ?**
Este autocarro vai para . . ?
Aysht owtohkahrroo va'ee para .. ?

200 **Which number bus goes to . . ?**
Qual é o número do autocarro que vai para . . ?
Kwal eh oo noomiroo doo owtohkahrroo ki va'ee para . . ?

201 **May I have a single (one-way)/return (round-trip)/day ticket/book of tickets?**
Pode-me dar um bilhete simples/ida e volta/diário/caderneta de bilhetes?
Pohd-mi dahr oong beelyayt seemplish/eeda ee vohlta/deeahreeoo/kadirnayta di beelyaytsh?

Taxis

202 **I would like to go to . . .**
How much will it cost?
Queria ir para . . .
Quanto custa?
Kireea eer para . . . kwngtoo kooshta?

203 **Please stop here.**
Pare aqui, por favor.
Pahr akee, poor favohr

204 **I would like to order a taxi today/tomorrow/at 2pm to go from . . . to . . .**
Queria um táxi para hoje/amanhã/ às duas da tarde para ir de . . . para . . .
Kireea oong tahksee para ohzhay/ ahmanyang/ahsh dooash da tahrd para eer de . . . para . . .

Asking the Way

205 **Excuse me, do you speak English?**
Desculpe, fala Inglês?
Dishkoolp, fahla eenglays?

206 **Excuse me, is this the right way to . . ?**
Desculpe é este o caminho certo para . . ?
Dishkoolp, eh aysht oo kameenyo sehrtoo para . . ?

207 **. . . the cathedral/the tourist information office/the castle/ the old town**
. . . a catedral/os serviços de informações turísticas (o turismo)/o castelo/a cidade velha
. . . er katidrahl/ oos sirveessoos de eemfoormasoyesh tooreehshteekash (oo tooreesmoo)/ oo kastehloo/ er seedahd vehlya.

208 **Can you tell me the way to the railway (railroad) station/ bus station/taxi rank (stand)/ city centre (downtown)/ beach?**

Pode-me indicar o caminho para a estação de caminho de ferro/a estação de autocarros/a paragem de táxis/o centro da cidade/a praia?

Podd-mi eendeecahr oo kameenyoo para er ishtasowng de kameenyo do fehrro/er ishtasowng di owtohkahrrosh/er parahzhayng de tahkseesh/oo sayntroo da seedahd/ er prahya?

209 **First/second left/right/ straight ahead.**

Primeira/segunda à esquerda/à direita/sempre em frente

Premayra/sigoonda ah ishkehrda/ ah deerayta/sayngpri ayng frayNti

210 **Where is the nearest police station/post office/doctor/ hospital/pharmacy?**

Onde é o posto da polícia/o correio/o médico/o hospital/a farmácia mais próximo?

Ohngdee eh oo pohshtoo da pooleesseea/oo koorrayoo/oo medeekoo/oo ohspeetahl/er farmasseah myish prohseemoo?

211 **Is it far?**

É longe?

Eh lohnzhi?

212 **Do I need to take a taxi/catch a bus?**

Preciso de apanhar um táxi/um autocarro?

Preseezoo di apanyahr oong tahksee/oong owtohkahrroo?

213 **Can you point to it on my map?**

Pode indicá-lo no meu mapa?

Pohd eendeecahloo noo mayo mahpa?

214 **Thank you for your help.**

Obrigado pela sua ajuda.

Ohbreegahdoo pehla sooa azhooda

SIGHTSEEING

215 **Where is the Tourist Information office?**

Onde é o Turismo?

Ohngdee eh oo tooreeshmoo?

216 **Where is the cathedral/ church/museum?**

Onde é a catedral/igreja/museu?

Ohngdee eh er katidrahl/ eegrayzha/moosayo?

217 **How much is the entrance (admission) charge?**

Qual é o preço da entrada?

Kwal eh oo preso do ayntrahda?

218 **Is there a discount for children/students/senior citizens?**

Há desconto para crianças/ estudantes/pessoas da terceira idade?

Ah dishkohngtoo para kreeangsash/ishtoodangtish/ pisoahsh da tersayra eedahd?

219 **What time does the next guided tour start?**
A que horas começa a próxima visita guiada?
Er ki orash koomehsa er prohseema veezeeta gueeahda?

220 **One/two adults/children, please.**
Um/dois adultos, uma/duas crianças, por favor.
Oong/doysh adooltoosh, ooma/dooash kreeangsash poor favohr.

221 **May I take photographs here?**
Posso tirar fotografias aqui?
Posso teerahr footoografeeash akee?

ENTERTAINMENT

222 **Can you recommend a good bar/nightclub?**
Pode recomendar um bom bar/clube nocturno?
Pohd rrikoomayngdahr oong bohm bahre/kloob nohtoornoo?

223 **Do you know what is on at the cinema (playing at the movies)/theatre at the moment?**
Sabe o que vai no cinema/teatro de momento?
Sahb oo ke va'ee noo seenayma/teeahtroo do momayngtoo?

224 **I would like to book (purchase) . . . tickets for the matinee/evening performance on Monday.**

Queria comprar . . . bilhetes para a sessão da tarde/noite, segunda-feira.
Kireea komprahr . . . beelyaytsh para er sessowngda tahrd/noyt, sigoonda-fayra.

225 **What time does the film/performance start?**
A que horas começa o filme/a sessão?
Er ki orash koomehsa oo film/er sesowng?

MEETING PEOPLE

226 **Hello/Goodbye.**
Olá/Adeus
Ohlah/adayoosh

227 **Good morning/good afternoon/good evening/goodnight.**
Bom dia/boa tarde/boa noite/boa noite
Bohm deea/boha tahrd/boha noyt

228 **Pleased to meet you.**
Muito prazer
Muhingtoo prazayr

229 **How are you?**
Como está?
Kohmoo istah?

230 **Fine, thank you. And you?**
Bem obrigado. E você?
Bayng ohbreegahdoo. ee vohsay?

231 **My name is . . .**
Chamo-me . . .
Shamoo-mi . . .

232 This is my friend/boyfriend/
girlfriend/husband/wife/
brother/sister.
Este é o meu/minha amigo/
amiga/namorado/namorada/
marido/mulher/irmão/irmã
*Aysht e oo mayoo/meenya
amighoo/amigha/namoorahdoo/
namoorahda/mareedoo/moolyer/
eermowng/eermang*

233 Where are you travelling to?
Para onde vai viajar?
Para ohngdee va'ee veeazhahr?

234 I am/we are going to . . .
Vou/vamos para . . .
Voh/vamoosh para . . .

235 How long are you travelling
for?
Vai para muito longe?
Va'ee para muhingtoo lohngzhe?

236 Where do you come from?
De onde vem?
Di ohngd vayng?

237 I am/we are from . . .
Sou/somos de . . .
Soh/sohmoosh di . . .

238 We're on holiday.
Estamos em férias.
Ishtahmoos ayng fehreeas

239 This is our first visit here.
Esta é a nossa primeira visita
aqui
Ehshta e er nossa

240 Would you like/May I have a
cigarette?
Quer um cigarro/posso fumar?

*Ker oong seegahrro/possoo
foomahr?*

241 I am sorry but I do not
understand.
Desculpe mas não entendo.
*Dishkoolp maysh nown
ayngtayngdoo.*

242 Please speak slowly.
Por favor, fale devagar.
Poor favohr fahl divagahr.

243 Do you mind if I smoke?
Importa-se se eu fumar?
Eemporta-si see ayoo foomahr?

244 Do you have a light?
Tem lume?
Tayng loome?

245 I am waiting for my husband/
wife/boyfriend/girlfriend.
Estou à espera do meu/minha
marido/mulher/namorado/
namorada.
*Ishtoh ah ishpehra doo mayoo/
meenyia mareedoo/moolyer/
namoorahdoo/namoorahda*

TRAVELLING WITH CHILDREN

246 Do you have a high chair/
baby-sitting service/cot?
Tem uma cadeira alta/serviço
de baby-sitting/cama de bébé?
*Tayng ooma kadayra ahlta/
sirveessoo di baby sitting/kama di
behbeh?*

247 Where is the nursery/
playroom?
Onde é a creche/infantário?

Ohngd e er kresh/eengfantahreeoo

248 Where can I warm the baby's bottle?

Onde posso aquecer o biberon do bébé?

Ohngd possoo akesayr oo beeberohng doo behbeh?

COMMUNICATIONS

Post

249 How much will it cost to send a letter/postcard/this package to Britain/Ireland/America/Canada/Australia/New Zealand?

Quanto custa mandar uma carta/postal/este pacote para Grã-Bretanha/Irlanda/América/Canadá/Austrália/Nova Zelândia?

Kwantoo kooshta mandahr ooma kahrta/pooshtahl/esht pakoht para grang-britanya/ eerlangda/ amehreeka/kanadah/owstrahleea/ nohva zelangdeea?

250 I would like one stamp/two stamps.

Queria um selo/dois selos.

Kireea oong saylo/doysh sayllosh

251 I'd like . . . stamps for postcards to send abroad, please.

Queria . . . selos para postais para o estrangeiro, por favor.

Kireea . . . sayloosh para pooshtiysh para o ishtrangzhayroo, poor favohr.

Phones

252 I would like to make a telephone call/reverse the charges to (make a collect call to) . . .

Queria fazer uma chamada/a pagar por quem recebe

Kireea fazayr ooma shamahda/er pagahr poor kayng ressebe

253 Which coins do I need for the telephone?

Que moedas preciso para telefonar?

Ki mwedash preseezoo para tilifoonahr?

254 The line is engaged (busy).

A linha está impedida.

A leenya istah eempideeda

255 The number is . . .

O número é . . .

Oo noomiroo e . . .

256 Hello, this is . . .

Está, aqui fala . . .

Ishtah, akee fahla . . .

257 May I speak to . . ?

Posso falar com . . ?

Possoo falahr kom . . .

258 He/She is not in at the moment. Can you call back?

Não está neste momento. Pode tornar a chamar?

Nown ishtah nayshte moomayntoo. pohd toornahr a shamahr?

P
O
R
T
U
G
U
E
S
E

248
↕
258

MONEY/SHOPPING

MONEY

259 I would like to change these travellers' cheques (travelers' checks)/this currency/this Eurocheque.

Queria trocar estes cheques de viagem/estas divisas/este Eurocheque.

Kireea trookahr aystsh shehkish di veeazhayng/ehshtash deeveezash/ayst ayroshek.

260 How much commission do you charge? (What is the service charge?)

Que comissão cobra?

Ke coomeessowng kohbra?

261 Can I obtain money with my MasterCard?

Posso levantar dinheiro com o meu MasterCard?

Possoo levangtahr deenyayroo kohm oo mayo mahstercahrd?

SHOPPING

Names of Shops and Departments

262 Livraria/Papelaria
Leevrareea/Papilareea
Bookshop/Stationery

263 Joalharia/Presentes
Zhooalyareea/Prizayntsh
Jeweller's/Gifts

264 Sapatos
Sapahtoosh
Shoes

265 Ferragens
Ferrahzhayngsh
Hardware

266 Antiguidades
Anteegweedadish
Antiques

267 Cabeleireiro (de homens)/(de senhoras)
Kabilayrayroo (di ohmayns)/(di sinyorash)
Hairdressers (men's)/(women's)

268 Tabacaria
Tabakareea
Tobacconist

269 Padaria
Padareea
Baker's

270 Supermercado
Soopermercahdoo
Supermarket

271 Fotografia
Footoografeea
Photoshop

272 Brinquedos
Breengkehdoosh
Toys

273 Agente de Viagens
Azhayngt di veeahzhayngsh
Travel Agent

274 Perfumarias
Pirfoomareeash
Toiletries

275 Discos
Deeshkoosh
Records

In the Shop

276 What time do the shops open/close?
A que horas abrem/fecham as lojas?
A kee orah abrayng/fayshown ash lohzhash

277 Where is the nearest market?
Onde é o mercado mais próximo?
Ohngdee eh oo mercahdoo myish prohseemoo?

278 Can you show me the one in the window/this one?
Pode mostrar-me aquele na janela/este
Pohd mooshtrahr-mi akehle na zhanehla/aysht

279 Can I try this on?
Posso provar este?
Possoo proovahr aysht?

280 What size is this?
Que tamanho (número) é este?
Ki tamanyo (noomiroo) eh ayst?

281 This is too large/too small/too expensive.
Este é muito grande/muito pequeno/muito caro.
Aysht eh muingtoo grangdi/ muingtoo pikaynoo/muingtoo kahroo

282 Do you have any others?
Tem outros
Tayng ohtroosh

283 My size is . . .
O meu tamanho (número) é . . .

Oo mayo tamanyo (noomiroo) eh . . .

284 Where is the changing room/childrens/cosmetic/ladieswear/menswear/food department?
Onde é o gabinete de prova/secção infantil/cosmética/roupa de senhora/roupa de homem/secção de alimentos?
Ohngdee eh oo gabeeneht di prohva/sehksowng eengfangteel/ koosmehteeca/rohpa di sinyora/ rohpa di omayng/seksowng di aleemayngtoosh

285 I would like . . .
Queria . . .
Kireea . . .

286 I would like a quarter of a kilo/half a kilo/a kilo of bread/ butter/cheese/ham/ tomatoes.
Queria duzentos e cinquenta gramas/meio quilo/um quilo de pão/manteiga/queijo/ fiambre/ tomate.
Kireea doozayntoosh ee seengkwayngta gramash/mayoo keeloo/ oong keeloo di powng/ mangtayga/kayzhoo/feeangbri/ toomaht

287 How much is this?
Quanto custa isto?
Kwantoo kooshta eeshtoo?

288 I'll take this one, thank you.
Levo este, obrigado
Lehvoo aysht, ohbreegahdoo

289 Do you have a carrier (shopping) bag?

Tem um saco de plástico com pegas?

Tayng oong sahkoo di plahshteekoo kohng pehgash?

290 Do you have anything cheaper/larger/smaller/of better quality?

Tem alguma coisa mais barata/maior/mais pequena/de melhor qualidade?

Tayngahlgooma kohyza myish barahta/mahyohr/myish peekayna/do melior kwaleedahd?

291 I would like a film for this camera.

Queria um rolo para esta máquina.

Kireea oongrohloo para ehshta mahkeena.

292 I would like some batteries, the same size as this old one.

Queria umas pilhas do mesmo tamanho que esta.

Kireea oomash peelyash doo maysmoo tamahnyo ki ehshta.

293 Would you mind wrapping this for me, please?

Importa-se de me embrulhar isto, por favor?

Eemporta-si di mi aymbroolyahr eeshtoo, poor favohr?

294 Sorry, but you seem to have given me the wrong change.

Desculpe mas parece que me deu o troco errado.

Dishkoolp maysh parehse ki mi dayoo oo trohcoo eerrahdoo.

MOTORING

Car Hire (Rental)

295 I have ordered (rented) a car in the name of . . .

Reservei um carro em nome de . . .

Rrizervay oongkahrrooay nohmdi

296 How much does it cost to hire (rent) a car for one day/two days/one week?

Quanto custa alugar um carro por um dia/dois dias/uma semana?

Kwantoo kooshta aloogahr oong kahrroo poor oong deea/doysh deeash/ooma simahna?

297 Is the tank already full of petrol (gas)?

O depósito já está cheio de gasolina?

Oo depohzeetoo zhah ishtah shayoo di gazooleena?

298 Is insurance and tax included? How much is the deposit?

O seguro e o imposto estão incluídos? Quanto é o depósito?

Oosigooro ee oo eempohshtoo ishtowng eenklooeehdoosh? kwantoo eh oo depohzeetoo?

299 By what time must I return the car?

289
↕
299

P
O
R
T
U
G
U
E
S
E

A que horas devo devolver o
carro?
*A ki orash devoo divolvehr oo
kahrroo?*

300 I would like a small/family
car with a radio/cassette
player.
Queria um carro pequeno/
familiar com rádio/leitor de
cassettes.
*Kireea oong kahrroo pikayni/
fameeleeahr kohng rahdeeoo/
laytohr do casehtsh*

Asking the Way

301 Excuse me, can you help me
please?
Desculpe, pode dar-me uma
ajuda?
*Dishkoolp, pohd dahr-mi ooma
azhooda?*

302 How do I reach the
motorway/main road?
Como vou para a autoestrada/
estrada principal?
*Kohngoo voh para a
owtoishtrahda/ishtrahda
preengseepahl?*

303 I think I have taken the
wrong turning.
Acho que virei no sítio errado.
*Ahshoo ki veeray noo seeteeoo
irradoo*

304 I am looking for this address.
Estou à procura desta morada.
*Ishtoh ah prohkoora deshta
moorahda.*

305 I am looking for the . . .
hotel.
Estou à procura do hotel . . .
Ishtou ah prokoora doo otel . . .

306 How far is it to . . .
from here?
A que distância daqui fica . . .
A ki deeshtangseea dakee feeka . . .

307 Carry straight on for . . .
kilometres.
Continui a direito por . . .
quilómetros.
*Kongteenooee a deeraytoo poor . . .
keelohmetrosh*

308 Take the next turning on the
right/left.
Vire na próxima à direita/esquerda
*Veer na prohseema ah deerayta/
ishkayrda*

309 Turn right/left at the next
crossroads/traffic lights.
Vire à direita/esquerda no
próximo cruzamento/semáforo
*veer ah deerayta/ishkayrda noo
prohseemoo kroozamengtoo/
simahfooroo*

310 You are going in the wrong
direction.
Vai na direcção errada.
Va'ee na deeresowng irrahda

Parking

311 How long can I park here?
Por quanto tempo posso
estacionar aqui?
*Poor kwantoo taympoo possoo
ishtaseeoonahr akee?*

312 Is there a car park near here?
Há um parque de
estacionamento aqui perto?
*Ah oong pahrki di
ishtaseeoonamayngtoo akee
pehrtoo?*

313 At what time does this car
park close?
A que horas fecha este parque
de estacionamento?
*A ki orash faysha aysht pahrk di
ishtaseeoonamayngtoo?*

Signs and Notices

314 Via única
Veea oohneeka
One way.

315 Entrada proibida
Ayntrahda proeebeeda
No entry.

316 Estacionamento proibido
Ishtaseeoonamayngto proeebeedoo
No parking.

317 Desvio
Dishveeoo
Detour (diversion)

318 Stop (paragem)
Stop (parahzhayng)
Stop.

319 Dê passagem
Deh passahzhayng
Give way (yield).

320 Estrada escorregadia
Ishtrahda iskorregadeea
Slippery road.

321 Ultrapassagem proibida
Ultrapassahzhayng proeebeeda
No overtaking.

At the Filling Station

322 Unleaded (lead-free)/
Standard/Premium
Sem chumbo/Normal/Super
Sayng shoongboo/normahl/sooper

323 Fill the tank please.
Encha o depósito por favor.
*Ayngsha oo depohzeetoo poor
favohr*

324 Do you have a road map of
this area?
Tem um mapa das estradas
desta zona?
*Tayng oong mahpa dash
ishtradash dehshya zona?*

325 How much is the car-wash?
Quanto é a lavagem do carro?
*Kwanto eh a lavazhayng doo
kahrroo*

Breakdowns

326 I've had a breakdown at . . .
Tive uma avaria em . . .
Teev ooma avareea ayng . . .

327 I am on the road from . . .
to . . .
Estou na estrada de . . .
para . . .
*Ishtoh na ishtrahda di . . .
para . . .*

328 I can't move the car. Can you send a tow-truck?

Não posso mover o carro. Pode mandar um reboque?

Nown possoo moovehr oo kahrroo. pohd mandahr oong ribok

329 I have a flat tyre.

Tenho um pneu furado.

Tayngoo oong pnayoo foorahdoo

330 The windscreen (windshield) has smashed/cracked.

O pára-brisas estilhaçou-se/rachou.

Oo pahra-breezash isteelyasoh-si/rrashoh.

331 There is something wrong with the engine/brakes/lights/steering/gearbox/clutch/exhaust.

Qualquer coisa está mal com o motor/os travões/os faróis/o volante/a caixa de velocidades/ a embraiagem/ o tubo de escape.

Kwalkehr kohiza ishtah mahl kohng oo mootohr/oosh travoyesh/oosh faroysh/oo voolangt/a kaisha dash vilooseedahdish/a aymbriyahzhayng

332 It's overheating.

Está a aquecer demais.

Istah a akehser demaish

333 It won't start.

Não arranca

Nown arrangka

334 Where can I get it repaired?

Onde posso mandá-lo arranjar?

Ohngd possoo mandahloo arrangzhahr?

335 Can you take me there?

Pode-me levar lá?

Pohdmi livahr lah?

336 Will it take long to fix?

Leva muito tempo a arranjar?

Lehva muingtoo tayngpoo a arrangzhahr?

337 How much will it cost?

Quanto vai custar?

Kwantoo va'ee kooshtahr?

Accidents

338 Can you help me? There has been an accident.

Pode-me ajudar? Houve um acidente.

Pohdmi azhoodahr? ohv oong aseedayngt

339 Please call the police/an ambulance.

Por favor chame a polícia/uma ambulância.

Poor favohr, shahm a pooleesya/ooma angboolansya

340 Is anyone hurt?

Há alguém ferido?

Ah ahlguayng fereedoo?

Traffic Offences

341 I'm sorry, I didn't see the sign.

Desculpe, não vi o sinal.

Dishkoolp nown vee oo seenahl

[342] **Must I pay a fine? How much?**
Tenho de pagar uma multa? De quanto?
Taynyoo di pagahr ooma moolta? di kwantoo?

[343] **Show me your documents.**
Mostre-me os seus documentos.
Mohshtrimi oosh sayosh dokoomayngtoosh

HEALTH

Pharmacy

[344] **Do you have anything for a stomachache/headache/sore throat/toothache?**
Tem qualquer coisa para dores de estômago/dores de cabeça/ dores de garganta/ dores de dentes?
Tayng kwalkehr kohiza para dohrish di ishtohmago/dohrish di kabehsa/ dohrish do gargangta/ dorish di dengtish?

[345] **I need something for diarrhoea (diarrhea)/ constipation/a cold/a cough/ insect bites/sunburn/travel (motion) sickness.**
Preciso de alguma coisa contra diarreia/prisão de ventre/ uma constipação/ tosse/picadas de insectos/queimaduras do sol/ enzhoo.
Preseezoo di ahlgooma kohiza kongtra deearraya/preezowng di ventre/ooma konshteepasowng/

tohs/peekahdash do eensetoosh/ kaymadoorash doo sohl/ingzho'oo

[346] **How much/how many do I take?**
Quanto/quantos devo tomar?
Kwantoo/kwantoosh dayvoo toomahr?

[347] **How often do I take it/them?**
Quantas vezes devo tomar isto?
Kwantash vehzesh dayvoo toomahr ishto?

[348] **How much does it cost?**
Quanto custa?
Kwantoo kooshta?

[349] **Can you recommend a good doctor/dentist?**
Pode recomendar um bom médico/dentista?
Pohd rrikoomayngdahr oong bohm mehdeekoo/dayngteeshta?

[350] **Is it suitable for children?**
É bom para crianças?
Eh bohm para kreeansash?

Doctor

[351] **I have a pain here/in my arm/ leg/chest/stomach.**
Tenho uma dor aqui/no braço/ na perna/no peito/no estômago.
Taynyoo ooma dohr akee noo brahsoo/na perna/noo ishtohmagoo.

352 Please call a doctor, this is an emergency.
Por favor, chame um médico. É uma emergência.
Poor favohr sahni oong mehdeekoo. eh ooma imerzhayngseea.

353 I would like to make an appointment to see a doctor.
Queria marcar uma consulta para um médico.
Kireea markahr ooma kongsoolta para oong mehdeekoo.

354 I am diabetic/pregnant.
Sou diabético(a)/estou grávida.
Soh deeabehteekoo (a)/ishtoh grahveeda

355 I need a prescription for . . .
Preciso de uma receita para . . .
Priseezoo di ooma rresayta para . .

356 Can you give me something to ease the pain?
Pode-me dar alguma coisa para as dores?
Pod-mi dahr ahlgwma kohiza para as dohrish?

357 I am/he is/she is allergic to penicillin.
Sou/ele é/ela é/ alérgico/ alérgica à penicilina.
Soh/ili eh/ ehla eh/alehrzheekoo/ alehrzheeka ah peneeseeleena

358 Does this hurt?
Isso faz doer?
Eesso fahsh dooayr?

359 You must/he must/she must go to hospital.
Você deve/ele deve/ele deve ir para o hospital.
Dev/dev/dev eer para oo ohspeetahl

360 Take these once/twice /three times a day.
Tome isto uma vez/duas vezes/ três vezes ao dia.
Tohmi ishtoo ooma vays/dooash vayzish/traysh vayzish ow deea

361 I am/he is/she is taking this medication.
Estou/ele está/ela está a tomar este medicamento.
Ishtoh/ishtah a toomahr aysht medeekamayngtoo

362 I have medical insurance.
Tenho seguro médico.
Taynyo sigooroo mehdeekoo

Dentist

363 I have toothache.
Tenho uma dor de dente.
Taynyo ooma dohr do daynteesh

364 My filling has come out.
O meu chumbo caiu.
Oo mayo shoongboo kaeehoo

365 I do/do not want to have an injection first.
Quero/não quero levar uma injecç#ao primeiro.
Kehroo/nown kehroo levahr ooma eenzhehsowng preemayroo.

EMERGENCIES

366 Help!
Socorro!
Sookohrroo!

367 Call an ambulance/a doctor/ the police!
Chame uma ambulância/um médico/a polícia!
Shami ooma angboolangsya/oong medeekoo/ a pooleesseeya.

368 I have had my travellers' cheques (travelers' checks)/ credit cards/purse/handbag/ rucksack (knapsack)/ luggage/wallet stolen.
Roubaram-me os meus cheques de viagem/cartões de crédito/a minha bolsa/ mala de mão/a minha mochila/bagagem/ carteira.
Rrohbahrowm̃-mi oosh mayos shehkish di veeahzhayng/ kartoyesh di kredeetoo/ a meenya bohlsa/mahla di mowng/a meenya moosheela/bagahzhayng/ kartayra.

369 Can you help me, I have lost my daughter/son?

Pode ajudar-me? Perdi a minha filha/o meu filho.
Pohdee azhoodahr-mi? perdee a meenya feelya/oo mayo feelyoo.

370 Please go away/leave me alone.
Por favor, vá-se embora/deixe-me em paz.
Poor favohr, vah-see ayngbohra/ daysh-mi ayng pahsh.

371 Fire!
Fogo!
Fohgoo!

372 I want to contact the British/ American/Canadian/Irish/ Australian/New Zealand/ South African consulate.
Quero contactar o consulado Britânico/Americano/ Canadiano/Irlandês/ Australiano/da Nova Zelândia/ Sul Africano.
Keroo kohntaktahr oo konsoolahdoo breetahngeekoo/ amireekanoo/kanadeeanoo/ eerlahngdays/ owshtraleeanoo/da nohva zeelangdeea/sool afreekanoo

P
O
R
T
U
G
U
E
S
E

367
↕
372

Introduction

Alone among the languages of Eastern Europe, Romanian is a Romance tongue, descended from Latin and therefore a distant cousin of French, Italian, Spanish and Portuguese. This is of more than academic interest, since the basic meaning of many words in written Romanian can be understood by someone with a knowledge of one of these other languages. Spoken Romanian is reminiscent of French, which is the most likely second language you will encounter, at least among older and better-educated Romanians. In some regions of the country Hungarian or German will be understood.

R
O
M
A
N
I
A
N

Addresses for travel and tourist information

Australia: *Consulate-General,* 333 Old South Head Road, Bondi, NSW 2026; tel: (2) 9365 5718.
UK: *Romanian National Tourist Office,* New Cavendish St, London, W1G 8TT; tel: (020) 7224 3692.
USA: *Romanian National Tourist Office,* 14 East 38th Street (12th Floor), New York, NY 10016; tel: (212) 545 8484.

ESSENTIALS

ESSENTIALS

Alphabet

A *Ah*	B *Beh*
C *Cheh*	D *Deh*
E *Eh*	F *Eff*
G *Djeh*	H *Hash*
I *Ee*	J *Zheu*
K *Kah*	L *Ell*
M *Em*	N *En*
O *Oh*	P *Peh*
Q *Kew*	R *Airr*
S *Ess*	T *Ten*
U *Oo*	V *Veh*
W *Dooblooveh*	X *Ecks*
Y *Ee-grek*	Z *Zed*

Basic Words and Phrases

1 **Yes**   **No**
   Da   Nu
   Dah   *Noo*

2 **Please**   **Thank you**
   Te rog   Multumesc
   Teh rohg   *Multzumesc*

3 **That's O.K.**   **Perhaps**
   E în regula   Poate
   Eh an rehgoolah *Pwahteh*

4 **To**   **From**
   La   De la
   Lah   *Deh lah*

5 **Here**   **There**
   Aici   Acolo
   Aich   *Acohlo*

6 **None**   **Also**
   Nici unul/una De asemenea
   Neech oonool/oona *Deh asehmehneya*

7 **How**   **When**
   Cum?   Când?
   Coom   *Cund*

8 **What**   **Why**
   Ce?   De ce?
   Cheh   *Deh cheh*

9 **I don't understand.**
   Nu înteleg.
   Noo antzehleg

10 **I don't speak Romanian.**
   Nu vorbesc româneste.
   Noo vorbesc romaneshteh

11 **Do you speak English?**
   Vorbiti englezeste?
   Vorbeetz englezeshteh?

12 **Can you please write it down?**
   Scrieti vă rog.
   Screeyetz vah rohg

ROMANIAN

01
↕
12

260

13 **Can you please speak more slowly?**
Vorbiti mai rar vă rog.
Vorbeetz my rar vah rohg.

14 **How much does it/this cost?**
Cît costa?
Kewt costa?

Days

15 **Monday**
Luni
Loony

Tuesday
Marti
Martz

16 **Wednesday**
Miercuri
Me-aircooree

Thursday
Joi
Zhoy

17 **Friday**
Vineri.
Vinairee

Saturday
Sâmbăta
Sumbahtah

18 **Sunday**
Duminiča
Doomeeneeka

Morning
Dimineata.
Deemeeneyatza

19 **Afternoon**
Dupa amiaža
Dupah amiazah.

Evening
Seară
Sara

20 **Night**
Noapte
Nwaphteh

Week
Săptamâňa
Saptamerna.

21 **Yesterday/Today/Tomorrow**
Ieri/Azi/Mâine
Eeyairee/Ahzee/Meu-eeneh

Numbers

22 **Zero**
Zero
Zehro

One
Unu.
Oonoo

23 **Two**
Doi
Doy

Three
Trei.
Tray

24 **Four**
Patru.
Patroo

Five
Cinci.
Chinch

25 **Six**
Sase.
Shaseh

Seven
Sapte.
Shapteh

26 **Eight**
Opt.
Opt

Nine
Noŭa
Nower

27 **Ten**
Zece
Zecheh

Eleven
Unsprezece.
Oonsprezecheh

28 **Twelve**
Doisprezece
Doysprezecheh

Thirteen
Treisprezece
Traysprezecheh

29 **Fourteen**
Paisprezece.
Pie-sprezecheh

Fifteen
Cincisprezece.
Cheenchsprezecheh

30 **Sixteen**
Saisprezece
Shy-sprezecheh

Seventeen
Saptesprezece
Shaptesprezecheh

31 **Eighteen**
Optsprezece
Optsprezecheh

Nineteen
Noŭasprezece
Nowahsprezecheh.

32 **Twenty**
Doŭazeci.
Douahzech.

Twenty-one
Doŭazeci si unu.
Duoahzech she oonoo.

33 **Twenty-two**
Doŭazeci si doi.
Douahzech she doy

Thirty
Treizeci.
Trayzech

R
O
M
A
N
I
A
N

13
↕
33

34 Forty **Fifty**
Patruzeci. Cincizeci.
Patroozech. *Cheench-zech*

35 Sixty **Seventy**
Saizeci Saptezeci
Shy-zech *Shaptezech*

36 Eighty **Ninety**
Optzeci Noŭazeci
Optzech *Nowahzech*

37 One hundred **Five hundred**
O suťa Cinci sute
Oh sooter *Chinch sooteh*

38 One thousand **One million**
O mie Un milion
Oh meeyeh *Oon milion*

Time

39 9.00
Noŭa
Nowa

40 9.05
Noŭa si cinci.
Nowa she chinch

41 9.10
Noŭa si zece.
Nowa she zecheh

42 9.15
Noŭa si un sfert.
Nowa she oon sfehrt

43 9.20
Noŭa si doŭazeci.
Nowa she dowazech

44 9.25
Noŭa si doŭazeci si cinci.
Nowa she dowazech she chinch

45 9.30
Noŭa si jumătate.
Nowa she zhoomahtateh

46 9.35
Zece faťa doŭazeci si cinci.
Zecheh fahrah dowazech she chinch

47 9.40
Zece faťa doŭazeci.
Zecheh fahrah dowazech

48 9.45
Zece faťa un sfert.
Zecheh fahrah oon sfehrt

49 9.50
Zece faťa zece.
Zecheh fahrah zecheh

50 9.55
Zece faťa cinci.
Zecheh fahrah chinch

51 12.00/Midday/Midnight
Doŭasprezece/Amiaža/Miezul noptii.
Dowasprezecheh/Amiazah/Meeyehzool noptz

52 What time is it?
Cât este ceasul?
Cut esteh cheyasool?

53 It is . . .
Este ora . . .
Esteh ora . . .

ARRIVING AND DEPARTING

Airport

54 Excuse me, where is the check-in desk for . . . airline?

ROMANIAN

34
↑
54

Scuzati-mă unde este ghiseul
liniei aeriene . . ?
*Scoozatz-mah, oondeh esteh gisherl
leeneeyeh aereeyehneh . . ?*

**55 What is the boarding gate/
time for my flight?**
Care este poarta/ora de
îmbarcare pentru zborul meu?
*Cahreh esteh pwarta/ora deh
umbarcareh pentroo zborool meu?*

**56 How long is the delay likely
to be?**
Cît de lungă poate fi întârzierea?
*Cut deh loongah pwateh fee
unterzeeyaireya?*

57 Where is the duty-free shop?
Unde este magazinul duty-free?
*Oondeh esteh magazinool duty-
free?*

**58 Which way is the baggage
reclaim?**
De unde se colectează bagajele?
*Deh oondeh seh colectayah-zah
bagazhehleh?*

**59 Where can I get the bus to
the city centre?**
De unde pot lua autobuzul spre
centru?
*Deh oondeh pot lwah autoboozul
spreh chentroo?*

Train Station

**60 Where is the ticket office/
information desk?**
Unde este ghiseul de bilete/
ghiseul de informatii?
Oondeh esteh gisherl deh bileteh/

gisherl deh informatzi?

**61 Which platform does the
train to . . . depart from?**
De la ce peron pleacă trenul spre
. . ?
*Deh la cheh pehron pleyacah
trehnool spreh . . ?*

62 Where is platform . . ?
Unde este peronul . . ?
Oondeh esteh peronool . . ?

63 When is the next train to . . ?
La ce ora pleacă următorul tren
spre . . ?
*La cheh orah pleyacah
oormahtorool tren spreh . . ?*

64 Is there a later train to . . ?
Mai este un alt tren spre . . ?
My esteh oon alt tren spreh . . ?

Port

65 How do I get to the port?
Cum ajung în port?
Coom azhung un port?

**66 When is the next sailing
to . . ?**
Când este viitoarea cursa
spre . . ?
*Cund esteh veetwareya coorsa
spreh . . ?*

**67 Can I catch an earlier ferry
with this ticket?**
Pot ua cu acest bilet un vas care
pleacă mai devreme?
*Pot ooah coo achest bilet oon vas
cahreh pleyacah my devrehmeh?*

Notices and Signs

55
↕
67

ROMANIAN

68
↕
88

68 **Bufet/Vagon restaurant.**
Buffet/Vagon restaurant
Buffet (Dining) Car

69 **Autobuz.**
Autobooz
Bus

70 **Apă potabilă/Apă ne potabila**
Apah potabilah/Apah neh potabilah
Drinking/Non-drinking water

71 **Intrare**
Intrareh
Entrance

72 **Iesire**
Yesheereh
Exit

73 **Informatii**
Informatzee
Information

74 **Birou de bagaje**
Beero deh bagazheh
Left Luggage (Baggage Claim)

75 **Dulapioare pentru bagaje**
Doolapeeyowahreh pentroo bagazheh
Luggage Lockers

76 **Oficiul postal**
Ofeecheeyool poshtal
Post Office

77 **Peron**
Pehron
Platform

78 **Gară**
Garah
Railway (Railroad) Station

79 **Aeroport**
Aeroport
Airport

80 **Port**
Port
Port

81 **Restaurant**
Restaurant
Restaurant

82 **Zona pentru fumători/ nefumători**
Zonah pentroo foomahtoree/ nehfoomahtoree
Smoking/Non-Smoking

83 **Telefon**
Telefon
Telephone

84 **Ghiseu de bilete**
Geesheeyoo deh bileteh
Ticket Office

85 **Ghiseu de înregistrare**
Geesheeyoo deh unredjeestrareh
Check-in Desk

86 **Orar**
Orar
Timetable (Schedule)

87 **Toalete**
Twaleht
Toilets (Restrooms)

88 **Barbati**
Bahrbatz
Gentlemen

89 Femei
Femay
Ladies'

90 Tramvai
Tramvye
Tram (Streetcar)

91 Metrou
Metro
Underground (Subway)

92 Sala de asteptare
Salah deh ashteptareh
Waiting-Room

Buying a Ticket

**93 I would like a first-class/
second-class single (one-
way)/return (round-trip)
ticket to . . .**
Un bilet de clasa întâi/a doua
dus/dus-întors pâña la . . . vă
rog.
*Oon bilett deh classa unteuy/ah
dowa dooss/dooss-untors peunah
la . . . vah rohg.*

**94 Is my rail pass valid on this
train/ferry/bus?**
Este permisul meu valabil pe
acest tren/vapor/autobuz?
*Esteh permeesool meh-oo valabil
peh achest tren/vapor/autobooz?*

**95 I would like an aisle/window
seat.**
Un loc pe coridor/lângă
fereastră vă rog.
*Oon lock peh coridor/lungah
fehreyastra, vah rohg.*

96 No smoking/smoking, please.
Pentru nefumători/fumători, vă
rog.
*Pentroo neh foomahtoree/
foomahtoree, vah rohg.*

**97 We would like to sit
together.**
Dorim să stăm împreuña
Doreem sa stahm umpreyunah.

**98 I would like to make a seat
reservation.**
Doresc ša rezerv un loc.
Doresc sa rezero oon lock

**99 I would like to reserve a
couchette/sleeper for one
person/two people/for my
family.**
Doresc ša rezerv o cuseťa/un pat
pentru o persoaña/două
persoane/familia mea, la vagonu
de dormit.
*Doresc sah rezero oh cooshetta/oon
pat pentroo oh persowahnah/
douah persowahneh/familia meya,
la vagonool deh dormeet.*

**100 I would like to reserve a
cabin.**
Doresc ša rezerv o cabiña
Doresc sa rezero oh cabinah.

Timetables (Schedules)

101 Sosiri
Soseeree
Arrive

102 Opriri la
Opreeree la
Calls (Stops) at

R
O
M
A
N
I
A
N

89
↕
102

ARRIVING AND DEPARTING

[103] **Bufet-Restaurant**
Boofet-Restaurant
Catering Service

[104] **Schimbati la . . .**
Skeembatz la
Change at . . .

[105] **Legătură**
Legahtoora
Connection

[106] **Zilnic**
Zilnic
Daily

[107] **La fiecare patruzeci de minute**
La fiehcareh patroozech deh minuteh
Every 40 Minutes

[108] **Clasa întâi**
Classa untuy
First-Class

[109] **La fiecare oră**
La fiehcareh orah
Hourly

[110] **Sânt recomandate rezervările**
Sunt rehcomandateh rezervahrileh
Seat reservations are recommended

[111] **Clasa a doua**
Classa a doua
Second-class

[112] **De plătit supliment**
Deh plahtit soopleement
Supplement Payable

[113] **Via/Prin**
Veeya/Preen
Via

Luggage

[114] **How much will it cost to send (ship) my luggage in advance?**
Cît mă costa dacă expediez bagajele în avans?
Cut mah costah dacah expediez bagazhehleh un avans?

[115] **Where is the left luggage (baggage claim) office?**
Unde este biroul de bagaje?
Oondeh esteh beerol deh bagazheh?

[116] **What time do you open/close?**
La ce ora deschideti/închideti?
La cheh ora deskidetz/unkidetz?

[117] **Where are the luggage trolleys (carts)?**
Unde sânt cărucioarele de bagaje?
Oondeh sunt cahroochioahrehleh deh bagazheh?

[118] **Where are the lockers?**
Unde sânt dulapioarele?
Oondeh sunt doolapeeyowahreleh?

[119] **I have lost my locker key.**
Am pierdut cheia de la dulapior
Am piehrdoot kaya deh la doolapior

On Board

120 Is this seat taken?
Este locul acesta ocupat?
Esteh locool achesta ocoopat?

121 Excuse me, you are sitting in my reserved seat.
Scuzati-mă, dar stati pe locul meu rezervat.
Scoozatz-mah, dar statz peh locool meyoo rezervat.

122 Which station is this?
La ce gaăa ne aflăm?
La cheh garah neh aflahm?

123 What time is this train/bus/ferry/flight due to arrive/depart?
La ce oa̋a urmează şa soseasča/şa plece/trenul/autobuzul/avionul/acesta?
La cheh orah oormeyazah sah soseyascah/sah plecheh/trenool/owtoboozool/avionool/achesta?

124 Will you wake me just before we arrive?
Sculati-mă vă rog înainte de sosire.
Sculatz-mah vah rohg unainteh deh soseereh.

Customs and Passports

125 Pasapoarteleh, vă rog!
Pashapoarteleh, vah rohg!
Passports, please!

126 I have nothing/wine/spirits (alcohol)/tobacco to declare.

Nu am nimic/vin/alcool/tigări/de declarat.
Noo am neemeek/veen/alcol/tzigahree/deh declarat.

127 I shall be staying for . . . days/weeks/months.
Voi sta . . . zile/săptămâni/luni.
Voy sta . . . zeeleh/sahptahmuni/loony.

AT THE TOURIST OFFICE

128 Do you have a map of the town/area?
Aveti o harţa a orasului/regiunii?
Avetz oh hartah a orashoolui/redjeeyoonee?

129 Can I reserve accommodation here?
Pot rezerva aici sederea?
Pot rezerva aich shehdehreya?

130 Do you have a list of accommodation?
Aveti o lisťa cu locuri disponibile?
Avetz oh listah coo locooree deesponeebeeleh?

ACCOMMODATION

Hotels

131 I have a reservation in the name of . . .
Am facut o rezervare pe numele . . .
Am fahcoot oh rezervareh peh numehleh . . .

ACCOMMODATION

132 I wrote to/faxed/telephoned
you last month/last week in . . .
V-am scris/faxat/telefonat/
luna/săptămâna trecută . . .
*Vam screece/faxat/telefonat/loona/
sahptahmurna trehcootah . . .*

133 Do you have any rooms free?
Aveti vreo cameră liberă?
Avetz vrehoh camerah leebehrah?

134 I would like to reserve a
single/double room with/
without bath/shower.
Doresc să rezerv o cameră cu pat
simplu/dublu cu/fără baie/dus.
*Doresc sah rezero oh camerah coo
pat seemploo/doobloo coo/fahrah
baieh/doosh.*

135 I would like bed and
breakfast/(room and) half
board/(room and) full board.
Doresc o cameră cu micul dejun/
semi pensiune/pensiune
*Doresc oh camerah coo meecool
dehzhoon/semi pensiuneh/
pensiuneh*

136 How much is it per night?
Cât costă pe noapte?
Cut costah peh nowapteh?

137 Is breakfast included?
Este micul dejun inclus în pret?
*Esteh meecool dehzhoon incloose
un pretz?*

138 May I see the room?
Pot să văo camera?
Pot sah vahd camehra?

139 Do you have any cheaper
rooms?
Aveti camere mai ieftine?
Avetz camehreh my yefteeneh?

140 I would like to take the
room.
Doresc să închiriez o camera.
*Doresc sah uncheeryez o
camehrah.*

141 I would like to stay for . . .
nights.
As dori să stau . . . nopti.
Ash doree sah stau . . . noptz.

142 The shower/light/tap doesn't
work.
Dusul/lumina/robinetul/este
defect.
*Dooshool/loomeenah/robinetool/
esteh dehfect.*

143 At what time/where is
breakfast served?
La ce ora/unde se serveste micul
dejun?
*La cheh orah/oondeh seh
serveshteh meecool dehzhoon?*

144 What time do I have to
check-out?
La ce oră trebuie să părăsesc
camera?
*La cheh orah trebooyeh sah
parahsesc camehra?*

145 Can I have the key to room
no . . ?
Dati-mi vă rog cheia de la
camera numărul . . .
*Datz-mee vah rohg kaya deh la
camehra noomahrool . . .*

146 My room number is . . .
Numărul camerei mele este . . .
Noomahrool camehrey mehleh esteh . . .

147 Do you accept travellers' cheques/Eurocheques/credit cards?
Acceptati cecuri de călătorie/ Eurocheques/cărti de credit?
Akcheptatz checooree deh cahlahtoreeyah/Eurocheques/ cahrtz deh credit?

148 May I have the bill please?
Nota de plata vă rog!
Nohta deh platah vah rohg!

149 Excuse me, I think there is a mistake in this bill.
Ma tem ča s-a strecurat o eroare în nota de plata
Mah tem cah sa strecoorat oh ero-arreh un nota deh platah.

Youth Hostels

150 How much is a dormitory bed per night?
Cât este un pat pe noapte în dormitor?
Cut esteh oon pat peh nowapteh un dormeetor?

151 I am/am not an HI member.
Nu sânt membru HI
Noo sunt membroo hash ee

152 May I use my own sleeping bag?
Pot folosi sacul meu de dormit?
Pot folosee sacool meyoo deh dormeet?

153 What time do you lock the doors at night?
La ce ora se închid portile?
La cheh orah seh unkhid portzeeleh?

Camping

154 May I camp here for the night/two nights?
Pot campa aici pentru o noapte/ doŭa nopti?
Pot campa aich pentroo oh nwapteh/douah noptz?

155 Where can I pitch my tent?
Unde pot instala cortul?
Oondeh pot instahla cortool?

156 How much does it cost for one night/week?
Cît costa pe noapte/pe săptamâna?
Cut costah peh nwapteh/peh sahptahmurnah?

157 Where can we park our caravan?
Unde putem parca caravana?
Oondeh pootem parca caravahna?

158 Where are the washing facilities?
Unde sânt lavabourile?
Oondeh sunt lavaboureeleh?

R
O
M
A
N
I
A
N

146
↑
158

EATING AND DRINKING

¹⁵⁹ Is there a restaurant/
supermarket/swimming pool
on site/nearby?
Există un restaurant/
supermarket/piscina la fata
locului/în apropiere?
*Existah oon restaurant/
supermarket/pischeenah la fatza
locooluoi/eun apropiereh?*

¹⁶⁰ Do you have a safety deposit
box?
Unde pot fi păstrate lucrurile de
valoare?
*Oondeh pot fee pahstrateh
loocroorileh deh valwareh?*

EATING AND DRINKING

Cafés and Bars

¹⁶¹ I would like a cup of/two
cups of/another coffee.
I would like a cup of/two
cups of/another tea.
O cafea/două cafele/altă cafea,
vă rog.
Uh ceai/două ceaiuri/alt ceai, vă
rog.
*Oh cafeya/douah cafehleh/altah
cafeya, vah rohg.*
*Oon cheai/douah cheaiooree/alt
cheai, vah rohg.*

¹⁶² With/without milk/sugar.
Cu/fără lapte/zahăr.
Coo/fahrah lapteh/zahahr.

¹⁶³ I would like a bottle/glass/
two glasses of mineral water/
red wine/white wine, please.

O sticla/un pahar/doua pahare
cu apa minerala/vin rosu/vin alb,
vă rog.
*O steeclah/oon pahar/dowah
pahareh coo apah minehralah/
veen roshoo/veen alb, vah rohg.*

¹⁶⁴ I would like a beer/two
beers, please.
O bere/două beri, vă rog.
O bereh/dowah beree, vah rohg.

¹⁶⁵ May I have some ice?
Gheață vă rog
Gheyatzah, vah rohg

¹⁶⁶ Do you have any matches/
cigarettes/cigars?
Aveti chibrituri/tigări/tigări de
foi?
*Avetz keebreetooree/tzigahree/
tzigahree deh foy?*

Restaurants

¹⁶⁷ Can you recommend a good/
inexpensive restaurant in this
area?
Îmi puteti recomanda un
restaurant bun/ieftin în aceasta
zonă?
*Eumi pootetz rehcomanda oon
restaurant boon/yefteen eun
acheyasta zona?*

¹⁶⁸ I would like a table for . . .
people.
Doresc ša rezerv o maša pentru .
. . persoane.
*Doresc sah rezerv oh masah
pentroo . . . perswaneh.*

169 Do you have a non-smoking area?

Există un loc pentru nefumători?

Existah oon loc pentroo nehfumahtoree?

170 Waiter/Waitress!

Chelner/chelneriţa

Kelner/Kelnehreetza.

171 Do you have a set menu/ children's menu/wine list?

Aveti un menu fix/un menu pentru copii/o lista cu vinuri?

Avetz oon mehnoo fix/oon mehnoo pentroo copii/oh leestah coo veenooree?

172 Do you have any vegetarian dishes, please?

Aveti mîncăruri pentru vegetarieni?

Avetz muncahrooree pentroo vegetaryehnee?

173 Are there any local specialities?

Există specialitaţi locale?

Existah spechialitahtz locaieh?

174 Are vegetables included?

Sânt legumele incluse în nota de plaţă?

Sunt legoomehleh inclooseh eun nota deh platah?

175 Could I have it well-cooked/ medium/rare please?

Doresc carnea bine prajiţa/nu foarte prajiţa/în sânge.

Doresc carneya beeneh prazheetah/ noo fwarteh prazheetah/un sundjeh.

176 What does this dish consist of?

Ce fel de mîncare este asta?

Cheh fehl deh muncahreh esteh asta?

177 I would like the set menu, please.

As dori un menu fix, va rog.

Ash doree oon mehnoo fix, vah rohg.

178 We have not been served yet.

N-am fost serviti înca

Nam fost serveetz uncah

179 Excuse me, this is not what I ordered.

Scuzati-mă n-am comandat asa ceva.

Scoozatz-mah, nam comandat asha chehva.

180 May I have some/some more bread/water/coffee/tea?

Pot avea mai multa pâine/apa/ cafea/mai mult ceai?

Pot aveya my mooltah peu-eeneh/ apah/cafeya/my moolt cheyai?

181 May I have the bill, please?

Nota de plaţă va rog.

Nota deh platah, vah rohg.

182 Does this bill include service?

E bacsisul inclus în nota de plaţă?

Eh bacshishool incloose un nota deh platah?

183 Do you accept travellers'
cheques (travelers' checks)/
Eurocheques/MasterCard/US
dollars?
Acceptati ceguri de călătorie/
Eurocheques/MasterCard/
Dolari americani?
*Akcheptatz checooree deh
cahlahtoreeyeh/ Eurocheque/
MasterCard/Dolaree
americahnee?*

184 Can I have a receipt, please?
Pot avea o chitanťa va rog?
*Pot aveya oh keetantzah va
rohg?*

185 Where is the toilet
(restroom), please?
Unde este toaleta, vă rog?
Oondeh esteh twalehta, vah rohg?

On the Menu

186 First courses
Primul fel
Preemool fel

187 Soups
Supe
Soopeh

188 Main courses
Felul principal
Feloool princheepal

189 Fish dishes
Pescărie
Pescahrieh

190 Meat dishes
Mâncăruri cu carne
Muncahrooree coo carneh

191 Vegetarian dishes
Mâncăruri cu legume
Muncahrooree coo legoomeh

192 Cheese
Brânža
Brunzah

193 Desserts
Deserturi
Dehsertooree

194 Specialities
Specialități culinare
Spechialitahtz coolinareh

GETTING AROUND

Public Transport

195 Where is the bus stop/coach
station/nearest metro
(subway) station?
Unde este statia de autobuz/
autocar/metrou, cea mai
apropiată?
*Oondeh esteh statzia deh
owtobooz/owtocar/metro, cheya
my apropiatah?*

196 When is the next/last bus
to . . ?
La ce oŕa vine următorul/ultimul
autobuz spre . . ?
*La cheh orah veeneh
oormahtorool/oolteemool
owtobooz spreh . . ?*

197 How much is the fare to the city centre (downtown)/ railway (railroad) station/ airport?
Cât costa biletul pâna-n centru/ pâna la gara/aeroport?
Cut costah biletool peunahn chentroo/peunah la garah/ aeroport?

198 Will you tell me when to get off?
Vreti ša-mi spuneti când ša cobor?
Vretz sah-mee spoonetz cund sah cobor?

199 Does this bus go to . . ?
Merge autobuzul˘asta la . . ?
Mehrdjeh owtoboozool ahsta la . . ?

200 Which number bus goes to . . ?
Care autobuz merge la . . ?
Careh owtobooz mehrdjeh la . . ?

201 May I have a single (one-way)/return (round-trip)/day ticket/book of tickets?
Un bilet dus/dus-întors/valabil 24 de ore/un abonament, ša rog.
Oon bilet doos/doos-untors/ valabil dwahzech deh oreh/oon abonament, vah rohg.

Taxis

202 I would like to go to . . . How much will it cost?
Vreau ša merg la . . ? Cât costa pâna la . . ?
Vreyow sah mairg la . . ? Cut costah pernah la . . ?

203 Please stop here.
Opriti aici, va rog.
Opreetz ayeechee, vah rohg.

204 I would like to order a taxi today/tomorrow/at 2pm to go from . . . to . . .
Doresc ša comand un taxi azi/ mâine/la ora doua dupa amiaža care ša mia duca de la . . . la . . .
Doresc sah comand oon taxi ahzee/meu-eeneh/la ora dowa doopah ameeyazah, careh sah mah ducah deh la . . . la . . .

Asking the Way

205 Excuse me, do you speak English?
Scuzati-mia Vorbiti englezeste?
Scoozatz-mah. Vorbeetz englehzeshteh?

206 Excuse me, is this the right way to . . ?
Scuzati-mia Asta este drumul spre . . ?
Scoozatz-mah. Asta esteh droomool spreh . . ?

207 . . . the cathedral/the tourist information office/the castle/ the old town
. . . catedrala/oficiul de informatii turistice/castelul/ orasul vechi?
. . . catedralah/ofeechiool deh informatzee tooristicheh/castelool/ orashool vehk?

208 Can you tell me the way to the railway (railroad) station/ bus station/taxi rank (stand)/ city centre (downtown)/ beach?

Vreti va rog ša-mi spuneti cum ajung la gară/statia de autobuz/ statia de taxiuri/în centru/la plajă

Vretz vah rohg sah-mee spoonetz koom azhoong la garah/statzia deh owtobooz/statzia deh taxiooree/un chentroo/la plazhah?

209 First/second left/right/ straight ahead.

Prima/a doua la stînga/dreapta/ drept înainte.

Preema/a dowa la stunga/ dreyapta/drept unainteh.

210 Where is the nearest police station/post office/doctor/ hospital/pharmacy?

Unde este postul de politie/ oficiul postal/doctorul/spital/ farmacie cel mai apropiat?

Oondeh esteh postool deh politzieh/ofeechiool poshtal/ doctorool/spital/farmachie chel my apropiat?

211 Is it far?

Este departe?

Esteh dehparteh?

212 Do I need to take a taxi/ catch a bus?

Trebuie ša iau un taxi/un autobuz?

Trebooyeh sah eeyow oon taxi/oon owtobooz?

213 Can you point to it on my map?

Puteti ša-mi arătati pe hartă?

Pootetz sa-mee arahtatz peh hartah?

214 Thank you for your help.

Multumesc pentru ajutor.

Mooltzoomesc pentroo azhootor.

SIGHTSEEING

215 Where is the Tourist Information office?

Unde este Oficiul de Informatii Turistice?

Oondeh esteh ofeechiool dee eenformatzee tooristicheh?

216 Where is the cathedral/ church/museum?

Unde este catedrala/biserica/ muzeul?

Oondeh esteh catedrahla/ bisehrica/moozeul?

217 How much is the entrance (admission) charge?

Cît costa intrarea?

Cut costah intrareya?

218 Is there a reduction for children/students/senior citizens?

Au copiii/studentii/bătrânii reducere?

Ow copeeyee/studentzee/ bahtreunee redoochehreh?

219 What time does the next guided tour start?

La ce oră începe următorul tur cu ghizi?

*La cheh orah unchehpeh
oormahtorool toor coo gheeze*

220 One/two adults/children,
please.
Un adult/doi adulti/copii, vă
rog
*Oon adoolt/doy adooltz/copeeyee,
vah rohg*

221 May I take photographs
here?
Am voie șa fotografiez aici?
Am voyeh sah fotografiez aich?

ENTERTAINMENT

222 Can you recommend a good
bar/nightclub?
Puteti recomanda un bar/club
de noapte bun?
*Pootetz rehcomanda oon bar/club
deh nwapteh boon?*

223 Do you know what is on at
the cinema (playing at the
movies)/theatre at the
moment?
Stiti cumva ce filme rulează/ce
piese se joacă în momentul de
fată?
*Shtitz coomva cheh feelmeh
rooleyahza/cheh peeyeseh seh
zhowacah un momentool deh
fatzah?*

224 I would like to book
(purchase) . . . tickets for the
matinée/evening
performance on Monday.
. . . bilete pentru matineul/seara
de luni, vă rog.

. . . *bileteh pentroo mateeneyool/
seyara deh loony, vah rohg.*

225 What time does the film/
performance start?
La ce ořa începe filmul/
spectacolul?
*La cheh orah unchehpeh feelmool/
spectacolool?*

MEETING PEOPLE

226 Hello/Goodbye.
Salut/La revedere.
Saloot/La revehdereh.

227 Good morning/good
afternoon/good evening/
goodnight.
Buňa dimineata/Buňa ziua/buňa
seara/noapte buňa
*Boonah deemeenayatz/Boonah
zeeyua/boonah seyara/nwapteh
boonah.*

228 Pleased to meet you.
Încântat de cunostința
Uncuntat deh coonoshteentzah.

229 How are you?
Ce mai faceti?
Cheh my fachetz?

230 Fine, thank you. And you?
Bine, multumesc. Dar
dumneavoastřa?
*Beeneh, mooltzoomesc. Dar
doomneyavowastrah?*

231 My name is . . .
Ma numesc . . .
Mah noomesc . . .

MEETING PEOPLE

232 This is my friend/boyfriend/
girlfriend/husband/wife/
brother/sister.
Va prezint prietenul/prietena/
sotul/sotia/fratele/sora.
*Vah prezint preeyetenool/
preeyetehna/sotzool/sotzia/
fratehleh/sora.*

233 Where are you travelling to?
Unde călatoriti?
Oondeh cahlatoritz?

234 I am/we are going to . . .
Călatoresc/călatorim la . . .
Cahlatoresc/cahlahtoreem la . . .

235 How long are you travelling
for?
Cît timp călatoriti?
Cut teemp cahlahtoritz?

236 Where do you come from?
De unde veniti?
Deh oondeh veneetz?

237 I am/we are from . . .
Sânt/sântem din . . .
Sunt/suntem deen . . .

238 We're on holiday.
Sântem în vacanta.
Suntem un vacantzah.

239 This is our first visit here.
Aceasta este prima noastră viziṭa
aici.
*Acheyasta esteh preema nwastrah
veezeetah aich*

240 Would you like/May I have a
cigarette?
Doriti/pot sa iau o tigară?
Doritz/pot sa iau oh tzigarah?

241 I am sorry but I do not
understand.
Ma scuzati dar nu înteleg.
Ma scoozatz dar noo untzehleg.

242 Please speak slowly.
Vorbiti mai rar vă rog.
Vorbeetz my rar vah rohg.

243 Do you mind if I smoke?
Pot aprinde o tigară?
Pot apreendeh oh tzigarah?

244 Do you have a light?
Aveti un foc?
Avetz oon fok?

245 I am waiting for my husband/
wife/boyfriend/girlfriend.
Îmi astept sotul/sotia/prietenul/
prietena.
*Eumi ashtept sotzool/sotza/
prietenool/prietehna.*

TRAVELLING WITH CHILDREN

246 Do you have a high chair/
baby-sitting service/cot?
Aveti un scaun pentru copii/un
serviciu baby-sitting/un pătut
pentru copii?
*Avetz oon scaun pentroo copee/oon
serveechioo baby-sitting/oon
pahtootz pentroo kopee?*

247 Where is the nursery/
playroom?
Unde este cresa/camera
copiilor?
*Oondeh esteh cresha/camehra
copeelor?*

COMMUNICATIONS

248 Where can I warm the baby's bottle?

Unde pot încălzi biberonul?

Oondeh pot uncahlzi beebehronool?

COMMUNICATIONS

Post

249 How much will it cost to send a letter/postcard/this package to Britain/Ireland/America/Canada/Australia/New Zealand?

Cât costă timbrul pentru a expedia o scrisoare/carte postală/pachetul acesta în Marea Britanie/Irlanda/America/Canada/Australia/Noua Zeelandă?

Cut costa timbrool pentroo ah expedhia oh scriswareh/karteh poshtala/paketool achesta un Mareya Britanyeh/Irlanda/Amehrica/Canada/Owstralia/Noua Zehlanda?

250 I would like one stamp/two stamps.

Un timbru/două timbre, vă rog.

Oon timbroo/douah timbreh, vah rohg.

251 I'd like ... stamps for postcards to send abroad, please.

... timbre pentru cărti postale de expediat în străinătate, vă rog.

... timbreh pentroo cartz poshtaleh deh expediat un strah-eenahtateh, vah rohg.

Phones

252 I would like to make a telephone call/reverse the charges to (make a collect call to) ...

Doresc să telefonez/cu taxa inverșa la ...

Doresc sah telefonez/coo taxah inversah la ...

253 Which coins do I need for the telephone?

Cu ce monede functioneaža telefonul?

Koo cheh monehdeh functzioneyazah telefonool?

254 The line is engaged (busy).

Numărul este ocupat.

Noomahrool esteh ocupat.

255 The number is ...

Numărul este ...

Noomahrool esteh ...

256 Hello, this is ...

Alo, ... sânt.

Alo, ... sunt.

257 May I speak to .. ?

Pot vorbi vă rog cu .. ?

Pot vorbee vah rohg coo .. ?

258 He/She is not in at the moment. Can you call back?

El/ea nu este aici pentru moment. Sunati vă rog mai târziu.

Yel/ya noo esteh aich pentroo moment. Soonatz vah rohg my turzioo

R O M A N I A N

248 ↑ 258

277

MONEY

²⁵⁹ I would like to change these travellers' cheques (travelers' checks)/this currency/this Eurocheque.

Vreau ša schimb aceste cecuri de călatorie/acesti bani/acest Eurocheque.

Vreyau sah skeemb acheshteh cecooree deh cahlahtoreeyeh/ achesht bahnee/achest Eurocheque.

²⁶⁰ How much commission do you charge? (What is the service charge?)

Cît este comisionul dumneavoastră?

Cut esteh comissionool doomneyavwastrah?

²⁶¹ Can I obtain money with my MasterCard?

Pot încasa bani cu MasterCard?

Pot uncasa bahnee coo MasterCard?

SHOPPING

Names of Shops and Departments

²⁶² Librărie/Papetărie

Leebrahrieh/Papetahrieh

Bookshop/Stationery

²⁶³ Bijuterii/Cadouri

Beezhootehrie/Kadoree

Jeweller's/Gifts

²⁶⁴ Încălțaminte

Euncahltzahmeenteh

Shoes

²⁶⁵ Ferometal

Feromehtahl

Hardware

²⁶⁶ Antichiťati

Antikitahtz

Antiques

²⁶⁷ Frizer/Coafor

Freezer/Cwafor

Hairdressers (men's)/(women's)

²⁶⁸ Tutungerie

Tootoondjerie

Tobacconist

²⁶⁹ Bruťarie

Brootahrie

Baker's

²⁷⁰ Supermarket

Supermarket

Supermarket

²⁷¹ Magazin fotografic

Magazeen fotografic

Photoshop

²⁷² Jucării

Zhoocahree

Toys

²⁷³ Agentie de voiaj

Agentzieh de voyazh

Travel Agent

²⁷⁴ Drogherie

Drogherie

Toiletries

²⁷⁵ Magazin de discuri

Magazeen deh deescooree

Records

R
O
M
A
N
I
A
N

259
↕
275

In the Shop

276 What time do the shops open/close?
La ce ora deschid/închid magazinele?
La cheh ora deskyd/unkyd magazeenehleh?

277 Where is the nearest market?
Unde este piata cea mai apropiata?
Oondeh esteh piatza cheya my apropiatah?

278 Can you show me the one in the window/this one?
Puteti sa mi-l/mi-o arătati pe cel/cea din vitriña/acesta/aceasta?
Pootetz sa mee-l/mee-o arahtatz peh chel/cheya deen veetreena/achesta/acheyasta?

279 Can I try this on?
Pot să-l/s-o încerc?
Pot sa-l/s-o unchairk?

280 What size is this?
Ce măsură are?
Cheh mahsoora areh?

281 This is too large/too small/too expensive.
E prea mare/prea mic/prea scump.
Eh preya mareh/preya meek/preya scoomp.

282 Do you have any others?
Aveti altii/altele?
Avetz altzee/altehleh?

283 My size is . . .
Măsura mea este . . .
Mahsoora meya esteh . . .

284 Where is the changing room/childrens/cosmetic/ladieswear/menswear/food department?
Unde este cabina de probă/raionul de confectii pentru copii/cosmetice/confectii pentru femei/bărbati/alimentara?
Oondeh esteh cabina deh prohbah/raionool deh confectzee pentroo copee/cosmeticheh/confectzee pentroo femay/bahrbatz/alimentahra?

285 I would like . . .
Dati-mi . . .
Datz-mee . . .

286 I would like a quarter of a kilo/half a kilo/a kilo of bread/ butter/cheese/ham/tomatoes.
Dati-mi un sfert/o jumătate/un kilogram de pâine/unt/brînză/suncă/rosii.
Datz-mee oon sfert/oh zhoomahtateh/oon keelogram deh peuineh/oont/breunzah/shooncah/roshee.

287 How much is this?
Cît costa?
Cut costah?

288 I'll take this one, thank you.
Îl iau pe acesta, multumesc.
Eul iau peh achesta, mooltzoomesc.

289 Do you have a carrier (shopping) bag?

Aveti o pungă de plastic?

Avetz oh pungah deh plastic?

290 Do you have anything cheaper/larger/smaller/of better quality?

Nu aveti nimic mai ieftin/mai mare/mai mic/de mai buňa calitate?

Noo avetz neemeek my yefteen/my mareh/my meek/deh my boonah calitahteh?

291 I would like a film for this camera.

Dati-mi vă rog un film pentru acest aparat.

Datz-mee vah rohg oon feelm pentroo achest aparat.

292 I would like some batteries, the same size as this old one.

Dati-mi vă rog niste baterii, de acceeasi mărime cu aceasta.

Datz-mee vah rohg neeshteh bateree, deh acheeyashi mahrimeh coo acheyasta.

293 Would you mind wrapping this for me, please?

Vreti vă rog s-o/ša-l ambalati?

Vretz vah rohg so/sahl ambalatz?

294 Sorry, but you seem to have given me the wrong change.

Ma scuzati dar am impresia čanu mi-ati dat restul corect.

Mah scoozatz dar am impresia cah noo mee-atz dat restool correct.

MOTORING

Car Hire (Rental)

295 I have ordered (rented) a car in the name of . . .

Am comandat/închiriat un automobil pe numele . . .

Am comandat/unkyriat oon automobeel peh noomehleh . . .

296 How much does it cost to hire (rent) a car for one day/two days/one week?

Cît cosťa închirierea unui automobil pe o zi/două zile/o šapťamâňa?

Cut costah unkyriereya oonui automobeel peh oh zee/dowah zeeleh/oh saptahmunah?

297 Is the tank already full of petrol (gas)?

I-ati făcut plinul?

Ee-atz fahcoot pleenool?

298 Is insurance and tax included? How much is the deposit?

Sânt asigurarea si taxa incluse? Cât este depozitul?

Sunt aseegurareya shee taxa incluseh? Cut esteh dehpositool?

299 By what time must I return the car?

Când trebuie ša înapoiez masina?

Cund trebooyeh sah unapoyez mashina?

300 I would like a small/family car with a radio/cassette player.

Vreau o masiňa miča/limuziňa cu radio/casetofoh.

Vreyau oh mashinah meecah/ leemoozeenah coo rahdio/ cassetofon.

Asking the Way

301 Excuse me, can you help me please?

Va rog frumos, puteti ša m̌a ajutati?

Vah rohg froomos, pootetz sah mah azhootatz?

302 How do I reach the motorway/main road?

În ce directie este autostrada/ soseaua natională?

Eun cheh directzieh esteh owtostrahda/shoseh-awua natzionalah?

303 I think I have taken the wrong turning.

Ma tem ča am luat cotitura gresiťa

Mah tem cah am lwat coteetoora greshitah.

304 I am looking for this address.

Caut aceasťa adreša

Caut acheyastah adresah.

305 I am looking for the . . . hotel.

Caut hotelul . . .

Caut hotelool . . .

306 How far is it to . . . from here?

Cât de departe de aici se afla . . ?

Cut deh dehparteh deh aich seh afla . . ?

307 Carry straight on for . . . kilometres.

Continuati drept înainte vreo . . . kilometri.

Continooatz drept unainteh vreh-oh . . . kilometree.

308 Take the next turning on the right/left.

Cotiti prima la dreapta/la stânga.

Cotitz preema la dreyapta/la stunga.

309 Turn right/left at the next crossroads/traffic lights.

Luati-o la dreapta/la stânga la prima intersectie/la primul semafor.

Lowatz-oh la dreyapta/la stunga la preema eentersectzieh/la preemool sehmafor.

310 You are going in the wrong direction.

Circulati în directie gresiťa

Cheercoolatz un directzieh gresheetah.

Parking

311 How long can I park here?

Cât timp pot parca aici?

Cut teemp pot parca aich?

312 Is there a car park near here?

Este vreun garaj prin apropiere?

Esteh vreh-oon garahzh preen apropeeyereh?

R
O
M
A
N
I
A
N

300
↕
312

281

313 At what time does this car park close?
La ce oŕa se închide garajul?
La cheh orah seh unkeedeh garazhool?

Signs and Notices

314 Sens unic
Sens ooneek
One way.

315 Intrarea interziša
Eentrareya eenterzeesah
No entry.

316 Stationarea interziša
Statzionareya eenterzeesah
No parking.

317 Deviatie
Deviatzieh
Detour (diversion)

318 Stop
Stop
Stop.

319 Dati prioritate
Datz prioritahteh
Give way (yield).

320 Pericol de derapaj
Pereecol deh dehrapazh
Slippery road.

321 Depăsirea interziša
Dehpahsheereya eenterzeesah
No overtaking.

At the Filling Station

322 Unleaded (lead-free)/ Standard/Premium
Benziña neetilaŕa/Standard/ Supercarburant
Benzeena neeteelahtah/Standard/ Supercarboorant

323 Fill the tank please.
Faceti plinul v̆a rog.
Fachetz pleenool vah rohg.

324 Do you have a road map of this area?
Aveti o harŕa a regiunii?
Avetz oh hartah ah redjeeyoonee?

325 How much is the car-wash?
Cât cosŕa sp̆alatul masinii?
Cut costah spahlatool mashineei?

Breakdowns

326 I've had a breakdown at . . .
Sânt în paña la . . .
Sunt un panah la . . .

327 I am on the road from . . . to . . .
Sânt pe soseaua de la . . . la . . .
Sunt pey shosehowua deh la . . . la . . .

328 I can't move the car. Can you send a tow-truck?
Nu pot porni automobilul. Puteti trimite o masiñacare šaña remorcheze?
Noo pot pornee owtomobeelool. Pootetz treemeeteh oh mashinah careh sah mah rehmorchezeh?

329 I have a flat tyre.
Am un cauciuc pe geanŕa
Am oon cowoochiook peh djeyantah.

³³⁰ **The windscreen (windshield) has smashed/cracked.**
Parbrizul este spart/crăpat.
Parbreezool esteh spart/crahpat.

³³¹ **There is something wrong with the engine/brakes/ lights/steering/gearbox/ clutch/exhaust.**
Motorul/frânele/farurile/ directia/cutia de viteze/ ambreiajul/esapamentul nu functioneaza
Motorool/fruneleh/farooreeleh/ deerectzia/cootia deh veetehzeh/ ambreyazhool/eshapamentool noo foonctzioneyazah.

³³² **It's overheating.**
Supraîncălzeste.
Sooprauncahlzeshteh.

³³³ **It won't start.**
Nu porneste.
Noo porneshteh.

³³⁴ **Where can I get it repaired?**
Unde o pot repara?
Oondeh oh pot rehpara?

³³⁵ **Can you take me there?**
Ma puteti transporta acolo?
Mah pootetz transporta acolo?

³³⁶ **Will it take long to fix?**
Cât timp va dura reparatia?
Cut teemp va doora rehparatzia?

³³⁷ **How much will it cost?**
Cît costă?
Cut costah?

Accidents

³³⁸ **Can you help me? There has been an accident.**
Vreti ša mía ajutati vă rog? Am avut un accident.
Vretz sah mah azhootatz vah rohg? Am avoot oon akcheedent.

³³⁹ **Please call the police/an ambulance.**
Chemati vă rog politia/ salvarea.
Kehmatz vah rohg poleetzia/ salvareya.

³⁴⁰ **Is anyone hurt?**
Sânt răniti?
Sunt rahneetz?

Traffic Offences

³⁴¹ **I'm sorry, I didn't see the sign.**
Îmi cer scuze dar n-am văzut semnul.
Eumi chair scoozeh dar nam vahzoot semnool.

³⁴² **Must I pay a fine? How much?**
Trebuie ša plătesc amendă? Cât costă?
Trebooyeh sah plahtesc amendah? Cut costah?

³⁴³ **Show me your documents.**
Arătati-mi hârtiile de identitate.
Arahtatz-mee hahrteeleh deh eedenteetahteh.

HEALTH

Pharmacy

344 Do you have anything for a
stomachache/headache/sore
throat/toothache?
Puteti ša-mi dati ceva pentru
dureri de stomac/dureri de cap/
dureri în gât/dureri de dinti?
*Pootetz sah-mee datz chehva
pentroo doorehree deh stomac/
doorehree deh cap/doorehree un
gut/doorehree deh deentz?*

345 I need something for
diarrhoea (diarrhea)/
constipation/a cold/a cough/
insect bites/sunburn/travel
(motion) sickness.
Am nevoie de un medicament
contra diareei/constipatiei/
răcelii/tusei/muscăturilor de
insecte/arsurilor de soare/răului
de călătorie.
*Am nevowyeh deh oon
medicament contra deeyareh-ee/
consteepatzee-ay/rachehlee/toosay/
mooshcatooreelor deh insecteh/
arsooreelor deh swahreh/rahwlui
deh cahlahtorieh.*

346 How much/how many do I
take?
Ce cantitate/câte iau?
Cheh cantitahteh/cuteh yow?

347 How often do I take it/them?
Cât de des iau medicamentul?
Cut deh des yow medeecamentool?

348 How much does it cost?
Cât costa
Cut costah

349 Can you recommend a good
doctor/dentist?
Puteti ša-mi recomandati un
doctor/dentist bun?
*Pootetz sah-mee rehcomandatz oon
doctor/denteest boon?*

350 Is it suitable for children?
Este indicat pentru copii?
Esteh eendeecat pentroo copee?

Doctor

351 I have a pain here/in my arm/
leg/chest/stomach.
Am o durere aici/în brat/picior/
piept/stomac.
*Am oh doorehreh aich/un bratz/
peechior/pee-ept/stomac.*

352 Please call a doctor, this is
an emergency.
Chemati vă rog un doctor de
urgenta
*Kehmatz vah rohg oon doctor deh
oordjentzah.*

353 I would like to make an
appointment to see a doctor.
Vreau ša văd un doctor.
Vreh-ow sah vahd oon doctor.

354 I am diabetic/pregnant.
Sânt diabetic/însărcinata
Sunt deeyabetic/unsahrcheenatah.

³⁵⁵ I need a prescription for . . .
Dati-mi vă rog o reteťa pentru . . .
Datz-mee vah rohg oh retzehtah pentroo . . .

³⁵⁶ Can you give me something to ease the pain?
Puteti ša-mi dati ceva contra durerilor?
Pootetz sa-mee datz chehva contra doorehreelor?

³⁵⁷ I am/he is/she is allergic to penicillin.
Sânt alergic/el este alergic/ea este alergiča la peniciliňa
Sunt alehrzheek/el esteh alerzheek/ eya esteh alerzheekah la peneecheeleenah

³⁵⁸ Does this hurt?
Doare?
Dwareh?

³⁵⁹ You must/he must/she must go to hospital.
Trebuie ša mergeti/el/ea trebuie ša mearǧa la spital.
Trebweh sah mehrdjetz/el/eya trebooyeh sah meyargah la spital.

³⁶⁰ Take these once/twice /three times a day.
Luati medicamentul o dať a/de douǎ ori/de trei ori pe zi.
Lowatz medeecamentool oh datah/ deh dowah oree/deh tray oree peh zee.

³⁶¹ I am/he is/she is taking this medication.
Iau/el ia/ea ia acest medicament.
Yow/el ya/eya ya achest medeecament.

³⁶² I have medical insurance.
Am asigurare medicaľa
Am aseegoorareh medeecalah.

Dentist

³⁶³ I have toothache.
Am o durere de dinti.
Am oh doorehreh deh deentz.

³⁶⁴ My filling has come out.
Am pierdut o plombǎ
Am peeyerdoot oh plombah.

³⁶⁵ I do/do not want to have an injection first.
Vreau/nu vreau un anestetic.
Vreh-aoo/noo vreh-aoo oon anestetik.

EMERGENCIES

³⁶⁶ Help!
Ajutor!
Azhootor!

³⁶⁷ Call an ambulance/a doctor/ the police!
Chemati salvarea/doctorul/ politia.
Kehmatz salvareya/doctorool/ politzia.

R
O
M
A
N
I
A
N

355
↕
367

285

368 I have had my travellers' cheques (travelers' checks)/ credit cards/purse/handbag/ rucksack (knapsack)/ luggage/wallet stolen.

Mi s-au furat cecurile de călatorie/cărtile de credit/ portmoneul/geanta/rucsacul/ valiza/portofelul.

Mee saow foorat cecooreeleh deh calatoreeyeh/cartzeeleh deh credit/ portmoneyool/djeyanta/ rooksacool/valeeza/portofelool.

369 Can you help me, I have lost my daughter/son?

Vreti sămă ajutati vă rog? Mi-am pierdut fetita/băiatul.

Vretz sah mah azhootatz vah rohg? Mee-am peeyerdoot fetitza/ bye-atool.

370 Please go away/leave me alone.

Va rog plecati de aici. Lăsati-mă în pace.

Vah rohg plecatz deh aich. Lasatz-mah un pacheh.

371 Fire!

Foc!

Foc!

372 I want to contact the British/ American/Canadian/Irish/ Australian/New Zealand/ South African consulate.

Vreau să contactez consulatul britanic/american/canadian/ irlandez/australian/neo zeelandez/sud african.

Vreyau sah contactez consoolatool britaneek/americahn/canadiahn/ eerlandez/owstraliahn/neyo zehlandez/sood africahn.

Introduction

Castilian Spanish, the official form of the language, is spoken all over Spain. Some regions also have their own official languages: Catalan in Catalonia and the Balearic Islands, Galego in Galicia and Basque in parts of the north-east. These are separate languages and not dialects of Spanish. In the popular tourist areas English is widely understood.

If using a Spanish dictionary, phone directory or other alphabetical listing, remember that words beginning with 'ch' come after all the other 'c's, and words starting with 'll' after all the other 'l's.

**S
P
A
N
I
S
H**

Addresses for travel and tourist information

Australia: *Embassy,* 15 Arkana St, Yarralumla, PO Box 9076; tel: (2) 73 3555. *Consulate-General,* Level 24 St Martin's Tower, 31 Market St, Sydney, NSW 2000; tel: (2) 261 2433.
South Africa: *Embassy,* 169 Pine St, Arcadia, Pretoria, 0083; tel: (12) 344 3875.
UK: *Spanish National Tourist Office,* 22–23 Manchester Square, London, W1M 5AP; tel: (020) 7486 8077.
USA: *Spanish National Tourist Office,* 666 Fifth Ave 35th, New York, NY 10103; tel: (212) 265 8822.

ESSENTIALS

ALPHABET

A	B
a	*be*
C	CH
ce	*che*
D	E
de	*e*
F	G
efey	*ge*
H	I
atchey	*ee latina*
J	K
hota	*ka*
L	LL
eley	*elyey*
M	N
emey	*eney*
Ñ	O
enyey	*o*
P	Q
pe	*cu*
R	RR
ere	*erre*
S	T
eseh	*te*
U	V
oo	*ubey*
W	X
ubey doble	*ekees*
Y	Z
ee greeayga	*theta*

Basic Words and Phrases

1. **Yes** / **No**
   Si / No
   Si / *noh*

2. **Please** / **Thank you**
   Por favor / Gracias
   Por fabor / *Gratheeas*

3. **That's O.K.** / **Perhaps**
   De acuerdo / Quizá
   Dey acwerdo / *Keetha*

4. **To** / **From**
   a / desde/de
   a / *desdey/dey*

5. **Here** / **There**
   Aquí / Allí
   akee / *ayee*

6. **None** / **Also**
   Ninguno/a / También
   Ningoono/a / *Tambeeyen*

7. **How?** / **When?**
   ¿Cómo? / ¿Cuándo?
   como / *cwandoe*

8. **What?** / **Why?**
   ¿Qué? / ¿Por qué?
   kay / *porkay*

9. **I don't understand.**
   No entiendo.
   Noh enteeyendo.

10. **I don't speak Spanish.**
    No hablo español.
    Noh ahblo espanyol.

11. **Do you speak English?**
    ¿Habla usted inglés?
    Ahbla oosteh eengless?

12 **Can you please write it down?**
Lo puede escribir, por favor?
Lo pwedeh escreebeer, porr fabor?

13 **Can you please speak more slowly?**
Quiere usted hablar más despacio?
Keyerehh oosteth ablar mas despathio?

14 **How much does it/this cost?**
Cuánto cuesta?
Kwanto kwesta?

Days

15 **Monday** **Tuesday**
Lunes Martes
Loones *Martes*

16 **Wednesday** **Thursday**
Miércoles Jueves
Meeyercoles *Hooebes*

17 **Friday** **Saturday**
Viernes Sábado
Beeyernes *Sabadoe*

18 **Sunday** **Morning**
Domingo Mañana
Domeengo *Manyana*

19 **Afternoon** **Evening**
Tarde Noche
Tardey *Nochey*

20 **Night** **Week**
Noche Semana
Nochey *Semanna*

21 **Yesterday/Today/Tomorrow**
Ayer/Hoy/Mañana
Ayer/Oy/Manyana

Numbers

22 **Zero** **One**
Cero Uno
Theroe *Oono*

23 **Two** **Three**
Dos Tres
Dos *Tres*

24 **Four** **Five**
Cuatro Cinco
Cwatro *Thinco*

25 **Six** **Seven**
Seis Siete
Seys *Seeyetey*

26 **Eight** **Nine**
Ocho Nueve
Ocho *Nwebey*

27 **Ten** **Eleven**
Diez Once
Deeyeth *Onthey*

28 **Twelve** **Thirteen**
Doce Trece
Dothey *Trethey*

29 **Fourteen** **Fifteen**
Catorce Quince
Catorthey *Keeyenthe*

30 **Sixteen** **Seventeen**
Dieciséis Diecisiete
Deeyetheeseys *Deeyetheeseeyetey*

31 **Eighteen** **Nineteen**
Dieciocho Diecinueve
Deeyetheoocho *Deeyetheenwebey*

32 **Twenty** **Twenty-one**
Veinte Veintiuno
Beintey *Beinteoono*

S
P
A
N
I
S
H

12
↕
32

289

33 Twenty-two **Thirty**
Veintidós Treinta
Beintedos *Treinta*

34 Forty **Fifty**
Cuarenta Cincuenta
Cwarenta *Thincwenta*

35 Sixty **Seventy**
Sesenta Setenta
Sesenta *Setenta*

36 Eighty **Ninety**
Ochenta Noventa
Ochenta *Nobenta*

37 One hundred **Five hundred**
Cien Quinientos
Thien *Keyneeyentos*

38 One thousand **One million**
Mil Un millón
Mil *Oon mellion*

Time

39 9.00
Las nueve
Nwebey

40 9.05
Las nueve y cinco
Nwebey ee thinco

41 9.10
Las nueve y diez
Nwebey ee deeyeth

42 9.15
Las nueve y cuarto
Nwebey ee quarto

43 9.20
Las nueve y veinte
Nwebey ee beinte

44 9.25
Las nueve y veinticinco
Nwebey ee beintethinco

45 9.30
Las nueve y media
Nwebey ee medeea

46 9.35
Las diez menos veinticinco
Deeyeth menos beinteethinco

47 9.40
Las diez menos veinte
Deeyeth menos beinte

48 9.45
Las diez menos cuarto
Deeyeth menos quarto

49 9.50
Las diez menos diez
Deeyeth menos deeyeth

50 9.55
Las diez menos cinco
Deeyeth menos thinco

**51 12.00/Midday/
Midnight**
Las doce/Mediodía/
Medianoche
*Las dothe/medeeodeea/
medeeanoche*

52 What time is it?
¿Qué hora es?
¿Kay ora es

53 It is . . .
Son las . . .
Son las . . .

ARRIVING AND DEPARTING

Airport

54 Excuse me, where is the check-in desk for . . . airline?
¿Perdone, dónde está la facturación de la línea . . ?
Perdoneh, dondeh estah el mostrador deh faktoorathion deh la leenya . . ?

55 What is the boarding gate/time for my flight?
¿Por qué puerta/a qué hora sale mi vuelo?
Porr keh pwerta/ah keh ora saleh mee bwehlo?

56 How long is the delay likely to be?
¿Cuánto lleva de retraso, aproximadamente?
Kwanto llieba deh rehtraso, aproksimadamenteh?

57 Where is the duty-free shop?
¿Dónde está el duty free?
Dondeh esta el duty free?

58 Which way is the baggage reclaim?
¿Por dónde se va a la recogida de equipajes?
Porr dondeh seh ba ah rekoheeda deh ekeypahess?

59 Where can I get the bus to the city centre?
¿De dónde sale el autobús al centro?
Deh dondeh saleh el outoboos al thentro?

Train Station

60 Where is the ticket office/information desk?
¿Dónde está la taquilla de billetes/la ventanilla de información?
¿Donde estaa la taakeellia dey beellietes/la bentaaneellia dey informatheeon?

61 Which platform does the train to . . . depart from?
¿De qué andén sale el tren para . . ?
¿Deke anden sale el tren para . . ?

62 Where is platform . . ?
¿Dónde está el andén . . ?
¿Donde esta el anden . . ?

63 When is the next train to . . ?
¿A qué hora sale el próximo tren para . . ?
¿A key ora sale el proxseemo tren para . . ?

64 Is there a later train to . . ?
¿Hay un tren más tarde para . . ?
¿Eye oon tren mass tarde para . . ?

Port

65 How do I get to the port?
¿Cómo se va al puerto?
¿Como se ba al pooerto?

66 When is the next sailing to . . ?
¿A qué hora zarpa el próximo transbordador para . . ?
¿A kay ora tharpa el proxeemo transbordador para?

S
P
A
N
I
S
H

54
↑
66

291

67 Can I catch an earlier ferry with this ticket?
¿Puedo coger un ferry más temprano con este billete?
Pwedo cogherr oon ferry mas temprano kon esteh billieteh?

Notices and Signs

68 Coche restaurante
Koche restaoorante
Buffet (Dining) Car

69 Autobús
Awtoeboos
Bus

70 Agua potable/Agua no potable
Agwa potable/agwa no potable
Drinking/Non-drinking water

71 Entrada
Entrada
Entrance

72 Salida
Saleeda
Exit

73 Información
Informatheeon
Information

74 Consigna
Consigna
Left Luggage (Baggage Claim)

75 Consigna automática
Consigna awtomateeka
Luggage Lockers

76 Oficina de Correos
Ofeetheena de korreos
Post Office

77 Vía
Veea
Platform

78 Estación de trenes
Estatheeon de tren
Railway (Railroad) Station

79 Aeropuerto
Aehropwerto
Airport

80 Puerto
Pwerto
Port

81 Restaurante
Restaoorante
Restaurant

82 Fumadores/No fumadores
Foomadoores/no foomadoores
Smoking/Non-smoking

83 Teléfono
Telephono
Telephone

84 Taquilla de billetes
Takeellia de beellietes
Ticket Office

85 Facturación
Faktoorathion
Check-in Desk

86 Horario
Orareeo
Timetable (Schedule)

87 Servicios
Serbeetheeos
Toilets (Restrooms)

88 Caballeros
Kaballieros

SPANISH

67
↕
88

Gentlemen

89 Señoras
Senyoras
Ladies'

90 Tranvía
Tranbeea
Tram (Streetcar)

91 Metro
Metro
Underground (Subway)

92 Sala de espera
Sala de espera
Waiting Room

Buying a Ticket

**93 I would like a first-class/
second-class single (one-
way)/return (round-trip)
ticket to . . .**
Quisiera un billete de primera
clase/de segunda clase/de ida/
de ida y vuelta a . . .
*Keyseeyera oon beelliete de premera
clase/dey segoonda clase/dey eeda/
dey eeda ee bwelta a . . .*

**94 Is my rail pass valid on this
train?**
Puedo usar mi pase en este
tren/ferry/autobús?
*Pwedo usar mee pasey en esteh
tren/ferry/outoboos?*

**95 I would like an aisle/window
seat.**
Me gustaría un asiento junto al
pasillo/de ventanilla.

*Me goosetareea oon aseeyento
hoontoe al paseellio/de
bentaneellya.*

**96 No smoking/smoking,
please.**
No fumadores/fumadores, por
favor.
*No foomadoores/foomadoores, por
farbor*

**97 We would like to sit
together.**
Nos gustaría sentarnos juntos.
*Nos goosetareea sentarnos
hoontos.*

**98 I would like to make a seat
reservation.**
Quisiera reservar una plaza.
Keyseeyera rehzerbar oona platha.

**99 I would like to reserve a
couchette/sleeper for one
person/two people/for my
family.**
Quisiera hacer una reserva en el
coche-literas/coche-camas para
una persona/dos personas/mi
familia.
*Keyseeyera ather oona resserba en
el koche-literas/koche-kama para
oona persawna/dos persawnas/
mee fameleeya.*

**100 I would like to reserve a
cabin.**
Quisiera reservar un
camarote.
*Keyseeyera rehzerbar oon
kamarote.*

S
P
A
N
I
S
H

89
↕
100

ARRIVING AND DEPARTING

Timetables (Schedules)

101 Llegada
Yeygada
Arrival

102 Para en
Para en
Calls (stops) at

103 Servicio de restauración
Serbeetheeo dey restawratheeon
Catering Service

104 Transbordo en
Transbordoe en
Change at

105 Correspondencia
Correespondenthia
Connection

106 Diario
Deeareeo
Daily

107 Cada 40 minutos
Kada cwarenta menootos
Every 40 Minutes

108 Primera clase
Preemera clase
First-class

109 Cada hora
Kada ora
Hourly

110 Se recomienda reservar plaza
Se rekomeenda reserbar platha
Seat reservations are
recommended

111 Segunda clase
Segoonda clase
Second-class

112 Hay que pagar suplemento
Eye ke pagar sueplemento
Supplement Payable

113 Por
Beea
Por

Luggage

114 How much will it cost to send
(ship) my luggage in
advance?
¿Cuánto costaría enviar mi
equipaje por adelantado?
*¿Cwantoe costareea enbeear mee
ekeypahe por adelantado?*

115 Where is the left luggage
(baggage claim) office?
¿Dónde está la consigna?
¿Donde esta la consinya?

116 What time do you open/
close?
¿A qué hora abren/cierran?
¿a kay ora abren/theeyeran?

117 Where are the luggage
trolleys (carts)?
¿Dónde están los carretillas para
el equipaje?
*¿Donde estan las karretillias para
el ekeypahe?*

118 Where are the lockers?
Dónde está la consigna
automática?
*Dondeh esta la konseegna
awtoematika?*

119 I have lost my locker key.
He perdido la llave de la
consigna automática.
*Ey perdeedo la lliabe de la consigna
awtoematecar.*

On Board

120 Is this seat taken?
¿Está libre este asiento?
¿Esta leebre este aseeyento?

121 Excuse me, you are sitting in
my reserved seat.
Perdone, pero se ha sentado en
mi asiento reservado.
*Perdone pero sey a sentado en mee
aseeyento resserbado.*

122 Which station is this?
¿Qué estación es esta?
¿Kay estatheeon es esta?

123 What time is this train/bus/
ferry/flight due to arrive/
depart?
A qué hora sale/llega este tren/
autobús/vuelo?
*Ah keh ora saleh/lliega esteh tren/
outoboos/bwelo?*

124 Will you wake me just before
we arrive?
¿Le importaría despertarme un
poco antes de llegar?
*¿Ley inportareea despertarme oon
poco antes de lliegar?*

Customs and Passports

125 ¡Los pasaportes, por favor!
¡Los pasaportes por farbor!
Passports, please!

126 I have nothing to declare. I
have wine/spirits (alcohol)/
tobacco to declare.
No tengo nada que declarar.
Tengo vino/licores/tabaco que
declarar.
*No tengo nada kay declarar.
Tengo beeno/leekores/tabaco kay
declarar.*

127 I shall be staying for . . .
days/weeks/months.
Me quedaré por . . . días/
semanas/meses.
*Mey keydarey por . . . deeas/
semanas/messes.*

128 Do you have a map of the
town/area?
¿Tiene un mapa de la ciudad/de
la zona?
*¿Teeyene oon mapa de la
theeoodath/de la thona?*

129 Can I reserve
accommodation here?
¿Puedo reservar alojamiento
aquí?
*¿Pwedo reserbar alohameeyento
akee?*

130 Do you have a list of
accommodation?
¿Tiene una lista de hoteles?
Teeyene oona leesta deh oteles?

S
P
A
N
I
S
H

119
↕
130

ACCOMMODATION

ACCOMMODATION

Hotels

131 I have a reservation in the name of . . .
Tengo una reserva a nombre de . . .
Tengo oona resserba a nonbre dey . . .

132 I wrote to/faxed/telephoned you last month/last week in . . .
El mes pasado/la semana pasada les escribí/envié un fax/llamé por teléfono
El mes passado/la sehmanna passada les eskreebee/embeeyeh oon faks/lliameh porr tehlehfono.

133 Do you have any rooms free?
¿Tienen habitaciones?
Teeyenen abeetathiones?

134 I would like to reserve a single/double room with/without bath/shower.
Quisiera reservar una habitación individual/doble con/sin baño/ducha.
keyseeyera resserbar oona abeetatheeon indeebeedooal/doeble con/sin banyo/doocha.

135 I would like bed and breakfast/(room and) half board/(room and) full board.
Me gustaría cama y desayuno/media pensión/pensión completa.

Mey goosetareea kama ee desayuno/medeea penseeon/penseon conpleta.

136 How much is it per night?
¿Cuánto cuesta por noche?
¿Cwantoe cwesta por noche?

137 Is breakfast included?
¿Está el desayuno incluido?
¿Esta el desayoonoh incleedo?

138 May I see the room?
¿Puedo ver la habitación?
¿Pwedo ber la abeetatheeon?

139 Do you have any cheaper rooms?
¿Tienen habitaciones más baratas?
¿Teeyenen abeetatheeones mass baratas?

140 I would like to take the room.
Me gustaría ocupar la habitación.
Mey goosetareea ocoopar la abeetatheeon.

141 I would like to stay for . . . nights.
Quisiera quedarme por . . . noches.
Keyseeyera keydarme por . . . noches.

142 The shower/light/tap doesn't work.
La ducha/luz/el grifo no funciona.
La dootcha/looth/el greefoh noh foonthiona.

143 At what time/where is breakfast served?

¿A qué hora/dónde se sirve el desayuno?

¿A kay ora/donde sey seervey el desayoono?

144 What time do I have to check-out?

¿A qué hora debo desalojar la habitación?

¿A kay ora debo desalohar la abeetatheeon?

145 Can I have the key to room number?

¿Me quiere dar la llave de la habitación número . . ?

Meh keyereh dahrr la lliubeh deh la abeetathion noomero . . ?

146 My room number is . . .

Mi habitación es el número . . .

me abeetatheeon es el noomero . . .

147 Do you accept travellers' cheques/Eurocheques/credit cards?

¿Aceptan cheques de viaje/ Eurocheques/tarjetas de crédito?

Atheptan tchekes deh biaheh/ ehwrotchekes/tarhetas deh credeeto?

148 May I have the bill please?

¿Por favor me da la cuenta?

¿Por farbor meh da la cwenta?

149 Excuse me, I think there is a mistake in this bill.

Oiga, me parece que la cuenta está mal.

Oyga, meh parethe keh la kwenta esta mal.

Youth Hostels

150 How much is a dormitory bed per night?

¿Cuánto cuesta una cama por noche?

¿Cwantoe cwesta oona kama por noche?

151 I am/am not an HI member.

Soy/no soy miembro de HI.

Soy/no soy meeyembro dey hachey ee.

152 May I use my own sleeping bag?

¿Puedo utilizar mi propio saco de dormir?

¿Pwedo ooteeleethar mee propeeo saco de dormeer?

153 What time do you lock the doors at night?

¿A qué hora cierran por la noche?

¿A kay ora theeyerran por la noche?

Camping

154 May I camp here for the night/two nights?

¿Puedo acampar aquí por esta noche/dos noches?

¿Pwedo acanpar akee por esta noche/dos noches?

S
P
A
N
I
S
H

143
↕
154

297

¹⁵⁵**Where can I pitch my tent?**
¿Dónde puedo montar la tienda?
¿Donde pwedo montar la teeyenda?

¹⁵⁶**How much does it cost for one night/week?**
¿Cuánto cuesta por noche/semana?
¿Cwantoee cwesta por noche/semana?

¹⁵⁷**Where can we park our caravan?**
¿Dónde podemos aparcar la caravana?
Dondeh pohdemos aparkahrr la carabana?

¹⁵⁸**Where are the washing facilities?**
¿Dónde están los aseos?
¿Donde estan los aseos?

¹⁵⁹**Is there a restaurant/supermarket/swimming pool on site/nearby?**
¿Hay algún restaurante/supermercado/alguna piscina por aquí/cerca?
¿Eye algoon restawrante/suepermerkadoe/algoona pistheena por akee/therca?

¹⁶⁰**Do you have a safety deposit box?**
¿Tienen cajafuerte?
¿Teeyenen kahafwerte?

EATING AND DRINKING

Cafés and Bars

¹⁶¹**I would like a cup of/two cups of/another coffee/tea.**
Quisiera una taza de/dos tazas de/otra taza de café/té.
Keyseeyera oona tatha dey/dos tathas/otra tatha dey kafey/te.

¹⁶²**With/without milk/sugar.**
Con/sin leche/azucar.
Con/seen leche/athoocar.

¹⁶³**I would like a bottle/glass/two glasses of mineral water/red wine/white wine, please.**
Quisiera una botella/un vaso/dos vasos de agua mineral/de vino tinto/de vino blanco, por favor.
Keyseeyera oona botellia/oon baso/dos basos dey agwa meneral/dey beeno tintoe/dey beeno blanco, por farbor.

¹⁶⁴**I would like a beer/two beers, please.**
Quisiera una cerveza/dos cervezas, por favor.
Keyseeyera oona therbeytha/dos therbeythas, por farbor.

¹⁶⁵**May I have some ice?**
¿Pueden ponerme hielo?
¿Pweden ponerme eeyelloe?

EATING AND DRINKING

166 Do you have any matches/ cigarettes/cigars?
¿Tienen cerillas/cigarrillos/ puros?
¿Teeyenen thereellias/ theegarrellios/pooros?

Restaurants

167 Can you recommend a good/ inexpensive restaurant in this area?
¿Puede recomendarme un buen/ restaurante barato en la zona?
¿Pwede recomendarme oon bwen/ restawrante barato en la thona?

168 I would like a table for . . . people.
Quisiera una mesa para . . . personas.
Keyseeyera oona mesa para . . . personas.

169 Do you have a non-smoking area?
¿Tiene una zona reservada para no fumadores?
Teeyene oona thona rehzerbada para noh foomadores?

170 Waiter/Waitress!
¡Camarero/Camarera!
¡Camareroe/camarera!

171 Do you have a set menu/ children's menu/wine list?
¿Tienen menú del Día/menú para niños/ la carta de vinos?
¿Teeyenen menoo del deea/menoo para neenios/la carta dey beenos?

172 Do you have any vegetarian dishes, please?
¿Dan comidas vegetarianas, por favor?
¿Dan comeedas behetareanas, por farbor?

173 Are there any local specialities?
¿Tienen especialidades del lugar?
¿Teeyenen espethialeedades del loogar?

174 Are vegetables included?
¿Están incluidas las verduras?
¿Estan eenklooeedas las berdooras?

175 Could I have it well-cooked/ medium/rare please?
Por favor, la carne bien cocida/ al punto/roja.
Porr fabor, la kahrrne beeyen kotheeda/al poontoh/roha.

176 What does this dish consist of?
¿Qué contiene este plato?
¿Kay conteeyene este platoe?

177 I would like the set menu, please.
Quisiera el menú del día, por favor.
Keyseeyera el menoo del deea, por farbor.

178 We have not been served yet.
Todavía no nos han servido.
Toedabeea no nos an serbeedoe.

179 Excuse me, this is not what I ordered.
Perdone, no he pedido esto.
Perdoneh, noh eh pedeedo esto.

S P A N I S H

166 ↑ 179

180 May I have some/some more
bread/water/coffee/tea?
¿Podría traerme/más pan/agua/
café/té?
*¿Pordreea trayerme/mass pan/
agwa/kafey/te?*

181 May I have the bill, please?
¿Podría traerme la cuenta por
favor?
*¿Pordreea trayerme la cwenta por
farbor?*

182 Does this bill include service?
¿Está incluido el servicio en la
cuenta?
*¿Esta inclueedoe el serbeetheeo en la
cwenta?*

183 Do you accept travellers'
cheques (travelers' checks)/
Eurocheques/MasterCard/US
dollars?
¿Aceptan cheques de viaje/
Eurocheques/MasterCard/
dólares americanos?
*¿Atheptan chekes de beeahe/
eurochekes/MasterCard/doelares
amereecarnos?*

184 Can I have a receipt, please?
¿Me quiere dar un recibo, por
favor?
*¿Meh keyereh dahrr oon
resgwardo, porr fabor?*

185 Where is the toilet
(restroom), please?
¿Dónde están los servicios, por
favor?
*¿Donde estan los serbeetheeos, por
farbor?*

On the Menu

186 First courses
Entradas
Entradas

187 Soups
Sopas
Sohpas

188 Main courses
Platos principales
Platos preentheepales

189 Fish dishes
Pescados
Peskados

190 Meat dishes
Carnes
Kahrrnes

191 Vegetarian dishes
Platos vegetarianos
Platos behetaryanos

192 Cheese
Queso
Kehso

193 Desserts
Postres
Postres

194 Specialities
Especialidades
Espetheealeedades

GETTING AROUND

Public Transport

195 Where is the bus stop/coach
station/nearest metro
(subway) station?

¿Dónde está la parada de autobuses/la estación de autobuses/la estación de metro más cercana?
¿Donde esta la parrada dey awtoebooses/la estatheeon dey awtoebooses/la estatheeon dey metro mass thercana?

196 When is the next/last bus to . . ?
¿A qué hora sale el próximo autobús/el último autobús para . . ?
¿A kay ora sale el proxseemo awtoeboos/el ultimo awtoeboos para . . ?

197 How much is the fare to the city centre (downtown)/railway (railroad) station/airport?
¿Cuánto cuesta el billete hasta el centro/la estación de trenes/el aeropuerto?
¿Cwantoe cwesta el beelliete asta el thentro/la estatheeon de trenes/el aeropwerto?

198 Will you tell me when to get off?
¿Podría decirme cuando tendré que bajar?
¿Poordreea detheerme cwandoe tendray kay bahar?

199 Does this bus go to . . ?
¿Es este el autobús de . . ?
¿Es este el awtoeboos de . . ?

200 Which number bus goes to . . ?
¿Cuál es el número del autobús que va a . . ?
¿Cwal es el noomero del awtoeboos kay ba a . . ?

201 May I have a single (one-way)/return (round-trip)/day ticket/multi-journey ticket?
¿Quisiera un billete de ida/de ida y vuelta/de día/tarjeta
¿Keyseeyera oon beelliete dey eeda/dey eda ee bwelta/dey dea/tarheyta?

Taxis

202 I would like to go to . . . How much will it cost?
Quisiera ir a . . . ¿Cuánto me costaría?
Keyseeyera eer a . . . ¿cwantoe me costarea?

203 Please stop here.
Por favor pare aquí.
Por farbor parey akee.

204 I would like to order a taxi today/tomorrow/at 2pm to go from . . . to . . .
Quisiera reservar un taxi para hoy/mañana/a las dos de la tarde para ir de . . a . . .
Keyseeyera resserbar oon taxsee para oy/manyana/a las dos de la tarde para eer dey . . . a . . .

S
P
A
N
I
S
H

196
↕
204

GETTING AROUND/SIGHTSEEING

Asking the Way

205 Excuse me, do you speak English?
Perdone, ¿habla usted inglés?
Perdoene, ¿abla oosteth ingles?

206 Excuse me, is this the right way to . . ?
Perdone, ¿por aquí se va a . . ?
Perdoneh, ¿porr akee seh bah ah . ?

207 . . . the cathedral/the tourist information office/the castle/the old town.
. . . la catedral/oficina de turísmo/el castillo/el casco antiguo.
. . . la katehdral/offeetheena deh toorismoe/el kasteellio/el kasko antigwo.

208 Can you tell me the way to the railway (railroad) station/bus station/taxi rank (stand)/city centre (downtown)/beach?
¿Puede decirme cómo se va a la estación de trenes/estación de autobuses/parada de taxis/al centro de la ciudad/a la playa?
¿Pwede detheerme como sey ba a la estatheeon de trenes/estatheeon dey awtoebooses/parada de taxsis/al thentroe de la theeoodath/a la playa?

209 First/second left/right/straight ahead.
Primera/segunda a la izquierda/derecha/todo seguido.
Preemera/segoonda a la eethkeyerda/derecha/toedoe segeedoe.

210 Where is the nearest police station/post office/doctor/hospital/pharmacy?
¿Dónde está la comisaría de policía/la oficina de correos/el médico/el hospital/la farmacia más cercana?
¿Donde esta la comeesarea dey poleetheea/la ofeetheena dey coreos/el meydico/ el ospeetal/ lah farmatheea mass thercarna?

211 Is it far?
¿Está lejos?
¿Esta lehos?

212 Do I need to take a taxi/a bus?
¿Necesito coger un taxi/un autobús?
¿Netheeseeto coher oon taxsee/oon aootoeboos?

213 Can you point to it on my map?
¿Puede señalármelo en el mapa?
¿Pwede senyarlarmeloe en el mapa?

214 Thank you for your help.
Muchas gracias por su ayuda.
Moochas gratheeas poor soo ayuda.

SIGHTSEEING

215 Where is the Tourist Information office?
¿Dónde está la oficina de información y turismo?
¿Donde esta la ofeetheena de informatheeon ee toorismo?

SIGHTSEEING/ENTERTAINMENT

216 Where is the cathedral/
church/museum?
¿Dónde está la catedral/la
iglesia/el museo?
*¿Donde esta la catedral/la
igleeseea/el mooseo?*

217 How much is the entrance
(admission) charge?
¿Cuánto cuesta la entrada?
¿Cwantoe cwesta la entrada?

218 Is there a discount for
children/students/senior
citizens?
¿Tienen descuento los niños/los
estudiantes/los jubilados?
*¿Teeyenen descwento los neenyos/
los estoodeeantes/los hubeelados?*

219 What time does the next
guided tour start?
¿A qué hora empieza la
siguiente guía?
*¿A kay ora enpeeyetha la
seegeeyente geea?*

220 One/two adults/children,
please.
Uno/dos adultos/niños, por
favor.
*Oonoh/dos adooltos/neenios
porfarbor.*

221 May I take photographs
here?
Puedo sacar fotos?
Pwedo sakar fotos?

ENTERTAINMENT

222 Can you recommend a good
bar/nightclub?
¿Puede recomendarme un bar
bueno/una discoteca buena?
*¿Pwede recomendarme oon bar
bweno/oona discoteca bwena?*

223 Do you know what is on at
the cinema (playing at the
movies)/theatre at the
moment?
¿Sabe lo que están dando en el
cine/en el teatro en estos
momentos?
*¿Sabe lo key estan dando en el
theenne/en el tayatro en estos
momentos?*

224 I would like to book
(purchase) . . . tickets for the
matinee/evening
performance on Monday.
Quisiera reservar . . . entradas
para la sesión de tarde/de noche
del lunes.
*Keyseeyera resserbar . . . entradas
para la seseeon dey tarde dey noche
del loones.*

225 What time does the film/
performance start?
¿A qué hora empieza la sesión/
la función?
*¿A key ora enpeeyetha la seseeon/
la foontheeon?*

S P A N I S H

216
↕
225

303

MEETING PEOPLE

226 Hello/Goodbye.
Hola/adiós.
Ola/adeeos.

227 Good morning/good
afternoon/good evening/
goodnight.
Buenos días/buenas tardes/
buenas noches.
*Bwenos dee-ahs/bwenas tarrdess/
bwenas notchess.*

228 Pleased to meet you.
Encantado de conocerle.
Encantadoe dey conotherle.

229 How are you?
¿Cómo está usted?
¿Como esta oosteth?

230 Fine, thank you. And you?
Bien, gracias. Y usted?
Beeyen, grathias. Ee oosteth?

231 My name is . . .
Me llamo . . .
Meh lliamo . . .

232 This is my friend/boyfriend/
girlfriend/husband/wife/
brother/sister.
Este es mi amigo/novio/novia/
marido/esposa/hermano/
hermana.
*Este es mee ameego/nobeeo/nobeea/
mareedo/esposa/ermano/ermana.*

233 Where are you travelling to?
¿A dónde viaja?
¿A donde beeaha?

234 I am/we are going to . . .

voy/vamos a . . .
Boy/bamos a . . .

235 How long are you travelling
for?
¿Cuánto tiempo van a viajar?
¿Cwantoe teaempo ban a beahar?

236 Where do you come from?
¿De dónde es usted?
¿Dey donde es oosteth?

237 I am/we are from . . .
Soy/somos de . . .
Soy/somos . . .

238 We're on holiday.
Estamos de vacación.
Estamos deh bakathion.

239 This is our first visit here.
Es la primera vez que venimos
aquí.
*Es la preemera beth keh benimos
akee.*

240 Would you like/May I have a
cigarette?
¿Quiere un cigarrillo/Me da un
cigarillo?
*¿Keyerey oon theegarrellio/Mey da
oon theegarrellio?*

241 I am sorry but I do not
understand.
Lo siento pero no entiendo.
Loh siento pero no entiendo.

242 Please speak slowly.
Por favor hable despacio.
Por farbor abley despathio.

243 Do you mind if I smoke?
¿Le molesta si fumo?
¿Ley molesta see foomo?

244 Do you have a light?
¿Tiene fuego?
¿Teeyene fwego?

245 I am waiting for my husband/
wife/boyfriend/girlfriend.
Estoy esperando a mi marido/
mujer/novio/novia.
*Estoy esperando a mee mareedo/
mooher/nobyoh/nobya.*

TRAVELLING WITH CHILDREN

246 Do you have a high chair/
babysitting service/cot?
¿Tienen sillas para bebés/
servicio de kanguro/cuna?
*¿Teeyenen seellias para bebes/
serbeetheeo de cangooro/coona?*

247 Where is the nursery/
playroom?
¿Dónde está la guardería/el
cuarto de niños?
*¿Donde esta la gwardereea/el
kwarto de neenyos?*

248 Where can I warm the baby's
bottle?
¿Dónde puedo calentar el
biberón?
¿Donde pwedo calentar el beeberron?

COMMUNICATIONS

Post

249 How much will it cost to
send a letter/postcard/this
package to Britain/Ireland/
America/Canada/Australia/
New Zealand?

¿Cuánto cuesta enviar esta
carta/postal/paquete a Gran
Bretaña/Irlanda/América/
Canadá/Australia/Nueva
Zelanda?
*¿Cwantoe cwesta enbeear esta
carta/pohstal/pakete a gran
bretannia/eerlandda/amereeca/
canada/awstralea/nweyba
theylanda?*

250 I would like one stamp/two
stamps.
Quisiera un sello/dos sellos.
Keyseeyera oon sellio/dos sellios.

251 I'd like . . . stamps for
postcards to send abroad,
please.
Quisiera . . . sellos para postales
al extranjero, por favor.
*Keysyera . . . sellios para postales
al estranhero, porr fabor.*

Phones

252 I would like to make a
telephone call/reverse the
charges to (make a collect
call to) . . .
Quisiera llamar por teléfono/
llamar a cobro revertido a . . .
*Keyseeyera lliamar por telephono/
lliamar a cobro rebertedo a . . .*

253 Which coins do I need for
the telephone?
¿Qué monedas necesito para el
teléfono?
*¿Kay monehdas netheseeto para el
telephono?*

S
P
A
N
I
S
H

244
↕
253

²⁵⁴ **The line is engaged (busy).**
La línea está comunicando.
La leeneea esta comooneecando.

²⁵⁵ **The number is . . .**
El número es el . . .
El noomero es el . . .

²⁵⁶ **Hello, this is . . .**
Hola, habla . . .
Ola, abla . . .

²⁵⁷ **May I speak to . . ?**
Puedo hablar con . . ?
Pwedo ablar kon . . ?

²⁵⁸ **He/She is not in at the moment. Can you call back?**
No está. ¿Quiere volver a llamar más tarde?
Noh esta. Keyereh bolber a lliamar mas tarrdeh?

MONEY

²⁵⁹ **I would like to change these travellers' cheques (travelers' checks)/this currency/this Eurocheque.**
Quisiera cambiar estos cheques de viaje/dinero/este Eurocheque.
Keyseeeeyera canbeear estos chekes de beeahe/denero/este eoorocheke.

²⁶⁰ **How much commission do you charge (What is the service charge)?**
¿Qué comisión recargan?
¿Kay comeeseeon recargan?

²⁶¹ **Can I obtain money with my MasterCard?**
¿Puedo sacar dinero con la tarjeta MasterCard?
¿Pwedo sacar deenero con la tarheta MasterCard?

SHOPPING

Names of Shops and Departments

²⁶² **Librería/Papelería**
Leebreree-ah/paplehree-ah
Bookshop/Stationery

²⁶³ **Joyería/Regalos**
Hoyeree-ah/regalos
Jeweller's/Gifts

²⁶⁴ **Zapatería**
Thapatos
Shoe Shop

²⁶⁵ **Ferretería**
Ferretehree-ah
Hardware

²⁶⁶ **Anticuario**
Antikwaryo
Antiques

²⁶⁷ **Peluquería (caballeros)/ (damas)**
Pelookeree-ah (kaballieros)/ (damas)
Hairdressers (men's)/(women's

²⁶⁸ **Estanco/Tabaquería**
Estanko/Tabakeree-ah
Tobacconist

²⁶⁹ **Panadería**
Panaderee-ah
Baker's

270 Supermercado
Soopermerkado
Supermarket

271 Tienda de fotos
Teeyenda deh fotos
Photoshop

272 Juguetería
Hoogetehree-ah
Toys

273 Agencia de viajes
Ahenthya deh byahes
Travel Agent

274 Artículos de tocador
Arteekoolos deh tokador
Toiletries

275 Discos
Deeskos
Records

In the Shop

276 What time do the shops open/close?
¿A qué hora abren/cierran las tiendas?
¿A kay ora abren/theeyerran las teeyendas?

277 Where is the nearest market?
Dónde está el mercado más próximo?
Dondeh kayda el merkado mas proksimo?

278 Can you show me the one in the window/this one?
Quiere enseñarme el del escaparate/este?

Keyereh ensehniarmeh el del eskaparateh/esteh?

279 Can I try this on?
¿Puedo probarme esto?
¿Pwedo probarme esto?

280 What size is this?
¿Qué talla es esta?
¿Kay tallia es esta?

281 This is too large/too small/too expensive.
Es muy grande/muy pequeño/muy caro.
Es mooy grandeh/mooy pekenio/mooy karo.

282 Do you have any others?
¿Tienen más?
¿Teeyenen mas?

283 My size is . . .
Ni número es el . . .
Mee noomero es el . . .

284 Where is the changing room/childrens/cosmetic/ladieswear/menswear/food department?
¿Dónde están los probadores/niños/perfumería/señoras/caballeros/sección de alimentos?
¿Donde estan los probadores/neenyos/perfoomereea/senyoras/caballieros/sectheeon dey alimentos?

285 I would like . . .
Me gustaría . . .
Meh goostaree-ah . . .

286 I would like a quarter of a kilo/half a kilo/a kilo of bread/ butter/cheese/ham/ tomatoes.
Quisiera un cuarto de kilo/ medio kilo/un kilo de pan/ mantequilla/queso/jamón/ tomates.
Keyseeyera oon cwarto dey kilo/ medio kilo/oon kilo dey pan/ mantekillia/keso/hamon/tomates.

287 How much is this?
¿Cuánto es?
¿Cwantoe es?

288 I'll take this one, thank you.
Me llevo éste.
Meh llievo esteh.

289 Do you have a carrier (shopping) bag?
¿Me da una bolsa por favor?
¿Meh da oona bolsa por farbor?

290 Do you have anything cheaper/larger/smaller/of better quality?
¿Tiene algo más barato/grande/ pequeño/de mejor calidad?
¿Teeyene algo mass baratto/ grande/pekenio/de mehor caleedath?

291 I would like a film for this camera.
Quisiera un rollo para esta cámara.
Keyseeyera oon rollio para esta camara.

292 I would like some batteries, the same size as this old one.
Quisiera pilas, del mismo tamaño que esta vieja.
Keyseeyera peelas, del mismo tamanio kay esta beeha.

293 Would you mind wrapping this for me, please?
¿Le importaría envolvermelo?
¿Le inportareea enbolbermelo?

294 Sorry, but you seem to have given me the wrong change.
Lo siento, pero no me ha dado la vuelta correcta.
Lo seeyento, pero no meh a dado la vwelta correcta.

MOTORING

Car Hire (Rental)

295 I have ordered (rented) a car in the name of . . .
Tengo un coche alquilado a nombre de . . .
Tengo oon koche alkeyladoe a nombre de . . .

296 How much does it cost to hire (rent) a car for one day/ two days/one week?
¿Cuánto cuesta alquilar un coche por un día/dos días/una semana?
¿Cwantoe cwesta alkeylar oon koche por oon deea/dos deeas/oona semanna?

297 Is the tank already full of
petrol (gas)?
¿Está el depósito de gasolina
lleno?
*¿Esta el deposeytoe de gasoleena
llieno?*

298 Is insurance and tax
included? ¿How much is the
deposit?
¿Está incluido en el precio los
impuestos y el seguro? ¿Cuánto
hay que poner de señal?
*¿Esta inclooeedoe en el pretheeo los
inpwestoes ee el segooro, cwantoee
eye kay poner de senial?*

299 By what time must I return
the car?
¿A qué hora debo entregar el
coche?
¿A kay ora debo entregar el koche?

300 I would like a small/family
car with a radio/cassette
player.
Quisiera un coche pequeño/
familiar con radio/casete.
*Keyseeyera oon koche pekenio/
familiar con radeeo/caset.*

Asking the Way

301 Excuse me, can you help me
please?
¿Perdone, me puede ayudar?
*¿Perdoneh, meh pwedeh
aiyoodahrr?*

302 How do I reach the
motorway/main road?
¿Por dónde se va a la autopista/

carretera principal?
*¿Porr dondeh seh ba a la
outopeesta/karretehrra printhipal?*

303 I think I have taken the
wrong turning.
Creo que me he equivocado de
camino.
*Kreoh keh meh eh ekeebokado deh
kameeno.*

304 I am looking for this address.
Busco esta dirección.
Boosko esta deerekthion.

305 I am looking for the . . . hotel.
Busco el hotel . . .
Boosko el ohtel . . .

306 How far is it to . . .
from here?
¿. . . queda muy lejos de aquí?
¿ . . kayda mooy lehos deh akee?

307 Carry straight on for . . .
kilometres.
Siga derecho unos . . .
kilómetros.
*Seega deretcho oonos . . .
keelometros.*

308 Take the next turning on the
right/left.
La próxima a la derecha/
izquierda.
*La proksima a la deretcha/
eethkyerda.*

309 Turn right/left at the next
crossroads/traffic lights.
Tire a la derecha/izquierda en el
próximo cruce/semáforo.
*Teereh a la deretcha/eethkyerda en
el proksimo croothe/sehmaforo.*

310 You are going in the wrong direction.
No se va por ahí.
Noh seh ba porr ah-ee.

Parking

311 How long can I park here?
¿Cuanto tiempo puedo aparcar aquí?
¿Kwanto teeyempo pwedo aparkar akee?

312 Is there a car park near here?
¿Hay un aparcamiento cerca de aquí?
¿Eye oon aparkameeyento therka deh akee?

313 At what time does this car park close?
¿A qué hora cierra este aparcamiento?
¿A keh ora thierra esteh aparkameeyento?

Signs and Notices

314 One way.
Sentido único.
Senteedo ooneeko.

315 No entry.
Prohibido el paso.
Proeebeedoh el passoh.

316 No parking.
Prohibido aparcar
Proeebeedo aparcar.

317 Detour (diversion)
Desvío
Desbeeyathion.

318 Stop.
Alto
Alto

319 Give way (yield).
Ceda el paso
Theda el paso

320 Slippery road.
Camino resbaladizo.
Kameeno resbaladeetho.

321 No overtaking.
Prohibido adelantar
Proybeedo adelantar

At the Filling Station

322 Unleaded (lead-free)/ Standard/Premium
Sin plomo/normal/extra
Seen plohmoh/normall/ekstra

323 Fill the tank please.
¿Me llena el tanque, por favor?
¿Meh lliena el tankeh porr fabor?

324 Do you have a road map of this area?
¿Tiene un mapa de carreteras de la zona?
¿Teeyene oon mapa deh karretehrras deh la thona?

325 How much is the car-wash?
¿Cuánto cuesta el lavado?
¿Kwanto kwesta el labahdo?

Breakdowns

326 I've had a breakdown at . . .
El coche se ha averiado en . . .
El cotcheh seh ah aberyado en . . .

327 I am on the road from . . .
to . . .
Estoy en la carretera de . . .
a . . .
Estoy en la karretehrra deh . . .
a . . .

328 I can't move the car. Can you
send a tow-truck?
El coche no se mueve. ¿Puede
enviar una grúa?
El cotcheh noh seh mwehbeh.
¿Pwedeh embeeyar oona groo-ah?

329 I have a flat tyre.
He tenido un pinchazo.
Eh tehneedo oom pintchatho.

330 The windscreen (windshield)
has smashed/cracked.
El parabrisas se ha hecho trizas/
se ha rajado.
El parabreesas seh ah etcho
treethas/seh ah rahado.

331 There is something wrong
with the engine/brakes/
lights/steering/gearbox/
clutch/exhaust.
El motor/los frenos/las luces/la
dirección/la caja de cambios/el
embrague/el escape no funciona
bien.
El motor/los frenos/las loothes/la
deerekthion/la caha deh cambyos/
el embrahge/el escape noh
foonthiona bien.

332 It's overheating.
Se sobrecalienta
Seh sobrekalienta.

333 It won't start.
No arranca.
Noh arranka

334 Where can I get it
repaired?
¿Dónde lo pueden arreglar?
¿Dondeh lo pweden arreglar?

335 Can you take me there?
¿Me puede llevar allí?
¿Meh pwedeh lliebar allyee?

336 Will it take long to fix?
¿Va a tardar mucho en
arreglarlo?
¿Ba a tardahrr mootcho en
arreglarlo?

337 How much will it cost?
¿Cuanto me va a cobrar?
¿Kwanto meh ba a kobrar?

Accidents

338 Can you help me? There has
been an accident.
¿Me puede ayudar? Ha habido
un accidente.
¿Meh pwedeh aiyoodahrr? Ah
ahbeedo oon akthidenteh.

339 Please call the police/an
ambulance.
Llame a la policía/ambulancia.
Lliameh a la poleethee-ah/
amboolanthia

340 Is anyone hurt?
¿Se ha lastimado alguién?
¿Seh ah lasteemado algyen?

S
P
A
N
I
S
H

327
↕
340

311

Traffic Offences

341 I'm sorry, I didn't see the sign.

Lo siento, no me fijé en la señal.

Lo seeyento, noh meh feeheh en el lehtrero.

342 Must I pay a fine? How much?

¿Tengo que pagar una multa? ¿Cuánto?

¿Tengo keh pagar oona moolta? ¿Kwanto?

343 Show me your documents.

Enséñeme sus documentos.

Ensehniemeh soos dokoomentos.

HEALTH

Pharmacy

344 Do you have anything for a stomachache/headache/sore throat/toothache?

¿Tienen algo para el dolor de estómago/cabeza/garganta/dientes?

¿Teeyenen algo para el doelor de estoemago/cabeetha/garganta deeyentes?

345 I need something for diarrhoea (diarrhea)/constipation/a cold/a cough/insect bites/sunburn/travel (motion) sickness.

Necesito algo contra la diarrea/el estreñimiento/el catarro/la tos/las picaduras de insectos/la quemadura del sol/el mareo.

Netheseeto algo contra la deearrea/el estrenyiemeeyento/el catarro/la tos/las peecadooras de insectos/la khemadoora del sol/el mareo.

346 How much/how many do I take?

¿Cuánto/cuántas tengo que tomar?

¿Cwantoe/cwantas tengo kay toemar?

347 How often do I take it/them?

¿Cada cuánto tiempo tengo que tomarlo/tomarlas?

¿Cada cwantoe teaenpo tengo kay toemarlo/toemarlas?

348 How much does it cost?

¿Cuánto cuesta?

¿Cwantoe cwesta?

349 Can you recommend a good doctor/dentist?

¿Puede recomendarme un buen médico/dentista?

¿Pwede recomendarmeh oon bwen meddeeco/denteesta?

350 Is it suitable for children?

¿Es adecuado para niños?

¿Es adecwado para neenios?

Doctor

351 I have a pain here/in my arm/leg/chest/stomach.

Tengo dolor aquí/en el brazo/la pierna/el pecho/el estómago.

Tengo oon doelor akee/en el bratho/la peeyerna/el pecho/el estomago.

S
P
A
N
I
S
H

341
↕
351

352 Please call a doctor, this is an emergency.
Por favor, llamen a un médico, es una emergencia.
Por farbor lliamen a oon meddeeco, es oona emerhentheea.

353 I would like to make an appointment to see a doctor.
Quisiera una cita para una consulta.
Keyseeyera oona thita para oona consoolta.

354 I am diabetic/pregnant.
Soy diabético(a)/estoy embarazada.
Soy deeabetteeko/estoy enbarathada.

355 I need a prescription for . . .
Necesito una receta para . . .
Netheseeto oona rethetta para . . .

356 Can you give me something to ease the pain?
¿Puede darme algo para aliviar el dolor?
¿Pwede darme algo para aleebear el doelor?

357 I am/he is/she is allergic to penicillin.
I am/he is/she is allergic to penicillin.
Soy/es alérgico/alérgica a la penicilina.
Soy alerheeko/alerheeka a la peneetheeleena.

358 Does this hurt?
¿Le duele esto?
¿Leh dweleh esto?

359 You must/he must/she must go to hospital.
Usted/él/ella tiene que ir al hospital.
Oosteth/el/ellia teeyene keh eer al ospeetal.

360 Take these once/twice/three times a day.
Tome esto una vez/dos/tres veces al día.
Tomeh esto oonah beth/dos/tres bethess al dee-ah.

361 I am/he is/she is taking this medication.
Estoy/está tomando este medicamento.
Estoy/esta tomando esteh medeekamento.

362 I have medical insurance.
Tengo seguro médico.
Tengo sehgooro mehdeeko.

Dentist

363 I have toothache.
Tengo dolor de muelas/me duelen las muelas.
Tengo dolor de mwelas/mey dwelen las mooeylas.

364 My filling has come out.
Se me ha caído un empaste.
Se meh a cayeedo oon enpaste.

365 I do/do not want to have an injection first.
Quiero/no quiero que me den una inyección.
Kiero/no kiero kay meh den oona inyechthion.

S
P
A
N
I
S
H

352
↑
365

EMERGENCIES

366 Help!
¡Socorro!
¡Sawkoro!

367 Call an ambulance/a doctor/
the police!
¡Llame a una ambulancia/un
médico/la policía!
*¡Lliame a oona anboolanthea/oon
meydico/la poletheea!*

368 I have had my travellers
cheques (traveler's checks)/
credit cards/purse/handbag/
rucksack (knapsack)/
luggage/wallet stolen.
Me han robado los cheques de
viaje/las tarjetas de crédito/el
bolso/la mochila/el equipaje/el
billetero.
*Meh an robadoe los chekes dey
beahe/las tarhetas dey credeeto/el
bolso/la mocheela/el ekeypahe/el
bellietero.*

369 Can you help me, I have lost
my daughter/son.
¿Puede ayudarme, se ha
extraviado mi hija/mi hijo.
*¿Pwede ajudarme, sey a
extrabeeado mee eekha/mee eekho?*

370 Please go away/leave me
alone.
Por favor váyase/déjeme en
paz.
Por farbor bayase/deheme en path.

371 Fire!
¡Fuego!
¡Fwegoh!

372 I want to contact the British/
American/Canadian/Irish/
Australian/New Zealand/
South African consulate.
Quisiera llamar al consulado
británico/americano/
candadiense/irlandés/de Nueva
Zelanda/surafricano.
*Keyseeyera lliamar al konsoolado
britaneeko/amehreekano/
kanadeyenseh/eerlandess/deh
nweba theylanda/surafrikano.*

Introduction

Turkish, brought to the shores of Europe from central-eastern Asia by the invading Ottomans, is unrelated to other European languages. Although it contains modern words borrowed from English, the main linguistic influence over the centuries has been Arabic.

Turkish uses a roman alphabet (albeit with a large number of accented characters) which was introduced in the 20th century as part of the modernising reforms which followed on the fall of the Ottoman Empire.

English, German and French are widely spoken in the cosmopolitan and tourist-frequented areas of Istanbul and the Aegean coast, but elsewhere you will need Turkish phrases.

Addresses for travel and tourist information

Australia: *Turkish Tourist Office,* Room 17, Level 3, 428 George Street, Sydney, NSW 2000; tel: (2) 92 233055.
Canada: *Turkish Tourist Office,* Constitution Square, 360 Albert St, Suite 801, Ottawa, Ontario, K1R 7X7; tel: (613) 230 8654.
UK: *Turkish Tourist Office,* First Floor, 170–173 Piccadilly, London, W1J 9EJ; tel: (020) 7629 7771/7355 4207.
USA: *Turkish Tourist Office,* 821 UN Plaza, New York, NY 10017; tel: (212) 687 2194/5/6.

T
U
R
K
I
S
H

ESSENTIALS

Alphabet

The letters Q, W and X are only used in describing foreign words.

A	B
ah	*beh*
C	D
jeh	*deh*
E	F
eh	*feh*
G	H
geh	*heh*
I	J
ee	*zheh*
K	L
keh	*leh*
M	N
meh	*neh*
O	P
o	*peh*
Q	R
qu	*reh*
S	T
seh	*teh*
U	V
u	*veh*
W	X
dueblueveh	*iks*
Y	Z
yeh	*zeh*

Basic Words and Phrases

1 **Yes** **No**
Evet Hayır
Evet *Hayer*

2 **Please** **Thank you**
Lütfen Tesekkür ederim
Luetphen *Teshekkuer ederim*

3 **That's O.K.** **Perhaps**
Bir sey değil Belki
Bir shey de'el *Belki*

4 **To** **From**
e/a den/dan
e/a *dan/den*

5 **Here** **There**
Burada Orada
Burada *Orada*

6 **None** **Also**
Hiç de/da
Hich *de/da*

7 **How** **When**
Nasıl Ne zaman
Nasel *Ne zaman*

8 **What** **Why**
Ne Neden
Ne *Neden*

9 **I don't understand.**
Anlamıyorum.
Anlameyourum.

10 **I don't speak Turkish.**
Türkçe bilmiyorum.
Tuerkche bilmiyourum.

11 **Do you speak English?**
İngilizce biliyor musunuz?
İnghilizh'dje biliyour musunuz?

TURKISH

01
↕
11

316

12 Can you please write it down?
Lütfen suraya yazar mısınız?
Luetfen shuraya yazar me'se'nez?

13 Can you please speak more slowly?
Lütfen biraz daha yavas konusur musunuz?
Luetfen biraz daha yavash konushur musunuz?

14 How much does it/this cost?
O/Bu kaç para?
O/Bu kach para?

Days

15 **Monday** **Tuesday**
Pazartesi Salı
Pazartesi *Salae*

16 **Wednesday** **Thursday**
Çarsamba Persembe
Charshamba *Pershembe*

17 **Friday** **Saturday**
Cuma Cumartesi
Djuma *Djumartesi*

18 **Sunday** **Morning**
Pazar Sabah
Pazar *Sabah*

19 **Afternoon** **Evening**
öğleden sonra Aksam
Oe'leden sonra *Aksham*

20 **Night** **Week**
Gece Hafta
Ghedje *Haphta*

21 **Yesterday/Today/Tomorrow**
Dün/Bugün/Yarın
Duen/Buguen/Yaren

Numbers

22 **Zero** **One**
Sıfır Bir
Saephaer *Beer*

23 **Two** **Three**
Iki Üç
Eki *Uech*

24 **Four** **Five**
Dört Bes
Doert *Besh*

25 **Six** **Seven**
Altı Yedi
Alte *Yedi*

26 **Eight** **Nine**
Sekiz Dokuz
Sekiz *Dokuz*

27 **Ten** **Eleven**
On On bir
On *On beer*

28 **Twelve** **Thirteen**
On iki On üç
On eki *On uech*

29 **Fourteen** **Fifteen**
On dört On bes
On doert *On besh*

30 **Sixteen** **Seventeen**
On altı On yedi
On alte *On yedi*

31 **Eighteen** **Nineteen**
On sekiz On dokuz
On sekiz *On dokuz*

TURKISH

12 ↕ 31

32 Twenty
Yirmi
Yirmi

Twenty-one
Yirmi bir
Yirmi beer

33 Twenty-two
Yirmi iki
Yirmi eki

Thirty
Otuz
Otuz

34 Forty
Kırk
Kaerk

Fifty
Elli
Elli

35 Sixty
Altmıs
Altmaesh

Seventy
Yetmis
Yetmish

36 Eighty
Seksen
Seksen

Ninety
Doksan
Doksan

37 One hundred
Yüz
Yuez

Five hundred
Bes yüz
Besh yuez

38 One thousand
Bin
Been

One million
Bir milyon
Beer million

Time

39 9.00
Dokuz
Dokuz

40 9.05
Dokuzu bes geçiyor
Dokuzu besh gechiyour

41 9.10
Dokuzu on geçiyor
Dokuzu on gechiyour

42 9.15
Dokuzu onbes geçiyor
Dokuzu onbesh gechiyour

43 9.20
Dokuzu yirmi geçiyor
Dokuzu yirmi gechiyour

44 9.25
Dokuzu yirmibes geçiyor
Dokuzu yirmibesh gechiyour

45 9.30
Dokuz buçuk
Dokuz buchuk

46 9.35
Ona yirmibes var
Ona yirmibesh var

47 9.40
Ona yirmi var
Ona yirmi var

48 9.45
Ona çeyrek var
Ona cheyrek var

49 9.50
Ona on var
Ona on var

50 9.55
Ona bes var
Ona besh var

51 12.00/Midday/Midnight
On iki/öğle üzeri/Gece yarısı
Oneki/Oe'le uezeri/ghedje yarese

52 What time is it?
Saat kaç?
Saat kach?

53 It is . . .
Saat . . .
Saat . . .

TURKISH

32
↓
53

318

ARRIVING AND DEPARTING

Airport

54 **Excuse me, where is the check-in desk for . . . airline?**
Afedersiniz, . . . havayollarının çekin bürosu neresi acaba?
Afedersiniz, . . . havayollarenen checkin buerosu ne'resi adjaba?

55 **What is the boarding gate/ time for my flight?**
Benim uçağımın binis kapısı neresi/binis saati kaç acaba?
Benim ucha'emen binish kapese neresi/binish saati kach adjaba?

56 **How long is the delay likely to be?**
Uçağın gecikme süresi ne kadar acaba?
Ucha'en gedjikme sueresi ne kadar adjaba?

57 **Where is the duty-free shop?**
Gümrüksüz mal satıs yeri neresi acaba?
Guemrueksuez mal satesh yeri ne'resi adjaba?

58 **Which way is the baggage reclaim?**
Bavulları alma yeri neresi acaba?
Bavullare alma yeri neresi adjaba?

59 **Where can I get the bus to the city centre?**
Kentin merkezine otobüs nereden kalkıyor acaba?
Kentin merkezine otobues nereden kalkeyor adjaba?

Train Station

60 **Where is the ticket office/ information desk?**
Bilet gisesi nerede?/ Enformasyon masası nerede?
Bilet gishesi nerede?/Enformasyon masase nerede?

61 **Which platform does the train to . . . depart from?**
. . . treni hangi perondan hareket ediyor?
. . . treni hangi perondan hareket ediyor?

62 **Where is platform . . ?**
. . . peronu nerede?
. . . peronu nerede?

63 **When is the next train to . . ?**
. . . treni ne zaman?
. . . treni ne zaman?

64 **Is there a later train to . . ?**
. . . a/e baska tren var mı?
. . . a/e bashka tren var mae?

Port

65 **How do I get to the port?**
Limana nasıl gidebilirim?
Leemana nasael gedebilirim?

66 **When is the next sailing to . . ?**
Bundan sonraki sefer kaçta?
Bundan sonraki sepher kachta?

T
U
R
K
I
S
H

54
↕
66

ARRIVING AND DEPARTING

67 **Can I catch an earlier ferry with this ticket?**
Bu biletle daha erken kalkan feribota binebilir miyim?
Bu biletle daha erken kalkan feribota binebilir miyim?

Notices and Signs

68 **Büfe vagonu**
Beufe vagonu
Buffet (Dining) Car

69 **Otobüs**
Otobeus
Bus

70 **Içilir/içilmez su**
Echilir/echilmez su
Drinking/Non-drinking water

71 **Giris**
Girish
Entrance

72 **Çıkıs**
Chekesh
Exit

73 **Enformasyon**
Enformasyon
Information

74 **Emanet**
Emanet
Left Luggage (Baggage Claim)

75 **Bagaj dolapları**
Bagadj dolaplare
Luggage Lockers

76 **Postane**
Postane
Post Office

77 **Peron**
Peron
Platform

78 **Estasion**
Istasyon
Railway (Railroad) Station

79 **Havaalanı**
Hava a'lane
Airport

80 **Liman**
Liman
Port

81 **Restoran**
Restoran
Restaurant

82 **Sigara içilir/içilmez**
Sigara echilir/echilmez
Smoking/Non-Smoking

83 **Telefon**
Telephon
Telephone

84 **Bilet gisesi**
Beelet ghishese
Ticket Office

85 **Çekin bürosu**
Checkin buerosu
Check-in Desk

86 **Tarife**
Tarife
Timetable (Schedule)

87 **Tuvaletler**
Tuvaletler
Toilets (Restrooms)

88 **Erkekler**
Erkekler
Gentlemen

89 **Bayanlar**
Baianlar
Ladies'

90 **Tramvay**
Trumvai
Tram (Streetcar)

91 **Metro**
Metro
Underground (Subway)

92 **Bekleme Odası**
Bekleme Odase
Waiting Room

Buying a Ticket

93 **I would like a first-class/
second-class single (one-
way)/return (round-trip)
ticket to . . .**
. . . e/a birinci/ikinci mevki
sadece gidis/gidis gelis bileti
istiyorum.
*. . . e/a beerindji/ekindji mevki
sadedje ghedish/ghedish ghelis
beelete estiyourum.*

94 **Is my rail pass valid on this
train?**
Benim tren pasom bu trende/
feribotta/otobüste geçer mi?
*Benim teren pasom bu terende/
feribotta/otobueste gecher mi?*

95 **I would like an aisle/window
seat.**

Pencere kenarında/koridor
tarafında bir yer istiyorum.
*Pendjere koridoor/kenaraenda
tarafaenda beer yer estiyourum.*

96 **No smoking/smoking, please.**
Sigara içilmez/sigara içilir,
lütfen
*Sigara icheler/sigara echelmez,
leutphen*

97 **We would like to sit together**
Yan yana oturmak istiyoruz.
Yan yana otoormak estiyouruz

98 **I would like to make a seat
reservation.**
Bir yer ayırtmak istiyorum.
Bir yer ayertmak istiyourum.

99 **I would like to reserve a
couchette/sleeper for one
person/two people/for my
family.**
Kusetlide/yataklıda bir kisilik/
iki kisilik/ailem için yer
ayırtmak istiyorum.
*Coushetleede/yataklaeda beer
kishelik/eki kishelik yer
ayeaertmak estiyourum.*

100 **I would like to reserve a
cabin.**
Bir kabin ayırtmak istiyorum.
Bir kabin ayertmak istiyourum.

Timetables (Schedules)

101 **Varış**
Vareash
Arrive

T
U
R
K
I
S
H

88
↑
101

321

ARRIVING AND DEPARTING

102 **. . . da durur**
. . . da durur
Calls (Stops) at

103 **Lokanta**
Lokanta
Catering Service

104 **. . . da değistirin**
. . . da de'shtirin
Change at

105 **Bağlantı**
Ba'lantae
Connection

106 **Günlük**
Geunleuk
Daily

107 **Her kırk dakikada bir**
Haer kerk dakekada beer
Every 40 Minutes

108 **Birinci mevki**
Beerindji mevke
First-class

109 **Saatte bir**
Sa'atte beer
Hourly

110 **Yer ayırtılması tavsiye edilir**
Yer ayertelmase tavsiye edilir
Seat reservations are recommended

111 **Ikinci mevki**
Ekinci mevki
Second-class

112 **Ek ücret ödenir**
Ek eudjret eadenir
Supplement Payable

113 **Üzerinden**
euzerinden
Via

Luggage

114 **How much will it cost to send (ship) my luggage in advance?**
Bagajımı önceden göndermek kaça mal olur?
Baghadjaemae eandjden geandermek kacha mal oleur?

115 **Where is the left luggage (baggage claim) office?**
Emanet nerede?
Emanet nerede?

116 **What time do you open/close?**
Ne zaman açıyorsunuz/kapatıyorsunuz?
Ne zaman achaeyoursunuz/kapataeyoursunuz?

117 **Where are the luggage trolleys (carts)?**
Bagaj troleyleri nerede?
Badghadj troleylere nerede?

118 **Where are the lockers?**
Kilitli dolaplar nerede acaba?
Kilitli dolaplar neresi adjaba?

119 **I have lost my locker key.**
Dolap anahtarımı kaybettim.
Dolap anahtaraeme kaibettim.

On Board

120 **Is this seat taken?**
Bu yer bos mu?
Bu yer bosh mu?

121 Excuse me, you are sitting in
my reserved seat.
Pardon, bana ayrılmıs yerde
oturuyorsunuz.
*Pardon, bana airaelmaesh yerde
oturuyorsunuz.*

122 Which station is this?
Bu hangi istasyon?
Bu hange istasion?

123 What time is this train/bus/
ferry/flight due to arrive/
depart?
Bu tren/feribot/uçak saat kaçta
gelecek/kalkacak?
*Bu teren/feribot/uchak sa't kachta
gelecek/kalkadjak?*

124 Will you wake me just
before we arrive?
Varmadan önce beni uyandırır
mısınız?
*Varmadan oendje beni
uyandaeraer maesaeniz?*

Customs and Passports

125 Pasaportlar, lütfen!
Pasaportlar luetphen!
Passports, please!

126 I have nothing/wine/
spirits (alcohol)/tobacco to
declare.
Gümrüğe tabi (hiçbir esyam
yok)/sarap/içki/tütün var.
*Geumreu'e tabe (hichbir eshiam
yok)/sharap/eachki/tuetuen var.*

127 I shall be staying for . . .
days/weeks/months.
. . . gün/hafta/ay kalacağım.
. . . guen/hafta/ai kaladja'em.

AT THE TOURIST OFFICE

128 Do you have a map of the
town/area?
Bu kentin/bölgenin haritası var
mı?
*Bu kentin/boelgenin haritasae var
mae?*

129 Can I reserve
accommodation here?
Burada kalacak yer ayırtabilir
miyim?
*Beurada kaladjak yer ayaertabeler
meyem?*

130 Do you have a list of
accommodation?
Kalacak yerlerin bir
listesi var mı?
*Kaladjak yerlerin bir
listesi var me?*

ACCOMMODATION

Hotels

131 I have a reservation in the
name of . . .
. . . adına rezervasyon
yaptırmıstım.
*. . . adaena rezervasyon
yaptaermaeshtaem.*

T
U
R
K
I
S
H

121
↕
131

ACCOMMODATION

132 I wrote to/faxed/telephoned you last month/last week in . . .
Geçen ay/geçen hafta size yazmıstım/faks çekmistim/ telefon etmistim.
Gechen ay/gechen hafta size yazmeshtem/fax chekmishtim/ telephon etmishtim.

133 Do you have any rooms free?
Hiç bos odanız var mı?
Hich bosh odanez var me?

134 I would like to reserve a single/double room with/ without bath/shower.
Bir/iki kisilik banyolu/banyosuz duslu/dussuz oda ayırtmak istiyorum.
Bir/iki kieshielik banyolu/dushlu banyosuz/dushsuz oda ayaertmak istiyourum.

135 I would like bed and breakfast/(room and) half board/(room and) full board.
Sadece kahvaltılı/kahvaltı ve bir öğün yemekli/üç öğün yemekli bir oda istiyorum.
Sadedje kahvaltaelae/kahvaltae ve beer oe'oen yemekli/euch oe'oen yemekli oda istiyourum.

136 How much is it per night?
Gecesi kaça?
Ghedjesi kacha?

137 Is breakfast included?
Kahvaltı dahil mı?
Kahvaltae dahil me?

138 May I see the room?
Odayı görebilir miyim?
Odayae goerebilir miim?

139 Do you have any cheaper rooms?
Daha ucuz odalarınız var mı?
Daha oodjuz odalaraenaez var me?

140 I would like to take the room
Odayı tutuyorum.
Odayae tootooyorum.

141 I would like to stay for . . . nights.
. . . gece kalmak istiyorum.
. . . gedje kalmak istiyourum

142 The shower/light/tap doesn't work.
Dus/elektrik/musluk bozuk galiba.
Dush/electric/musluk bozuk ga'liba.

143 At what time/where is breakfast served?
Kahvaltı servisi nerede/ne zaman?
Kahvaltee servisi nerede/ne zaman?

144 What time do I have to check-out?
Saat kaçta ayrılmam lazım?
Sa'at kachta ayraelmam lazaem?

145 Can I have the key to room no . . ?
. . . numaralı odanın anahtarını rica ediyorum.
. . . numarale odanen anakhtarene ridja ediyourum.

146 My room number is . . .
Oda numaram . . .
Oda numaram . . .

147 Do you accept travellers'
cheques/Eurocheques/credit
cards?
Seyahat çeki/Euroçek/kredi
kartı kabul ediyor musunuz?
*Seyahat cheki/Eurocheck/kredi
karte kabul ediyor musunuz?*

148 May I have the bill please?
Hesabı, lütfen
Hesabee, luetphen.

149 Excuse me, I think there is a
mistake in this bill.
Afedersiniz, bu hesapta bir
yanlıslık var galiba.
*Afedersiniz, bu hesapta bir
yanleshlek var ga'liba.*

Youth Hostels

150 How much is a dormitory
bed per night?
Bir gecelik yatakhane ücreti ne
kadar?
*Beer ghedjelik yatakhane uedjreti
ne kadar?*

151 I am/am not an HI member.
Uluslararası Gençlik Hostelleri
Birliği üyesiyim/üyesi değilim.
*Euluslararasae Ghenchlik Hostelleri
Beerli'e ueyesiim/ueyesi deelim.*

152 May I use my own sleeping
bag?
Kendi uyku tulumumu
kullanabilir miyim?

*Kendi uyku tulumumu kullanabilir
miyim?*

153 What time do you lock the
doors at night?
Gece kapıları kaçta
kilitliyorsunuz?
*Ghedje kapaelarae kachta
kilitliyoursunuz?*

Camping

154 May I camp here for the
night/two nights?
Burada bu gece/iki gece kamp
yapabilir miyim?
*Burada bu ghedje/eki ghedje kamp
yapabilir miyim?*

155 Where can I pitch my tent?
Çadırımı nereye kurabilirim?
*Chadaeraemae nereye
kurabilirim?*

156 How much does it cost for
one night/week?
Bir geceliği/bir haftalığı kaça?
*Beer ghedjeli'e/beer haftalae'e
kacha?*

157 Where can we park our
caravan?
Karavanımızı nereye park
edebiliriz?
*Karava'nemezhe nereye park
edebiliriz?*

158 Where are the washing
facilities?
Yıkanma yerleri nerede?
Yaekanma yerleri nerede?

T
U
R
K
I
S
H

146
↕
158

325

159 Is there a restaurant/
supermarket/swimming pool
on site/nearby?
Burada/yakında bir restoran/
çarsı/yüzme havuzu var mı?
*Burada/yakaenda bir restoran,
charshae/yuezme havuzu var
mae?*

160 Do you have a safety deposit
box?
Kıymetli esya için kasanız var
mı?
*Kaeymetli eshia eachin kasanaez
var mae?*

EATING AND DRINKING

Cafés and Bars

161 I would like a cup of/two
cups of/another coffee/tea.
Bir fincan/iki fincan/bir fincan
daha kahve/çay istiyorum.
*Beer findjan/eki findjan/beer
findjan daha kahve/chai
istiyourum.*

162 With/without milk/sugar.
Sütlü/sekerli (with), sütsüz/
sekersiz (without)
*Suetlue/shekerli, suetsuez/
shekersiz.*

163 I would like a bottle/glass/
two glasses of mineral water/
red wine/white wine, please.
Bir sise/bardak/iki sise maden
suyu/kırmızı sarap/beyaz sarap
lütfen.

*Beer shishe/bardak/eki shishe
maden suyu/kaermaezae sharap/
beyaz sharap luetphen.*

164 I would like a beer/two
beers, please.
Bir bira/iki bira lütfen.
Beer beera/eki beera luetphen.

165 May I have some ice?
Biraz buz alabilir miyim?
Biraz buz alabilir miyim?

166 Do you have any matches/
cigarettes/cigars?
Kibritiniz/sigaranız/puronuz
var mı?
*Kibritiniz/sigaranaez/pueronuz
var m?*

Restaurants

167 Can you recommend a good/
inexpensive restaurant in this
area?
Bu bölgede iyi/ucuz bir restoran
tavsiye eder misiniz?
*Bu boelgede eyi/udjuz beer
restoran tavsiye eder misiniz?*

168 I would like a table for . . .
people.
. . . lik bir masa istiyorum.
. . . lik beer masa istiyourum.

169 Do you have a non-smoking
area?
Sigara içilmeyen bir yeriniz var
mı?
*Sighara ichilmeyen bir yeriniz var
me?*

170 Waiter/Waitress!
Garson
Garson

171 Do you have a set menu/ children's menu/wine list?
Yemek listesi/çocuklar için yemek listesi/sarap listesi var mı?
Yemek listesi/chodjuklar ichin yemek listesi/sharap listesi var mae?

172 Do you have any vegetarian dishes, please?
Etsiz yemekleriniz var mı?
Etsiz yemekleriniz var mae?

173 Are there any local specialities?
Bu bölgeye has yemekler var mı?
Bu boelgheye has yemekler var me?

174 Are vegetables included?
Garnitür de dahil mi?
Garnituer de dahil mi?

175 Could I have it well-cooked/ medium/rare please?
İyice kızartılmıs/Normal/Az pismis olsun lütfen.
Iyidje kezartelmesh/Normal/Az pishmish olsun luetfen.

176 What does this dish consist of?
Bu yemeğin içinde neler var?
Bu yeme'en ichinde neler var?

177 I would like the set menu, please.
Tabldot lütfen.

Tabldot luetphen.

178 We have not been served yet.
Bize hala servis yapılmadı.
Bize hala servis yapaelmadae.

179 Excuse me, this is not what I ordered.
Afedersiniz, benim ısmarladığım bu değildi.
Afedersiniz, benim esmarlade'em bu de'ildi.

180 May I have some/some more bread/water/coffee/tea?
Biraz/biraz daha ekmek/su/ kahve/çay verir misiniz?
Beeraz/beeraz daha ekmek/su/ kahve/chai verir misiniz?

181 May I have the bill, please?
Hesap, lütfen?
Hesap, luetphen?

182 Does this bill include service?
Servis bu hesaba dahil mi?
Servis bu hesaba dahil mi?

183 Do you accept travellers' cheques (travelers' checks)/ Eurocheques/MasterCard/US dollars?
Seyahat çeki/Mastır kart/ Amerikan doları alıyor musunuz?
Seyahat cheki/master cart/ american dolarae alaeyour musunuz?

184 Can I have a receipt, please?
Bir makbuz rica etsem?
Bir makbuz ridja etsem?

EATING AND DRINKING

185 Where is the toilet (restroom), please?
Tuvalet nerede acaba?
Tuvalet nerede adjaba?

On the Menu

186 First courses
Aperitifler
Aperitifler

187 Soups
Çorbalar
Chorbalar

188 Main courses
Ana yemekler
An'a yemekler

189 Fish dishes
Balık yemekleri
Balek yemekleri

190 Meat dishes
Et yemekleri
Et yemekleri

191 Vegetarian dishes
Sebze yemekleri
Sebze yemekleri

192 Cheese
Peynir
Peynir

193 Desserts
Tatlılar
Tatlelar

194 Specialities
Buraya özgü yemekler
Buraya oezgue yemekler

GETTING AROUND

Public Transport

195 Where is the bus stop/coach station/nearest metro (subway) station?
Otobüs durağı/otobüs terminali/en yakın metro istasyonu nerede?
Otobues dura'ae/otobues terminali/en yakaen metro istasionu nerede?

196 When is the next/last bus to . . ?
. . . e/a bundan sonraki otobüs ne zaman?
. . . e/a bundan sonrakee otobues ne zaman?

197 How much is the fare to the city centre (downtown)/railway (railroad) station/airport?
Sehir merkezine/tren istasyonuna/hava alanına bilet kaça?
Shehir merkezine/tren istasionuna/hava alanaena bilet kacha?

198 Will you tell me when to get off?
Ne zaman ineceğimi söyler misiniz?
Ne zaman enedje'emi soeyler misiniz?

199 Does this bus go to . . ?
Bu otobüs . . . a/e gidiyor mu?
Bu otobues . . . a/e gidiyour mu?

200 Which number bus goes
to . . ?

. . . ya/ye kaç numaralı
otobüs gidiyor?

*. . . ye/ya kach numaralae
otobues gidiyour?*

201 May I have a single (one-
way)/return (round-trip)/day
ticket/book of tickets?

Gidis/gidis-gelis/günlük/koçan
halinde bilet istiyorum?

*Gidish/gidish-gelish/guenleuk/
kochan halinde bilet istiyourum?*

Taxis

202 I would like to go to . . . , how
much will it cost?

. . . a/e gitmek istiyorum, kaç
para tutar?

*. . . a/e ghitmek istiyourum, kach
para tutar?*

203 Please stop here.

Burada durur musunuz?

Burada durur musunuz.

204 I would like to order a taxi
today/tomorrow/at 2pm to
go from . . . to . . .

Bugün/yarın öğleden sonra saat
2'ye . . . den/dan . . . e/a taksi
ısmarlamak istiyorum.

*Buguen/yaraen oe'leden sonra
sa'at ikiye . . . den/dan . . . e/a taxi
aesmarlamak istiyourum.*

Asking the Way

205 Excuse me, do you speak
English?

Afedersiniz, Ingilizce biliyor
musunuz?

*Afedersiniz, engilizdje biliyor
musunuz?*

206 Excuse me, is this the right
way to . . ?

Afedersiniz, . . .'e/a/ye/ya
buradan mı gidilir?

*Afedersiniz, . . .'e/a/ye/ya
buradan me gidilir?*

207 . . . the cathedral/the tourist
information office/the castle/
the old town

. . . Katedral/turist
enformasyon bürosu/sato/eski
sehir

*. . . Cathedral/tourist
enformasyon buerosu/shato/eski
shehir*

208 Can you tell me the way to
the railway station/bus
station/taxi rank (stand)/city
centre (downtown)/beach?

Istasyona/otobüs terminaline/
taksi durağına/sehir merkezine/
plaja nasıl gidilir, söyler misiniz?

*Estasyona/otobues terminaline/
taxi dura'aena/shehir merkezine/
paeladja nasael ghidilir, soeyler
misiniz?*

T
U
R
K
I
S
H

200
↑
208

209 First/second left/right/
straight ahead.
Birinci/soldan ikinci/sağda/
dosdoğru.
*Beerindji/soldan ekindji/sa'da/
dosdo'ru.*

210 Where is the nearest police
station/post office/doctor/
hospital/pharmacy?
En yakın polis karakolu/
postane/doktor/hastane/eczane
nerede?
*En yakaen polis karakolu/
postaine/hastaine/eczaine nerede?*

211 Is it far?
Uzak mı?
Uzak mae?

212 Do I need to take a taxi/
catch a bus?
Taksiye mi/otobüse mi binmem
gerekli?
*Taxiye me/otobuese me binmem
gherekle?*

213 Can you point to it on my map?
Haritamın üzerinde gösterebilir
misiniz?
*Haritamaen uezerinde goesterebilir
misiniz?*

214 Thank you for your help.
Yardımınız için teşekkür ederim.
*Yardaemaenaez ichin teshekkuer
ederim.*

SIGHTSEEING

215 Where is the Tourist
Information office?

Turist enformasyon bürosu
nerede?
*Tourist enformasion buerosu
nerede?*

216 Where is the cathedral/
church/museum?
Katedral/Kilise/Müze nerede?
Catedral/Kilise/Mueze nerede?

217 How much is the admission
charge?
Giriş ücreti ne kadar?
Gherish eudjreti ne kadar?

218 Is there a reduction for
children/students/senior
citizens?
Çocuklara/öğrencilere/yaşlılara
indirim var mı?
*Chodjuklara/eurendjilere/
yashlaelara endirim var mae?*

219 What time does the next
guided tour start?
Bundan sonraki kılavuzlu tur ne
zaman başlıyor?
*Bundan sonraki khaelavuzlu tour
ne zaman bashlaeyour?*

220 One/two adults/children,
please.
Bir/iki büyük/çocuk, lütfen.
*Beer/eki bueyuek/chodjuk,
luetphen.*

221 May I take photographs
here?
Burada resim çekebilir miyim?
Burada resim chekebilir miyim?

ENTERTAINMENT

222 Can you recommend a good bar/nightclub?
Iyi bir bar/gece kulübü tavsiye edebilir misiniz?
Eyi bir bar/gedje kuluebue tavsiye edebilir misiniz?

223 Do you know what is on at the cinema (playing at the movies)/theatre at the moment?
Su anda sinemada/tiyatroda ne oynuyor?
Shu anda sinemada/teyatroda ne oynuyor?

224 I would like to book (purchase) . . . tickets for the matinee/evening performance on Monday.
Pazartesi günü öğle seansı/ aksam için . . . bilet ayırtmak istiyorum.
Pazartesi guenue oe'le seansae/ aksham ichin . . . bilet ayaertmak istiyourum.

225 What time does the film/ performance start?
Film/gösteri kaçta başlıyor?
Film/goesteri kachta bashleyour?

MEETING PEOPLE

226 Hello/Goodbye.
Merhaba/Hoşça kal
Merhaba/hoshcha kal

227 Good morning/good afternoon/good evening/ goodnight.
Günaydın/merhaba/iyi aksamlar/iyi geceler.
Guenayden/merhaba/iyi akshamlar/iyi gedjler.

228 Pleased to meet you.
Tanıştığımıza memnun oldum.
Tanaeshtae'maeza memnun oldum.

229 How are you?
Nasılsınız?
Nasaelsaenaez?

230 Fine, thank you. And you?
Tesekkür ederim, iyiyim. Siz nasılsınız?
Teshekkuer ederim, iyiyim. Siz naselsenez?

231 My name is . . .
Adım . . .
Adaem . . .

232 This is my friend/boyfriend/ girlfriend/husband/wife/ brother/sister.
Bu benim arkadaşım/erkek arkadaşım/kız arkadaşım/ kocam/karım/erkek kardeşim/ kız kardeşim
Bu benim arkadashaem/erkek arkadashaem/kaez arkadashaem/ kodjam/karaem/erkek kardeshaem/kaez kardeshaem

233 Where are you travelling to?
Nereye gidiyorsunuz?
Nereye ghidiyoursunuz?

T
U
R
K
I
S
H

222
↕
233

331

MEETING PEOPLE

234 I am/we are going to . . .
Ben/biz . . . e/a gidiyoruz.
Ben/beez . . . e/a ghidiyoruz.

235 How long are you travelling
for?
Kaç günlük bir geziye
çıkıyorsunuz?
*Kach guenluek beer gheziye
chekeyoursunuz?*

236 Where do you come from?
Neredensiniz?
Neredensiniz?

237 I am/we are from . . .
. . . den/dan
. . . den/dan

238 We're on holiday.
Tatildeyiz.
Tatildeyiz.

239 This is our first visit here.
İlk defa buraya geliyoruz.
Ilk def'a buraya geliyouruz.

240 Would you like/May I have a
cigarette?
Sigara alır mısınız?/Sigara
alabilir miyim?
*Sigara aler mesenez?/Sigara
alabilir miyim?*

241 I am sorry, but I do not
understand.
Kusura bakmayın,
anlamıyorum.
*Kusura bakmayaen,
anlameyourum.*

242 Please speak slowly.
Lütfen ağır ağır (tane tane/tek
tek) söyleyin.

*Luetphen a'ar a'ar (tane tane/tek
tek) soeyleyin.*

243 Do you mind if I smoke?
Sigara içmem sizi rahatsız eder
mi?
*Sigara ichmem sizi rahatsaez eder
mi?*

244 Do you have a light?
Kibritiniz/çakmağınız var mı?
Kibritiniz/chakma'anaez var mae?

245 I am waiting for my husband/
wife/boyfriend/girlfriend.
Kocamı/esimi/erkek
arkadasımı/kız arkadasımı
bekliyorum.
*Kodjame/eshimi/erkek
arkadasheme/kez arkadasheme
bekliyorum.*

TRAVELLING WITH CHILDREN

246 Do you have a high chair/
baby-sitting service/cot?
Bebek için sandalye/çocuk
bakım servisi/karyola var mı?
*Bebek ichin sandalie/chodjuk
bakem servisi/kariola var mae?*

247 Where is the nursery/
playroom?
Çocuk yuvası/oyun odası
nerede?
*Chodjuk yuvase/oyun odase
nerede?*

248 Where can I warm the baby's
bottle?
Biberonu nerede ısıtabilirim?
Beeberonu nerede aesetabilirim?

COMMUNICATIONS

Post

249 How much will it cost to send a letter/postcard/this package to Britain/Ireland/America/Canada/Australia/New Zealand?
İngiltere'ye/İrlanda'ya/Amerika'ya/Kanada'ya/Avustralya'ya/Yeni Zelanda'ya mektup/kartpostal/bu paket kaça gider?
Inghiltere'ye/Erlanda'ya/Amerika'ya/Kanada'ya/Avustralia'ya/Yeni Zelanda'ya mektup/cartpostal/bu paket kacha geder?

250 I would like one stamp/two stamps.
Bir pul/iki pul istiyorum.
Bir pul/eki pul istiyourum.

251 I'd like . . . stamps for postcards to send abroad, please.
Yurt dışına kartpostal göndermek için . . . pul rica ediyorum.
Yurt deshena kartpostal goendermek ichin . . . pul ridja ediyourum.

Phones

252 I would like to make a telephone call/reverse the charges to (make a collect call to) . . .
Telefon etmek/ telefon etmek istiyorum.
Telephon etmek/telephon etmek istiyourum.

253 Which coins do I need for the telephone?
Telefon için hangi parayı kullanmam lazım?
Telephon ichin hangi parayae kullanmam lazaem?

254 The line is engaged (busy).
Hat meşgul.
Hat meshgul

255 The number is . . .
Numara . . .
Numara . . .

256 Hello, this is . . .
Alo, ben . . .
Alo, ben . . .

257 May I speak to . . ?
. . .'i/ı/yi/yı rica edecektim.
. . .'i/e/yi/ye ridja ededjektim.

258 He/She is not in at the moment. Can you call back?
Kendisi şimdi burada değil. Daha sonra arar mısınız?
Kendisi shimdi burada de'il. Daha sonra arar mesenez?

TURKISH

249 ↑ 259

MONEY/SHOPPING

MONEY

259 I would like to change these travellers' cheques (travelers' checks)/this currency/this Eurocheque.
Bu seyahat çeklerini/bu parayı/bu Euro çeki bozdurmak istiyorum.
Bu sey'ahat cheklerini/bu paray/bu Euro cheki bozdurmak istiyourum.

260 How much commission do you charge (what is the service charge)?
Ne kadar komisyon alıyorsunuz?
Ne kadar komision alaeyorsunuz?

261 Can I obtain money with my MasterCard?
Master Kartla para alabilir miyim?
Mastaer Cartla para alabilir miyim?

SHOPPING

Names of Shops and Departments

262 Kitapçı/kırtasiyeci
Kitapche/kertasiyedji
Bookshop/Stationery

263 Mücevheratçı/Hediyelik esya
Muedjevheratche/Hediyelik eshya
Jeweller's/Gifts

264 Ayakkabılar/ayakkabı
Ayakka'belar/ayakka'be
Shoes

265 Hırdavat
Herdavat
Hardware

266 Antika esya
Antika eshya
Antiques

267 Erkek berberi/Kadın berberi
Erkek berberi/Kaden berberi
Hairdressers (men's)/(women's)

268 Sigara bayii/tütüncü
Sighara bayee/tuetuendjue
Tobacconist

269 Hamur isleri/Fırın
Hamur ishleri/Feren
Baker's

270 Süpermarket
Suepermarket
Supermarket

271 Fotoğrafçı
Photo'rafche
Photoshop

272 Oyuncaklar
Oyundjaklar
Toys

273 Seyahat Acentası
Seyahat Adjenta'se
Travel Agent

274 Makyaj malzemeleri
Makiazh maldzemeleri
Toiletries

275 Plaklar
Pilaklar
Records

In the Shop

276 What time do the shops open/close?
Dükkanlar ne zaman açılır/kapanır?
Duekkanlar ne zaman acheler/kapanaer?

277 Where is the nearest market?
En yakın alısveris merkezi/pazar neresi?
En yaken aleshverish merkedzi/padzar neresi?

278 Can you show me the one in the window/this one?
Vitrindekini/bunu görmek istiyorum.
Vitrindekini/bunu goermek istiyourum.

279 Can I try this on?
Bunu prova edebilir miyim?
Bunu prova edebilir miim?

280 What size is this?
Bunun numarası kaç?
Bunun numarase kach?

281 This is too large/too small/too expensive.
Bu çok büyük/çok küçük/çok pahalı.
Bu chok bueyuek/chok kuechuek/chok paha'le.

282 Do you have any others?
Baska çesitleriniz de var mı?
Bashka cheshitleriniz de var me?

283 My size is . . .
Benim ölçüm . . .
Benim oelchuem . . .

284 Where is the changing room/childrens/cosmetic/ladieswear/menswear/food department?
Giyinme odaları/çocuk/kozmetik esya/bayan giysileri/erkek giysileri/yiyecek bölümü nerede?
Giyinme odalarae/chodjuk/kozmetik eshia/bayan giysileri/erkek giysileri/yiyedjek boeluemue nerede?

285 I would like . . .
. . . istiyorum/rica edecektim.
. . . istiyourum/ridja ededjektim.

286 I would like a quarter of/half a kilo/a kilo of bread/ butter/cheese/ham/tomatoes.
Ikiyüzelli gram/yarım kilo/bir kilo ekmek/tereyağ/peynir/jambon/domates istiyorum.
Ekiyuezelli gram/yarem kilo/bir kilo ekmek/tereya' peinir/djambon/domates estiyourum.

287 How much is this?
Kaça?
Kacha?

288 I'll take this one, thank you.
Bunu alacağım, tesekkür ederim.
Bunu aladja'em, teshekkuer ederim.

T
U
R
K
I
S
H

276
↑
288

335

289 Do you have a carrier
(shopping) bag?
Plastik torbanız var mı?
Plastic torbanez var me?

290 Do you have anything
cheaper/larger/smaller/of
better quality?
Daha ucuz/büyük/küçük/iyi
kalite bir seyiniz var mı?
*Daha eudjuz/bueyuek/kuechuek/
eyi kalite bir sheyiniz var mi?*

291 I would like a film for this
camera.
Bu makineye bir film
istiyorum.
*Bu makineye bir film
istiyourum.*

292 I would like some batteries,
the same size as this old
one.
Bunlarla aynı büyüklükte yeni
pil istiyorum.
*Bunlarla ayne bueyuekluekte peel
istiyourum.*

293 Would you mind wrapping
this for me, please?
Lütfen bunu sarar mısınız?
Luetphen bunu sarar mesenez?

294 Sorry, but you seem to have
given me the wrong change.
Kusura bakmayın ama paranın
üstünü yanlış verdiniz.
*Kusura baknayen ama paranen
uestuenue yanlesh verdiniz.*

MOTORING

Car Hire (Rental)

295 I have ordered (rented) a car
in the name of . . .
. . . adına araba ısmarladım.
. . . adaena araba aesmarladaem.

296 How much does it cost to
hire (rent) a car for one day/
two days/one week?
Bir günlük/iki günlük/bir
haftalık araba kiralama ücreti ne
kadar?
*Beer guenluek/eki guenluek/beer
haftalaek araba kiralama eudjreti
ne kadar?*

297 Is the tank already full of
petrol (gas)?
Benzin deposu dolu mu?
Benzin deposu dolu mu?

298 Is insurance and tax
included? How much is the
deposit?
Sigorta ve vergi dahil mi?
Depozit ne kadar?
*Sigorta ve verghi dahil me?
Depozit ne kadar?*

299 By what time must I return
the car?
Arabayı ne zamana kadar geri
getirmem lazım?
*arabayae ne zamana kadar geri
ghetirmem lazaem?*

300 I would like a small/family car with a radio/cassette player.

Radyolu/teypli küçük bir araba/ aile arabası istiyorum.

Radiolu/teipli kuechuk beer araba/ aile arabasae istiyourum.

Asking the Way

301 Excuse me, can you help me please?

Afedersiniz, sizden bir ricada bulunacaktım.

Afedersiniz, sizden bir ridjada bulunadjaktem.

302 How do I reach the motorway/main road?

Otobana/ana yola nasıl çıkabilirim?

Autoba'na/ana yola nasel chekabilirim?

303 I think I have taken the wrong turning.

Galiba yanlış yerden/kavsaktan dönüs yaptım.

Ga'liba yanlesh yerden/ kavshaktan doenuesh yaptem.

304 I am looking for this address.

Su adresi arıyorum.

Shu adresi a'reyourum.

305 I am looking for the . . . hotel.

. . . oteli/otelini arıyorum.

. . . oteli/otelini a'reyourum.

306 How far is it to . . . from here?

Buradan . . .'e/a/ye/ya mesafe/

uzaklık ne kadar?

Buradan . . .'e/a/ye/ya mesa'fe/ uzhaklek ne kadar?

307 Carry straight on for . . . kilometres.

Dosdoğru . . . kilometre daha gidin/sürün.

Dosdo'ru . . . kilometre daha ghidin/sueruen.

308 Take the next turning on the right/left.

Bundan sonraki sapaktan/ dönemeçten sağa/sola dönün/ sapın.

Bundan sonra'ki sapaktan/ doenemechten sa'a/sola doenuen/ sa'pen.

309 Turn right/left at the next crossroads/traffic lights.

Bundan sonraki kavsaktan/trafik ısıklarından sağa/sola sapın.

Bundan sonra'ki kavshaktan/ traffic eshekla'rendan sa'a/sola sapen.

310 You are going in the wrong direction.

Ters yönde gidiyorsunuz.

Ters yoende ghidiyoursunuz.

Parking

311 How long can I park here?

Burada ne kadar süreyle/kaç saat park edebilirim.

Burada ne kadar suereyle/kach sa't park edebilirim?

MOTORING

³¹² **Is there a car park near here?**
Yakınlarda bir otopark var mı?
Yakenlarda bir autopark var me?

³¹³ **At what time does this car park close?**
Bu otopark saat kaçta kapanıyor?
Bu autopark sa't kachta kapa'neyor?

Signs and Notices

³¹⁴ **Tek yön**
Tek yoen
One way

³¹⁵ **Girilmez/Girmek yasaktır**
Ghirilmez/Girmek yasakter
No entry

³¹⁶ **Park yapılmaz/Park etmek yasaktır**
Park yapelmaz/Park etmek yasakter
No parking

³¹⁷ **Zorunlu sapış**
Zhorunlu sapesh
Detour (diversion)

³¹⁸ **Dur!**
Dur!
Stop!

³¹⁹ **Yol ver**
Yol ver
Give way (yield)

³²⁰ **Kaygan yol**
Kayghan yol
Slippery road

³²¹ **Sollama yapılmaz.**
Sol'lama yapelmez
No overtaking

At the Filling Station

³²² **Unleaded (lead-free)/ Standard/Premium**
Kursunsuz/Normal/Süper
Kurshunsuz/Normal/Sueper

³²³ **Fill the tank please.**
Depoyu doldurun lütfen.
Depoyu doldurun luetfen.

³²⁴ **Do you have a road map of this area?**
Sizde bu yörenin yol haritası var mı?
Sizde bu yoerenin yol harita'se var me?

³²⁵ **How much is the car-wash?**
Araba kaça yıkanıyor?
Araba kacha yeka'neyor?

Breakdowns

³²⁶ **I've had a breakdown at . . .**
. . .'de/da arabam bozuldu.
. . .'de/da arabam bozhuldu.

³²⁷ **I am on the road from . . . to . . .**
. . .'den/dan . . .'e/a/ye/ya giden yol üzerindeyim.
. . .'den/dan . . .'e/a/ye/ya ghiden yol uezerindeyim.

328 I can't move the car.
Can you send a tow-truck?
Arabayı çekemiyorum. Bir çekme aracı gönderebilir misiniz?
Arabaye che'kemiyourum. Bir chekme aradje goenderebilir misiniz?

329 I have a flat tyre.
Lastiğim patladı.
Lasti'im patla'de.

330 The windscreen (windshield) has smashed/cracked.
Ön cam kırıldı/çatladı.
Oen djam ke'relde/chatla'de.

331 There is something wrong with the engine/brakes/lights/steering/gearbox/clutch/exhaust.
Motorda/frenlerde/ısıklarda/direksiyonda/vites kutusunda/debriyajda/egzosta bir arıza var galiba.
Motorda/frenlerde/esheklerde/direxiyonda/vites kutusunda/debriyazhda/eghzosta bir areza var ga'liba.

332 It's overheating.
Motor fazla ısınmıs/su kaynatıyor.
Motor fazla esenmesh/su kayna'teyor.

333 It won't start.
Araba çalısmıyor/Mars basmıyor.

Araba chaleshmeyor/Marsh basmeyor.

334 Where can I get it repaired?
Nerede tamir ettirebilirim?
Ne're'de tamir etti'rebilirim?

335 Can you take me there?
Beni oraya götürebilir misiniz?
Beni oraya goetuerebilir misiniz?

336 Will it take long to fix?
Tamiri/takması uzun sürer mi?
Tamiri/takma'se uzhun suerer mi?

337 How much will it cost?
Kaça çıkar/malolur?
Kacha chekar/malolur?

Accidents

338 Can you help me? There has been an accident.
Bir kaza oldu. Bana yardım edebilir misiniz?
Bir kazha oldu. Bana yardem e'debilir misiniz?

339 Please call the police/an ambulance.
Lütfen polisi/bir ambulans çağırın.
Luetfen polisi/bir ambulans cha'eren.

340 Is anyone hurt?
Yaralı var mı?
Yara'le var me?

T U R K I S H

328 ↑ 340

339

MOTORING/HEALTH

Traffic Offences

³⁴¹ **I'm sorry, I didn't see the sign.**
Özür dilerim, isareti görmedim.
Oezuer dilerim, isha'reti goermedim.

³⁴² **Must I pay a fine? How much?**
Para cezası mı ödemem gerekiyor? Kaç para?
Para djeza'se me oedemem ghe'rekiyor? Kach para?

³⁴³ **Show me your documents.**
Ehliyetinizi/belgelerinizi gösterin.
Ehliyetinizhi/belghe'lerinizhi goesterin.

HEALTH

Pharmacy

³⁴⁴ **Do you have anything for a stomachache/headache/sore throat/toothache?**
Mide/bas ağrısı/boğaz ağrısı/dis ağrısı için bir ilacınız var mı?
Mee'de/bash a'raesae/bo'az a'raesae/dish a'raesae ichin bir eladjaenaez var mae?

³⁴⁵ **I need something for diarrhoea (diarrhea)/constipation/a cold/a cough/insect bites/sunburn/travel (motion) sickness.**
Ishal/kabız/soğuk algınlığı/öksürük/böcek ısırması/günes yanığı/otobüs tutması için bir sey istiyorum.
Eshaal/kabaez/so'uk algaenlae'ae/oeksueruek/boedjek aesaermasae/guenesh yanae'ae/otobues tutmasae ichin bir shei estiyourum.

³⁴⁶ **How much/how many do I take?**
Ne kadar/kaç tane alayım?
Ne kadar/kach tane alayeem?

³⁴⁷ **How often do I take it/them?**
Ne kadar aralıklarla alayım?
Ne kadar aralaeklarla alayeem?

³⁴⁸ **How much does it cost?**
Kaç para?
Kach para?

³⁴⁹ **Can you recommend a good doctor/dentist?**
Iyi bir doktor/disçi tavsiye edebilir misiniz?
Eyi bir doktor/dishchi tavsiye edebilir misiniz?

³⁵⁰ **Is it suitable for children?**
Çocuklara uygun mu?
Chodjuklara uygun mu?

Doctor

³⁵¹ **I have a pain here/in my arm/leg/chest/stomach.**
Suram/kolum/ayağım/göğsüm/karnım ağrıyor.
Shuram/kolum/aya'aem/goe'suem/karnaem a'raeyour.

HEALTH/EMERGENCIES

352 Please call a doctor, this is an emergency!
Lütfen doktor çağırın, acil bir vak'a!
Luetphen doktor cha'raen, adjil beer vak'a!

353 I would like to make an appointment to see a doctor.
Doktoru görmek için randevu almak istiyorum.
Doctoru goermek ichin randevu almak estiyourum.

354 I am diabetic/pregnant.
Seker hastasıyım/hamileyim.
Sheker hastasaeyaem/hamileyim.

355 I need a prescription for . . .
. . . için reçete istiyorum.
. . . ichin rechete estiyorum.

356 Can you give me something to ease the pain?
Ağrıyı azaltacak bir şey verebilir misiniz?
A'raeyae azaltadjak bershey verebilir misiniz?

357 I am/he is/she is allergic to penicillin.
Benim/onun/onun penisiline karşı alerjim/alerjisi var.
Benim/onun/onun penicillin'e karshe allergim/allergisi var.

358 Does this hurt?
Acıtıyor mu?
Adje'teyor mu?

359 You must/he must/she must go to hospital.
Hastaneye gitmelisiniz/gitmeli.

Hasta'neye ghitmelisiniz/ghitmeli.

360 Take these once/twice /three times a day.
Bundan günde bir/iki/üç kere alın.
Bundan guende bir/iki/uech ke're a'len.

361 I am/he is/she is taking this medication.
Ben/o/o bu ilaçları alıyorum/alıyor.
Ben/o/o bu ilachla're a'leyourum.

362 I have medical insurance.
Sağlık sigortam var.
Sa'lek sighortam var.

Dentist

363 I have toothache.
Disim ağrıyor.
Dishim a'raeyour.

364 My filling has come out.
Dolgum düstü.
Dolgum dueshtue.

365 I do/do not want to have an injection first.
önceden iğne istiyorum/istemiyorum.
Oendjeden e'ne estiyourum/estemiyourum.

EMERGENCIES

366 Help!
Imdat!/Yardım!
Imdat/Yardaem!

T
U
R
K
I
S
H

352
↑
366

341

EMERGENCIES

367 Call an ambulance/a doctor/
the police!
Ambulans/doktor/polis çağırın!
Ambulance/doctor/police cha'ren!

368 I have had my travellers'
cheques (travelers' checks)/
credit cards/purse/handbag/
rucksack (knapsack)/
luggage/wallet stolen.
Seyahat çeklerim/kredi
kartlarım/çantam/el çantam/sırt
çantam/bagajım/cüzdanım
çalındı.
*Sey'ahat cheklerim/credi
cartlarem/chantam/el chantam/
saert chantam/bagadjem/
djuezdanem chalendae.*

369 Can you help me, I have lost
my daughter/son?
Bana yardım eder misiniz,
kızımı/oğlumu kaybettim.
*Bana yardem eder misiniz,
kezeme/o'lumu kaybettim.*

370 Please go away/leave me
alone.
Lütfen gidin/beni yalnız
bırakın.
*Luetphen ghidin/beni yalnaez
baeraken.*

371 Fire!
Yangın!
Yanghen!

372 I want to contact the British/
American/Canadian/Irish/
Australian/New Zealand/
South African consulate.
İngiliz/Amerikan/Kanada/
İrlanda/Avustralya/Yeni
Zelanda/Güney Afrika
konsolosluğuyla görüsmek
istiyorum.
*Inghilizh/Amerikan/Kanada/
Irlanda/Yeni Zhelanda/Gueney
Afrika konsoloslu'yla goerueshmek
istiyourum.*

TURKISH

367
↕
372

342

International Time

Winter time: last weekend in September–last weekend in March.
Summer time: last weekend in March–last weekend in September.
*GMT all year.   **GMT + 2 all year.

WINTER: SUMMER:	GMT GMT + 1	GMT + 1 GMT + 2	GMT + 2 GMT + 3	GMT + 3 GMT + 4
	Canary Isles Faroes Iceland* Ireland Portugal UK	Albania Austria Belgium Bosnia Croatia Czech Republic Denmark France Germany Hungary Italy Luxembourg Macedonia Malta Netherlands Norway Poland Slovakia Slovenia Spain Sweden Switzerland Yugoslavia	Belarus Bulgaria Cyprus Estonia** Finland Greece Kaliningrad Latvia Lithuania** Moldova Romania Turkey Ukraine	Russia (European, except Kaliningrad)

Midnight depart	= 0000
1 am	= 0100
5am	= 0500
5.30 am	= 0530
11am	= 1100
12 noon	= 1200
1 pm	= 1300
3.45 pm	= 1545
Midnight arrive	= 2400

Weather

The weather in Europe is generally mild and pleasant although it varies greatly between the north and the south and between the east and the west. Temperature is also affected by altitude.

Highest = Average highest daily temperature in °C.
Lowest = Average lowest daily temperature in °C.

	London	Rome	Stockholm	Budapest
JANUARY				
Highest	6	12	2	0
Lowest	1	4	-4	-5
Rain days	15	8	7	8
APRIL				
Highest	13	20	17	7
Lowest	4	8	6	0
Rain days	13	6	8	6
JULY				
Highest	22	31	28	21
Lowest	12	18	16	13
Rain days	13	3	7	9
OCTOBER				
Highest	14	23	16	9
Lowest	6	11	7	4
Rain days	16	9	8	9

TEMPERATURE

°C	°F		°C	°F
-20	-4		10	50
-15	5		15	59
-10	14		20	68
-5	23		25	77
0	32		30	86
5	41		35	95
			40	104

Conversion formulae
$$°C \times 9 \div 5 + 32 = °F$$
$$1 \text{ Deg. } °C = 1.8 \text{ Deg. } °F$$
$$1 \text{ Deg. } °F = 0.55 \text{ Deg. } °C$$

DISTANCES (approx conversions)
1 kilometre (km) = 1000 metres (m); 1 metre = 100 centimetres (cm)

Metric	Imperial/US	Metric	Imperial/US	Metric	Imperial/US
1	3/8ths in.	10m	33 ft (11 yd)	3 km	2 miles
50 cm	20 in.	20 m	66 ft (22 yd)	4 km	2½ miles
1 m	6 ft 6 in.	50 m	164 ft (54 yd)	5 km	3 miles
2 m	6 ft 6 in.	100 m	330 ft (110 yd)	10 km	6 miles
3 m	10 ft	200 m	660 ft (220 yd)	20 km	12½ miles
4m	13 ft	250 m	820 ft (275 yd)	25 km	15½ miles
5m	16 ft 6 in.	300 m	984 ft (330 yd)	30 km	18½ miles
6m	19 ft 6 in.	500 m	1640 ft (550 yd)	40 km	25 miles
7m	23 ft	750 m	½ mile	50 km	31 miles
8m	26 ft	1 km	5/8ths mile	75 km	46 miles
9m	29 ft (10 yd)	2 km	1½ miles	100 km	62 miles

WEIGHT

Kilograms	Pounds
1	2.205
2	4.405
3	6.614
4	8.818
5	11.023
6	13.227
7	15.432
8	17.636
9	19.840
10	22.045
15	33.068
20	44.889
50	110.225
100	220.450

1 kilogram (kg)	=	1000 grammes (g)
100g	=	3.5 oz.
1 oz.	=	28.35 g.
1 lb	=	453.60 g.

FLUID MEASURES

Litres	Imp. gal.	US gal.
5	1.1	1.3
10	2.2	2.6
15	3.3	3.9
20	4.4	5.2
25	5.5	6.5
30	6.6	7.8
35	7.7	9.1
40	8.8	10.4
45	9.9	11.7
50	11.0	13.0

1 litre (l)	=	0.88 imp. quarts
1 litre (l)	=	1.06 US quarts
1 imp. quart	=	1.14 l
1 imp. gallon	=	4.55 l
1 US quart	=	0.95 l
1 US gallon	=	3.81 l

REFERENCE SECTION

LADIES' CLOTHES SIZES

UK	France	Italy	Rest of Europe	USA
10	36	38	34	8
12	38	40	36	10
14	40	42	38	12
16	42	44	40	14
18	44	46	42	16
20	46	48	44	18
22	48	50	46	20

LADIES' SHOE SIZES

UK	Europe	USA
3	36	4.5
4	37	5.5
5	38	6.5
6	39	7.5
7	40	8.5
8	41	9.5

MEN'S SHOE SIZES

UK	Europe	USA
6	40	7
7	41	8
8	42	9
9	43	10
10	44	11
11	45	12
12	46	13

MEN'S SUIT SIZES

UK	Europe	USA
36	46	36
38	48	38
40	50	40
42	52	42
44	54	44
46	56	46

MEN'S SHIRT SIZES

UK	Europe	USA
14	36	14
15	38	15
15.5	39	15.5
16	41	16
16.5	42	16.5
17	43	17

Index

INDEX

READER SURVEY

If you found this phrasebook useful – or if you didn't – please help us to improve future editions by taking part in our reader survey. Every returned form will be acknowledged, and to show our appreciation we will give you £1 off your next purchase of a Thomas Cook publication. Just take a few minutes to complete and return this form to:

The Editor, European 12-Language Phrasebook, Thomas Cook Publishing, PO Box 227, The Thomas Cook Business Park, Units 19–21, Coningsby Road, Peterborough PE3 8XX, UK.

When did you buy this book?

Where did you buy it? (Please give town/city and if possible name of retailer).

When did you/do you intend to travel in Europe?

For how long?

Did you/will you travel on business or for pleasure?

Which countries did you/do you intend to visit?

Did you/will you travel by:
☐ Organised coach tour   ☐ Car   ☐ Rail

Did you/do you intend to also purchase any of the following travel publications for your trip?
☐ Thomas Cook European Timetable
☐ A title from the Thomas Cook Traveller series
☐ Independent Traveller's Europe or Your Passport to Safer Travel
☐ Other guidebooks/maps. Please specify:

READER SURVEY

Please rate the following features of the European Travel Phrasebook for their value to you:
(Circle the 1 for 'little or no use,' 2 for 'useful,' 3 for 'very useful'):

The map on page 6	1	2	3
The introduction to each language section	1	2	3
The phonetic spellings	1	2	3
The index	1	2	3

Please use this space to list any additional phrases you would find useful

_____
_____
_____
_____

Please use this space to tell us about any features that in your opinion could be changed, improved, or added in future editions of the book, or any other comments you would like to make concerning the book:

_____
_____
_____

Your age category:
☐ under 30   ☐ 30–50   ☐ over 50

Your name: Mr/Mrs/Miss/Ms   First name or initials:

Last name:

Your full address (please include postal code or zip code):

_____
_____
_____
_____

Your daytime telephone number: